Hana & Hina
AFTER ♥ SCHOOL

story & art
MILK MORINAGA

1

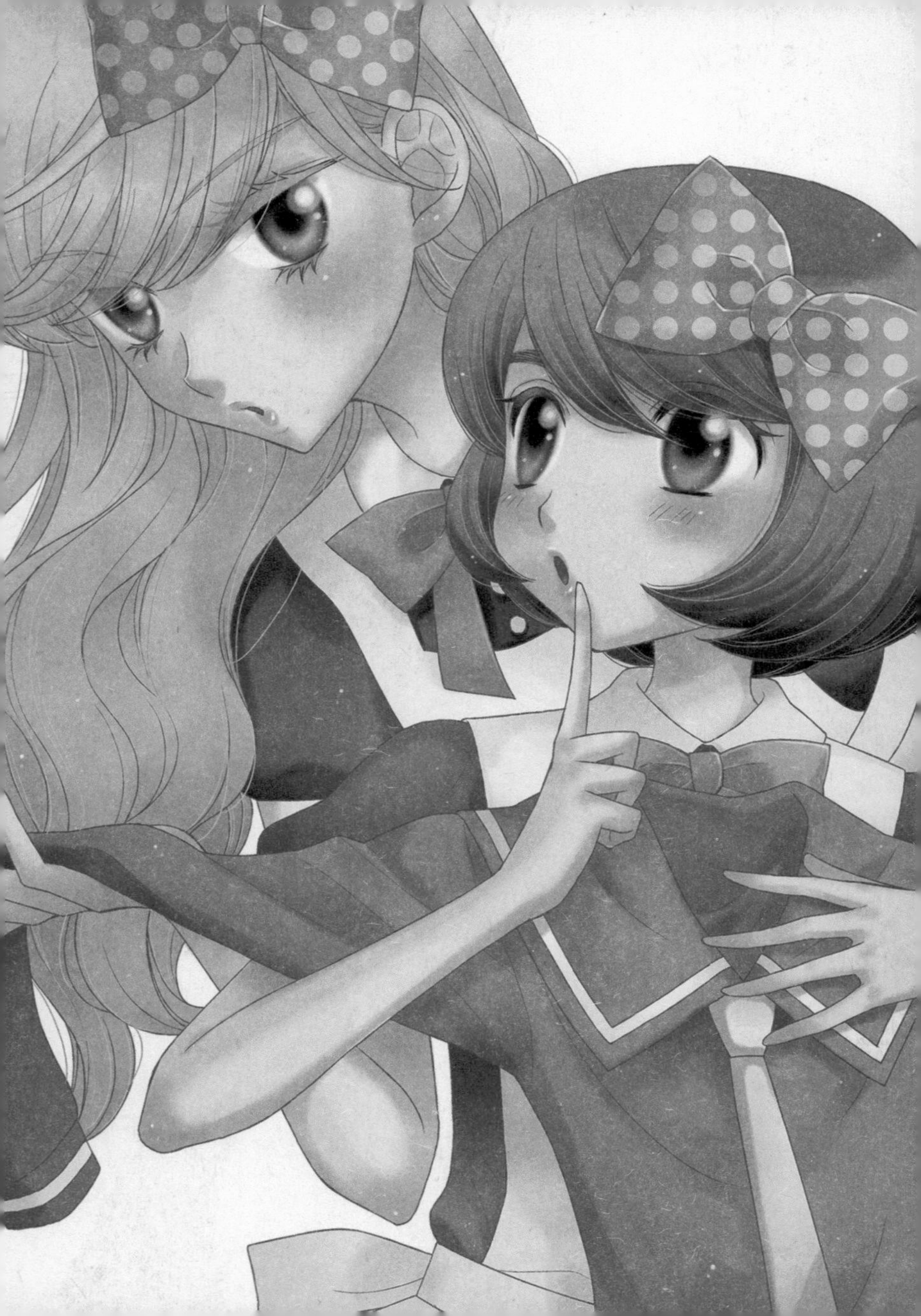

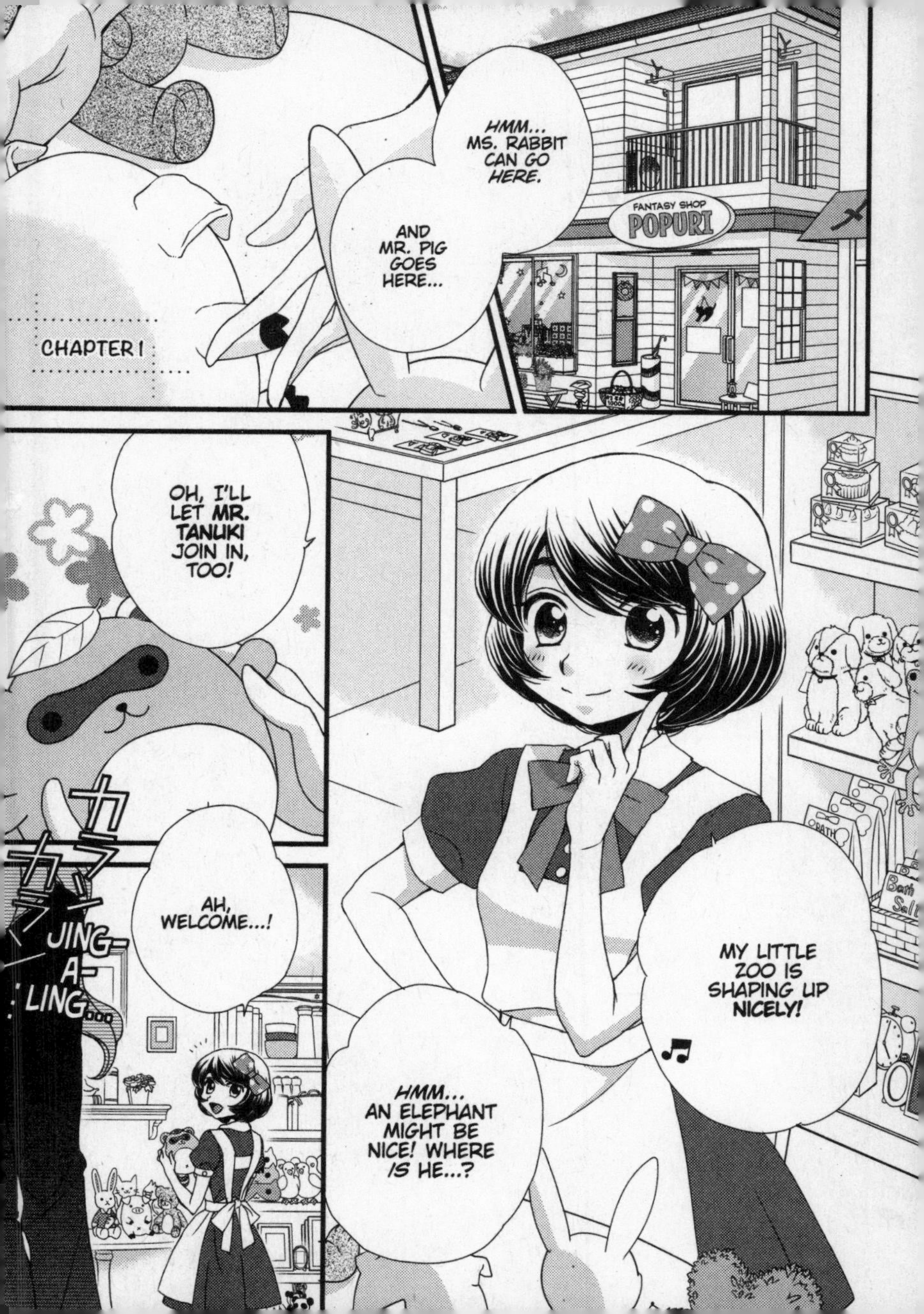
HMM... MS. RABBIT CAN GO HERE.
AND MR. PIG GOES HERE...
FANTASY SHOP
POPURI
CHAPTER 1
MY LITTLE ZOO IS SHAPING UP NICELY!
HMM... AN ELEPHANT MIGHT BE NICE! WHERE IS HE...?
OH, I'LL LET MR. TANUKI JOIN IN, TOO!
JING-A-LING...
AH, WELCOME...!

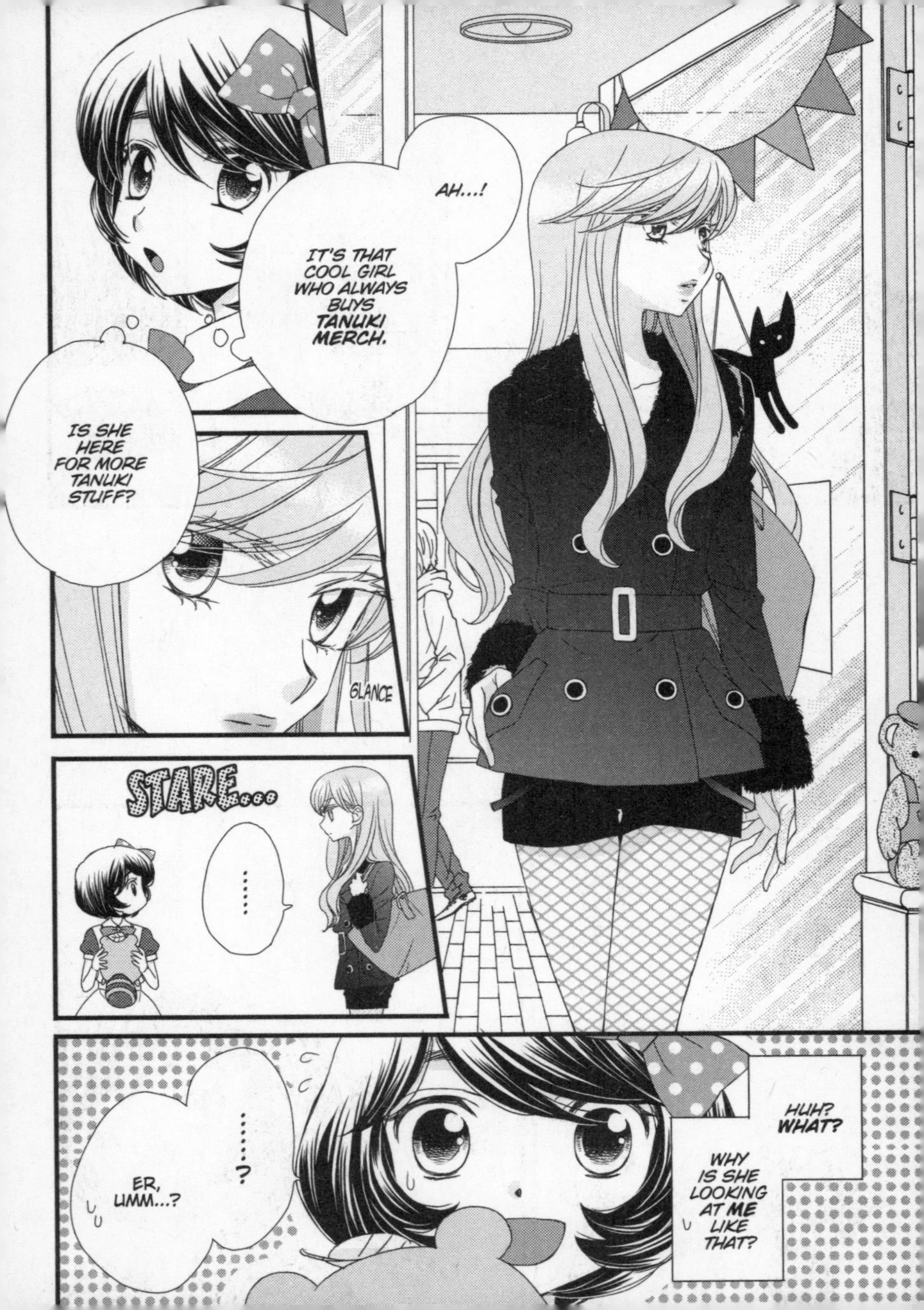
AH...!
IT'S THAT COOL GIRL WHO ALWAYS BUYS TANUKI MERCH.
IS SHE HERE FOR MORE TANUKI STUFF?
GLANCE
STARE...
......
HUH? WHAT?
WHY IS SHE LOOKING AT ME LIKE THAT?
......?
ER, UMM...?

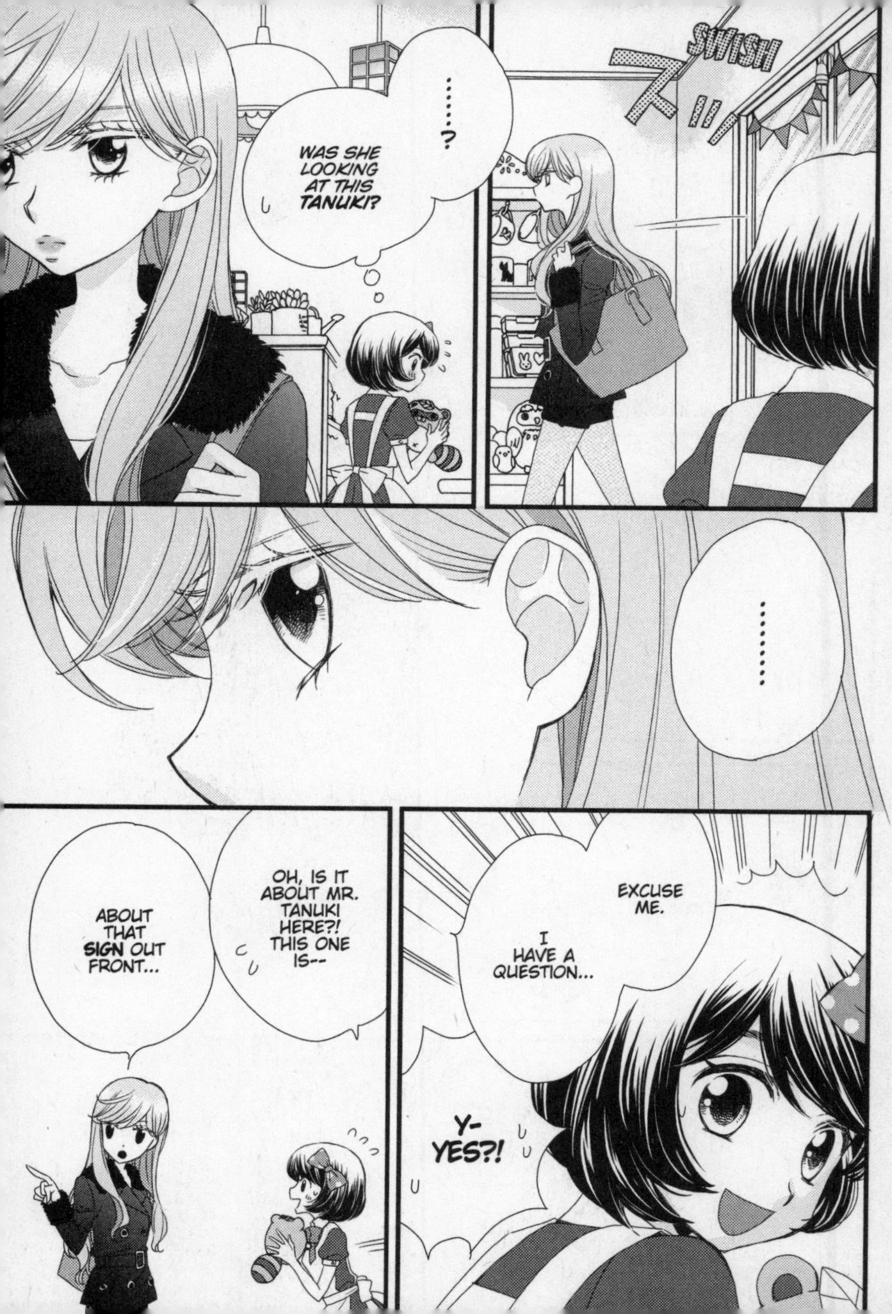
SWISH
......?
WAS SHE LOOKING AT THIS TANUKI?
......
EXCUSE ME.
I HAVE A QUESTION...
Y- YES?!
OH, IS IT ABOUT MR. TANUKI HERE?! THIS ONE IS--
ABOUT THAT SIGN OUT FRONT...

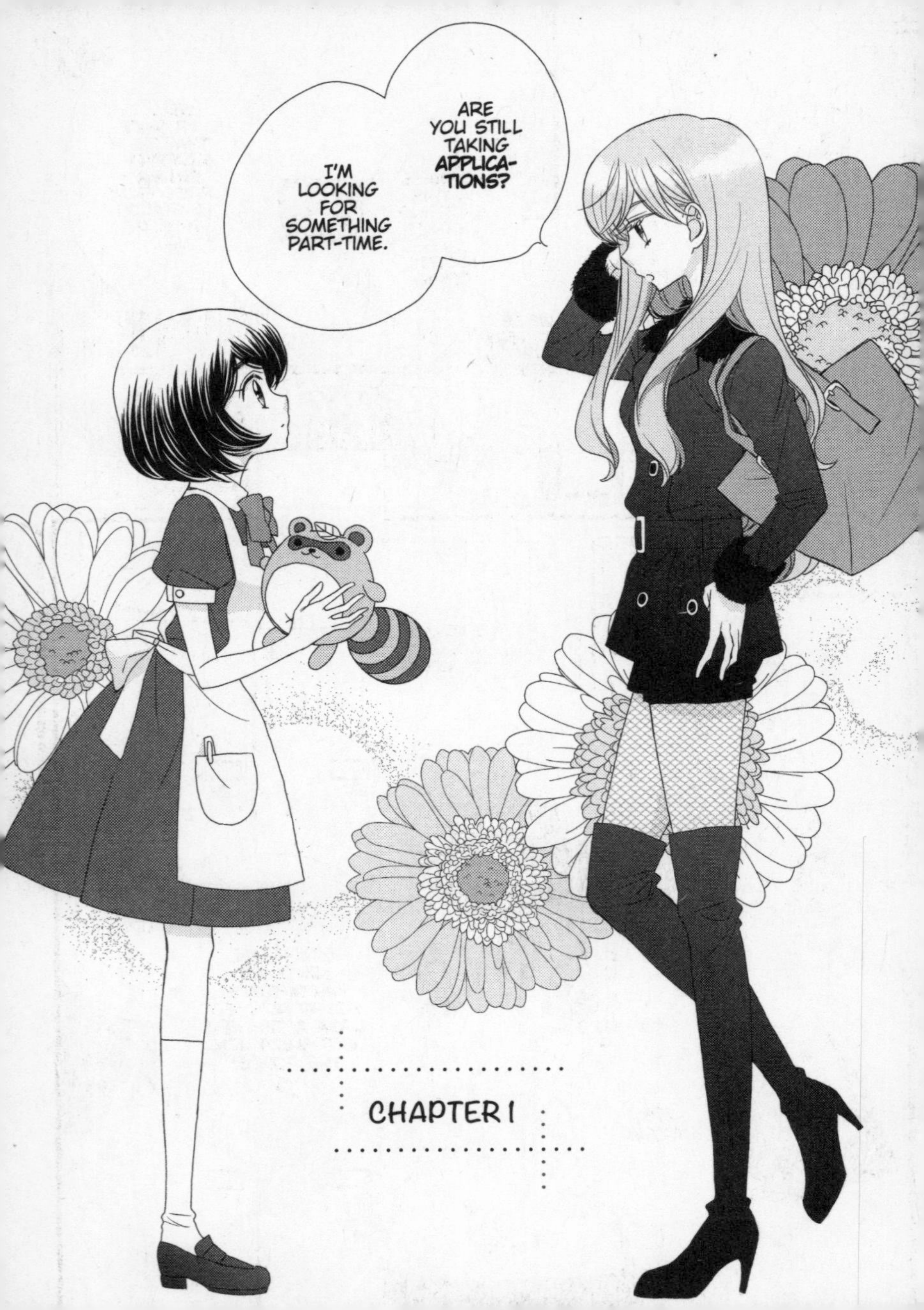
ARE YOU STILL TAKING APPLICATIONS?
I'M LOOKING FOR SOMETHING PART-TIME.
CHAPTER 1

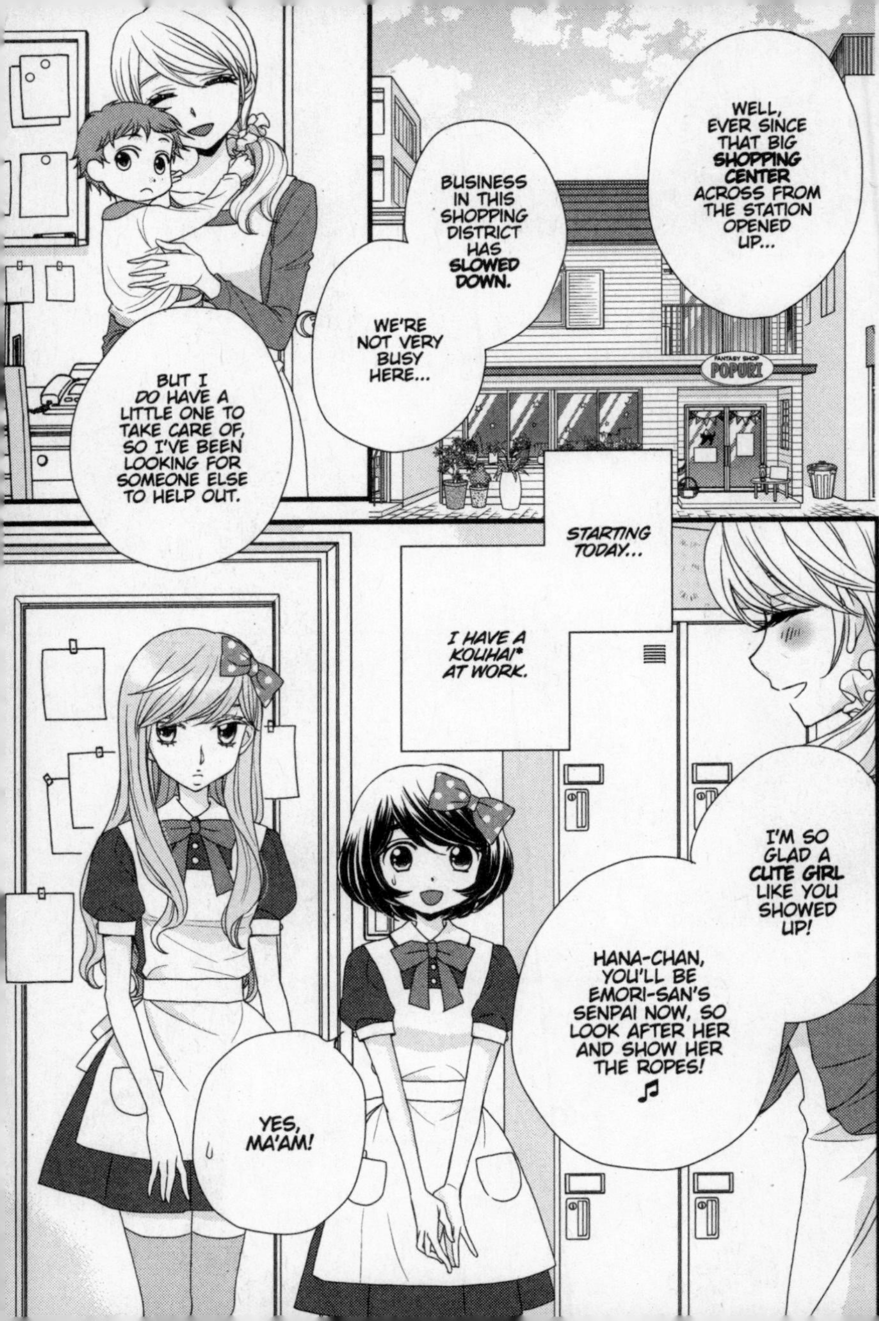
WELL, EVER SINCE THAT BIG SHOPPING CENTER ACROSS FROM THE STATION OPENED UP...
BUSINESS IN THIS SHOPPING DISTRICT HAS SLOWED DOWN.
WE'RE NOT VERY BUSY HERE...
FANTASY SHOP POPURI
BUT I DO HAVE A LITTLE ONE TO TAKE CARE OF, SO I'VE BEEN LOOKING FOR SOMEONE ELSE TO HELP OUT.
STARTING TODAY...
I HAVE A KOUHAI* AT WORK.
I'M SO GLAD A CUTE GIRL LIKE YOU SHOWED UP!
HANA-CHAN, YOU'LL BE EMORI-SAN'S SENPAI NOW, SO LOOK AFTER HER AND SHOW HER THE ROPES! ♫
YES, MA'AM!

*A kouhai is a younger schoolmate or junior person at work.

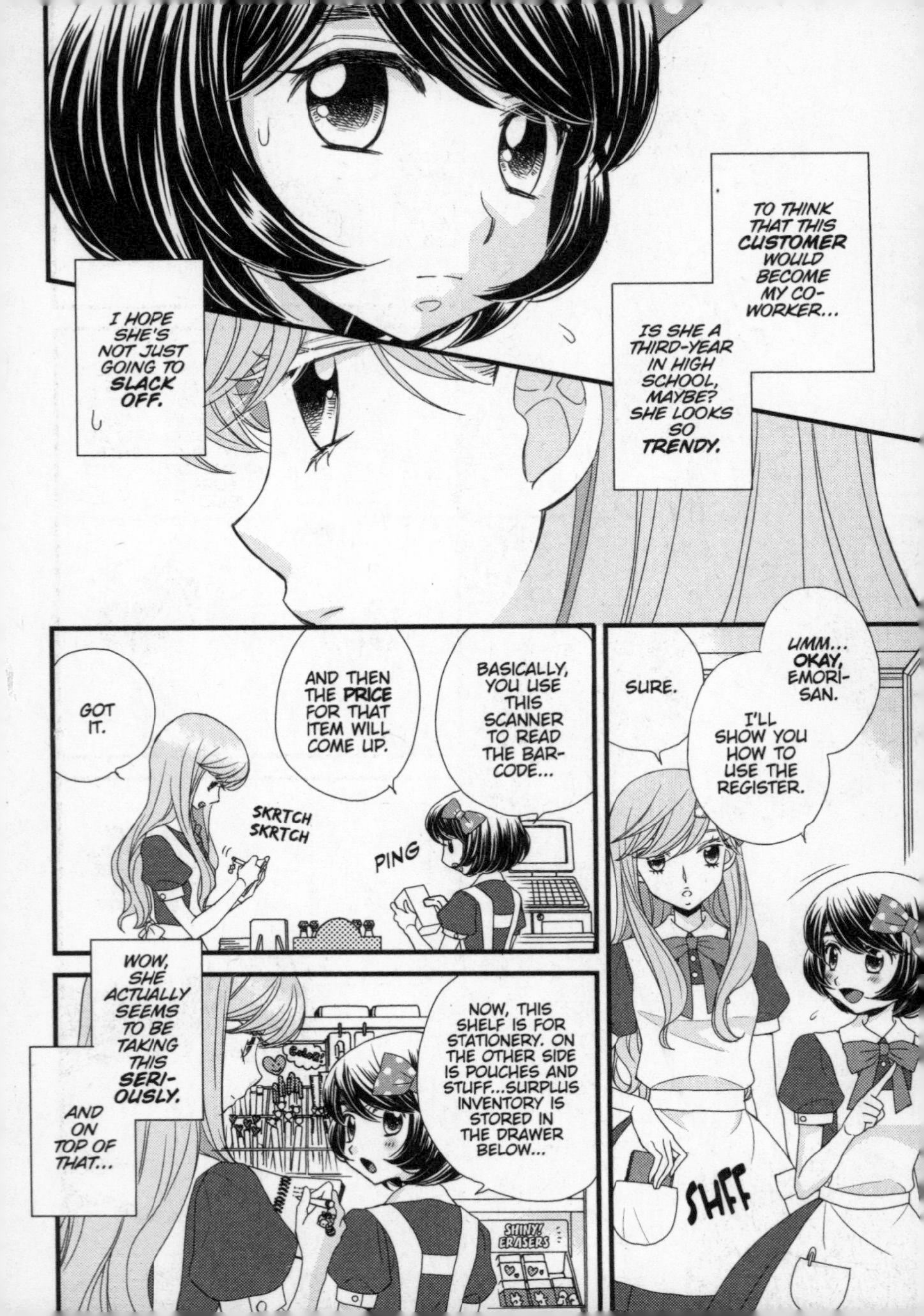
TO THINK THAT THIS CUSTOMER WOULD BECOME MY CO-WORKER...
IS SHE A THIRD-YEAR IN HIGH SCHOOL, MAYBE? SHE LOOKS SO TRENDY.
I HOPE SHE'S NOT JUST GOING TO SLACK OFF.
UMM... OKAY, EMORI-SAN.
I'LL SHOW YOU HOW TO USE THE REGISTER.
SURE.
SHFF
BASICALLY, YOU USE THIS SCANNER TO READ THE BAR-CODE...
AND THEN THE PRICE FOR THAT ITEM WILL COME UP.
PING
SKRTCH SKRTCH
GOT IT.
NOW, THIS SHELF IS FOR STATIONERY. ON THE OTHER SIDE IS POUCHES AND STUFF...SURPLUS INVENTORY IS STORED IN THE DRAWER BELOW...
WOW, SHE ACTUALLY SEEMS TO BE TAKING THIS SERIOUSLY.
AND ON TOP OF THAT...
SHINY! ERASERS

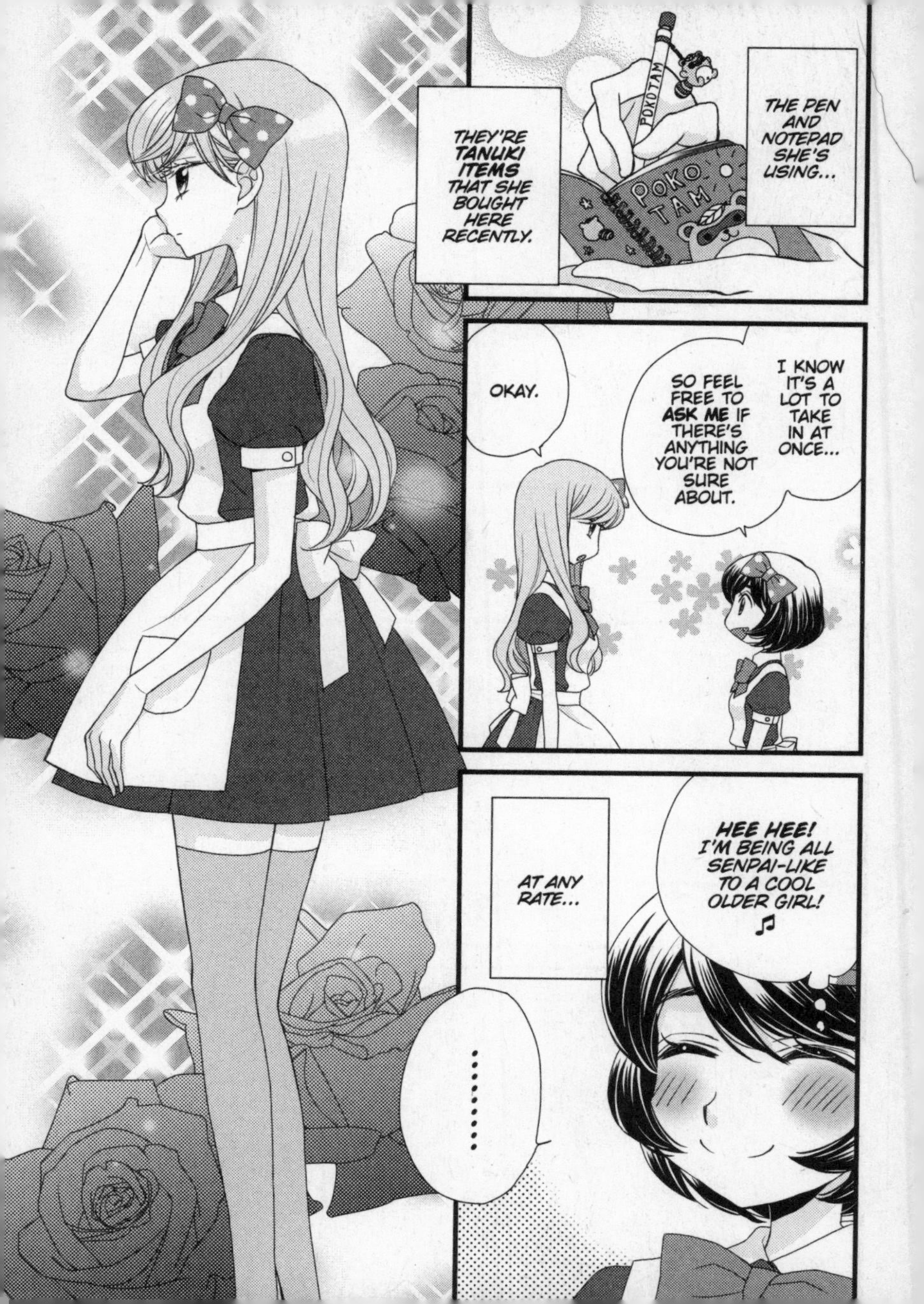
THE PEN AND NOTEPAD SHE'S USING...
POKOTAM
POKO TAM
THEY'RE TANUKI ITEMS THAT SHE BOUGHT HERE RECENTLY.
I KNOW IT'S A LOT TO TAKE IN AT ONCE...
SO FEEL FREE TO ASK ME IF THERE'S ANYTHING YOU'RE NOT SURE ABOUT.
OKAY.
HEE HEE! I'M BEING ALL SENPAI-LIKE TO A COOL OLDER GIRL! ♪
AT ANY RATE...
......

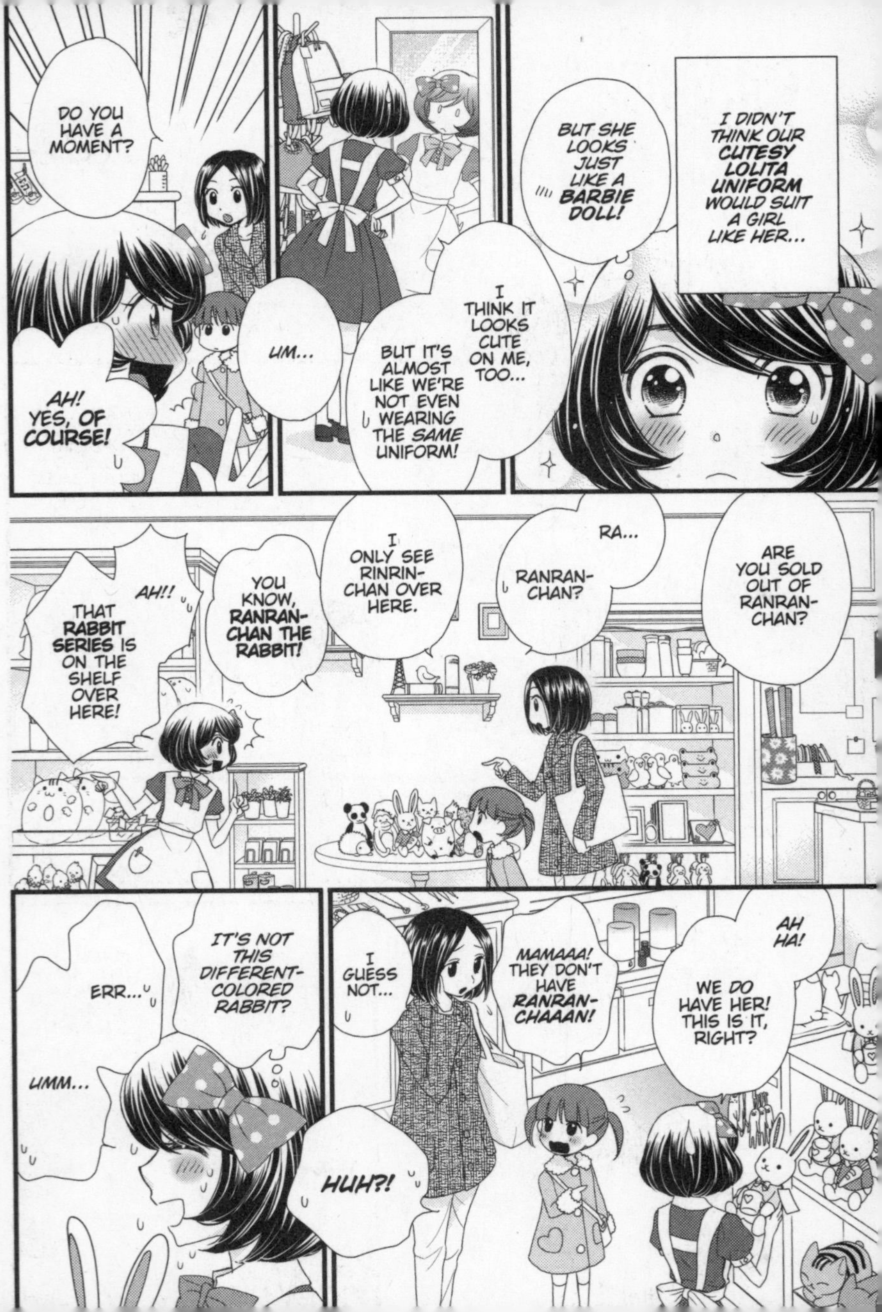
I DIDN'T THINK OUR CUTESY LOLITA UNIFORM WOULD SUIT A GIRL LIKE HER...
BUT SHE LOOKS JUST LIKE A BARBIE DOLL!
I THINK IT LOOKS CUTE ON ME, TOO...
BUT IT'S ALMOST LIKE WE'RE NOT EVEN WEARING THE SAME UNIFORM!
DO YOU HAVE A MOMENT?
UM...
AH! YES, OF COURSE!
ARE YOU SOLD OUT OF RANRAN-CHAN?
RA...
RANRAN-CHAN?
I ONLY SEE RINRIN-CHAN OVER HERE.
YOU KNOW, RANRAN-CHAN THE RABBIT!
AH!!
THAT RABBIT SERIES IS ON THE SHELF OVER HERE!
AH HA!
WE DO HAVE HER! THIS IS IT, RIGHT?
MAMAAA! THEY DON'T HAVE RANRAN-CHAAAN!
I GUESS NOT...
IT'S NOT THIS DIFFERENT-COLORED RABBIT?
ERR...
UMM...
HUH?!

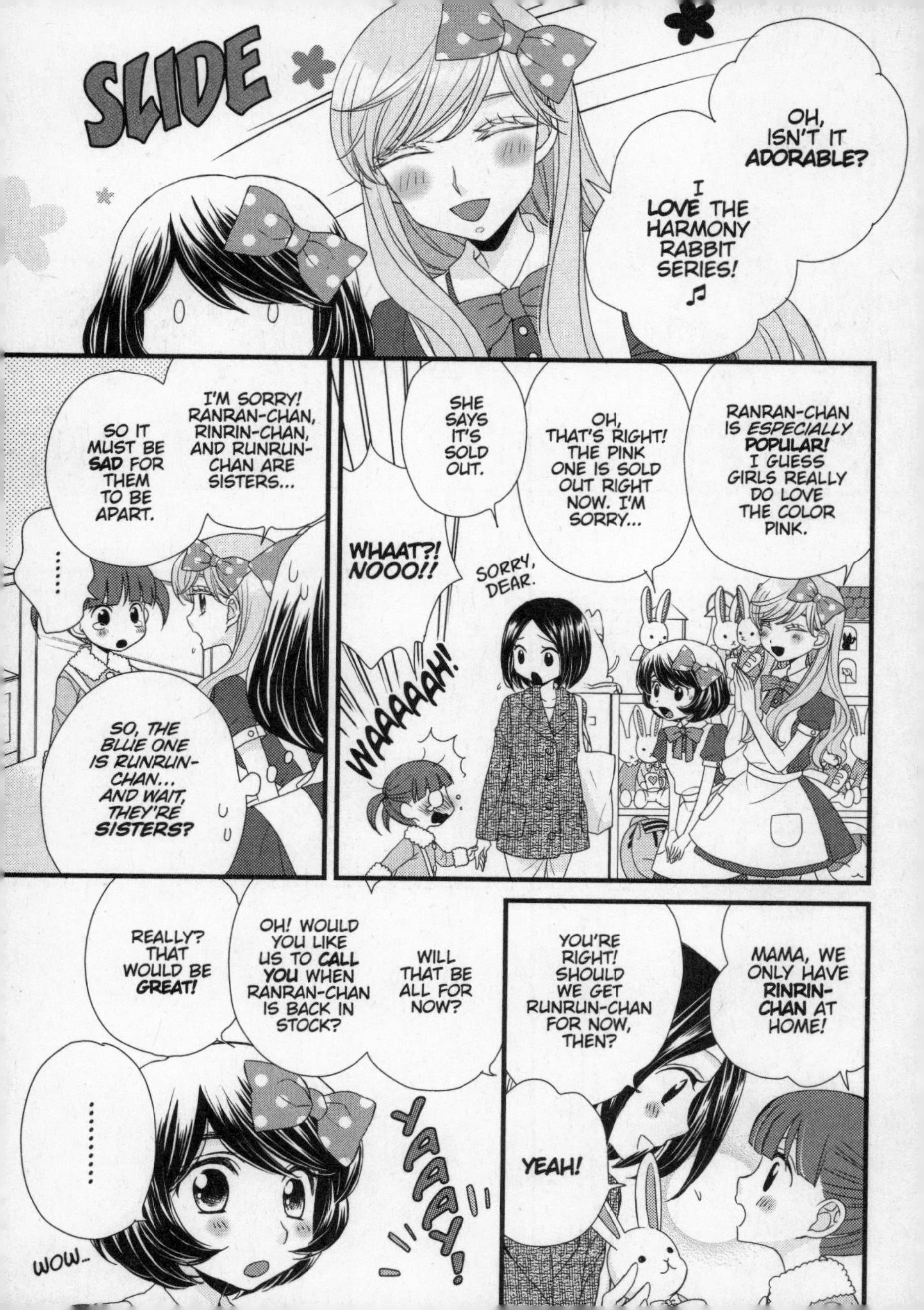
OH, ISN'T IT ADORABLE?
I LOVE THE HARMONY RABBIT SERIES! ♪
SLIDE
RANRAN-CHAN IS ESPECIALLY POPULAR! I GUESS GIRLS REALLY DO LOVE THE COLOR PINK.
OH, THAT'S RIGHT! THE PINK ONE IS SOLD OUT RIGHT NOW. I'M SORRY...
SHE SAYS IT'S SOLD OUT.
SORRY, DEAR.
WHAAT?! NOOO!!
WAAAAAAH!
I'M SORRY! RANRAN-CHAN, RINRIN-CHAN, AND RUNRUN-CHAN ARE SISTERS...
SO IT MUST BE SAD FOR THEM TO BE APART.
......
SO, THE BLUE ONE IS RUNRUN-CHAN... AND WAIT, THEY'RE SISTERS?
MAMA, WE ONLY HAVE RINRIN-CHAN AT HOME!
YOU'RE RIGHT! SHOULD WE GET RUNRUN-CHAN FOR NOW, THEN?
YEAH!
WILL THAT BE ALL FOR NOW?
OH! WOULD YOU LIKE US TO CALL YOU WHEN RANRAN-CHAN IS BACK IN STOCK?
REALLY? THAT WOULD BE GREAT!
......
WOW...

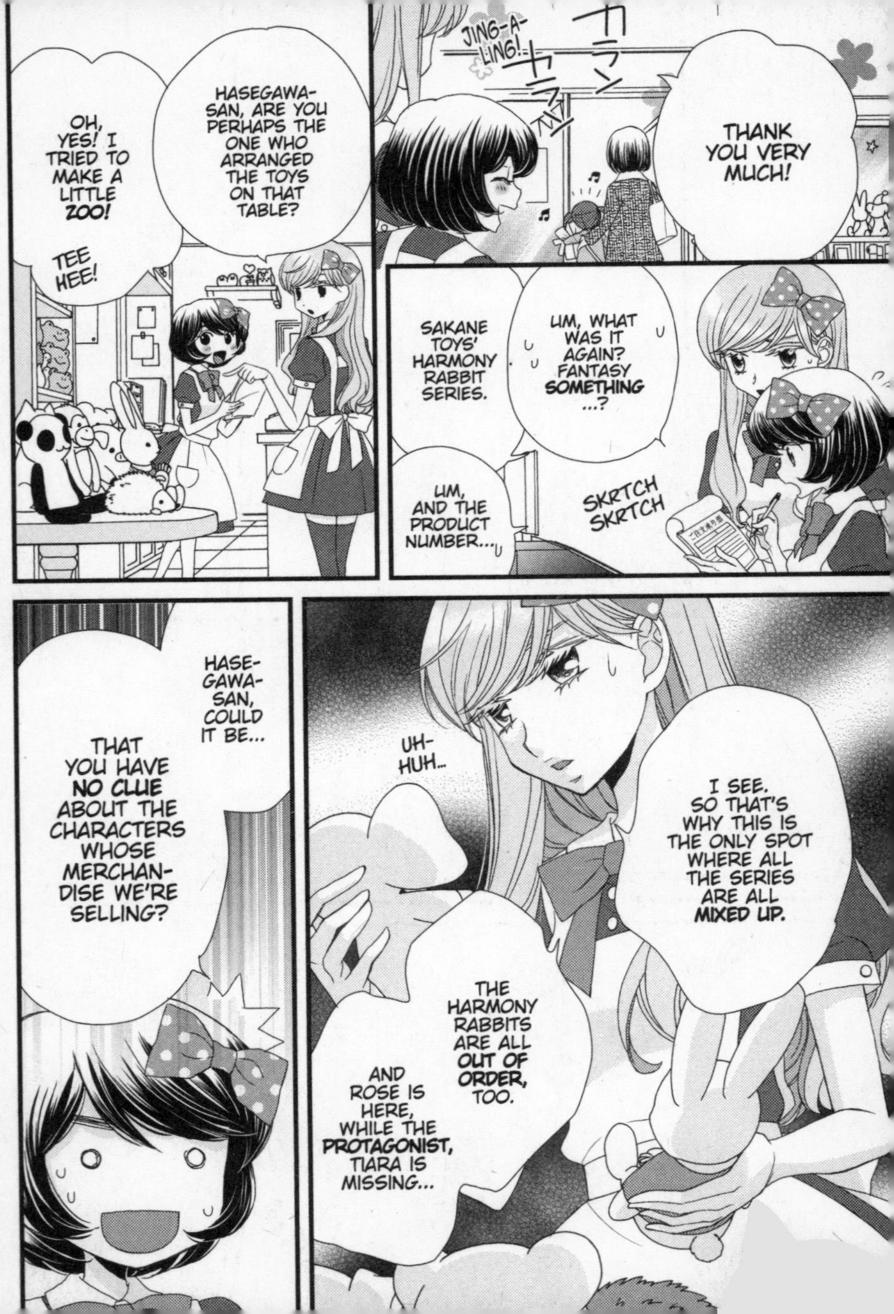
JING-A-LING!
THANK YOU VERY MUCH!
UM, WHAT WAS IT AGAIN? FANTASY SOMETHING...?
SAKANE TOYS' HARMONY RABBIT SERIES.
UM, AND THE PRODUCT NUMBER...
SKRTCH SKRTCH
HASEGAWA-SAN, ARE YOU PERHAPS THE ONE WHO ARRANGED THE TOYS ON THAT TABLE?
OH, YES! I TRIED TO MAKE A LITTLE ZOO!
TEE HEE!
I SEE. SO THAT'S WHY THIS IS THE ONLY SPOT WHERE ALL THE SERIES ARE ALL MIXED UP.
UH-HUH...
THE HARMONY RABBITS ARE ALL OUT OF ORDER, TOO.
AND ROSE IS HERE, WHILE THE PROTAGONIST, TIARA IS MISSING...
HASE-GAWA-SAN, COULD IT BE...
THAT YOU HAVE NO CLUE ABOUT THE CHARACTERS WHOSE MERCHANDISE WE'RE SELLING?

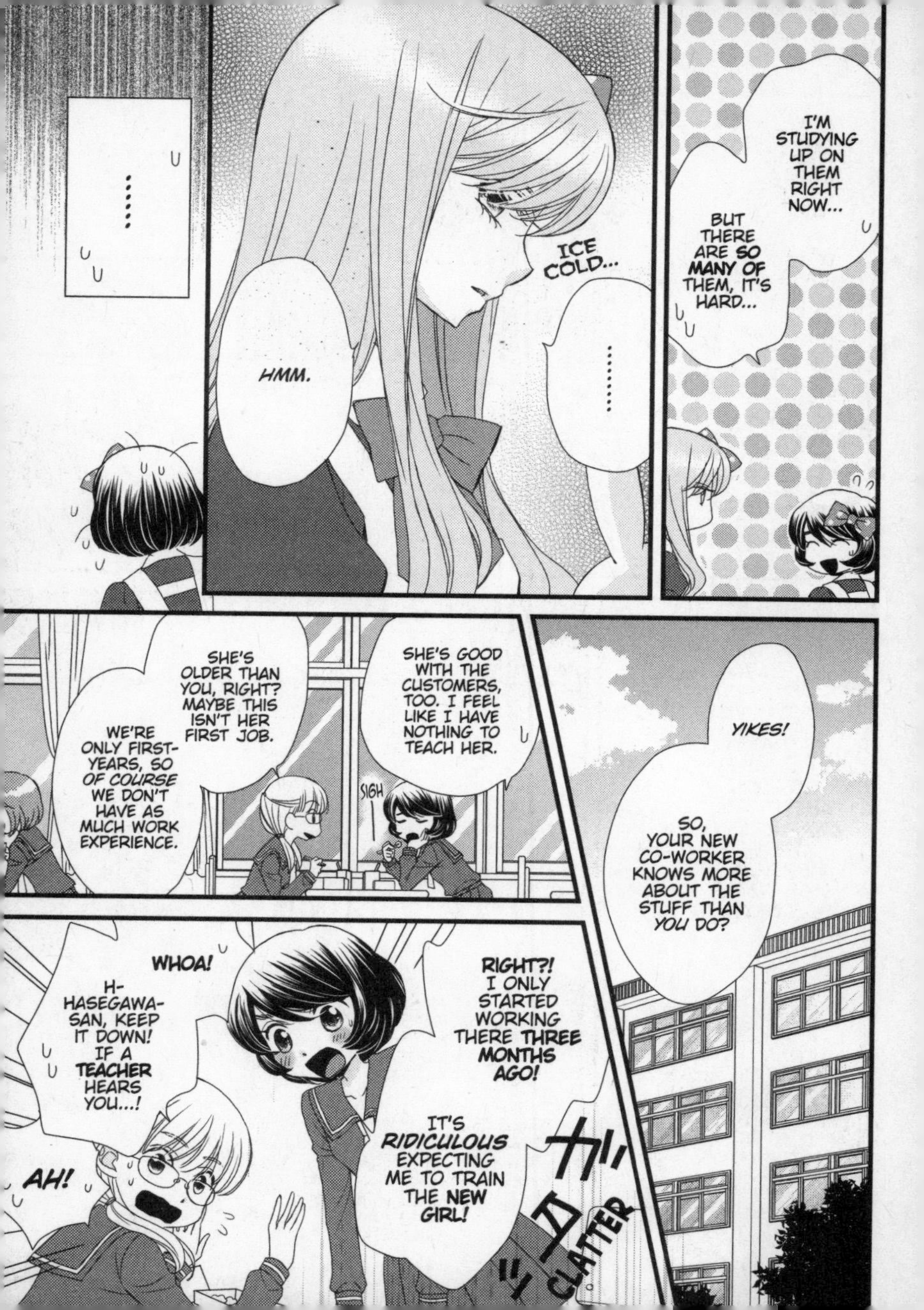

I'M STUDYING UP ON THEM RIGHT NOW...
BUT THERE ARE SO MANY OF THEM, IT'S HARD...
ICE COLD...
......
HMM.
......
YIKES!
SO, YOUR NEW CO-WORKER KNOWS MORE ABOUT THE STUFF THAN YOU DO?
SHE'S GOOD WITH THE CUSTOMERS, TOO. I FEEL LIKE I HAVE NOTHING TO TEACH HER.
SIGH
SHE'S OLDER THAN YOU, RIGHT? MAYBE THIS ISN'T HER FIRST JOB.
WE'RE ONLY FIRST-YEARS, SO OF COURSE WE DON'T HAVE AS MUCH WORK EXPERIENCE.
RIGHT?! I ONLY STARTED WORKING THERE THREE MONTHS AGO!
IT'S RIDICULOUS EXPECTING ME TO TRAIN THE NEW GIRL!
CLATTER
WHOA!
H-HASEGAWA-SAN, KEEP IT DOWN! IF A TEACHER HEARS YOU...!
AH!

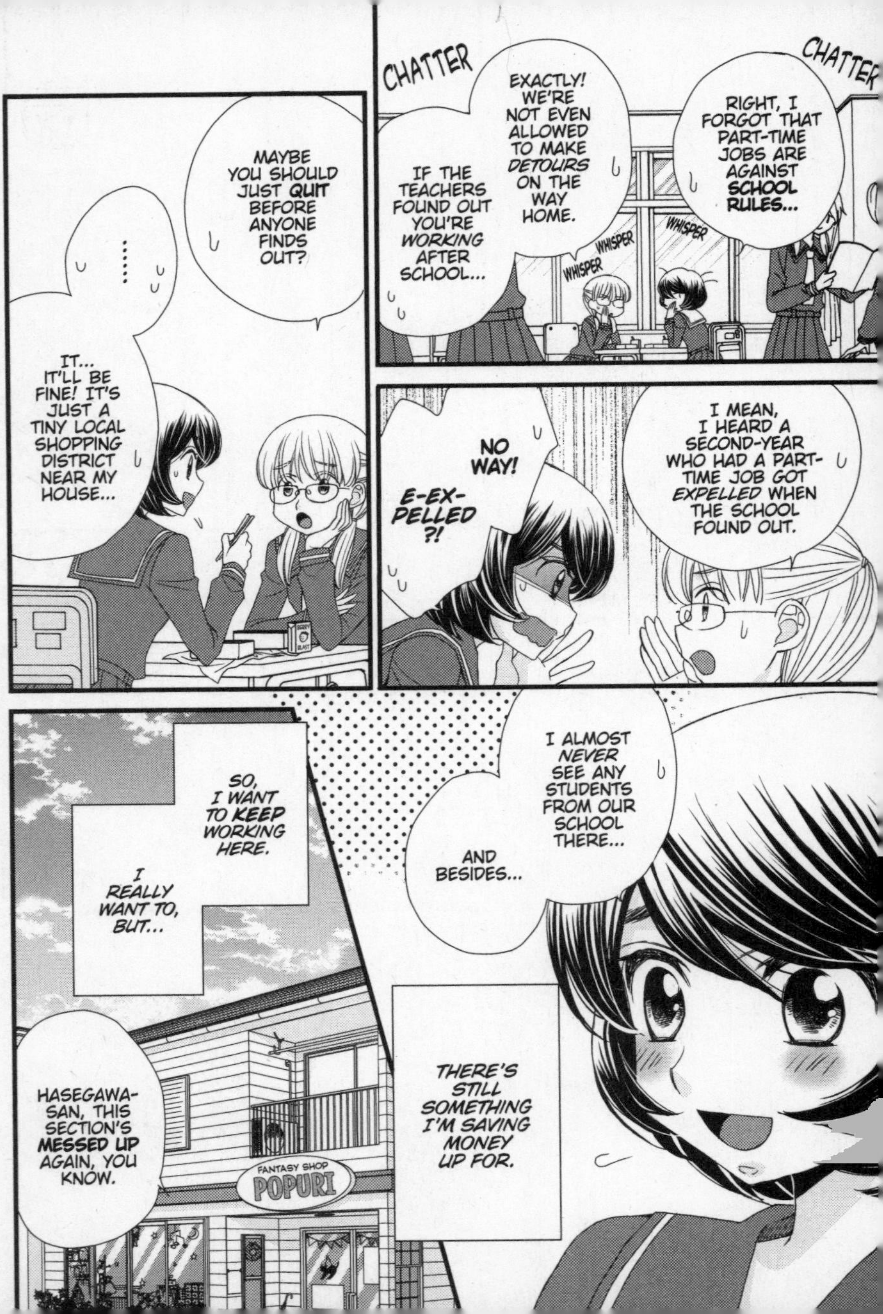
CHATTER
RIGHT, I FORGOT THAT PART-TIME JOBS ARE AGAINST **SCHOOL RULES...**
CHATTER
EXACTLY! WE'RE NOT EVEN ALLOWED TO MAKE *DETOURS* ON THE WAY HOME.
IF THE TEACHERS FOUND OUT YOU'RE *WORKING* AFTER SCHOOL...
WHISPER
WHISPER
WHISPER
I MEAN, I HEARD A SECOND-YEAR WHO HAD A PART-TIME JOB GOT *EXPELLED* WHEN THE SCHOOL FOUND OUT.
NO WAY!
E-EX-PELLED ?!
MAYBE YOU SHOULD JUST **QUIT** BEFORE ANYONE FINDS OUT?
......
IT... IT'LL BE FINE! IT'S JUST A TINY LOCAL SHOPPING DISTRICT NEAR MY HOUSE...
I ALMOST *NEVER* SEE ANY STUDENTS FROM OUR SCHOOL THERE...
AND BESIDES...
THERE'S STILL SOMETHING I'M SAVING MONEY UP FOR.
*SO, I WANT TO **KEEP** WORKING HERE.*
I REALLY WANT TO, BUT...
FANTASY SHOP
POPURI
HASEGAWA-SAN, THIS SECTION'S **MESSED UP** AGAIN, YOU KNOW.

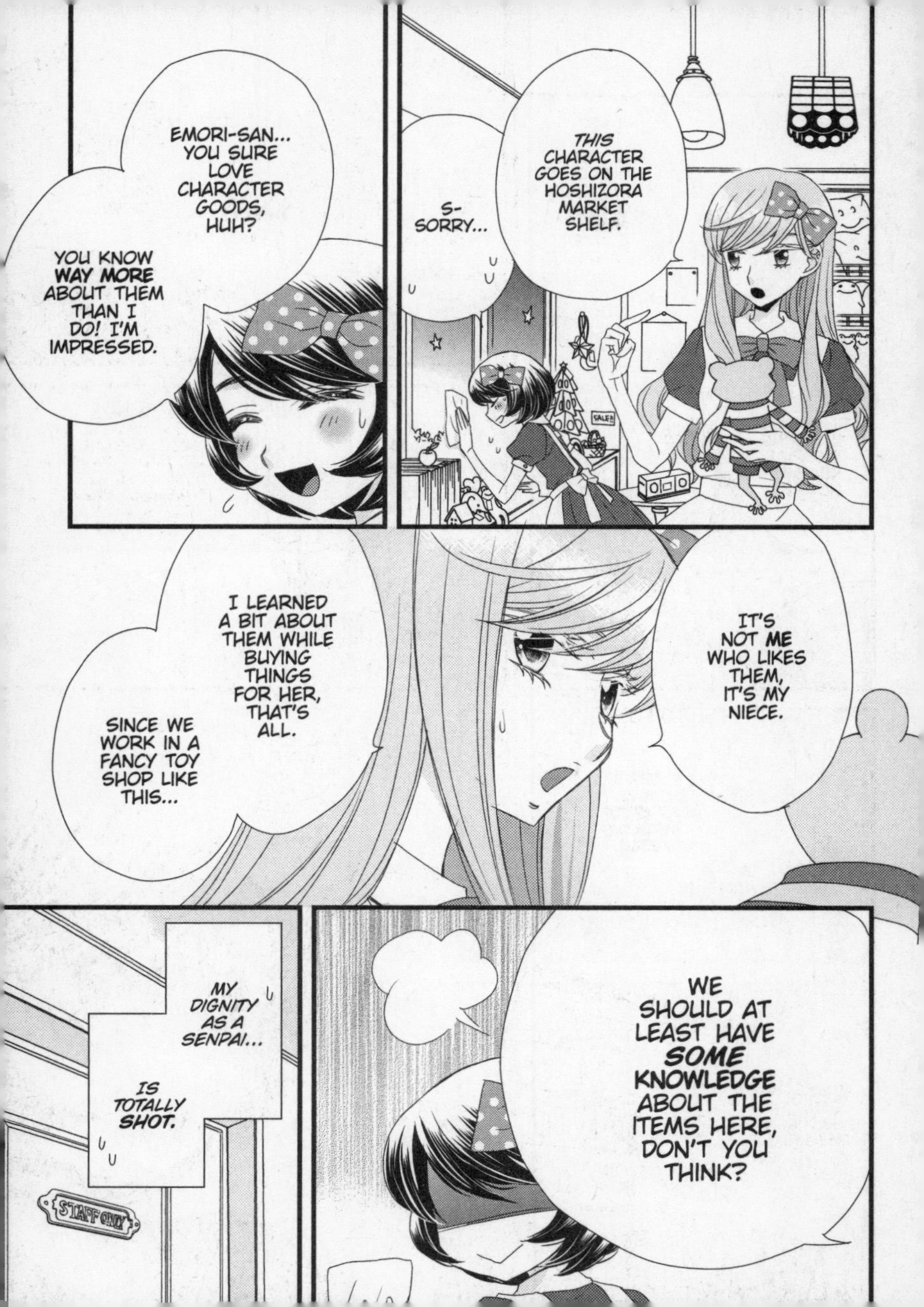
THIS CHARACTER GOES ON THE HOSHIZORA MARKET SHELF.
S-SORRY...
EMORI-SAN... YOU SURE LOVE CHARACTER GOODS, HUH?
YOU KNOW WAY MORE ABOUT THEM THAN I DO! I'M IMPRESSED.
IT'S NOT ME WHO LIKES THEM, IT'S MY NIECE.
I LEARNED A BIT ABOUT THEM WHILE BUYING THINGS FOR HER, THAT'S ALL.
SINCE WE WORK IN A FANCY TOY SHOP LIKE THIS...
WE SHOULD AT LEAST HAVE SOME KNOWLEDGE ABOUT THE ITEMS HERE, DON'T YOU THINK?
MY DIGNITY AS A SENPAI...
IS TOTALLY SHOT.
STAFF ONLY

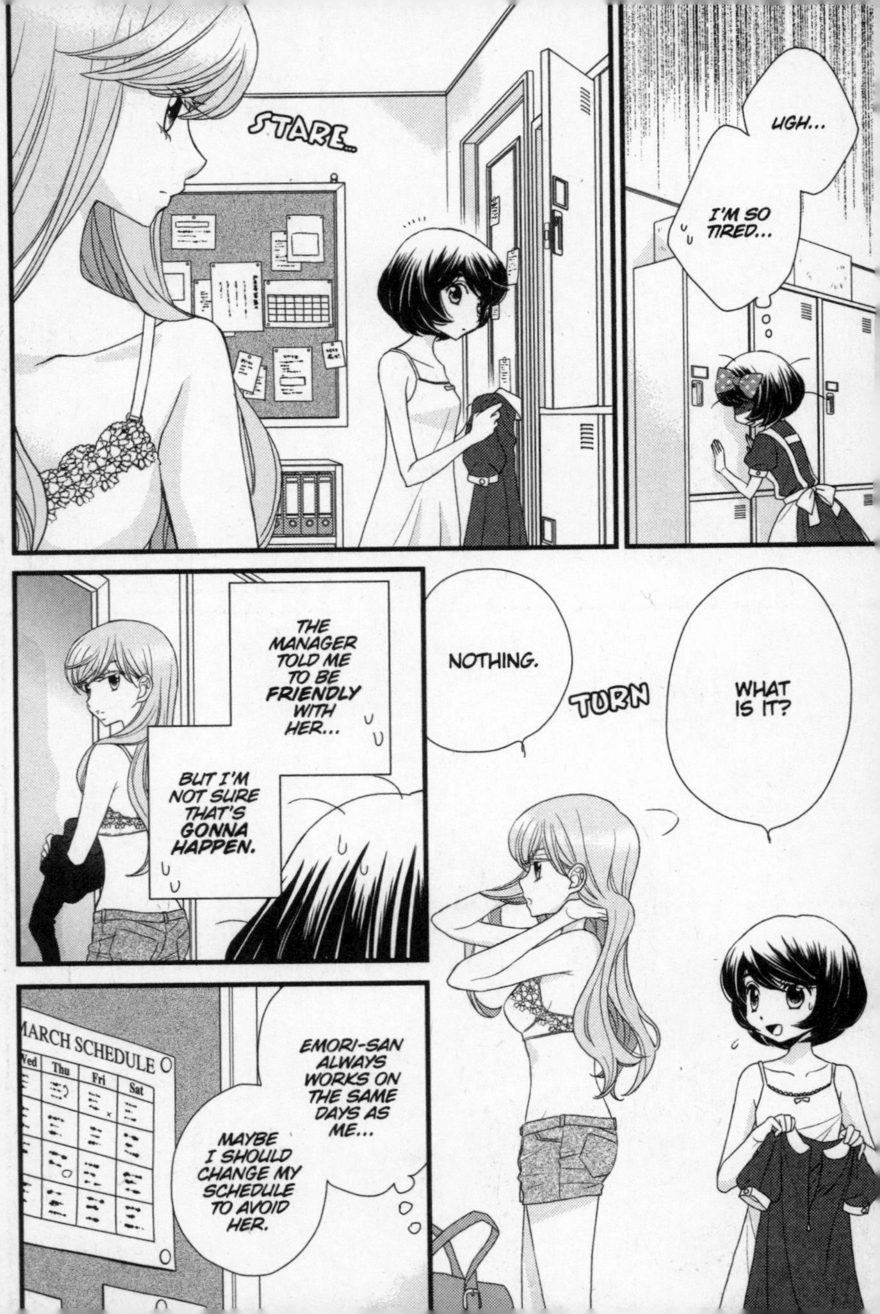

UGH...
I'M SO TIRED...
STARE...
WHAT IS IT?
TURN
NOTHING.
THE MANAGER TOLD ME TO BE FRIENDLY WITH HER...
BUT I'M NOT SURE THAT'S GONNA HAPPEN.
EMORI-SAN ALWAYS WORKS ON THE SAME DAYS AS ME...
MAYBE I SHOULD CHANGE MY SCHEDULE TO AVOID HER.
MARCH SCHEDULE
Wed Thu Fri Sat

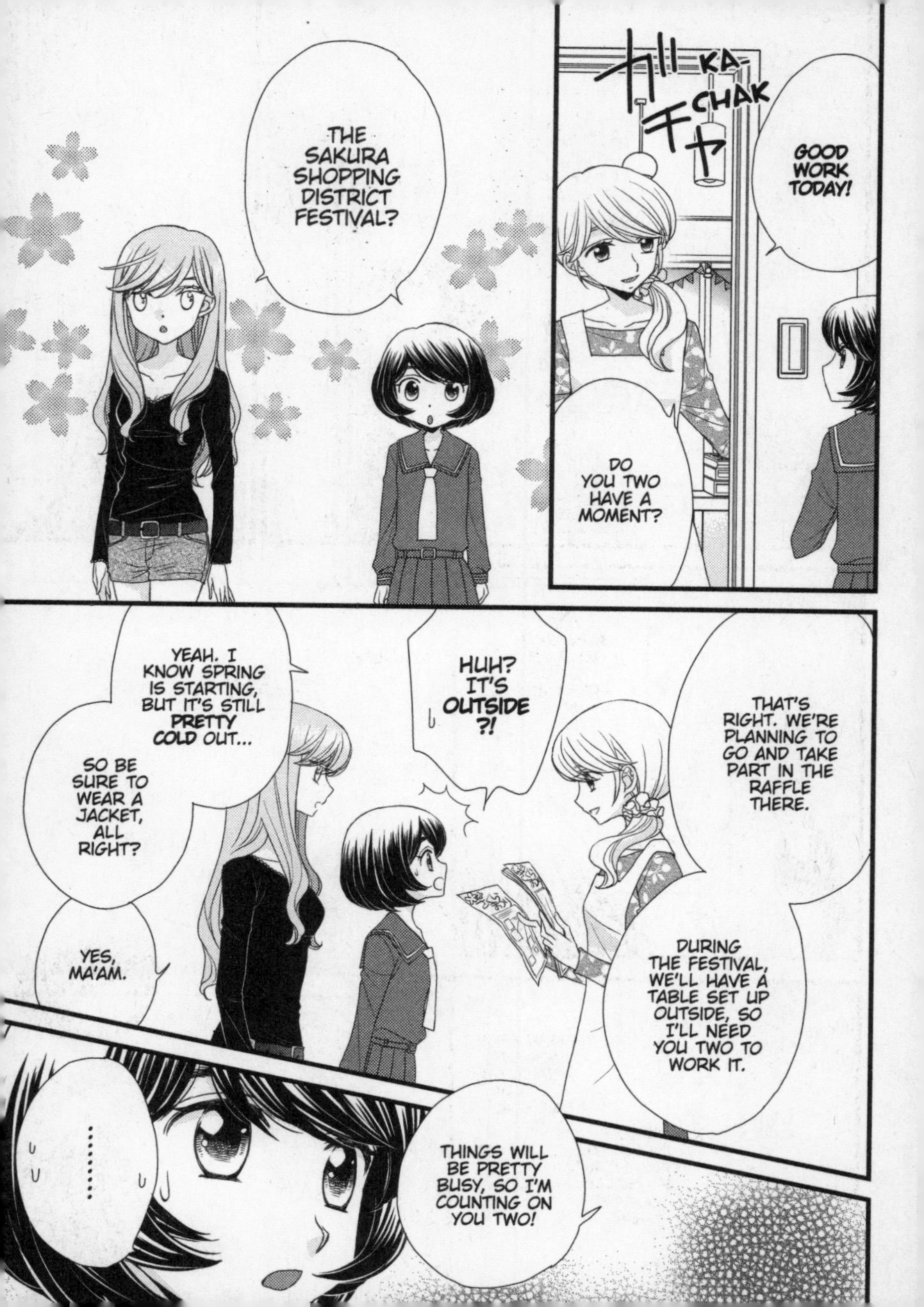
KA CHAK
GOOD WORK TODAY!
DO YOU TWO HAVE A MOMENT?
THE SAKURA SHOPPING DISTRICT FESTIVAL?
THAT'S RIGHT. WE'RE PLANNING TO GO AND TAKE PART IN THE RAFFLE THERE.
DURING THE FESTIVAL, WE'LL HAVE A TABLE SET UP OUTSIDE, SO I'LL NEED YOU TWO TO WORK IT.
THINGS WILL BE PRETTY BUSY, SO I'M COUNTING ON YOU TWO!
HUH? IT'S OUTSIDE?!
YEAH. I KNOW SPRING IS STARTING, BUT IT'S STILL PRETTY COLD OUT...
SO BE SURE TO WEAR A JACKET, ALL RIGHT?
YES, MA'AM.
....

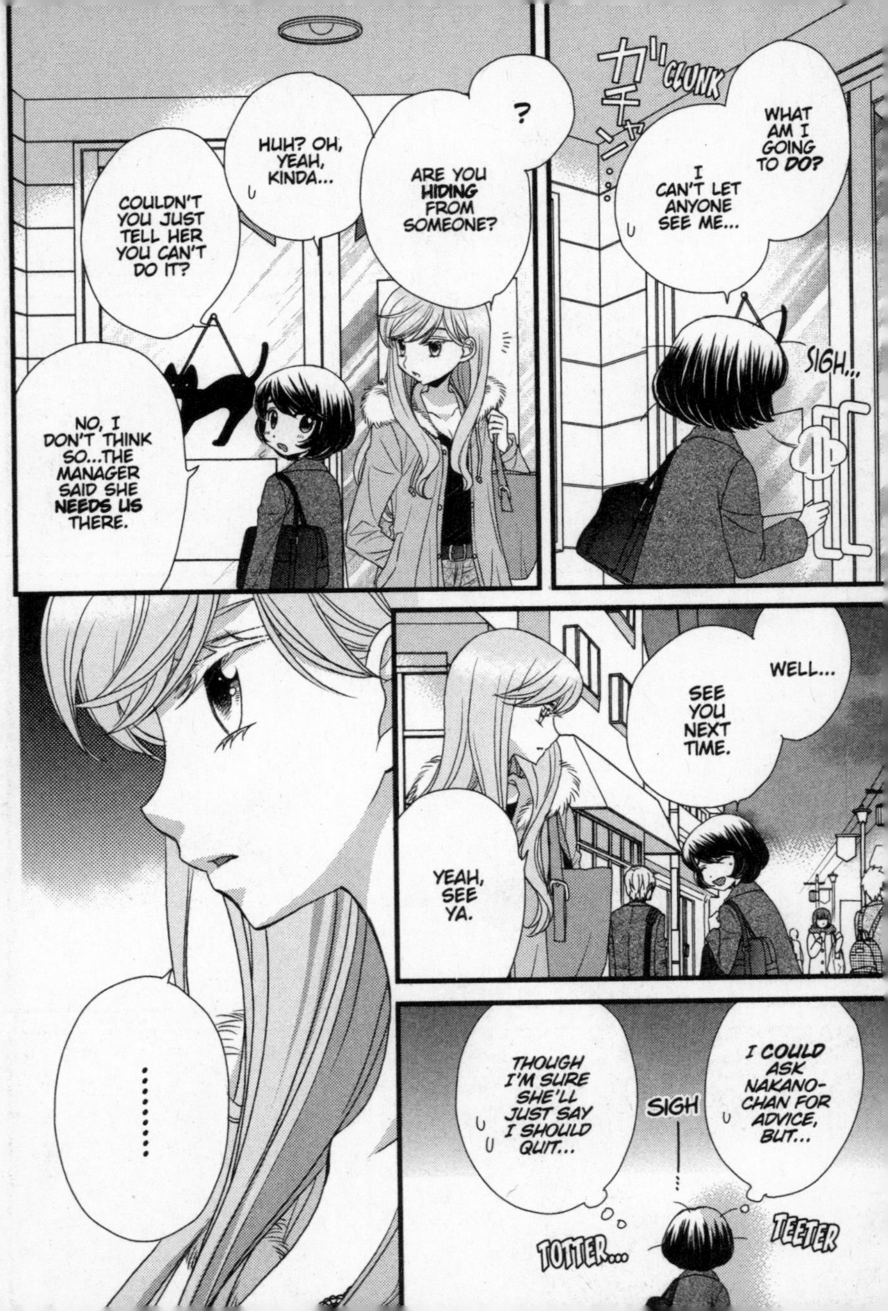
CLUNK
カチャン
WHAT AM I GOING TO DO?
I CAN'T LET ANYONE SEE ME...
SIGH...
?
ARE YOU HIDING FROM SOMEONE?
HUH? OH, YEAH, KINDA...
COULDN'T YOU JUST TELL HER YOU CAN'T DO IT?
NO, I DON'T THINK SO...THE MANAGER SAID SHE NEEDS US THERE.
WELL...
SEE YOU NEXT TIME.
YEAH, SEE YA.
I COULD ASK NAKANO-CHAN FOR ADVICE, BUT...
SIGH
THOUGH I'M SURE SHE'LL JUST SAY I SHOULD QUIT...
TEETER
TOTTER...
....

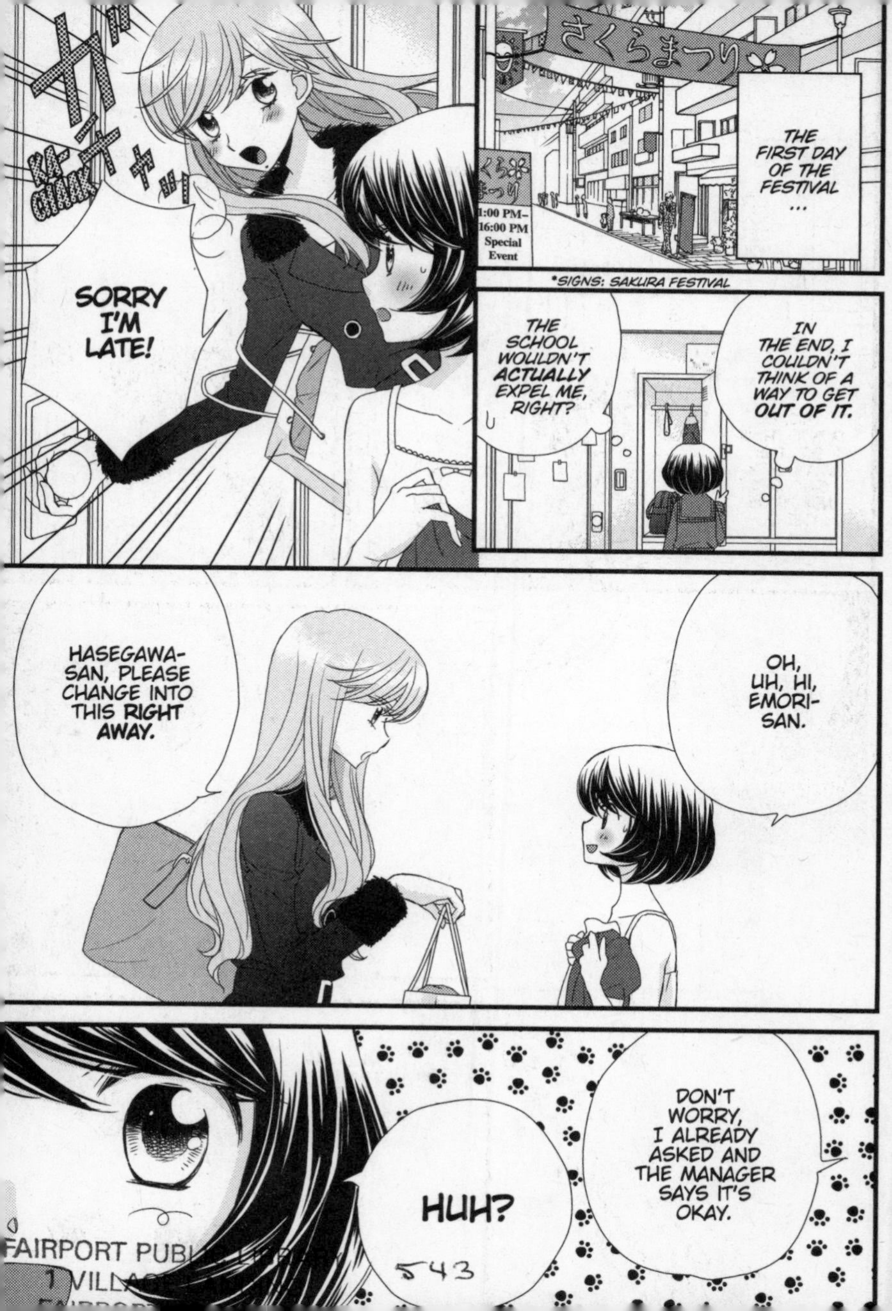
さくらまつり
くら まつり
1:00 PM–16:00 PM Special Event
THE FIRST DAY OF THE FESTIVAL ...
*SIGNS: SAKURA FESTIVAL
IN THE END, I COULDN'T THINK OF A WAY TO GET OUT OF IT.
THE SCHOOL WOULDN'T ACTUALLY EXPEL ME, RIGHT?
KA-CHINK
SORRY I'M LATE!
OH, UH, HI, EMORI-SAN.
HASEGAWA-SAN, PLEASE CHANGE INTO THIS RIGHT AWAY.
DON'T WORRY, I ALREADY ASKED AND THE MANAGER SAYS IT'S OKAY.
HUH?

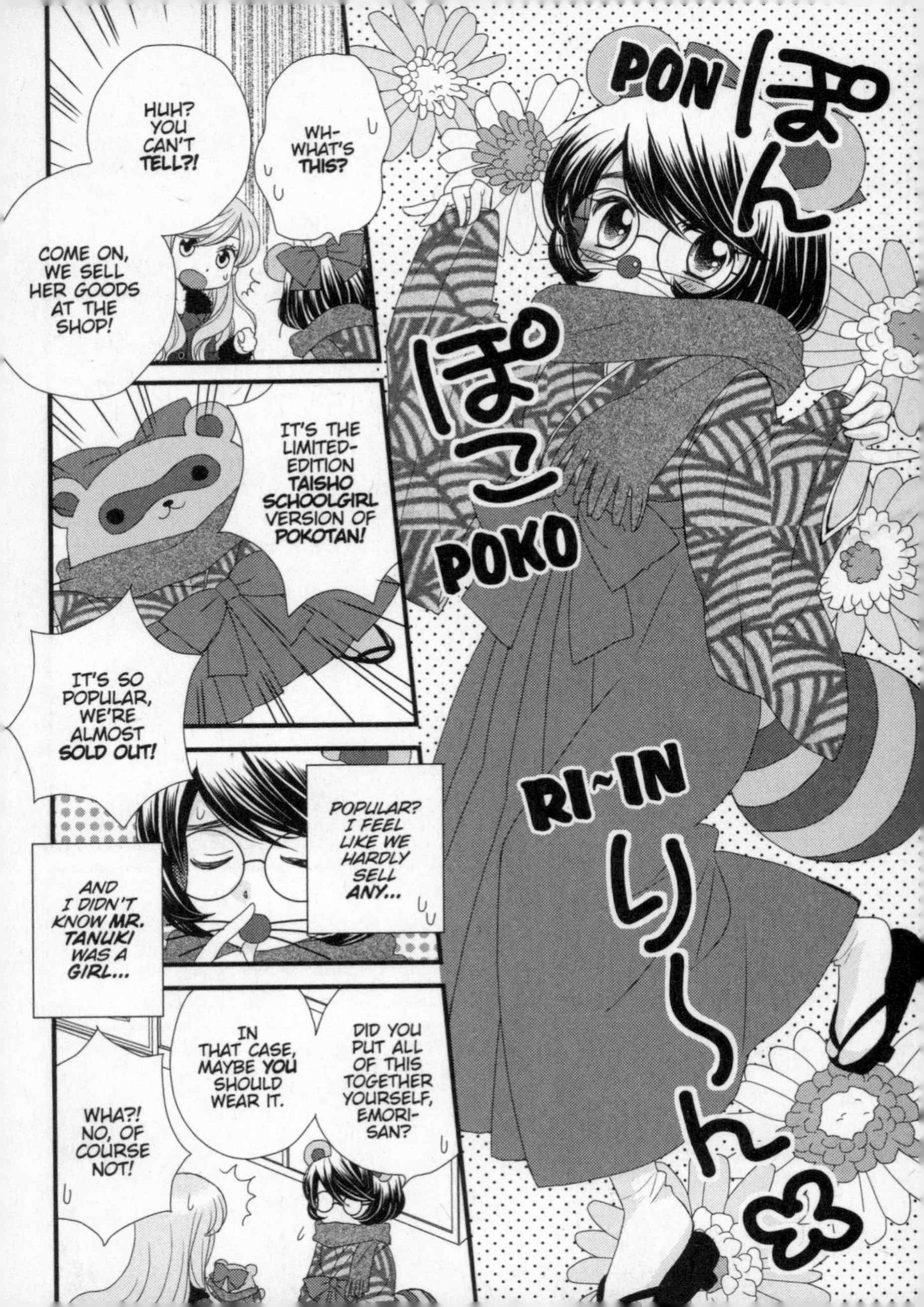

PON ぽん
ぽこ POKO
RI~IN りーん
WH-WHAT'S THIS?
HUH? YOU CAN'T TELL?!
COME ON, WE SELL HER GOODS AT THE SHOP!
IT'S THE LIMITED-EDITION TAISHO SCHOOLGIRL VERSION OF POKOTAN!
IT'S SO POPULAR, WE'RE ALMOST SOLD OUT!
POPULAR? I FEEL LIKE WE HARDLY SELL ANY...
AND I DIDN'T KNOW MR. TANUKI WAS A GIRL...
DID YOU PUT ALL OF THIS TOGETHER YOURSELF, EMORI-SAN?
IN THAT CASE, MAYBE YOU SHOULD WEAR IT.
WHA?! NO, OF COURSE NOT!

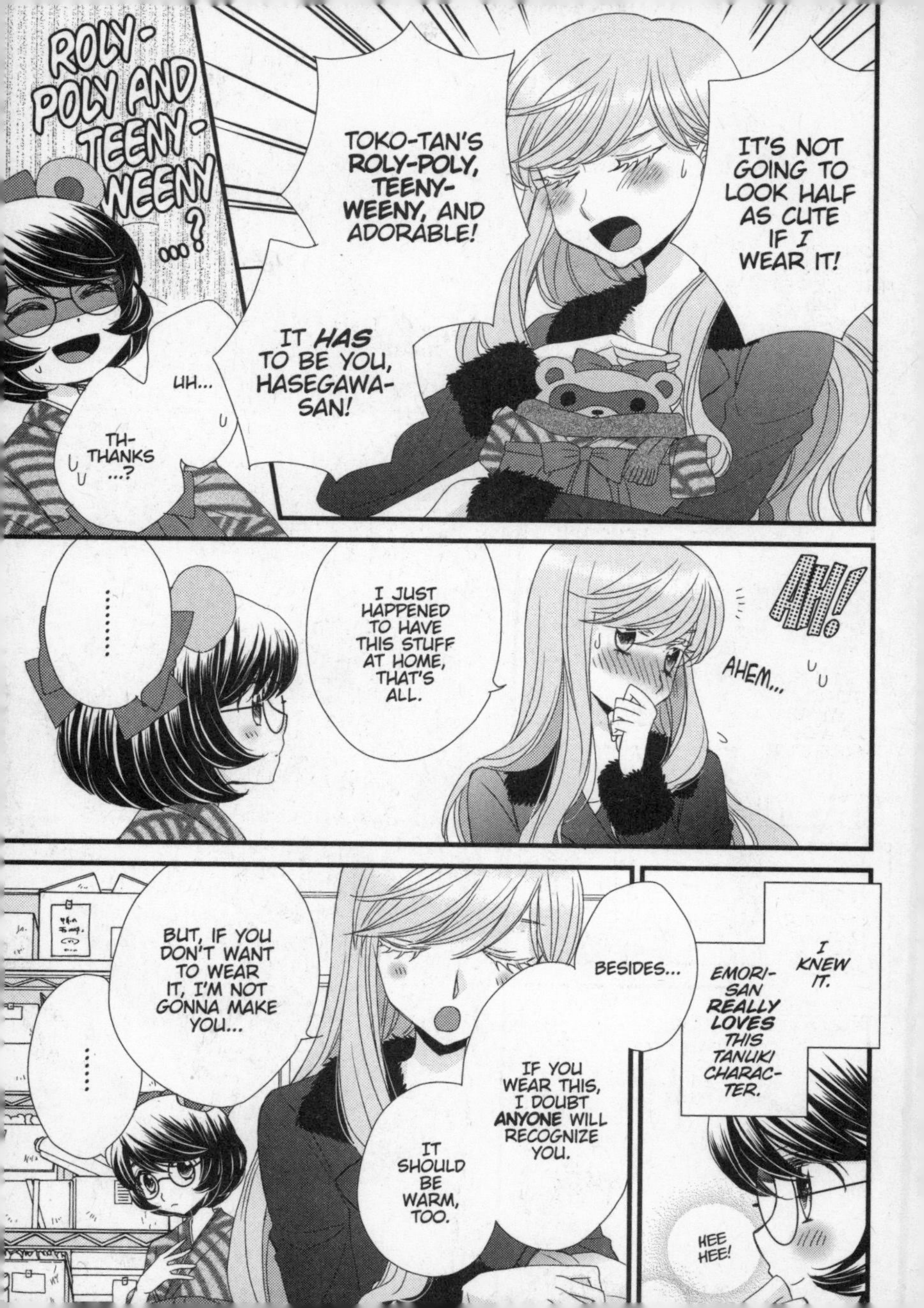
IT'S NOT GOING TO LOOK HALF AS CUTE IF *I* WEAR IT!
TOKO-TAN'S ROLY-POLY, TEENY-WEENY, AND ADORABLE!
IT **HAS** TO BE YOU, HASEGAWA-SAN!
ROLY-POLY AND TEENY-WEENY ...?
UH...
TH-THANKS ...?
AH!
AHEM...
I JUST HAPPENED TO HAVE THIS STUFF AT HOME, THAT'S ALL.
......
I KNEW IT.
EMORI-SAN **REALLY LOVES** THIS TANUKI CHARACTER.
HEE HEE!
BESIDES...
IF YOU WEAR THIS, I DOUBT **ANYONE** WILL RECOGNIZE YOU.
IT SHOULD BE WARM, TOO.
BUT, IF YOU DON'T WANT TO WEAR IT, I'M NOT GONNA MAKE YOU...
......

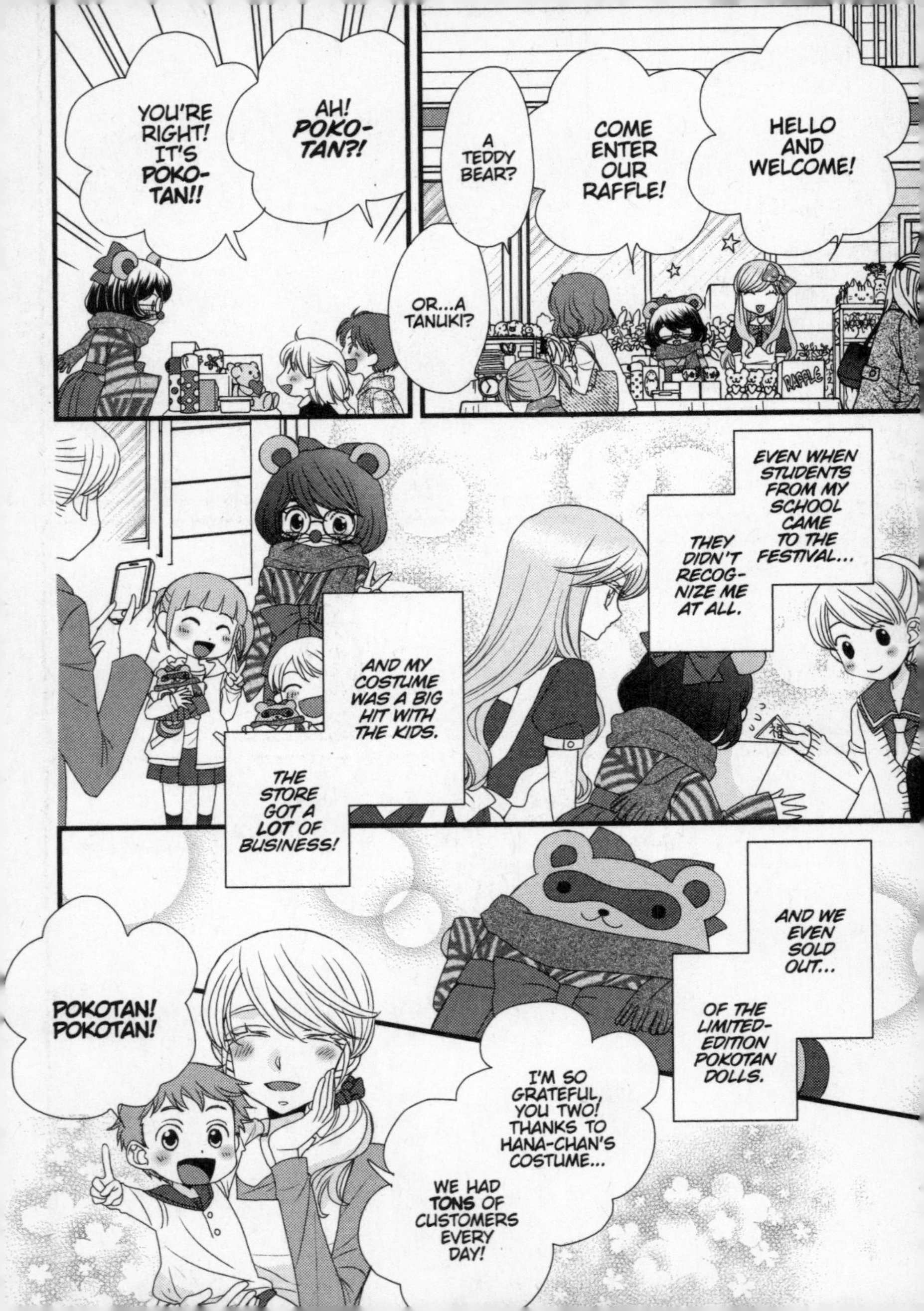
HELLO AND WELCOME!
COME ENTER OUR RAFFLE!
A TEDDY BEAR?
OR...A TANUKI?
RAFFLE
AH! POKO-TAN?!
YOU'RE RIGHT! IT'S POKO-TAN!!
EVEN WHEN STUDENTS FROM MY SCHOOL CAME TO THE FESTIVAL...
THEY DIDN'T RECOG-NIZE ME AT ALL.
AND MY COSTUME WAS A BIG HIT WITH THE KIDS.
THE STORE GOT A LOT OF BUSINESS!
AND WE EVEN SOLD OUT...
OF THE LIMITED-EDITION POKOTAN DOLLS.
I'M SO GRATEFUL, YOU TWO! THANKS TO HANA-CHAN'S COSTUME...
WE HAD TONS OF CUSTOMERS EVERY DAY!
POKOTAN! POKOTAN!

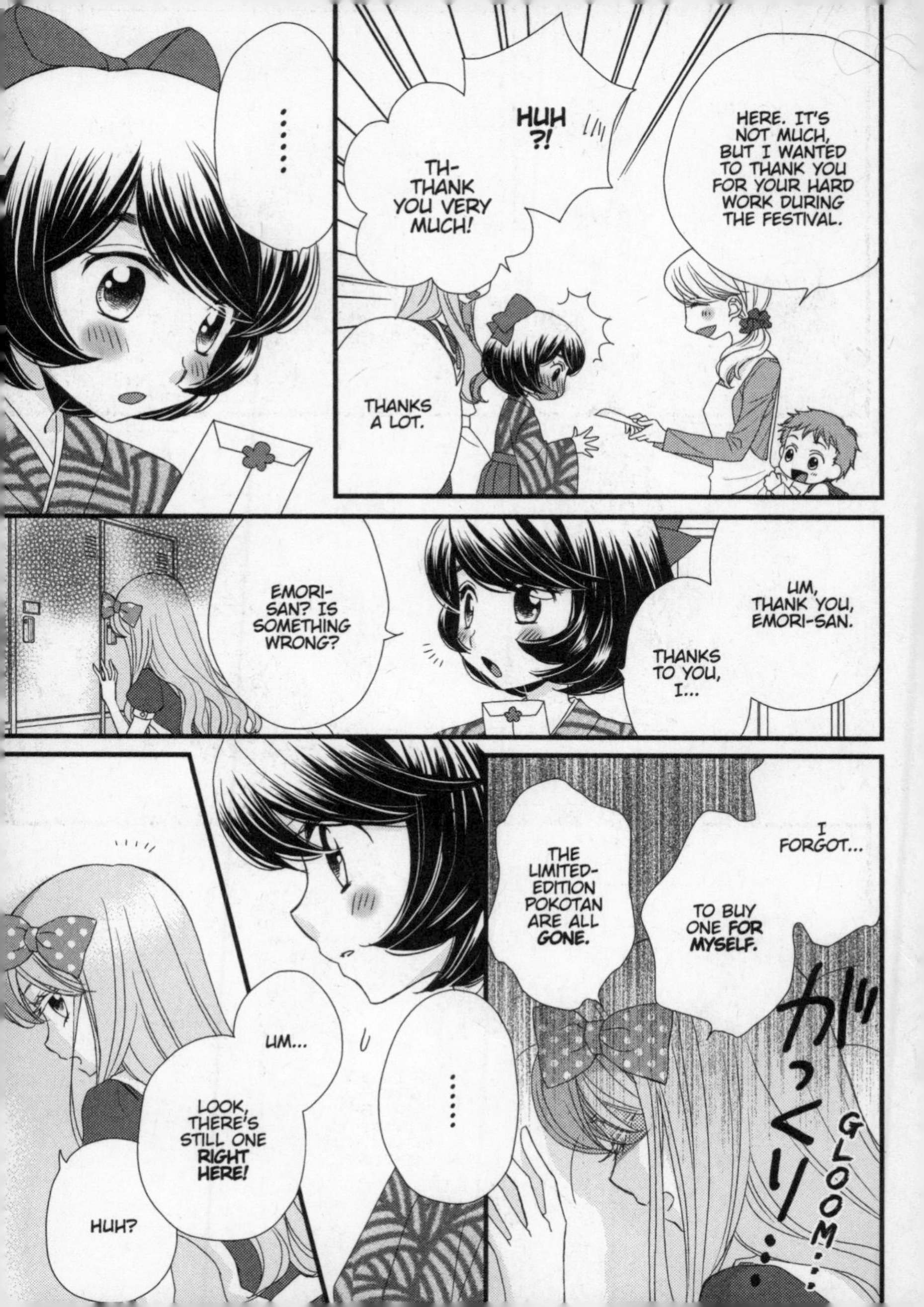
HERE. IT'S NOT MUCH, BUT I WANTED TO THANK YOU FOR YOUR HARD WORK DURING THE FESTIVAL.
HUH ?!
TH-THANK YOU VERY MUCH!
THANKS A LOT.
......
UM, THANK YOU, EMORI-SAN.
THANKS TO YOU, I...
EMORI-SAN? IS SOMETHING WRONG?
I FORGOT...
TO BUY ONE FOR MYSELF.
THE LIMITED-EDITION POKOTAN ARE ALL GONE.
がっくり
GLOOM...
......
UM...
LOOK, THERE'S STILL ONE RIGHT HERE!
HUH?

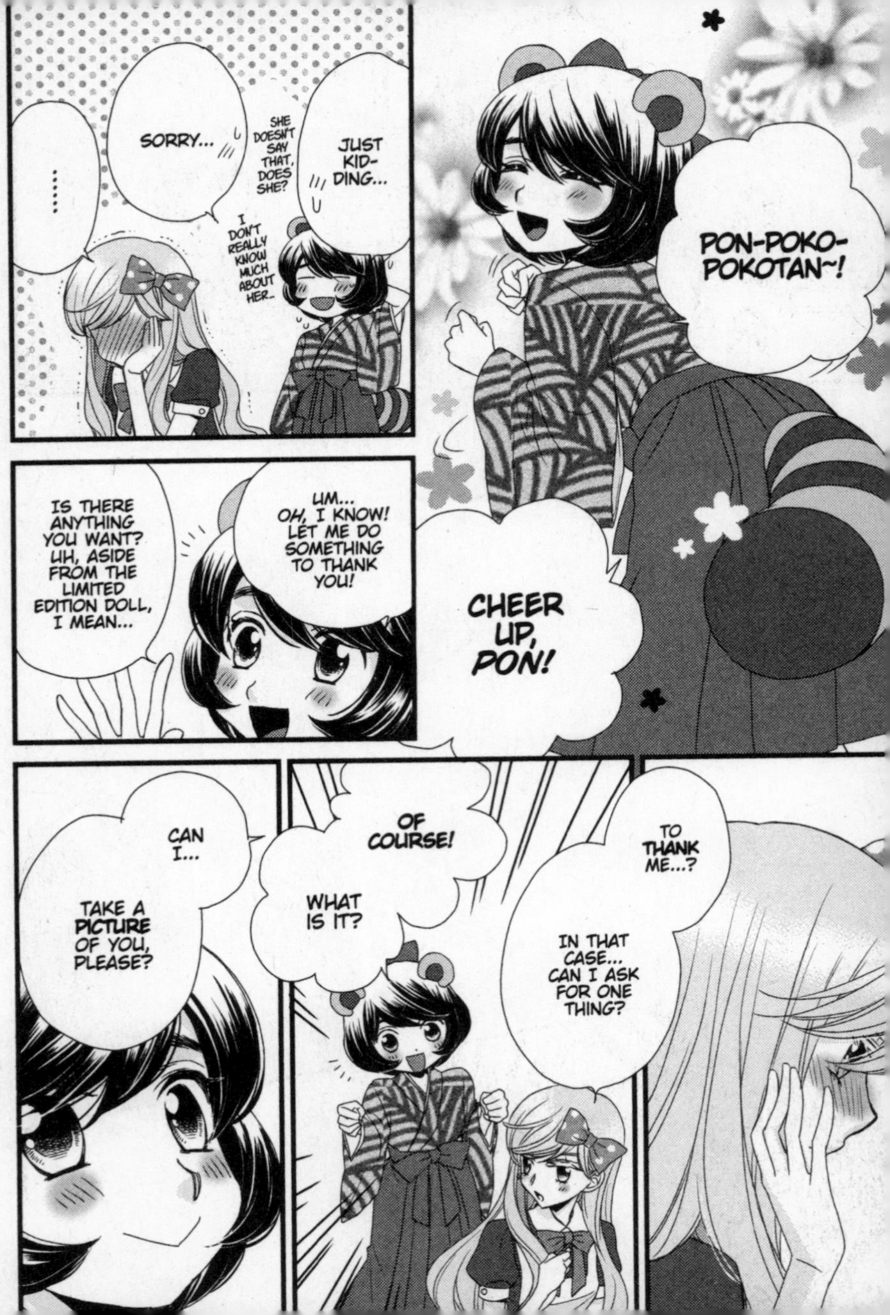
PON-POKO-POKOTAN~!
CHEER UP, PON!
JUST KID-DING...
SHE DOESN'T SAY THAT, DOES SHE?
I DON'T REALLY KNOW MUCH ABOUT HER...
SORRY...
......
UM... OH, I KNOW! LET ME DO SOMETHING TO THANK YOU!
IS THERE ANYTHING YOU WANT? UH, ASIDE FROM THE LIMITED EDITION DOLL, I MEAN...
TO THANK ME...?
IN THAT CASE... CAN I ASK FOR ONE THING?
OF COURSE!
WHAT IS IT?
CAN I...
TAKE A PICTURE OF YOU, PLEASE?

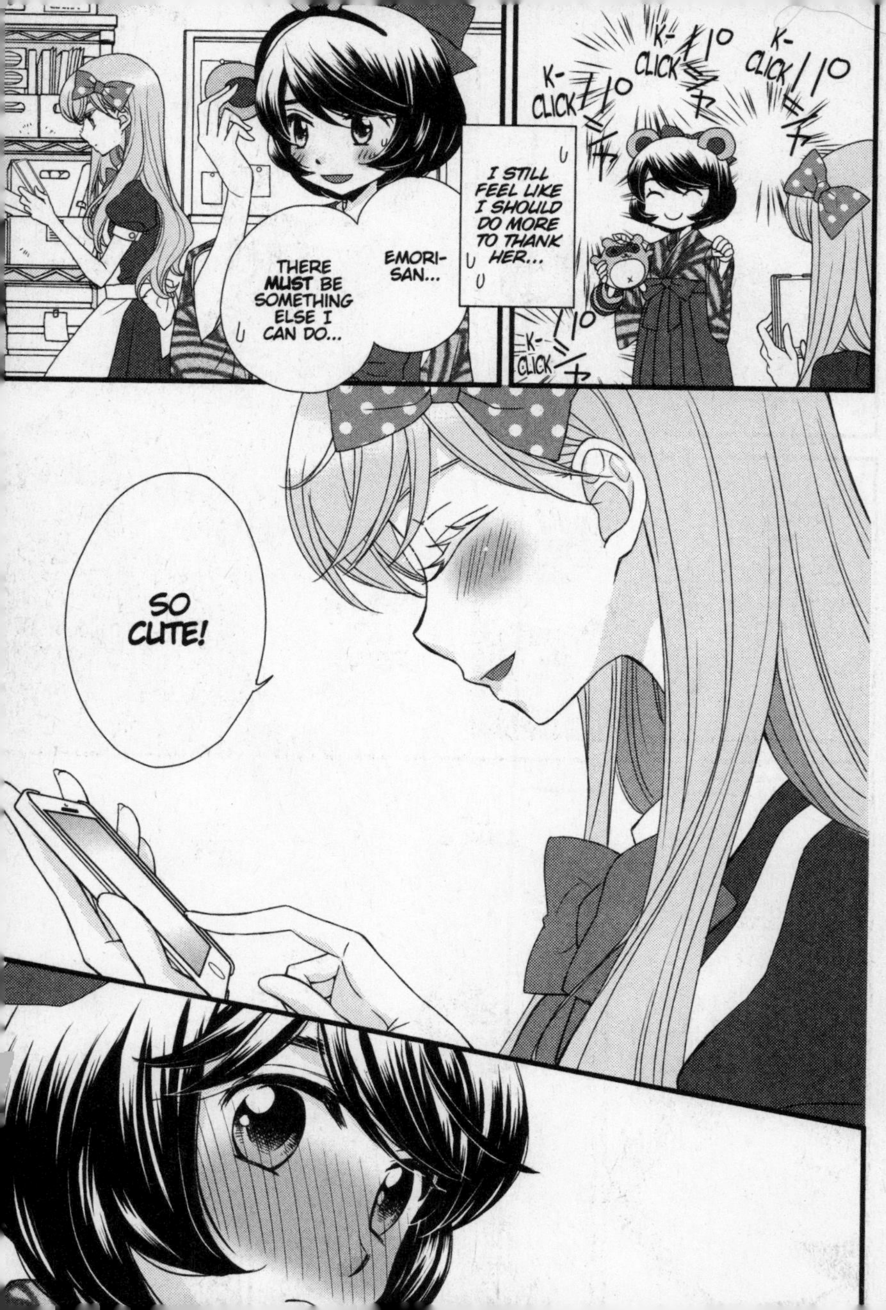
K-CLICK
K-CLICK
K-CLICK
I STILL FEEL LIKE I SHOULD DO MORE TO THANK HER...
K-CLICK
EMORI-SAN...
THERE MUST BE SOMETHING ELSE I CAN DO...
SO CUTE!

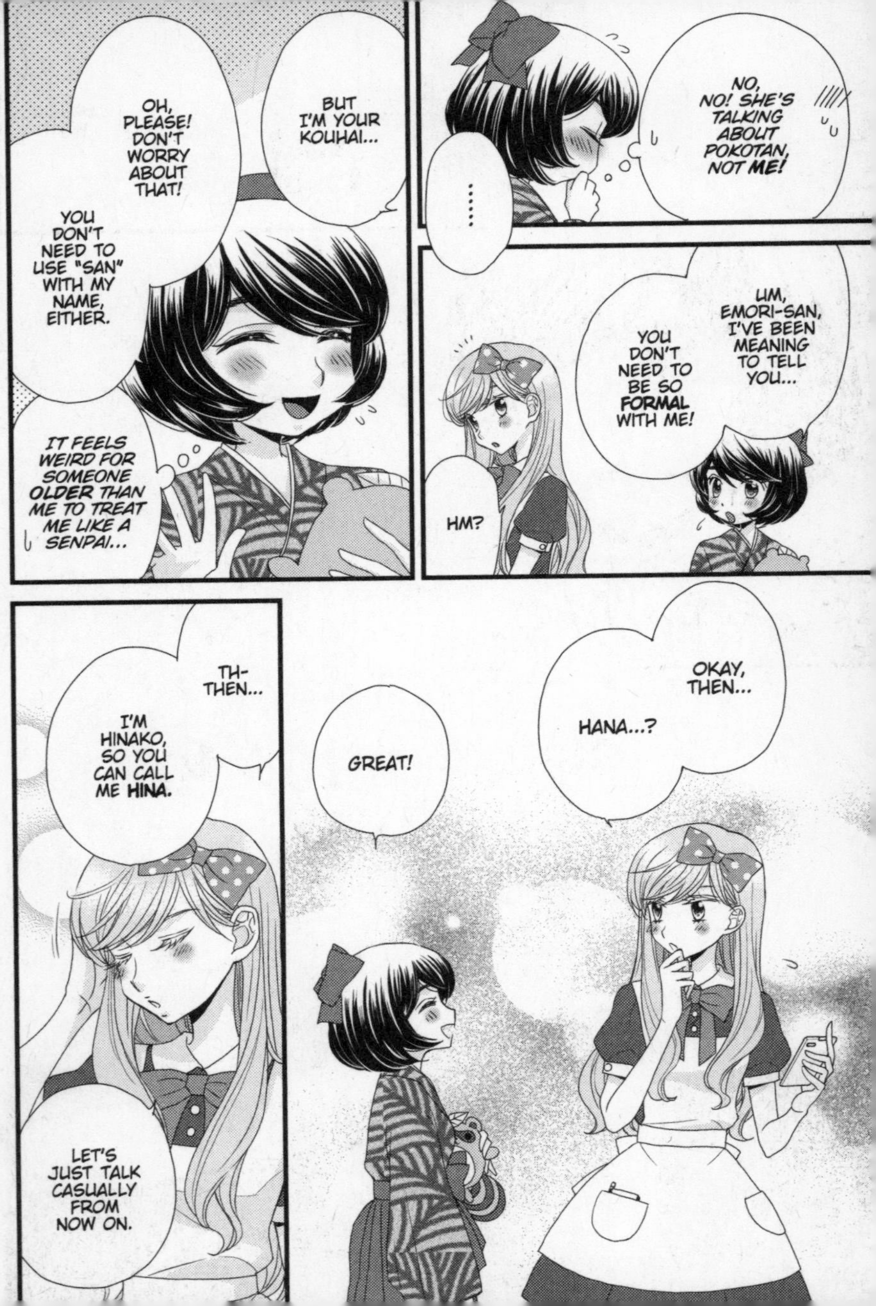
NO, NO! SHE'S TALKING ABOUT POKOTAN, NOT ME!
......
UM, EMORI-SAN, I'VE BEEN MEANING TO TELL YOU...
YOU DON'T NEED TO BE SO FORMAL WITH ME!
HM?
BUT I'M YOUR KOUHAI...
OH, PLEASE! DON'T WORRY ABOUT THAT!
YOU DON'T NEED TO USE "SAN" WITH MY NAME, EITHER.
IT FEELS WEIRD FOR SOMEONE OLDER THAN ME TO TREAT ME LIKE A SENPAI...
OKAY, THEN...
HANA...?
GREAT!
TH-THEN...
I'M HINAKO, SO YOU CAN CALL ME HINA.
LET'S JUST TALK CASUALLY FROM NOW ON.

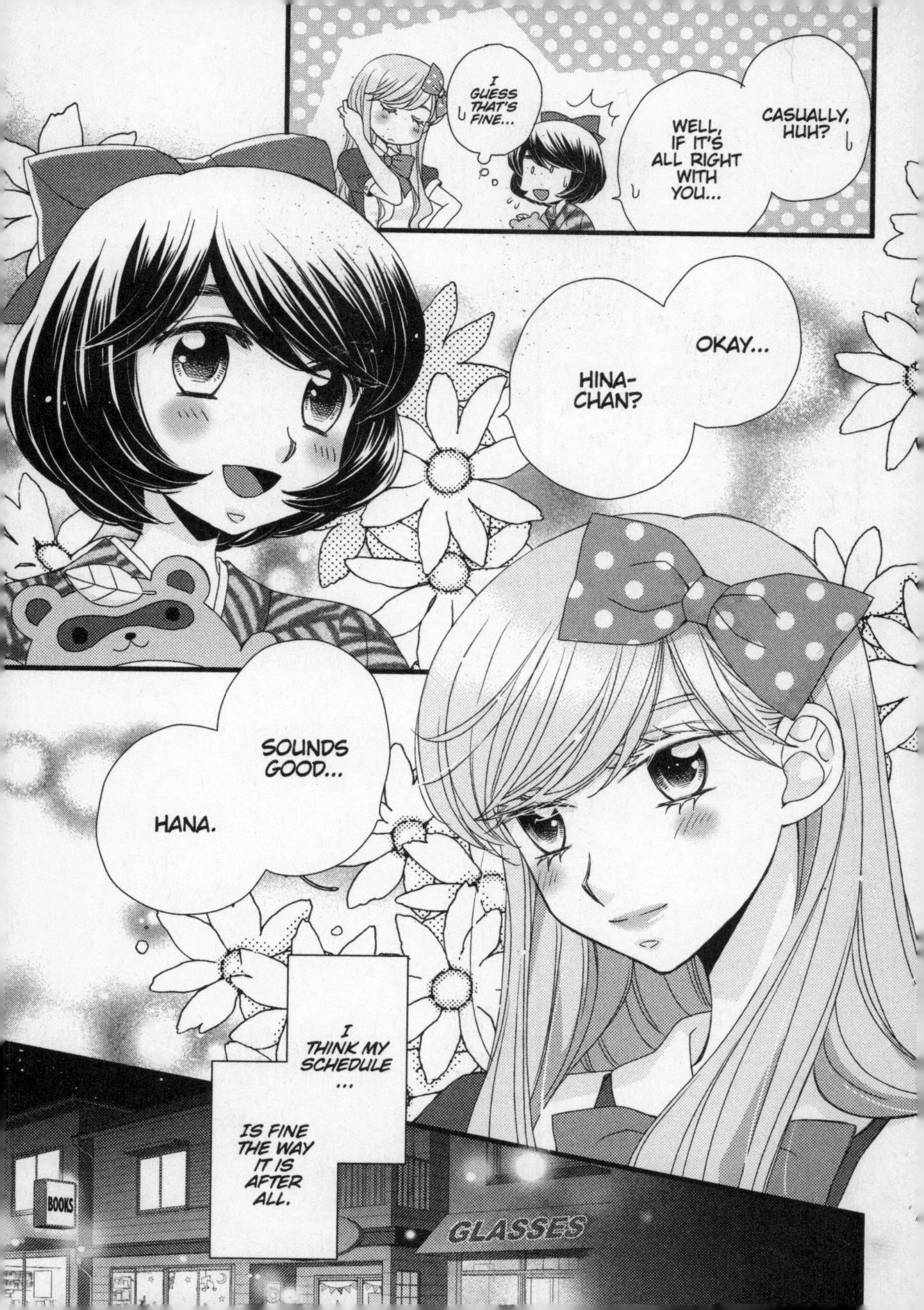
CASUALLY, HUH?
WELL, IF IT'S ALL RIGHT WITH YOU...
I GUESS THAT'S FINE...
OKAY...
HINA-CHAN?
SOUNDS GOOD...
HANA.
I THINK MY SCHEDULE ...
IS FINE THE WAY IT IS AFTER ALL.
GLASSES
BOOKS

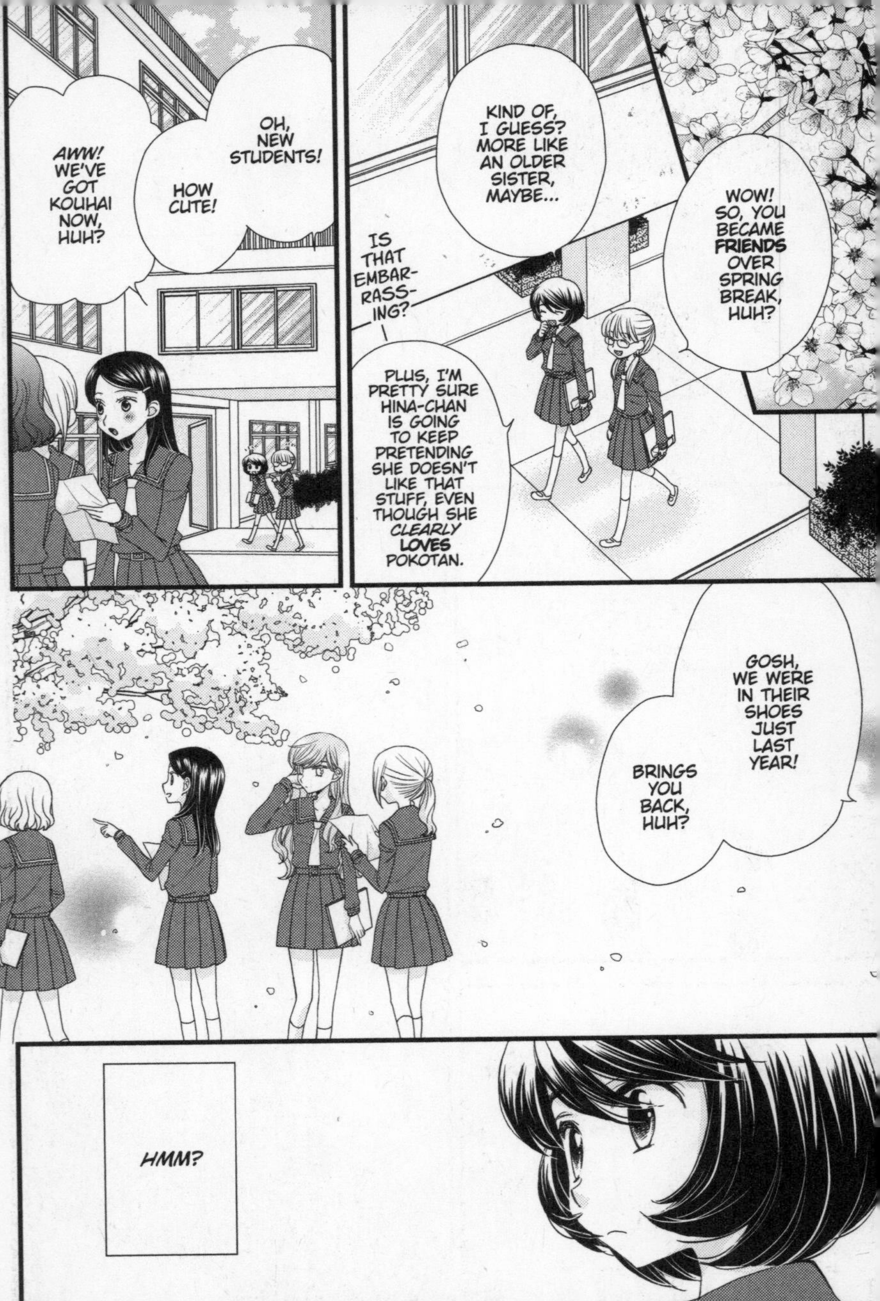
WOW! SO, YOU BECAME FRIENDS OVER SPRING BREAK, HUH?
KIND OF, I GUESS? MORE LIKE AN OLDER SISTER, MAYBE...
IS THAT EMBARRASSING?
PLUS, I'M PRETTY SURE HINA-CHAN IS GOING TO KEEP PRETENDING SHE DOESN'T LIKE THAT STUFF, EVEN THOUGH SHE CLEARLY LOVES POKOTAN.
OH, NEW STUDENTS!
HOW CUTE!
AWW! WE'VE GOT KOUHAI NOW, HUH?
GOSH, WE WERE IN THEIR SHOES JUST LAST YEAR!
BRINGS YOU BACK, HUH?
HMM?

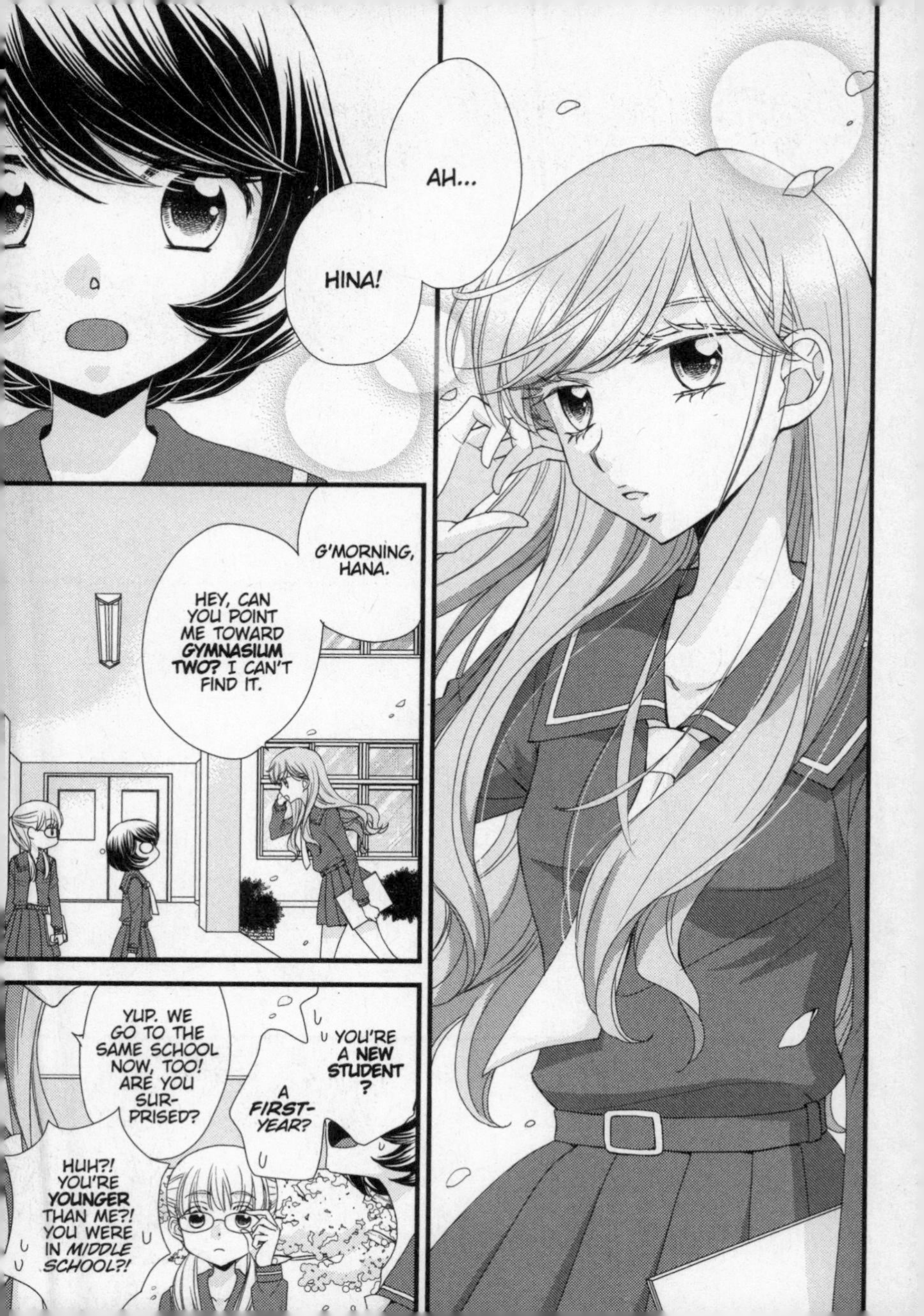
AH...
HINA!
G'MORNING, HANA.
HEY, CAN YOU POINT ME TOWARD GYMNASIUM TWO? I CAN'T FIND IT.
YOU'RE A NEW STUDENT?
A FIRST-YEAR?
YUP. WE GO TO THE SAME SCHOOL NOW, TOO! ARE YOU SURPRISED?
HUH?! YOU'RE YOUNGER THAN ME?! YOU WERE IN MIDDLE SCHOOL?!

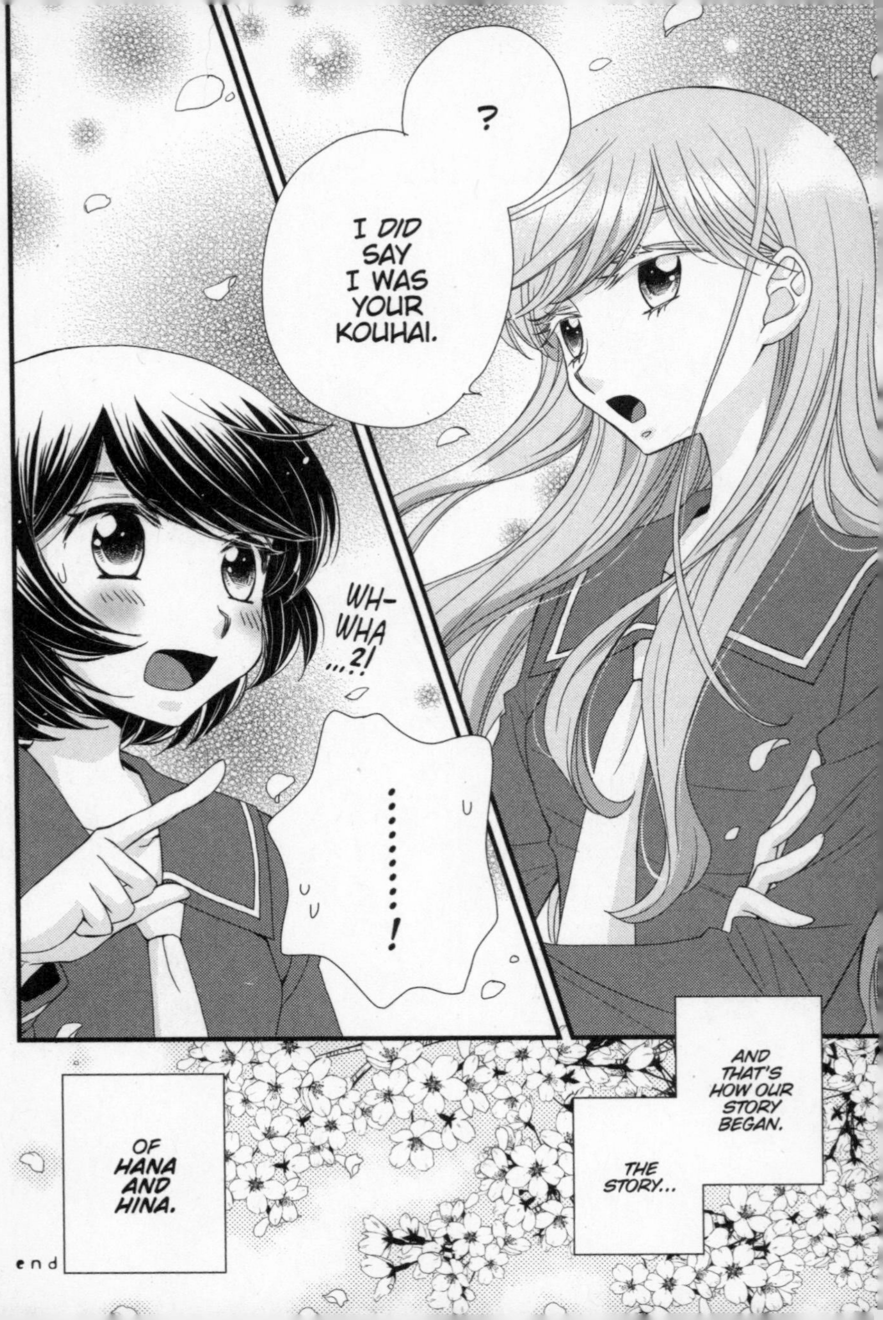
?
I DID SAY I WAS YOUR KOUHAI.
WH- WHA ...?!
.......!
AND THAT'S HOW OUR STORY BEGAN.
THE STORY...
OF HANA AND HINA.
end

Hana & Hina AFTER ♡ SCHOOL

Hana & Hina AFTER♡SCHOOL

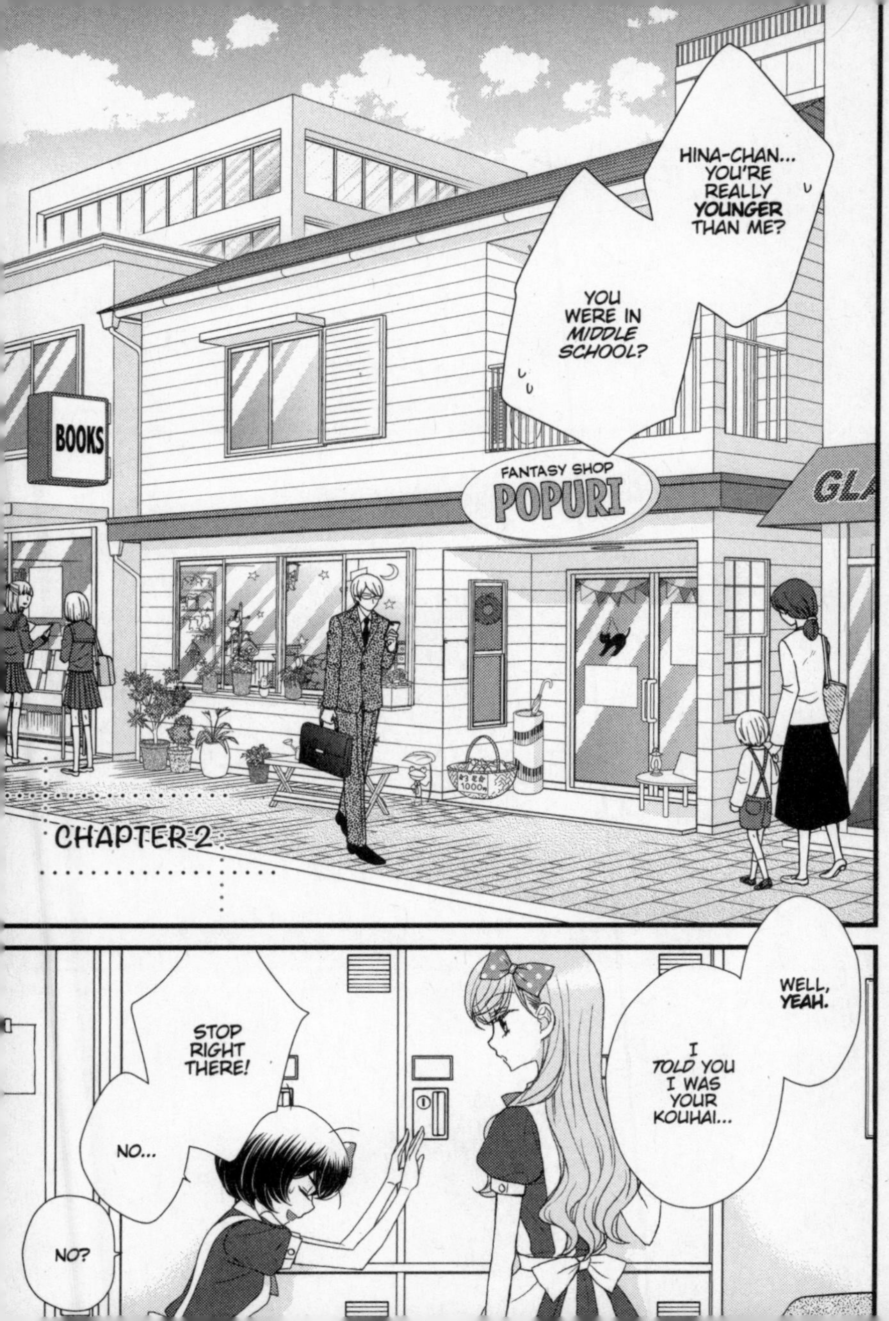
HINA-CHAN... YOU'RE REALLY **YOUNGER** THAN ME?
YOU WERE IN *MIDDLE SCHOOL?*
BOOKS
FANTASY SHOP POPURI
CHAPTER 2
WELL, **YEAH.**
I *TOLD* YOU I WAS YOUR KOUHAI...
STOP RIGHT THERE!
NO...
NO?

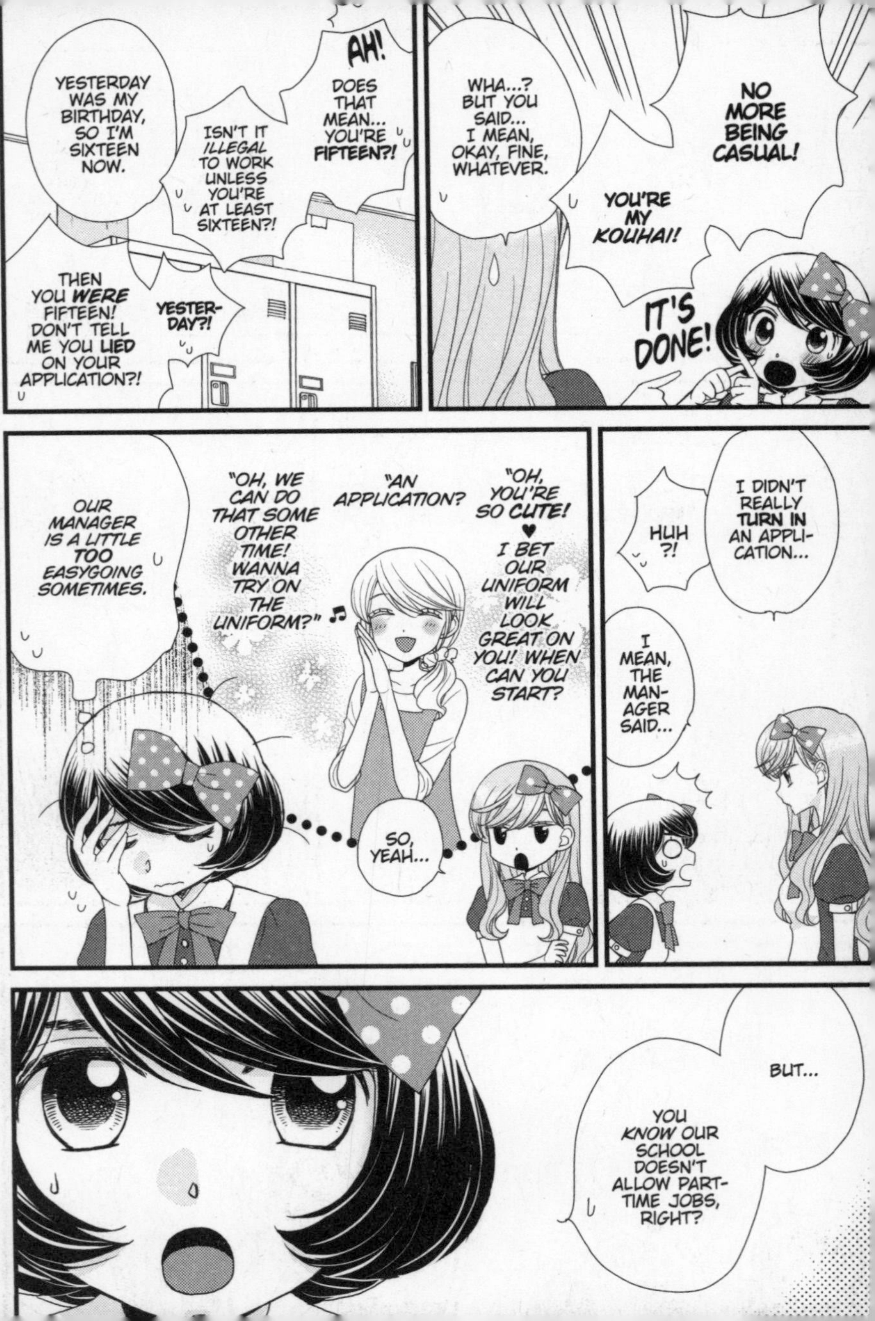
NO MORE BEING CASUAL!
YOU'RE MY KOUHAI!
IT'S DONE!
WHA...? BUT YOU SAID... I MEAN, OKAY, FINE, WHATEVER.
AH!
DOES THAT MEAN... YOU'RE FIFTEEN?!
YESTERDAY WAS MY BIRTHDAY, SO I'M SIXTEEN NOW.
ISN'T IT ILLEGAL TO WORK UNLESS YOU'RE AT LEAST SIXTEEN?!
YESTER-DAY?!
THEN YOU WERE FIFTEEN! DON'T TELL ME YOU LIED ON YOUR APPLICATION?!
I DIDN'T REALLY TURN IN AN APPLI-CATION...
HUH?!
I MEAN, THE MAN-AGER SAID...
"OH, YOU'RE SO CUTE! ♥ I BET OUR UNIFORM WILL LOOK GREAT ON YOU! WHEN CAN YOU START?
"AN APPLICATION?
"OH, WE CAN DO THAT SOME OTHER TIME! WANNA TRY ON THE UNIFORM?" ♪
SO, YEAH...
OUR MANAGER IS A LITTLE TOO EASYGOING SOMETIMES.
BUT...
YOU KNOW OUR SCHOOL DOESN'T ALLOW PART-TIME JOBS, RIGHT?

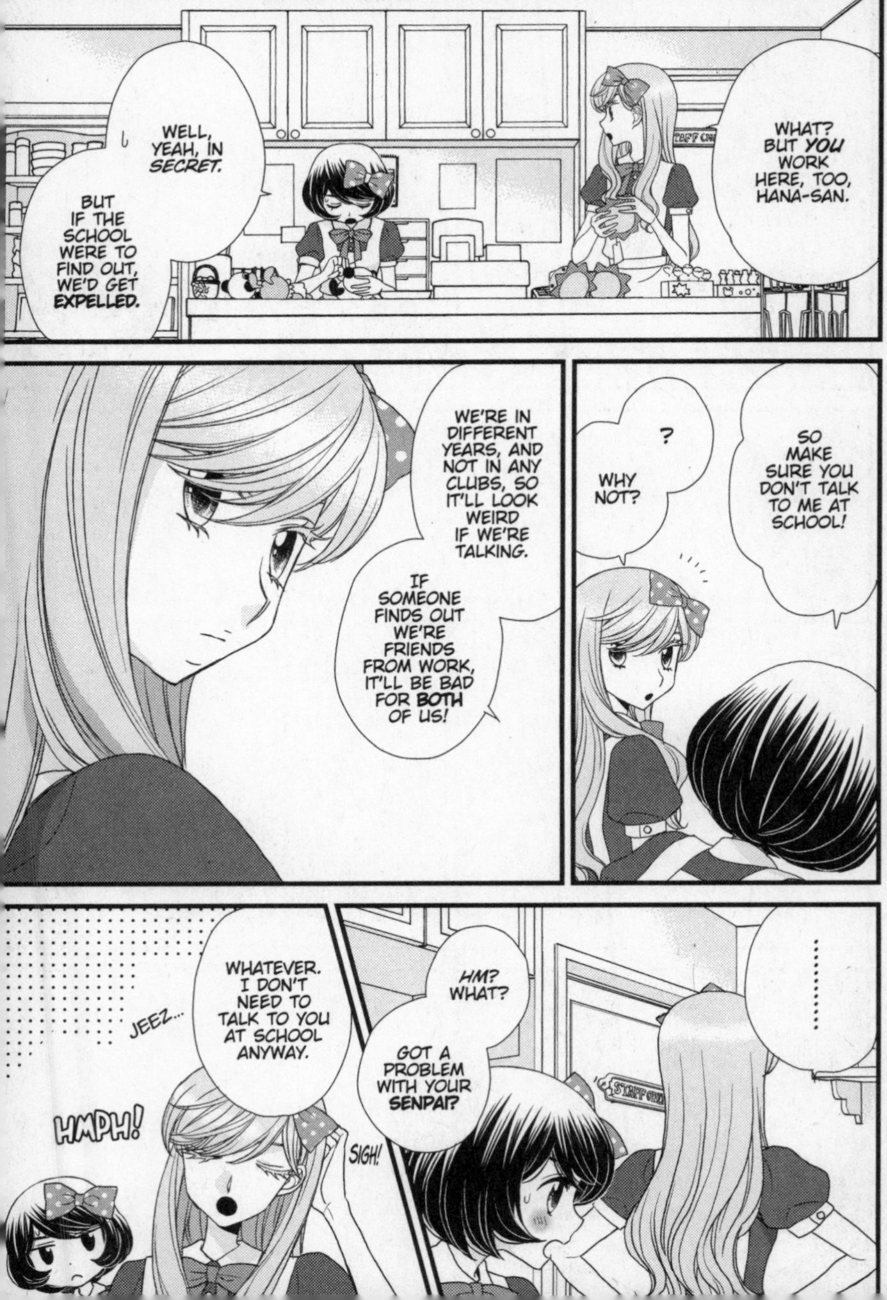
WHAT? BUT YOU WORK HERE, TOO, HANA-SAN.
WELL, YEAH, IN SECRET.
BUT IF THE SCHOOL WERE TO FIND OUT, WE'D GET EXPELLED.
SO MAKE SURE YOU DON'T TALK TO ME AT SCHOOL!
?
WHY NOT?
WE'RE IN DIFFERENT YEARS, AND NOT IN ANY CLUBS, SO IT'LL LOOK WEIRD IF WE'RE TALKING.
IF SOMEONE FINDS OUT WE'RE FRIENDS FROM WORK, IT'LL BE BAD FOR BOTH OF US!
......
HM? WHAT?
GOT A PROBLEM WITH YOUR SENPAI?
SIGH!
WHATEVER. I DON'T NEED TO TALK TO YOU AT SCHOOL ANYWAY.
JEEZ...
HMPH!

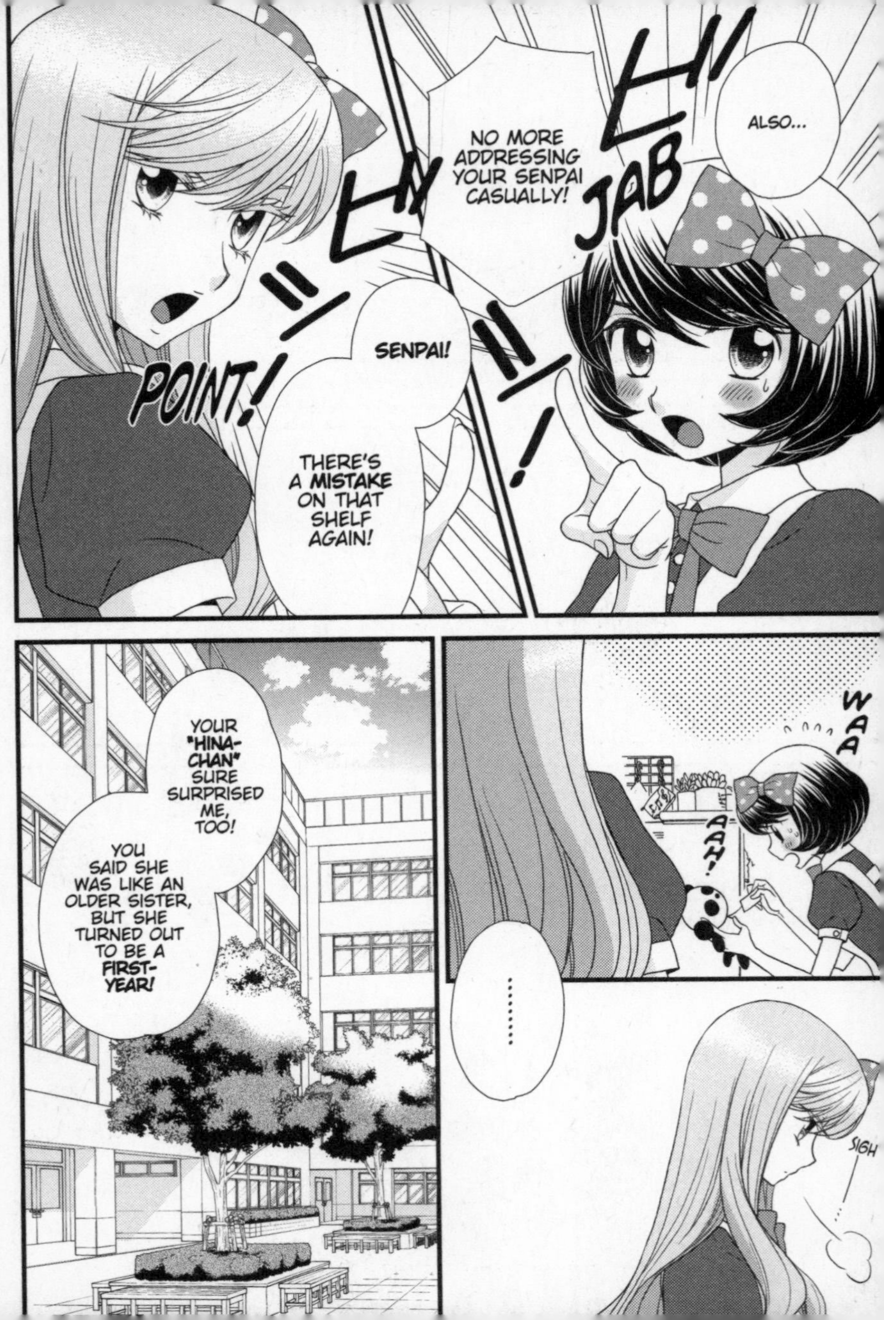
ALSO...
JAB
NO MORE ADDRESSING YOUR SENPAI CASUALLY!
SENPAI! THERE'S A MISTAKE ON THAT SHELF AGAIN!
POINT!
WAA
AAH!
......
SIGH
...
YOUR "HINA-CHAN" SURE SURPRISED ME, TOO!
YOU SAID SHE WAS LIKE AN OLDER SISTER, BUT SHE TURNED OUT TO BE A FIRST-YEAR!

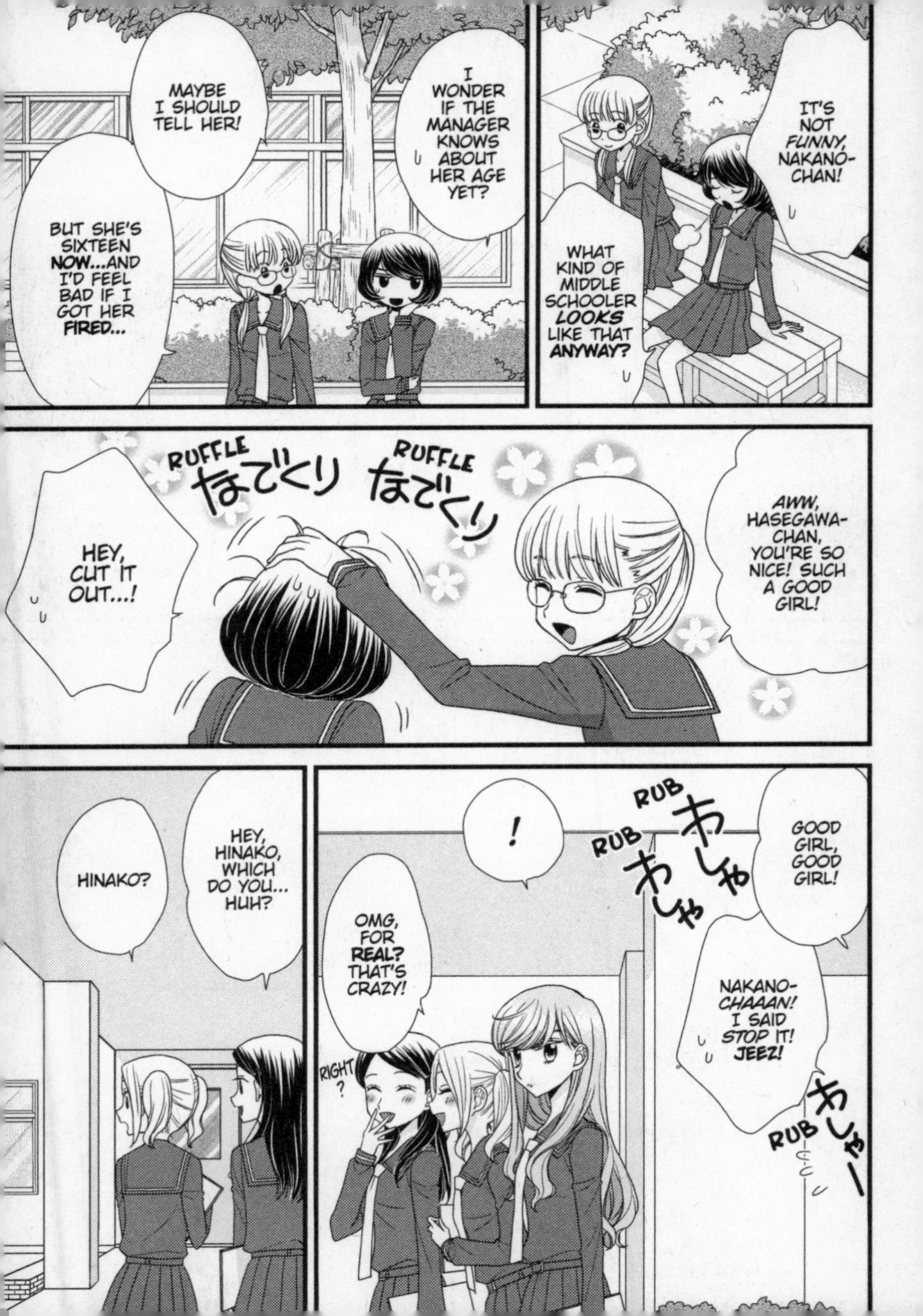
IT'S NOT *FUNNY*, NAKANO-CHAN!
WHAT KIND OF MIDDLE SCHOOLER **LOOKS** LIKE THAT **ANYWAY?**
I WONDER IF THE MANAGER KNOWS ABOUT HER AGE YET?
MAYBE I SHOULD TELL HER!
BUT SHE'S SIXTEEN **NOW**...AND I'D FEEL BAD IF I GOT HER **FIRED**...
AWW, HASEGAWA-CHAN, YOU'RE SO NICE! SUCH A GOOD GIRL!
RUFFLE なでくり
RUFFLE なでくり
HEY, CUT IT OUT...!
GOOD GIRL, GOOD GIRL!
RUB わしゃ
RUB わしゃ
NAKANO-*CHAAAN!* I SAID *STOP IT!* **JEEZ!**
RUB わしゃー
!
OMG, FOR **REAL?** THAT'S CRAZY!
RIGHT?
HEY, HINAKO, WHICH DO YOU... HUH?
HINAKO?

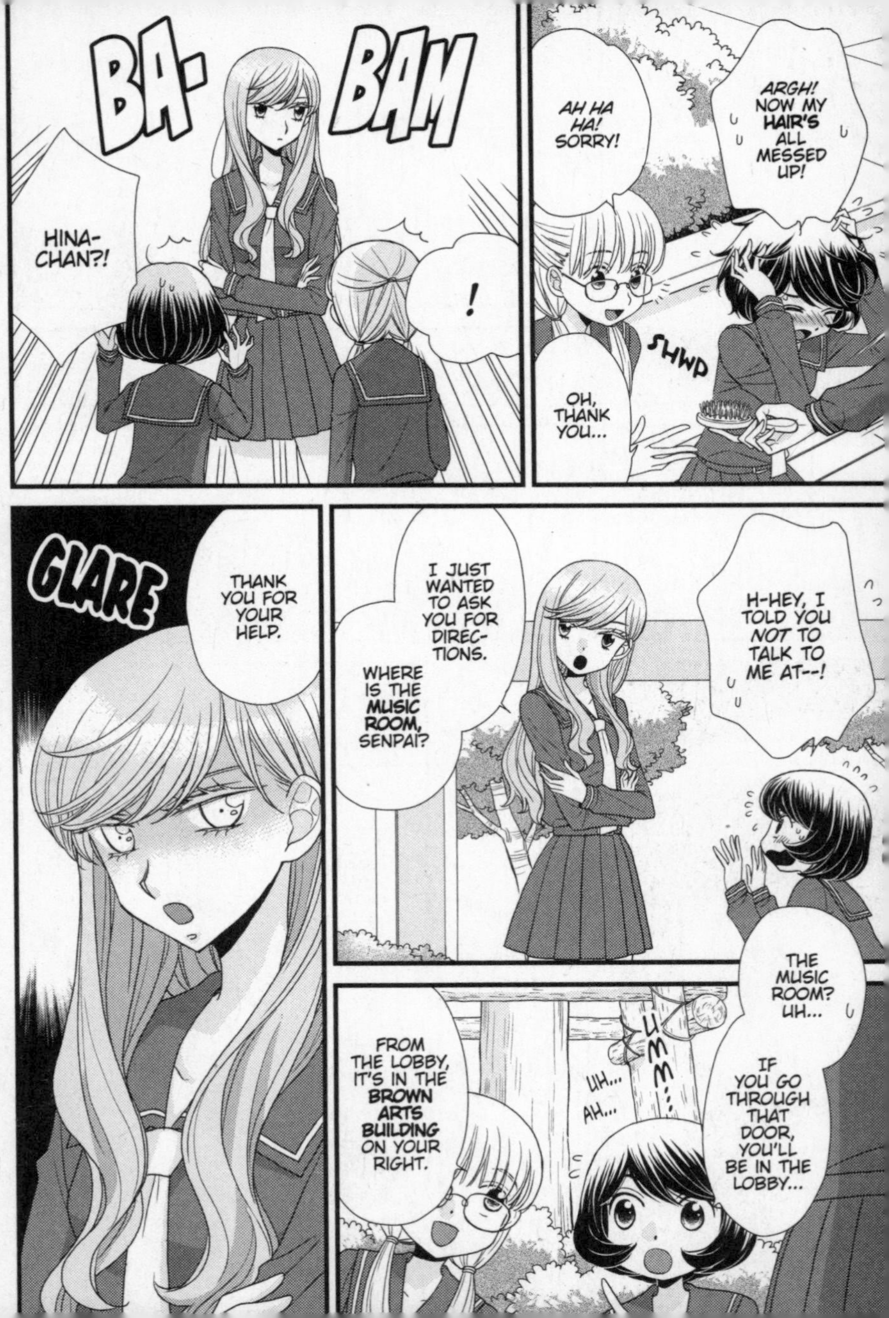
ARGH! NOW MY HAIR'S ALL MESSED UP!
AH HA HA! SORRY!
SHWP
OH, THANK YOU...
BA-BAM
!
HINA-CHAN?!
H-HEY, I TOLD YOU NOT TO TALK TO ME AT--!
I JUST WANTED TO ASK YOU FOR DIRECTIONS.
WHERE IS THE MUSIC ROOM, SENPAI?
THE MUSIC ROOM? UH...
IF YOU GO THROUGH THAT DOOR, YOU'LL BE IN THE LOBBY...
UMM...
UH... AH...
FROM THE LOBBY, IT'S IN THE BROWN ARTS BUILDING ON YOUR RIGHT.
GLARE
THANK YOU FOR YOUR HELP.

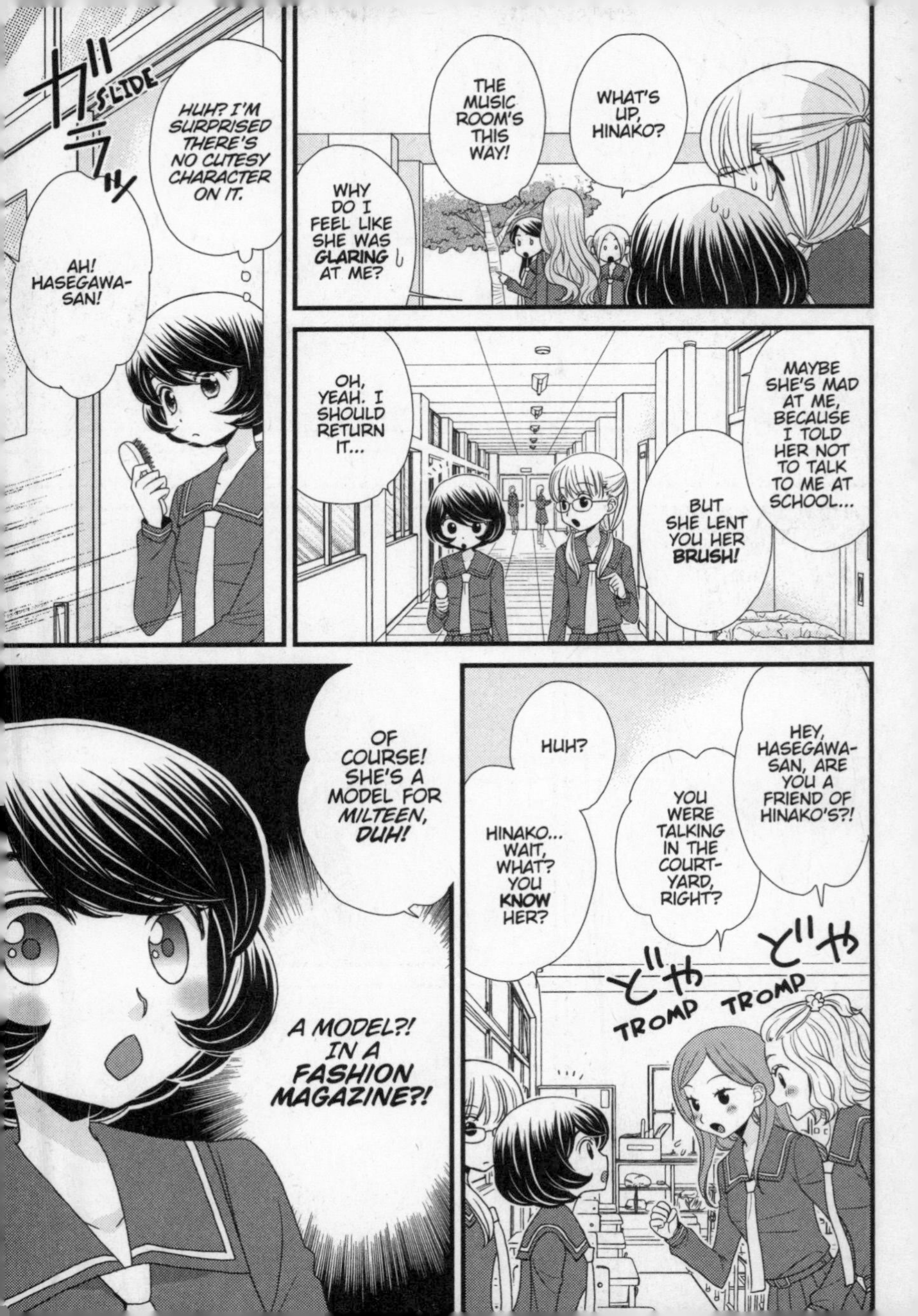
WHAT'S UP, HINAKO?
THE MUSIC ROOM'S THIS WAY!
WHY DO I FEEL LIKE SHE WAS GLARING AT ME?
MAYBE SHE'S MAD AT ME, BECAUSE I TOLD HER NOT TO TALK TO ME AT SCHOOL...
BUT SHE LENT YOU HER BRUSH!
OH, YEAH. I SHOULD RETURN IT...
SLIDE
HUH? I'M SURPRISED THERE'S NO CUTESY CHARACTER ON IT.
AH! HASEGAWA-SAN!
HEY, HASEGAWA-SAN, ARE YOU A FRIEND OF HINAKO'S?!
YOU WERE TALKING IN THE COURTYARD, RIGHT?
HUH?
HINAKO... WAIT, WHAT? YOU KNOW HER?
どやどや
TROMP TROMP
OF COURSE! SHE'S A MODEL FOR MILTEEN, DUH!
A MODEL?! IN A FASHION MAGAZINE?!

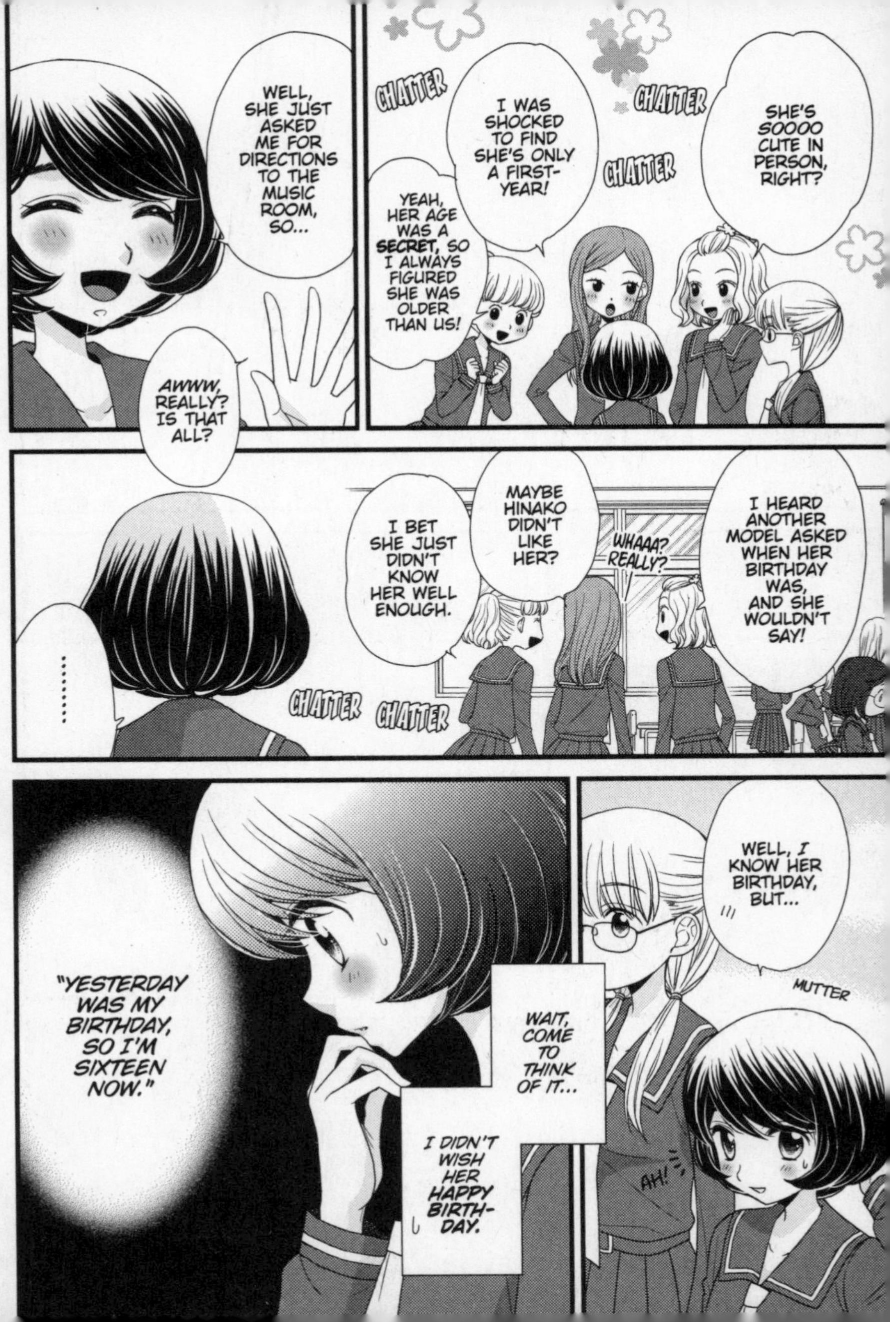
SHE'S SOOOO CUTE IN PERSON, RIGHT?
CHATTER
I WAS SHOCKED TO FIND SHE'S ONLY A FIRST-YEAR!
CHATTER
CHATTER
YEAH, HER AGE WAS A SECRET, SO I ALWAYS FIGURED SHE WAS OLDER THAN US!
WELL, SHE JUST ASKED ME FOR DIRECTIONS TO THE MUSIC ROOM, SO...
AWWW, REALLY? IS THAT ALL?
I HEARD ANOTHER MODEL ASKED WHEN HER BIRTHDAY WAS, AND SHE WOULDN'T SAY!
WHAAA? REALLY?
MAYBE HINAKO DIDN'T LIKE HER?
I BET SHE JUST DIDN'T KNOW HER WELL ENOUGH.
CHATTER
CHATTER
....
WELL, I KNOW HER BIRTHDAY, BUT...
MUTTER
AH!
WAIT, COME TO THINK OF IT...
I DIDN'T WISH HER HAPPY BIRTHDAY.
"YESTERDAY WAS MY BIRTHDAY, SO I'M SIXTEEN NOW."

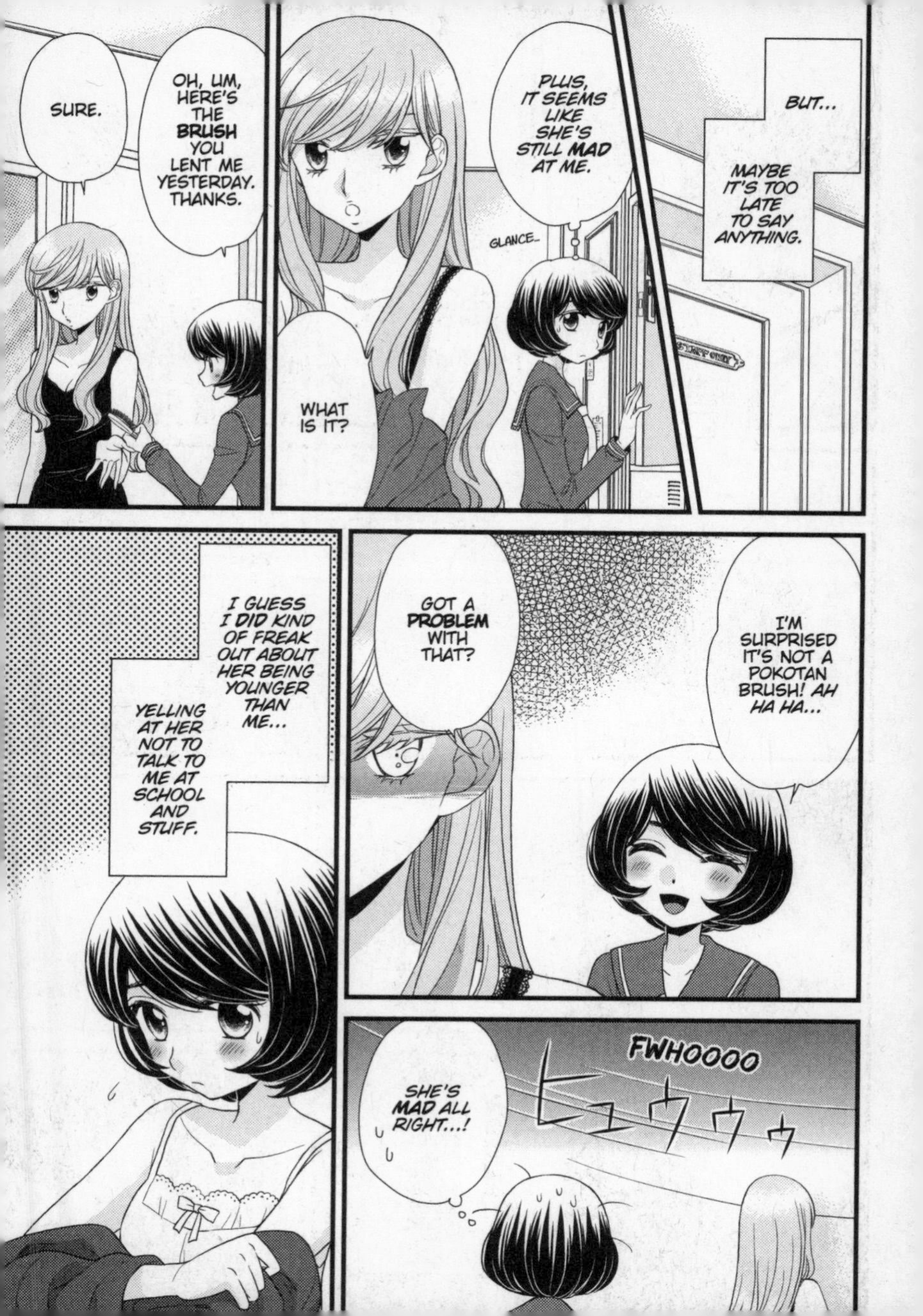
BUT...
MAYBE IT'S TOO LATE TO SAY ANYTHING.
PLUS, IT SEEMS LIKE SHE'S STILL MAD AT ME.
GLANCE...
WHAT IS IT?
OH, UM, HERE'S THE BRUSH YOU LENT ME YESTERDAY. THANKS.
SURE.
I'M SURPRISED IT'S NOT A POKOTAN BRUSH! AH HA HA...
GOT A PROBLEM WITH THAT?
FWHOOOO
SHE'S MAD ALL RIGHT...!
I GUESS I DID KIND OF FREAK OUT ABOUT HER BEING YOUNGER THAN ME...
YELLING AT HER NOT TO TALK TO ME AT SCHOOL AND STUFF.

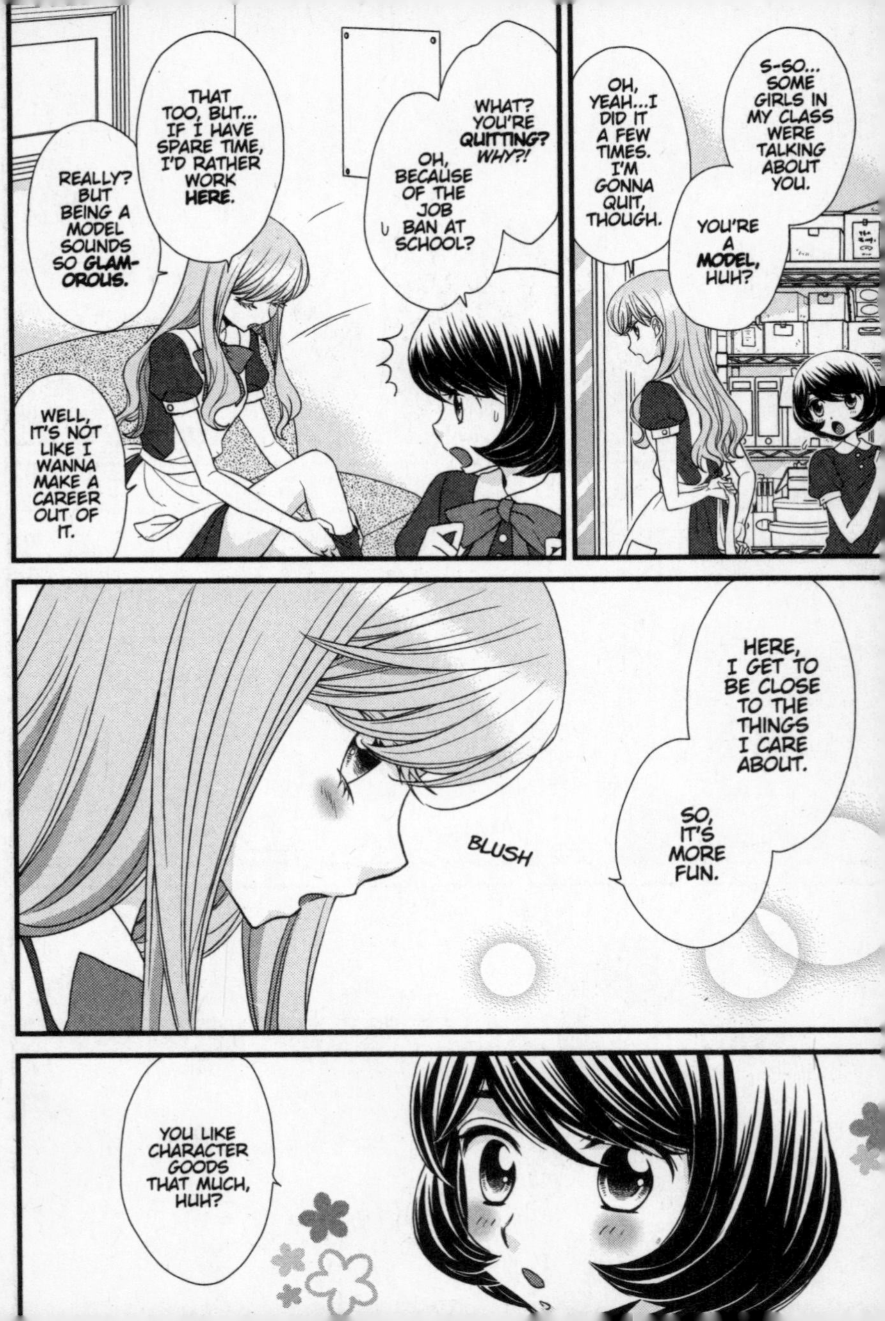
S-SO... SOME GIRLS IN MY CLASS WERE TALKING ABOUT YOU.
YOU'RE A MODEL, HUH?
OH, YEAH...I DID IT A FEW TIMES. I'M GONNA QUIT, THOUGH.
WHAT? YOU'RE QUITTING? WHY?!
OH, BECAUSE OF THE JOB BAN AT SCHOOL?
THAT TOO, BUT... IF I HAVE SPARE TIME, I'D RATHER WORK HERE.
REALLY? BUT BEING A MODEL SOUNDS SO GLAMOROUS.
WELL, IT'S NOT LIKE I WANNA MAKE A CAREER OUT OF IT.
HERE, I GET TO BE CLOSE TO THE THINGS I CARE ABOUT.
SO, IT'S MORE FUN.
BLUSH
YOU LIKE CHARACTER GOODS THAT MUCH, HUH?

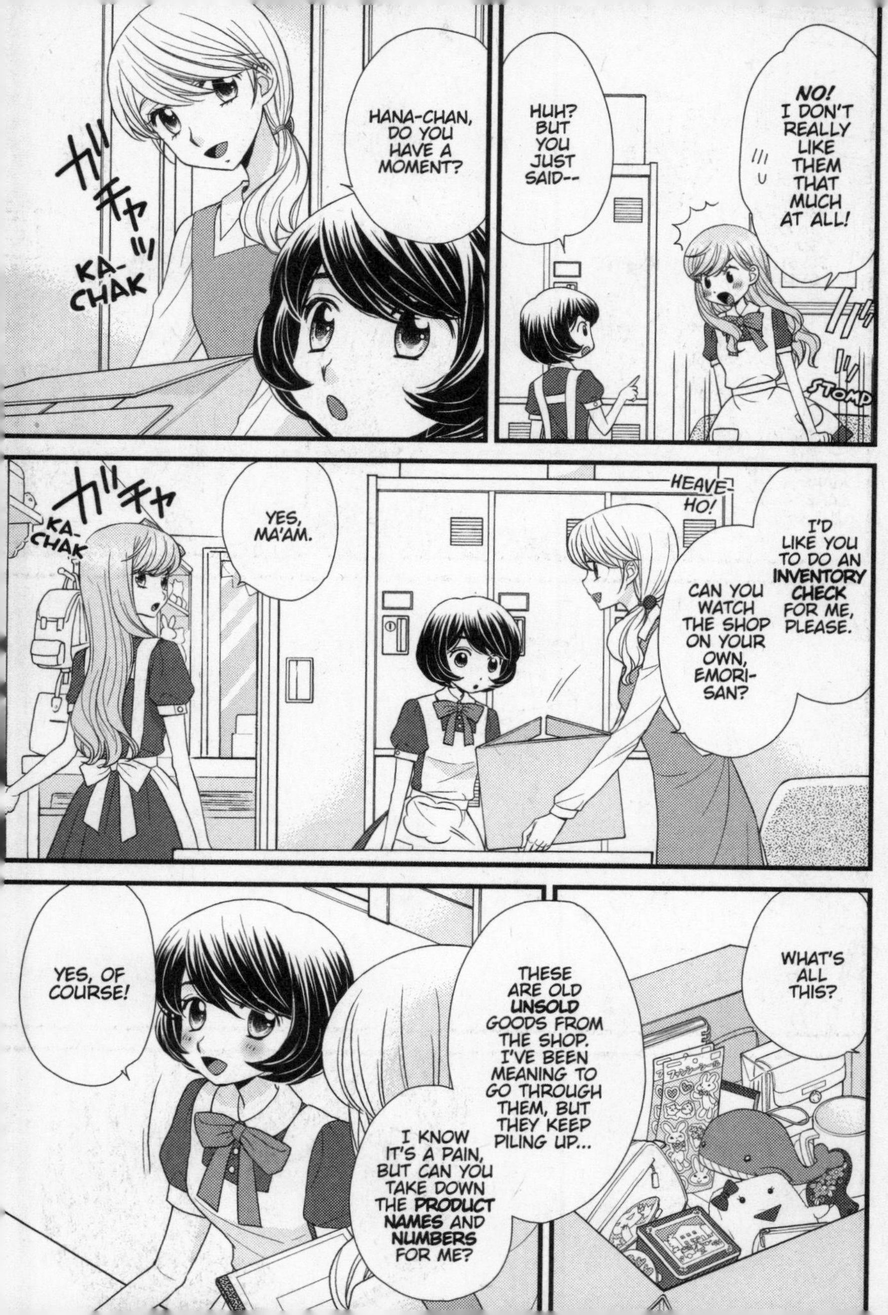
NO! I DON'T REALLY LIKE THEM THAT MUCH AT ALL!
HUH? BUT YOU JUST SAID--
STOMP
KA-CHAK
HANA-CHAN, DO YOU HAVE A MOMENT?
I'D LIKE YOU TO DO AN INVENTORY CHECK FOR ME, PLEASE.
CAN YOU WATCH THE SHOP ON YOUR OWN, EMORI-SAN?
HEAVE-HO!
YES, MA'AM.
KA-CHAK
WHAT'S ALL THIS?
THESE ARE OLD UNSOLD GOODS FROM THE SHOP. I'VE BEEN MEANING TO GO THROUGH THEM, BUT THEY KEEP PILING UP...
I KNOW IT'S A PAIN, BUT CAN YOU TAKE DOWN THE PRODUCT NAMES AND NUMBERS FOR ME?
YES, OF COURSE!

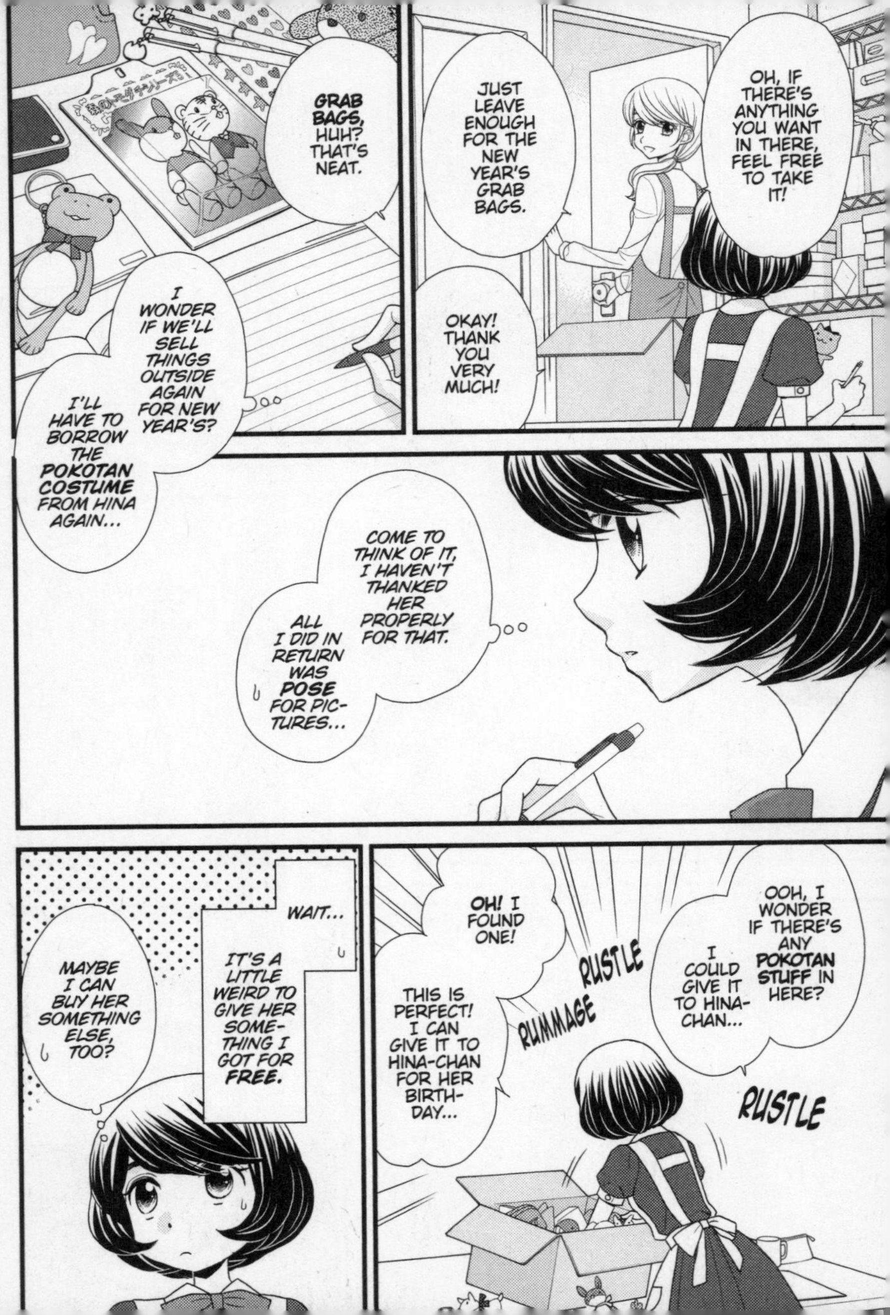
OH, IF THERE'S ANYTHING YOU WANT IN THERE, FEEL FREE TO TAKE IT!
JUST LEAVE ENOUGH FOR THE NEW YEAR'S GRAB BAGS.
OKAY! THANK YOU VERY MUCH!
GRAB BAGS, HUH? THAT'S NEAT.
I WONDER IF WE'LL SELL THINGS OUTSIDE AGAIN FOR NEW YEAR'S?
I'LL HAVE TO BORROW THE POKOTAN COSTUME FROM HINA AGAIN...
COME TO THINK OF IT, I HAVEN'T THANKED HER PROPERLY FOR THAT.
ALL I DID IN RETURN WAS POSE FOR PICTURES...
OOH, I WONDER IF THERE'S ANY POKOTAN STUFF IN HERE?
I COULD GIVE IT TO HINA-CHAN...
RUSTLE
RUMMAGE
RUSTLE
OH! I FOUND ONE!
THIS IS PERFECT! I CAN GIVE IT TO HINA-CHAN FOR HER BIRTHDAY...
WAIT...
IT'S A LITTLE WEIRD TO GIVE HER SOMETHING I GOT FOR FREE.
MAYBE I CAN BUY HER SOMETHING ELSE, TOO?

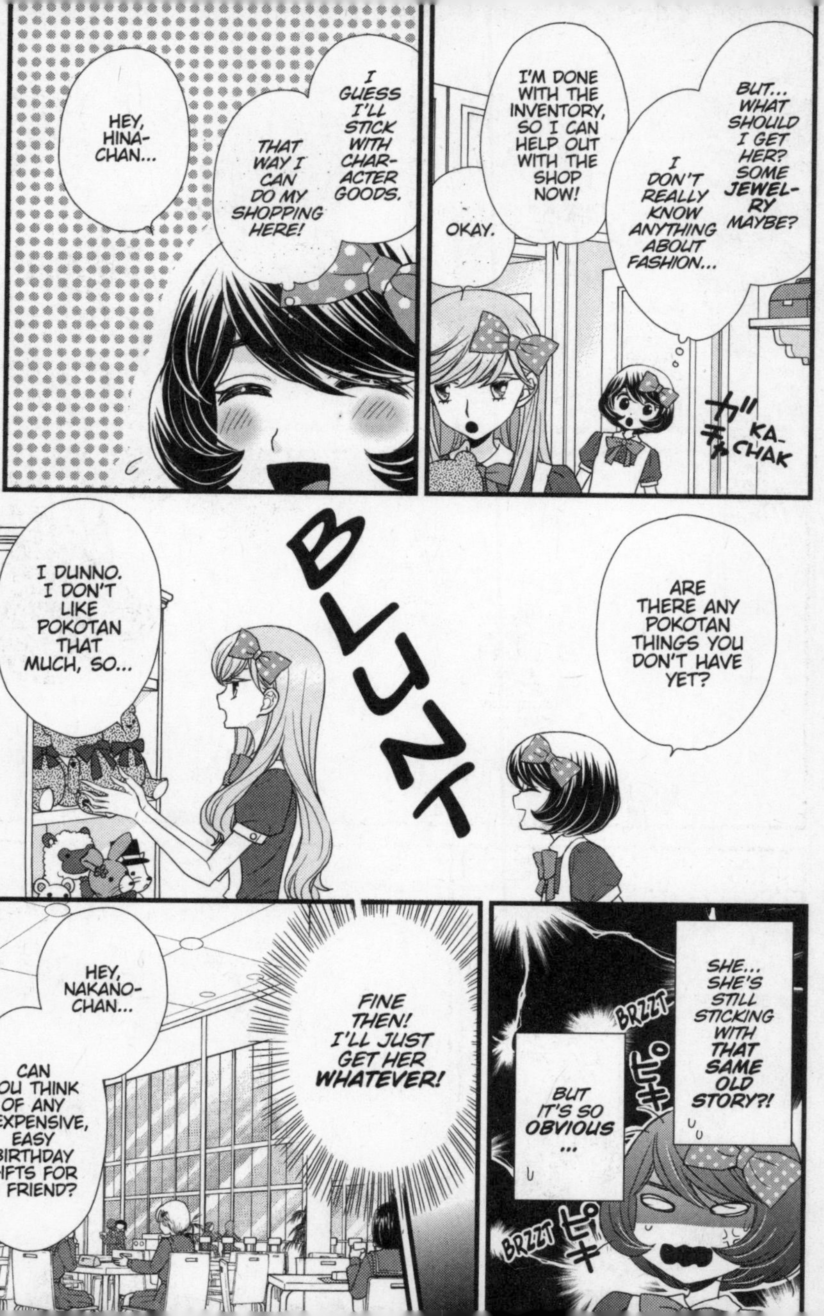
BUT... WHAT SHOULD I GET HER? SOME JEWELRY MAYBE?
I DON'T REALLY KNOW ANYTHING ABOUT FASHION...
I'M DONE WITH THE INVENTORY, SO I CAN HELP OUT WITH THE SHOP NOW!
OKAY.
KA-CHAK
I GUESS I'LL STICK WITH CHARACTER GOODS.
THAT WAY I CAN DO MY SHOPPING HERE!
HEY, HINA-CHAN...
ARE THERE ANY POKOTAN THINGS YOU DON'T HAVE YET?
BLUNT
I DUNNO. I DON'T LIKE POKOTAN THAT MUCH, SO...
SHE... SHE'S STILL STICKING WITH THAT SAME OLD STORY?!
BUT IT'S SO OBVIOUS...
BRZZT
BRZZT
FINE THEN! I'LL JUST GET HER WHATEVER!
HEY, NAKANO-CHAN...
CAN YOU THINK OF ANY INEXPENSIVE, EASY BIRTHDAY GIFTS FOR A FRIEND?

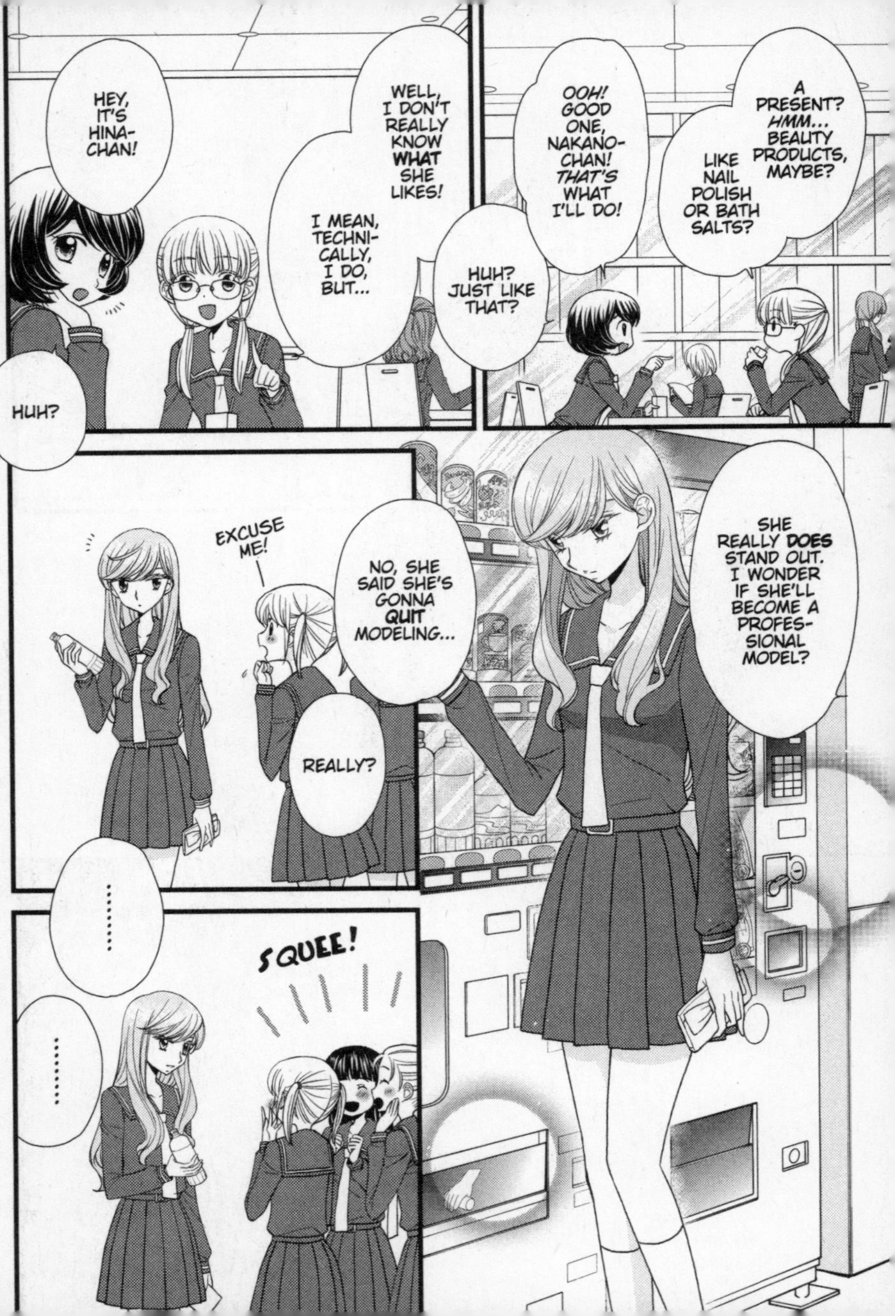
A PRESENT? HMM... BEAUTY PRODUCTS, MAYBE?
LIKE NAIL POLISH OR BATH SALTS?
OOH! GOOD ONE, NAKANO-CHAN! THAT'S WHAT I'LL DO!
HUH? JUST LIKE THAT?
WELL, I DON'T REALLY KNOW WHAT SHE LIKES!
I MEAN, TECHNICALLY, I DO, BUT...
HEY, IT'S HINA-CHAN!
HUH?
SHE REALLY DOES STAND OUT. I WONDER IF SHE'LL BECOME A PROFESSIONAL MODEL?
NO, SHE SAID SHE'S GONNA QUIT MODELING...
EXCUSE ME!
REALLY?
......
SQUEE!
......

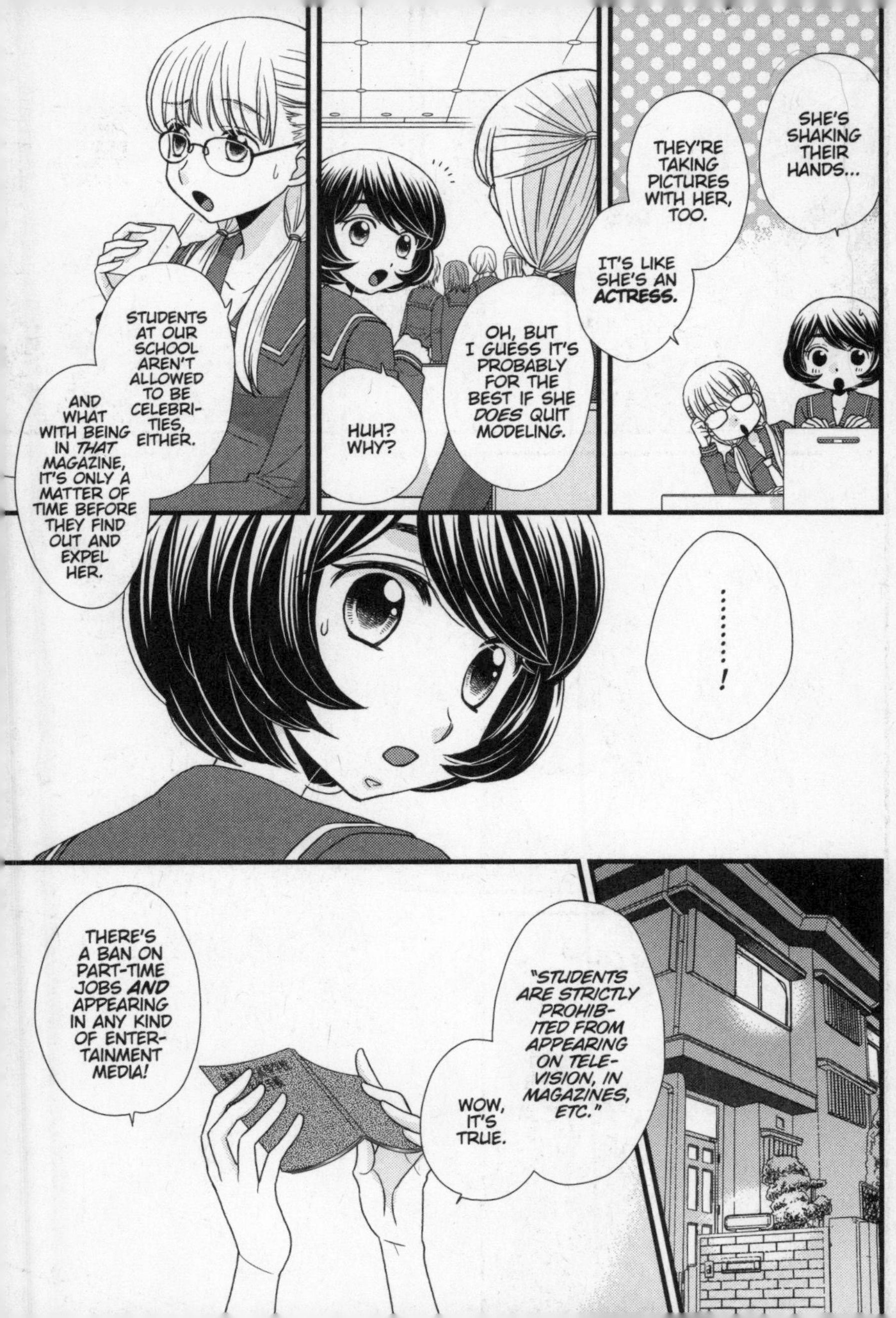
SHE'S SHAKING THEIR HANDS...
THEY'RE TAKING PICTURES WITH HER, TOO.
IT'S LIKE SHE'S AN **ACTRESS.**
OH, BUT I GUESS IT'S PROBABLY FOR THE BEST IF SHE *DOES* QUIT MODELING.
HUH? WHY?
STUDENTS AT OUR SCHOOL AREN'T ALLOWED TO BE CELEBRITIES, EITHER.
AND WHAT WITH BEING IN *THAT* MAGAZINE, IT'S ONLY A MATTER OF TIME BEFORE THEY FIND OUT AND EXPEL HER.
......!
"STUDENTS ARE STRICTLY PROHIBITED FROM APPEARING ON TELEVISION, IN MAGAZINES, ETC."
WOW, IT'S TRUE.
THERE'S A BAN ON PART-TIME JOBS ***AND*** APPEARING IN ANY KIND OF ENTERTAINMENT MEDIA!

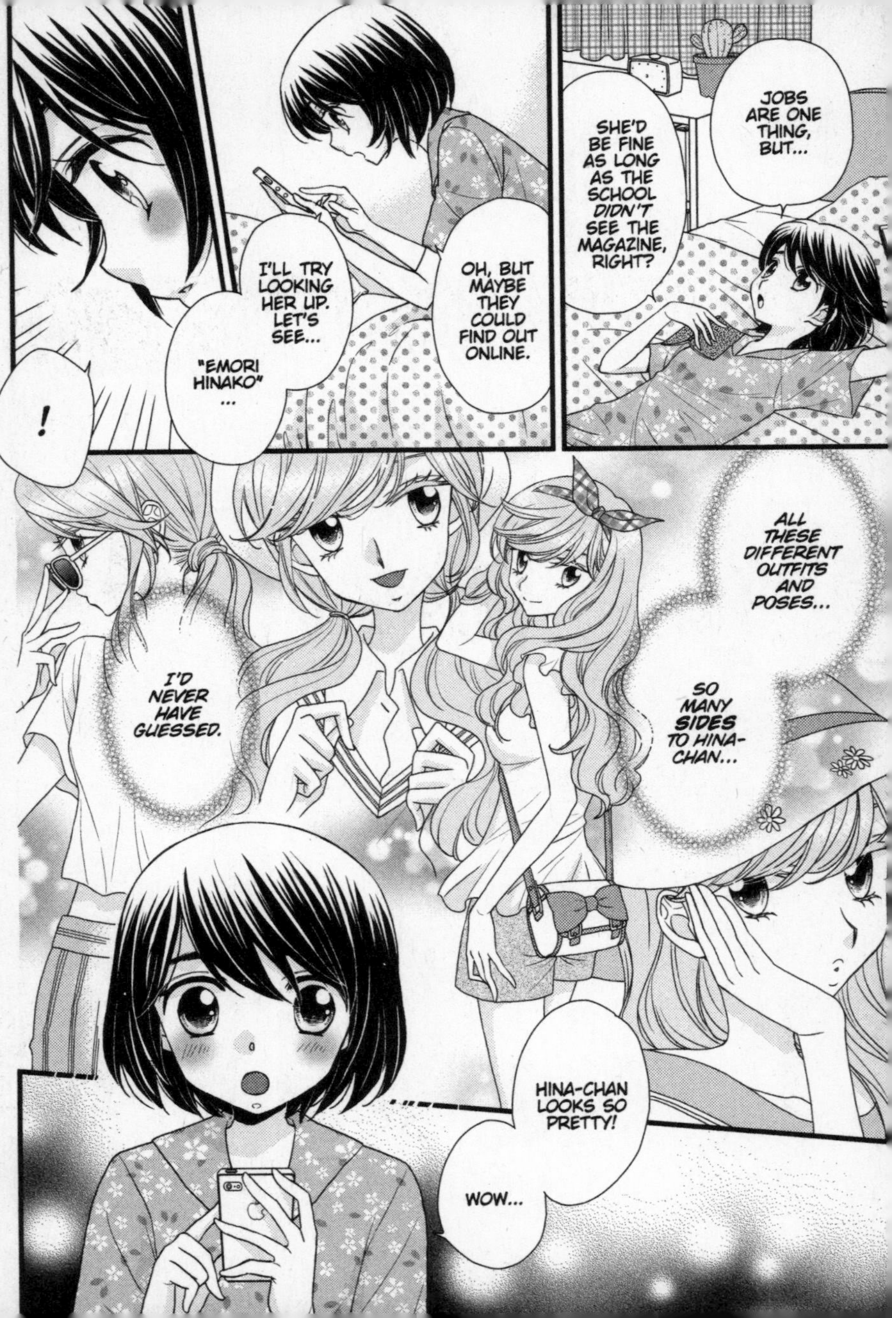
JOBS ARE ONE THING, BUT...
SHE'D BE FINE AS LONG AS THE SCHOOL DIDN'T SEE THE MAGAZINE, RIGHT?
OH, BUT MAYBE THEY COULD FIND OUT ONLINE.
I'LL TRY LOOKING HER UP. LET'S SEE...
"EMORI HINAKO"...
!
ALL THESE DIFFERENT OUTFITS AND POSES...
SO MANY SIDES TO HINA-CHAN...
I'D NEVER HAVE GUESSED.
HINA-CHAN LOOKS SO PRETTY!
WOW...

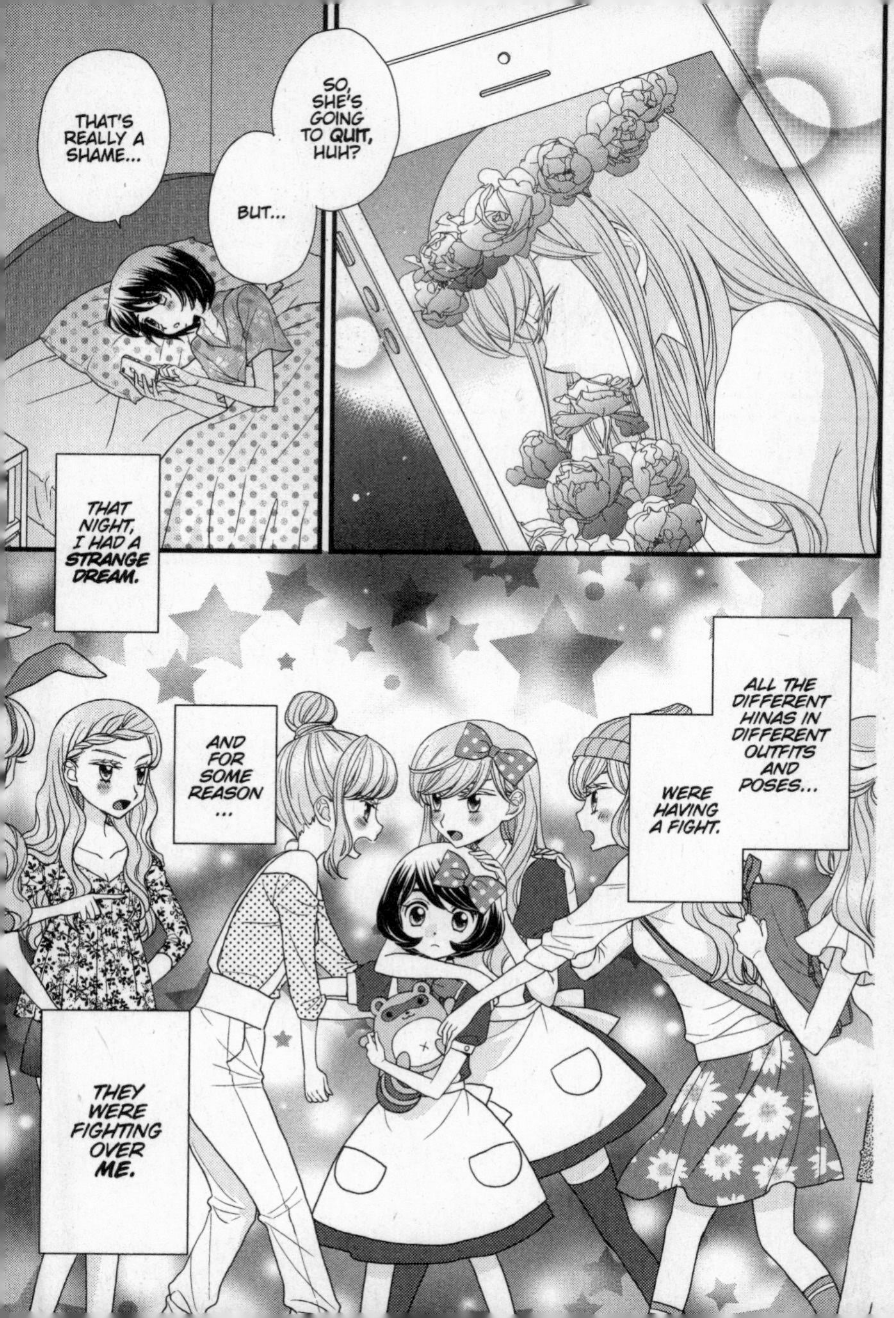
SO, SHE'S GOING TO QUIT, HUH?
BUT...
THAT'S REALLY A SHAME...
THAT NIGHT, I HAD A STRANGE DREAM.
ALL THE DIFFERENT HINAS IN DIFFERENT OUTFITS AND POSES...
WERE HAVING A FIGHT.
AND FOR SOME REASON...
THEY WERE FIGHTING OVER ME.

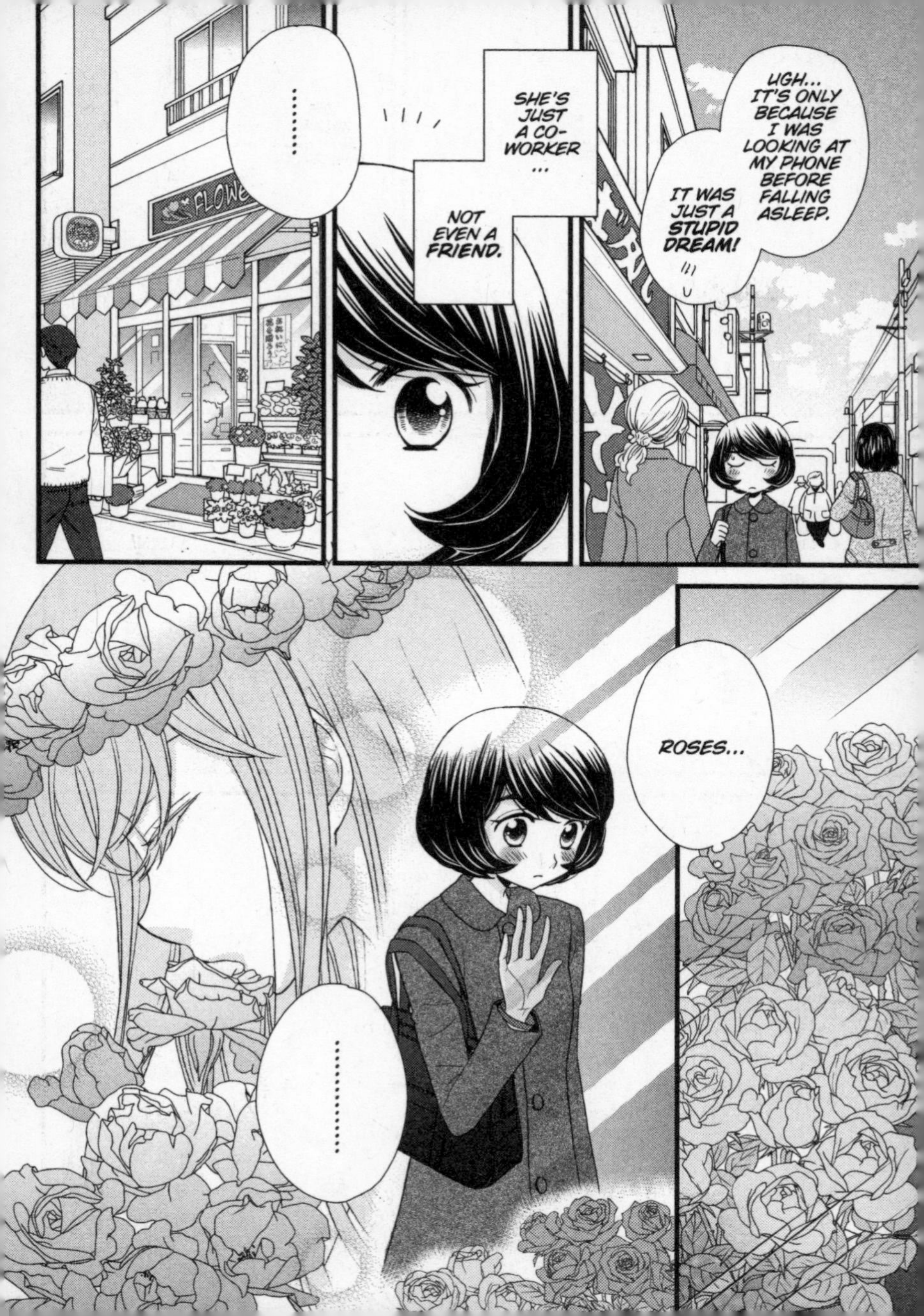

UGH... IT'S ONLY BECAUSE I WAS LOOKING AT MY PHONE BEFORE FALLING ASLEEP.
IT WAS JUST A STUPID DREAM!
SHE'S JUST A CO-WORKER ...
NOT EVEN A FRIEND.
....
ROSES...
....

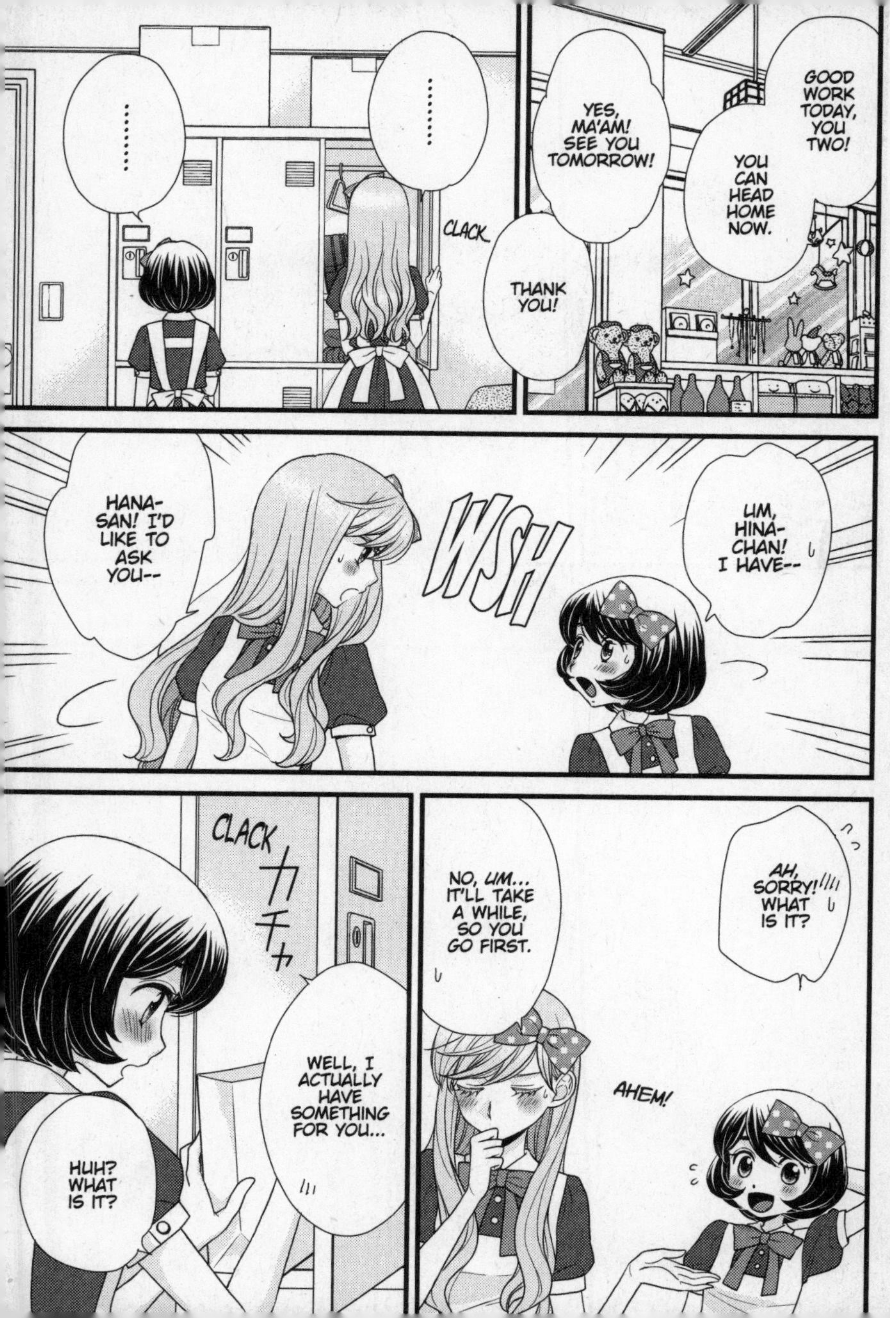
GOOD WORK TODAY, YOU TWO!
YOU CAN HEAD HOME NOW.
YES, MA'AM! SEE YOU TOMORROW!
THANK YOU!
CLACK
......
......
UM, HINA-CHAN! I HAVE--
WSH
HANA-SAN! I'D LIKE TO ASK YOU--
AH, SORRY! WHAT IS IT?
AHEM!
NO, UM... IT'LL TAKE A WHILE, SO YOU GO FIRST.
CLACK
カチャ
WELL, I ACTUALLY HAVE SOMETHING FOR YOU...
HUH? WHAT IS IT?

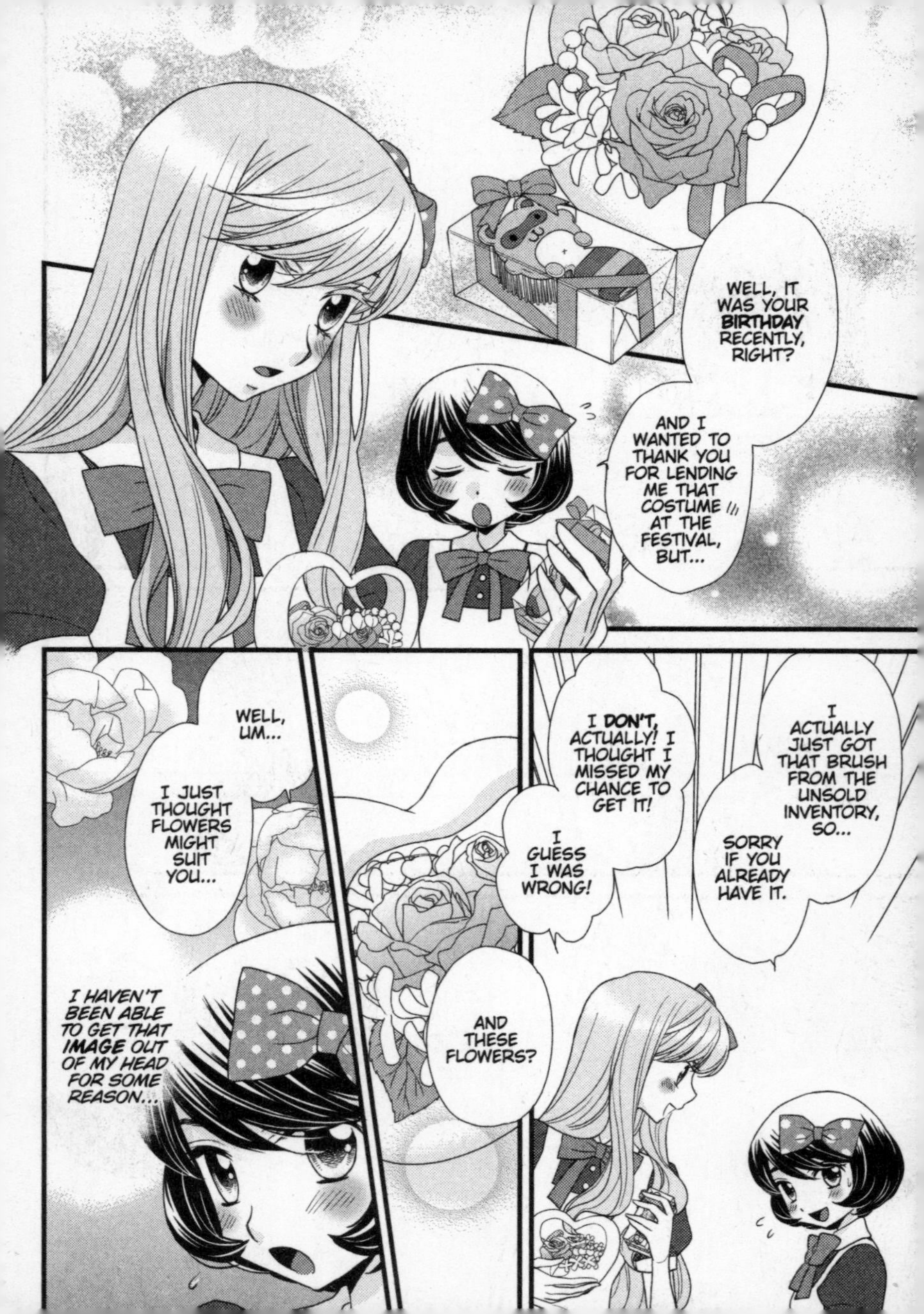
WELL, IT WAS YOUR **BIRTHDAY** RECENTLY, RIGHT?
AND I WANTED TO THANK YOU FOR LENDING ME THAT COSTUME AT THE FESTIVAL, BUT...
I ACTUALLY JUST GOT THAT BRUSH FROM THE UNSOLD INVENTORY, SO...
SORRY IF YOU ALREADY HAVE IT.
I **DON'T**, ACTUALLY! I THOUGHT I MISSED MY CHANCE TO GET IT!
I GUESS I WAS WRONG!
AND THESE FLOWERS?
WELL, UM...
I JUST THOUGHT FLOWERS MIGHT SUIT YOU...
*I HAVEN'T BEEN ABLE TO GET THAT **IMAGE** OUT OF MY HEAD FOR SOME REASON...*

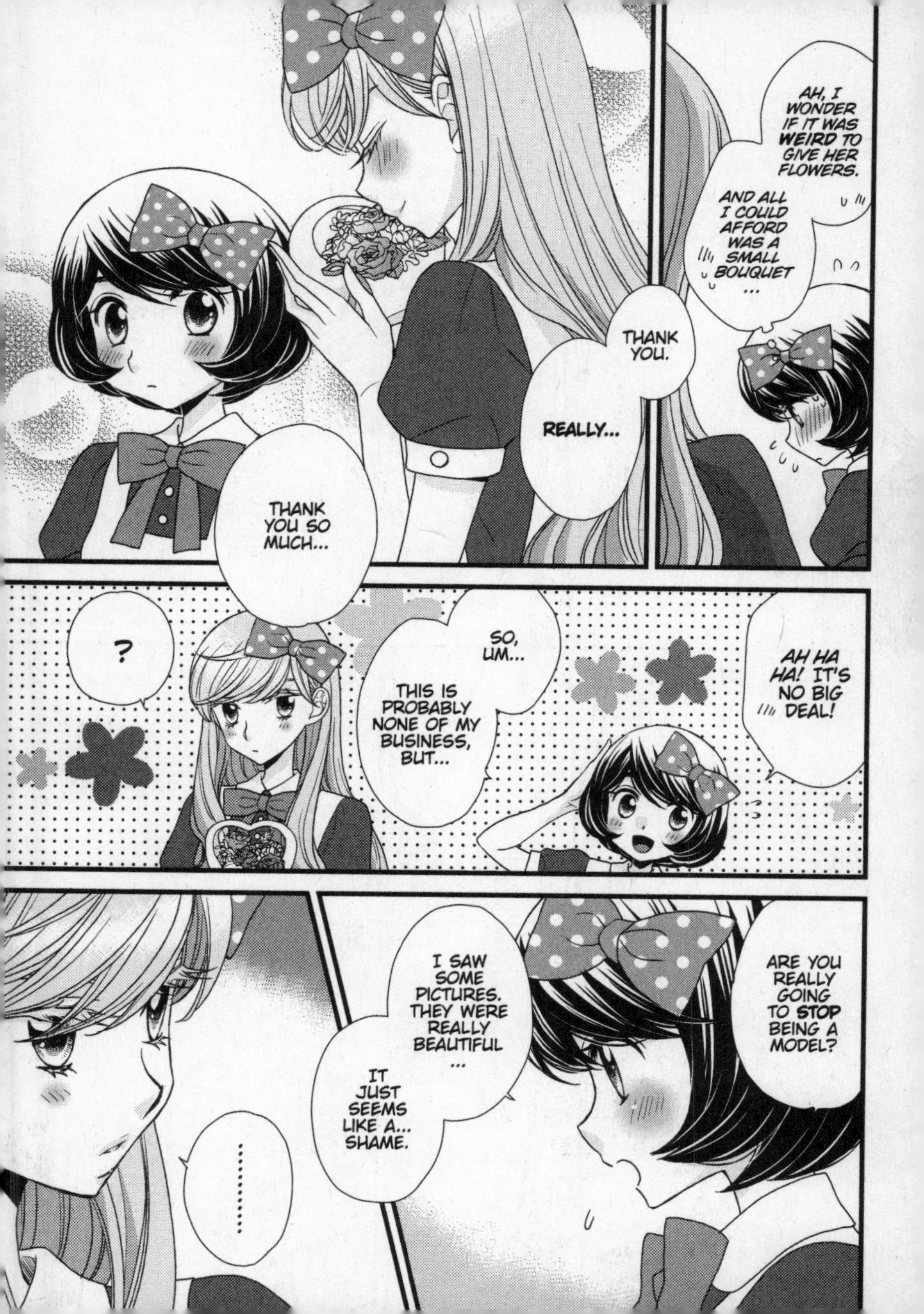
AH, I WONDER IF IT WAS WEIRD TO GIVE HER FLOWERS.
AND ALL I COULD AFFORD WAS A SMALL BOUQUET ...
THANK YOU.
REALLY...
THANK YOU SO MUCH...
AH HA HA! IT'S NO BIG DEAL!
SO, UM...
THIS IS PROBABLY NONE OF MY BUSINESS, BUT...
?
ARE YOU REALLY GOING TO STOP BEING A MODEL?
I SAW SOME PICTURES. THEY WERE REALLY BEAUTIFUL ...
IT JUST SEEMS LIKE A... SHAME.
....

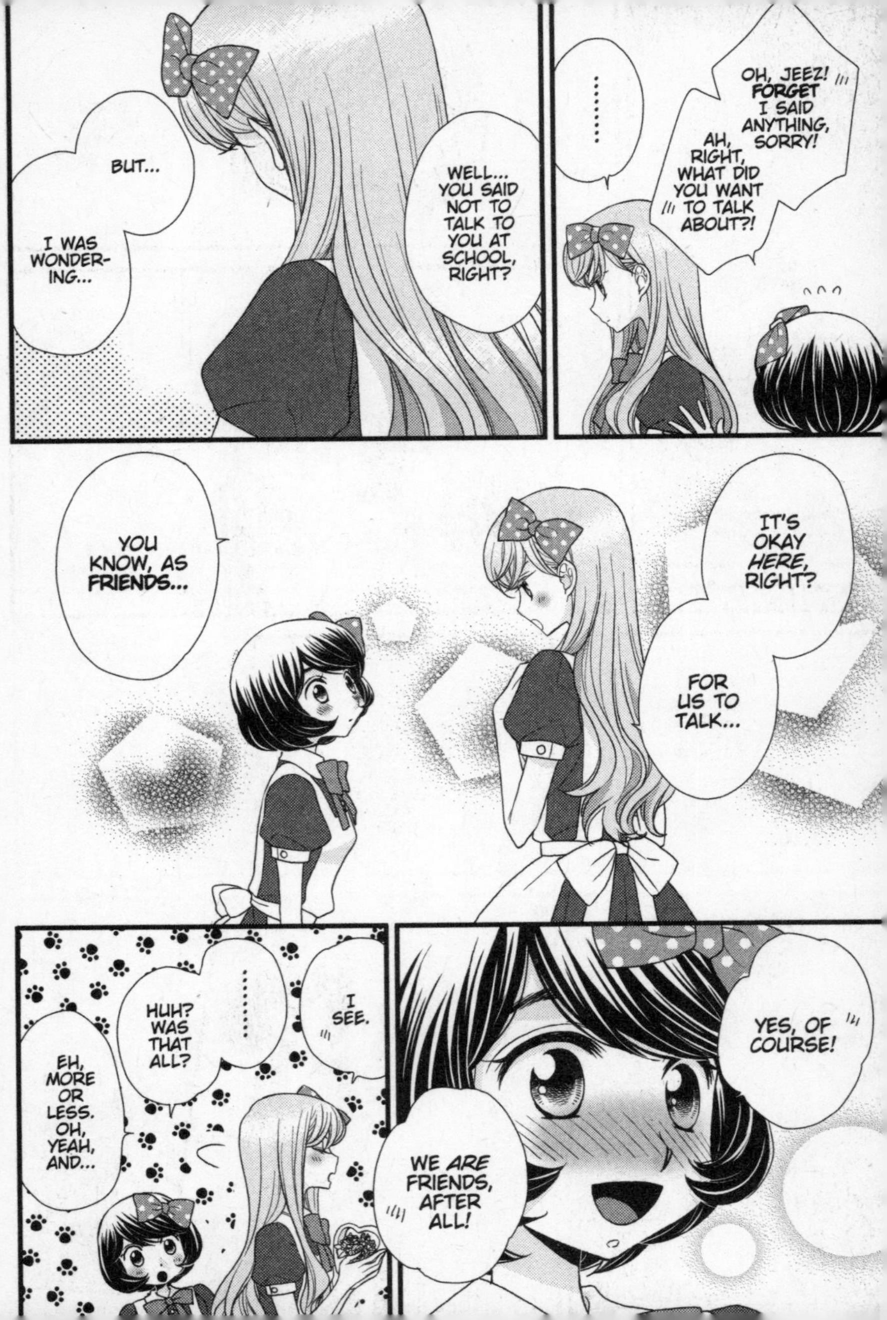
OH, JEEZ! FORGET I SAID ANYTHING, SORRY!
......
AH, RIGHT, WHAT DID YOU WANT TO TALK ABOUT?!
WELL... YOU SAID NOT TO TALK TO YOU AT SCHOOL, RIGHT?
BUT...
I WAS WONDER-ING...
IT'S OKAY *HERE*, RIGHT?
FOR US TO TALK...
YOU KNOW, AS FRIENDS...
YES, OF COURSE!
WE *ARE* FRIENDS, AFTER ALL!
I SEE.
......
HUH? WAS THAT ALL?
EH, MORE OR LESS. OH, YEAH, AND...

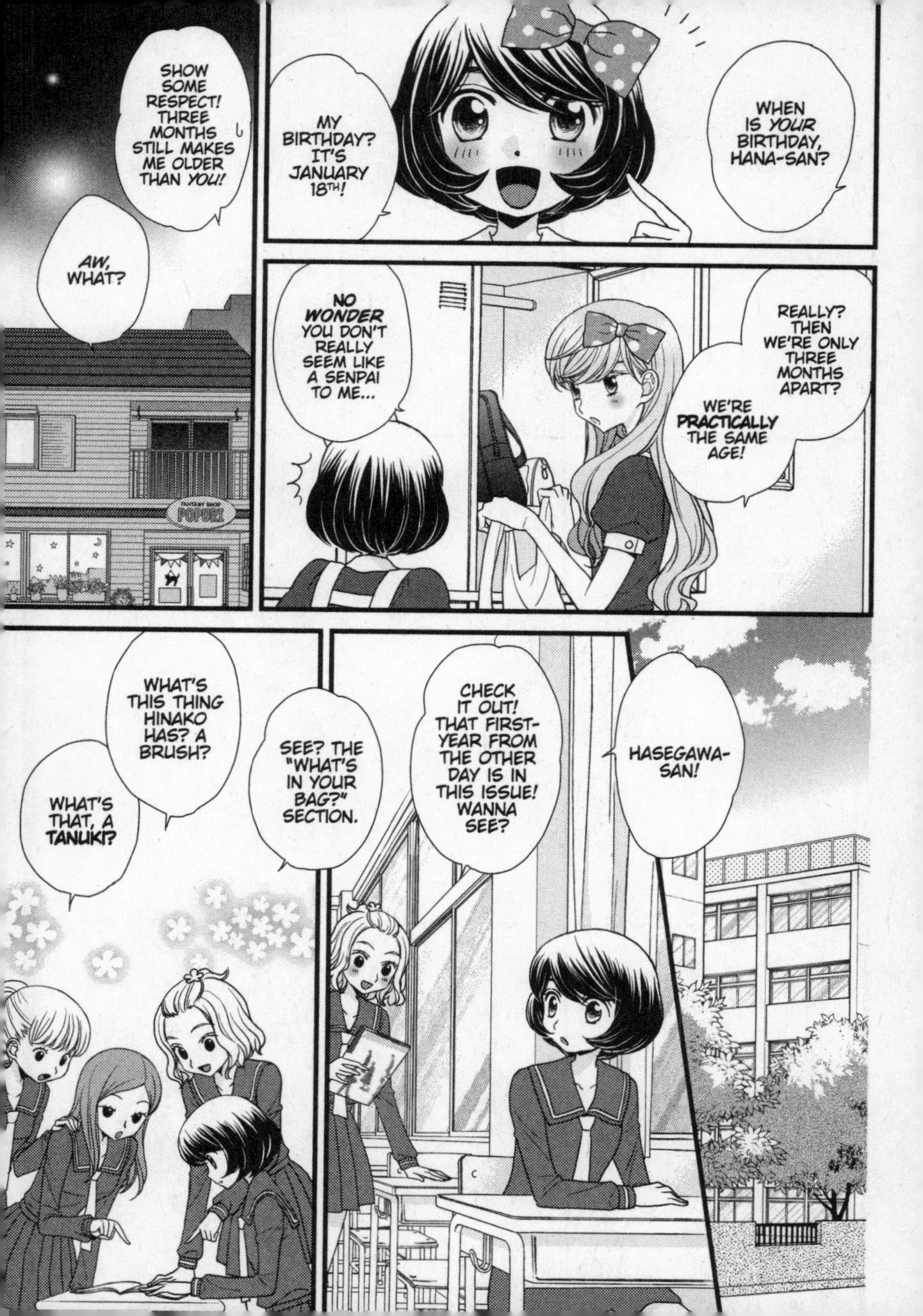
WHEN IS YOUR BIRTHDAY, HANA-SAN?
MY BIRTHDAY? IT'S JANUARY 18TH!
REALLY? THEN WE'RE ONLY THREE MONTHS APART?
WE'RE PRACTICALLY THE SAME AGE!
NO WONDER YOU DON'T REALLY SEEM LIKE A SENPAI TO ME...
SHOW SOME RESPECT! THREE MONTHS STILL MAKES ME OLDER THAN YOU!
AW, WHAT?
POPURI
HASEGAWA-SAN!
CHECK IT OUT! THAT FIRST-YEAR FROM THE OTHER DAY IS IN THIS ISSUE! WANNA SEE?
SEE? THE "WHAT'S IN YOUR BAG?" SECTION.
WHAT'S THIS THING HINAKO HAS? A BRUSH?
WHAT'S THAT, A TANUKI?

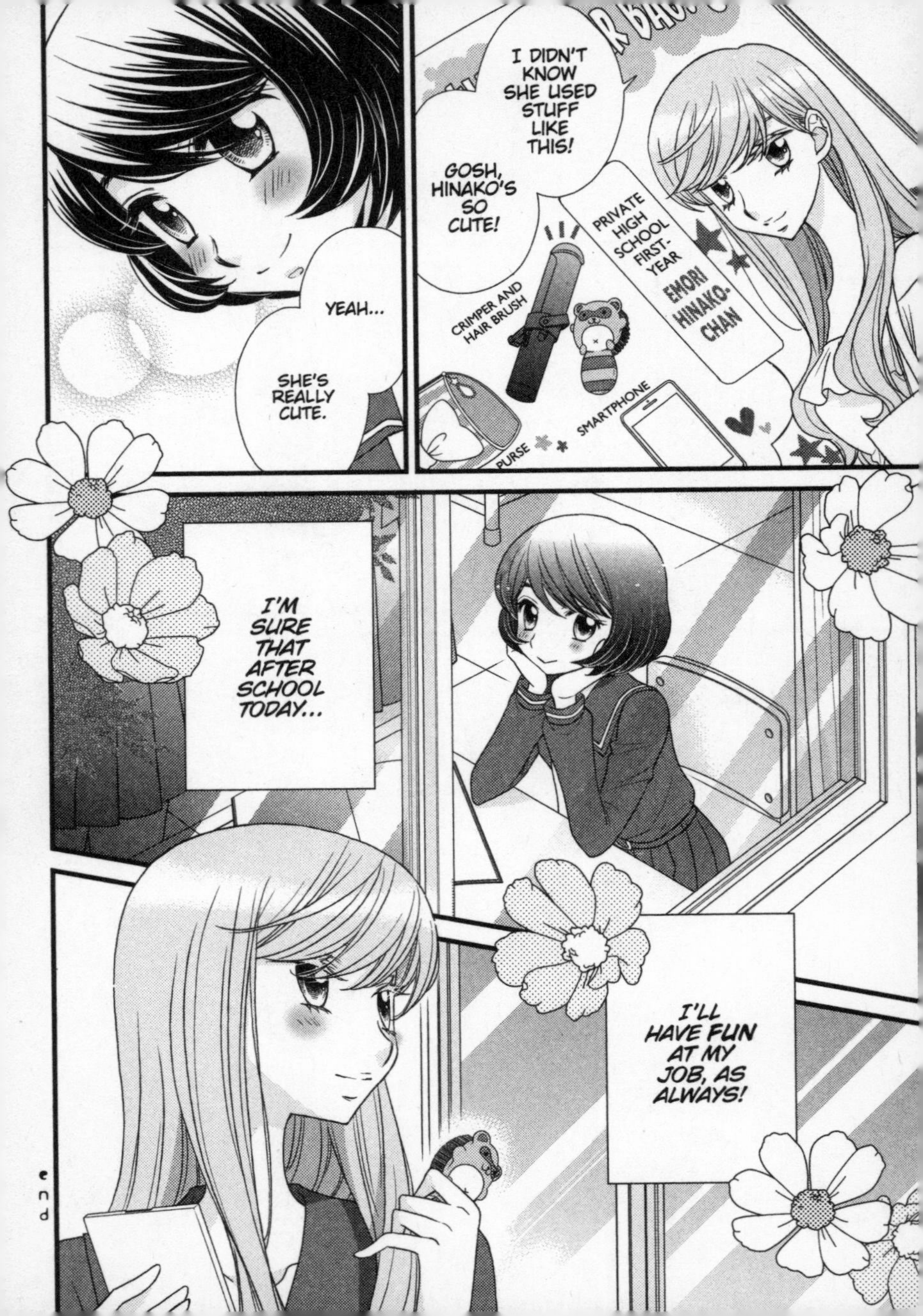
I DIDN'T KNOW SHE USED STUFF LIKE THIS!
GOSH, HINAKO'S SO CUTE!
PRIVATE HIGH SCHOOL FIRST-YEAR
EMORI HINAKO-CHAN
CRIMPER AND HAIR BRUSH
SMARTPHONE
PURSE
YEAH...
SHE'S REALLY CUTE.
I'M SURE THAT AFTER SCHOOL TODAY...
I'LL HAVE FUN AT MY JOB, AS ALWAYS!
end

Hana & Hina AFTER ♥ SCHOOL

Hana & Hina AFTER ♡ SCHOOL

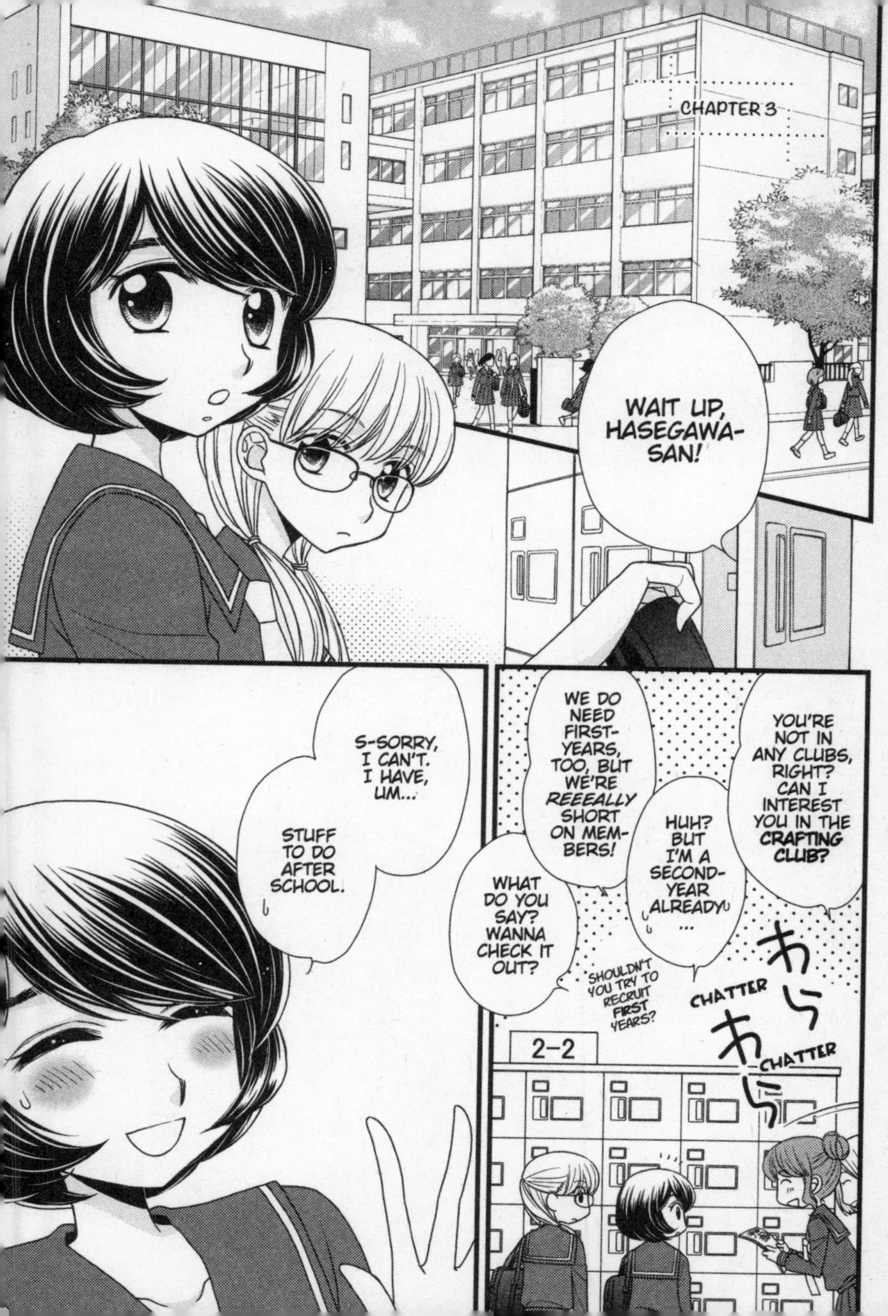
CHAPTER 3
WAIT UP, HASEGAWA-SAN!
YOU'RE NOT IN ANY CLUBS, RIGHT? CAN I INTEREST YOU IN THE **CRAFTING CLUB?**
HUH? BUT I'M A SECOND-YEAR ALREADY...
WE DO NEED FIRST-YEARS, TOO, BUT WE'RE *REEEALLY* SHORT ON MEMBERS!
WHAT DO YOU SAY? WANNA CHECK IT OUT?
SHOULDN'T YOU TRY TO RECRUIT **FIRST** YEARS?
わら CHATTER
わら CHATTER
2-2
S-SORRY, I CAN'T. I HAVE, UM...
STUFF TO DO AFTER SCHOOL.

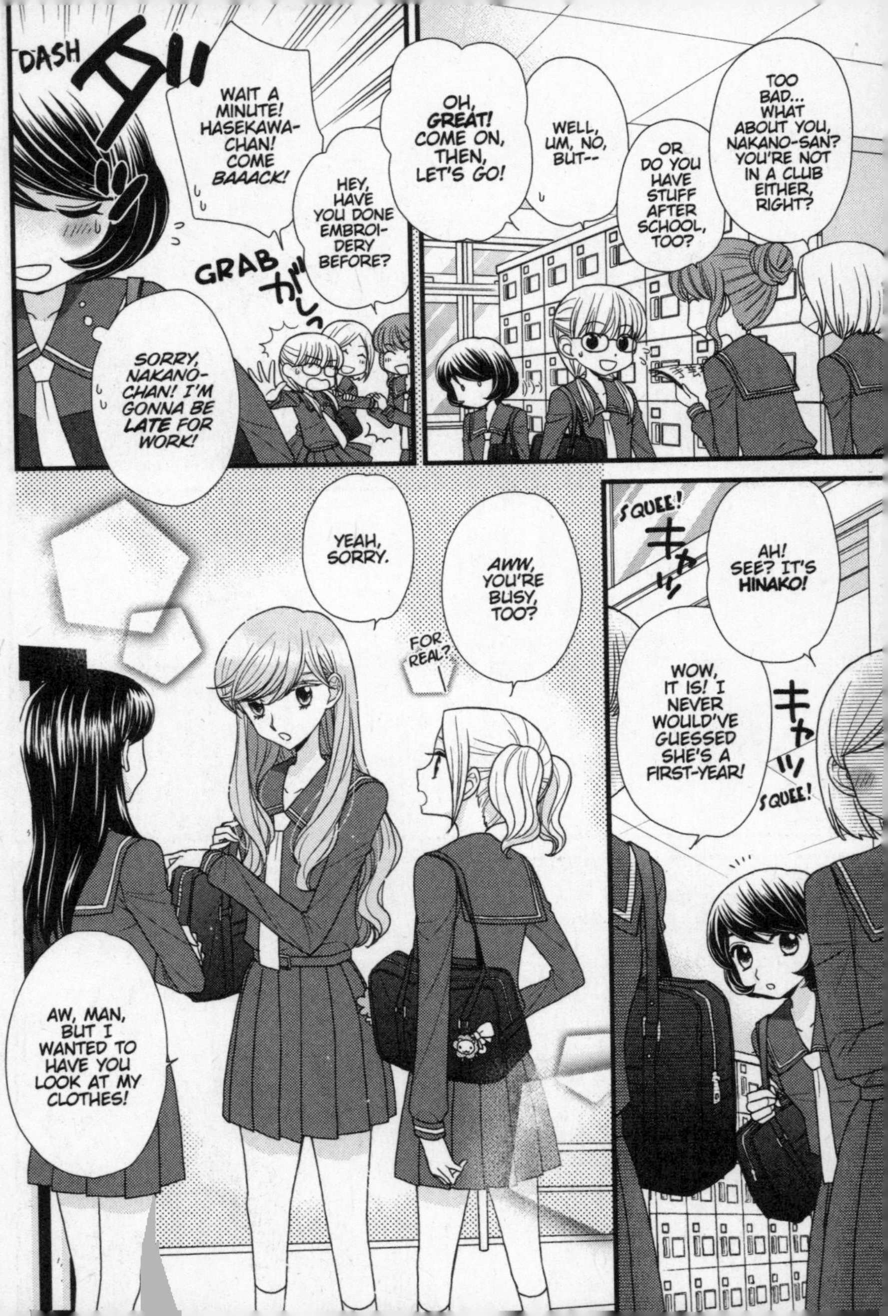
TOO BAD... WHAT ABOUT YOU, NAKANO-SAN? YOU'RE NOT IN A CLUB EITHER, RIGHT?
OR DO YOU HAVE STUFF AFTER SCHOOL, TOO?
WELL, UM, NO, BUT--
OH, GREAT! COME ON, THEN, LET'S GO!
HEY, HAVE YOU DONE EMBROIDERY BEFORE?
GRAB
WAIT A MINUTE! HASEKAWA-CHAN! COME BAAACK!
DASH
SORRY, NAKANO-CHAN! I'M GONNA BE LATE FOR WORK!
SQUEE!
AH! SEE? IT'S HINAKO!
WOW, IT IS! I NEVER WOULD'VE GUESSED SHE'S A FIRST-YEAR!
SQUEE!
AWW, YOU'RE BUSY, TOO?
FOR REAL?
YEAH, SORRY.
AW, MAN, BUT I WANTED TO HAVE YOU LOOK AT MY CLOTHES!

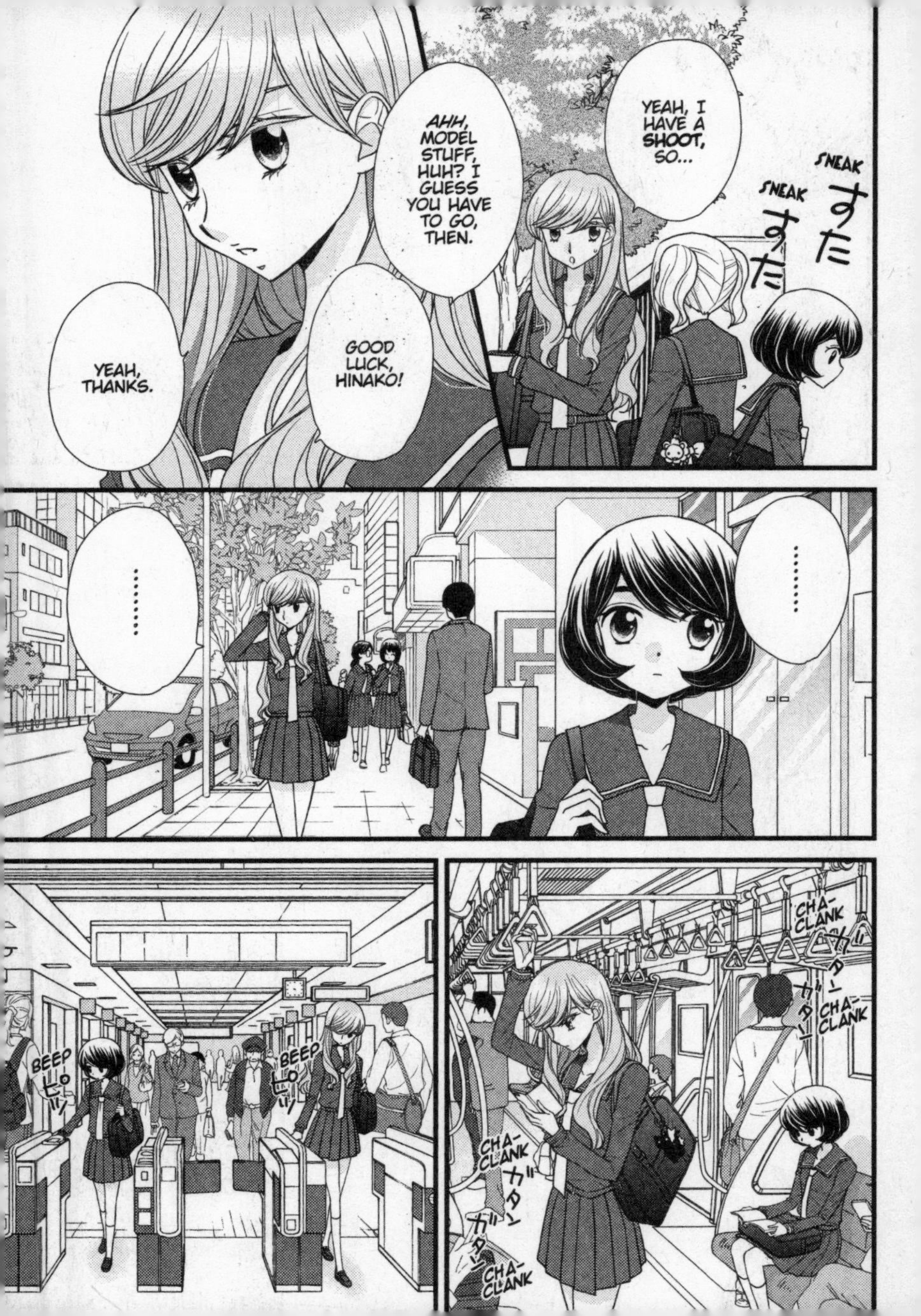
YEAH, I HAVE A SHOOT, SO...
SNEAK
すた
SNEAK
すた
AHH, MODEL STUFF, HUH? I GUESS YOU HAVE TO GO, THEN.
GOOD LUCK, HINAKO!
YEAH, THANKS.
......
......
CHA-CLANK
ガタン
CHA-CLANK
ガタン
CHA-CLANK
ガタン
CHA-CLANK
ガタン
BEEP
ピッ
BEEP
ピッ

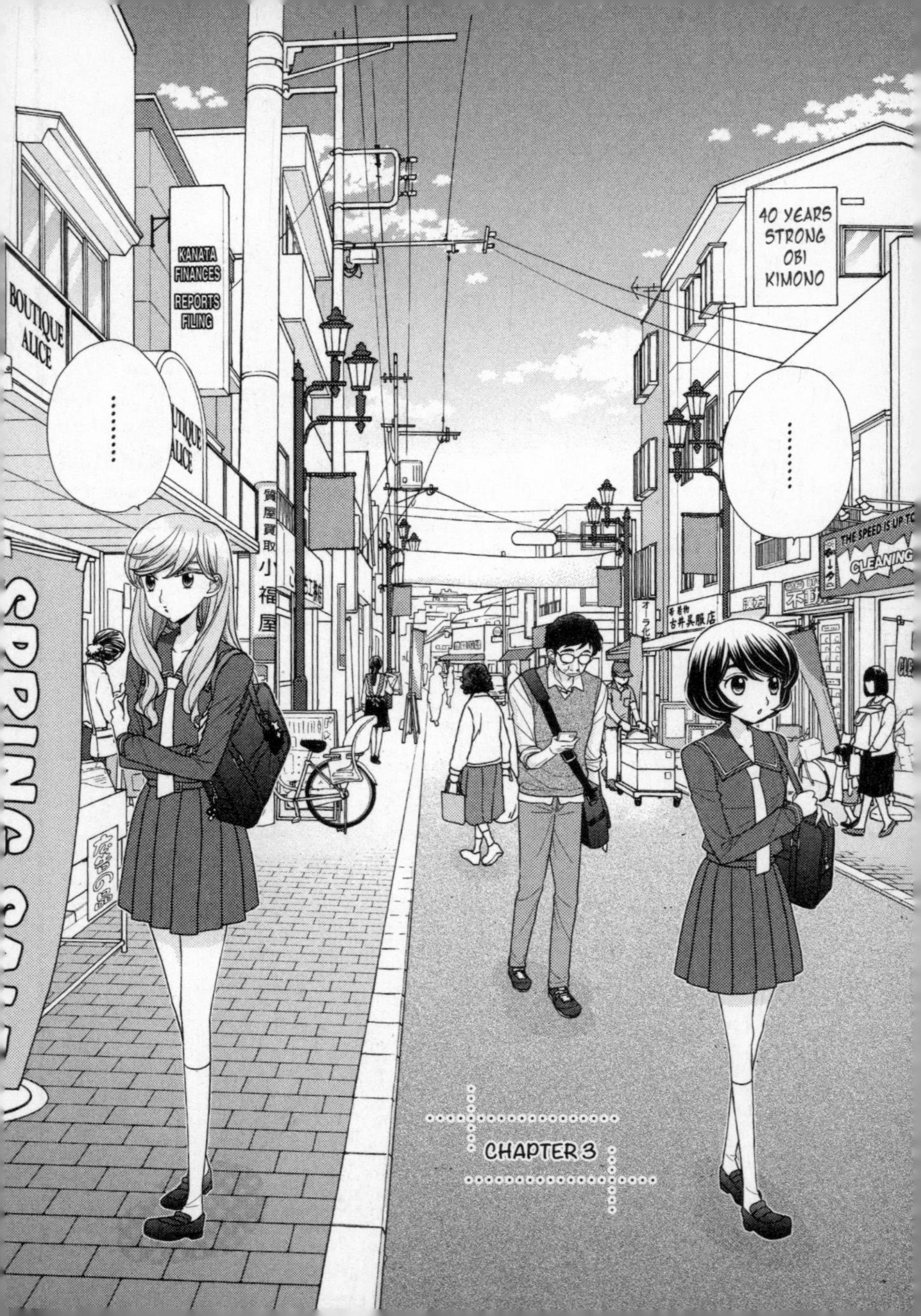
40 YEARS STRONG OBI KIMONO
......
THE SPEED IS UP TO
CLEANING
CHAPTER 3
KANATA FINANCES
REPORTS FILING
BOUTIQUE ALICE
BOUTIQUE ALICE
......

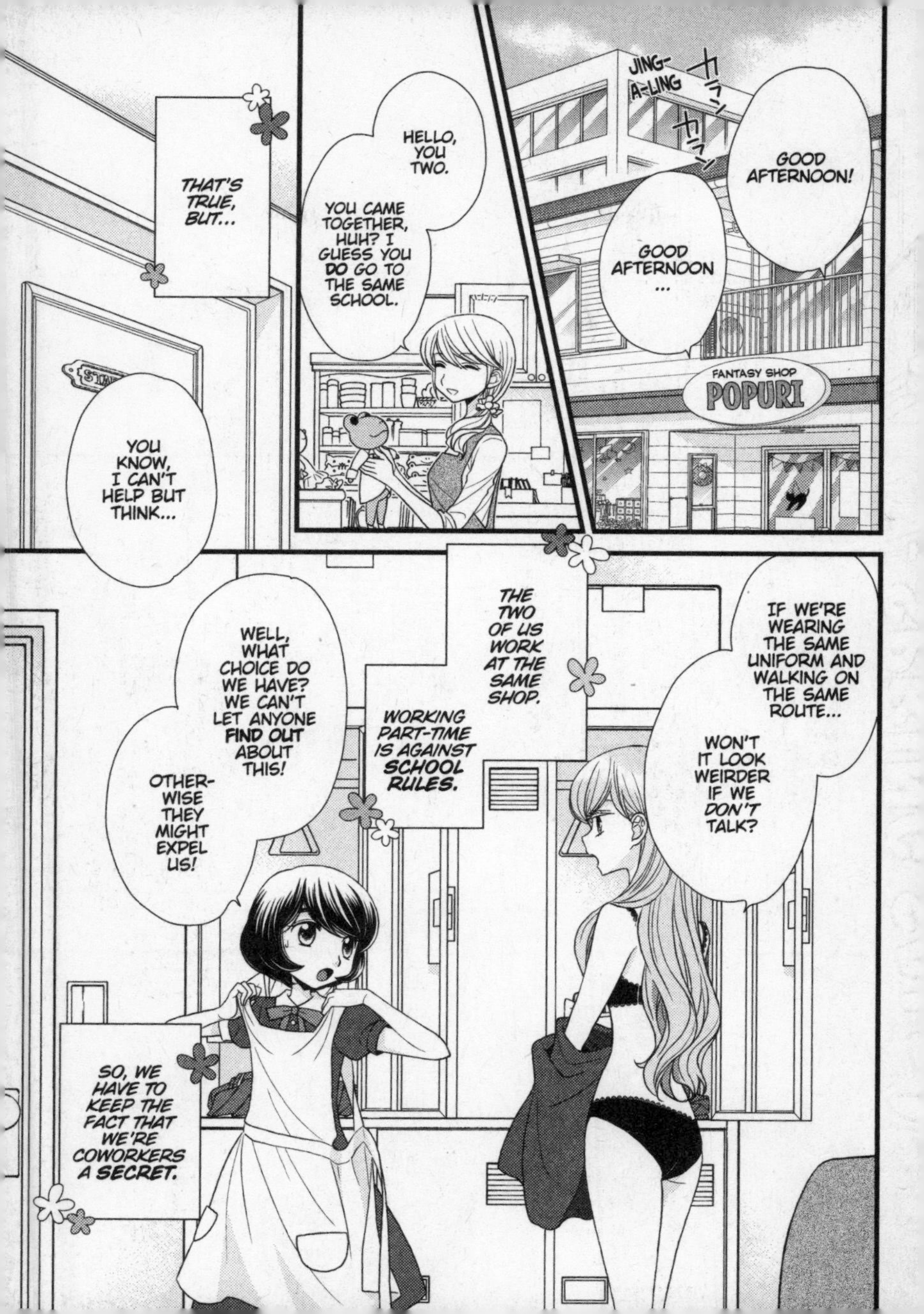
JING-A-LING
GOOD AFTERNOON!
GOOD AFTERNOON...
FANTASY SHOP POPURI
HELLO, YOU TWO.
YOU CAME TOGETHER, HUH? I GUESS YOU DO GO TO THE SAME SCHOOL.
THAT'S TRUE, BUT...
YOU KNOW, I CAN'T HELP BUT THINK...
IF WE'RE WEARING THE SAME UNIFORM AND WALKING ON THE SAME ROUTE...
WON'T IT LOOK WEIRDER IF WE DON'T TALK?
THE TWO OF US WORK AT THE SAME SHOP.
WORKING PART-TIME IS AGAINST SCHOOL RULES.
WELL, WHAT CHOICE DO WE HAVE? WE CAN'T LET ANYONE FIND OUT ABOUT THIS!
OTHER-WISE THEY MIGHT EXPEL US!
SO, WE HAVE TO KEEP THE FACT THAT WE'RE COWORKERS A SECRET.

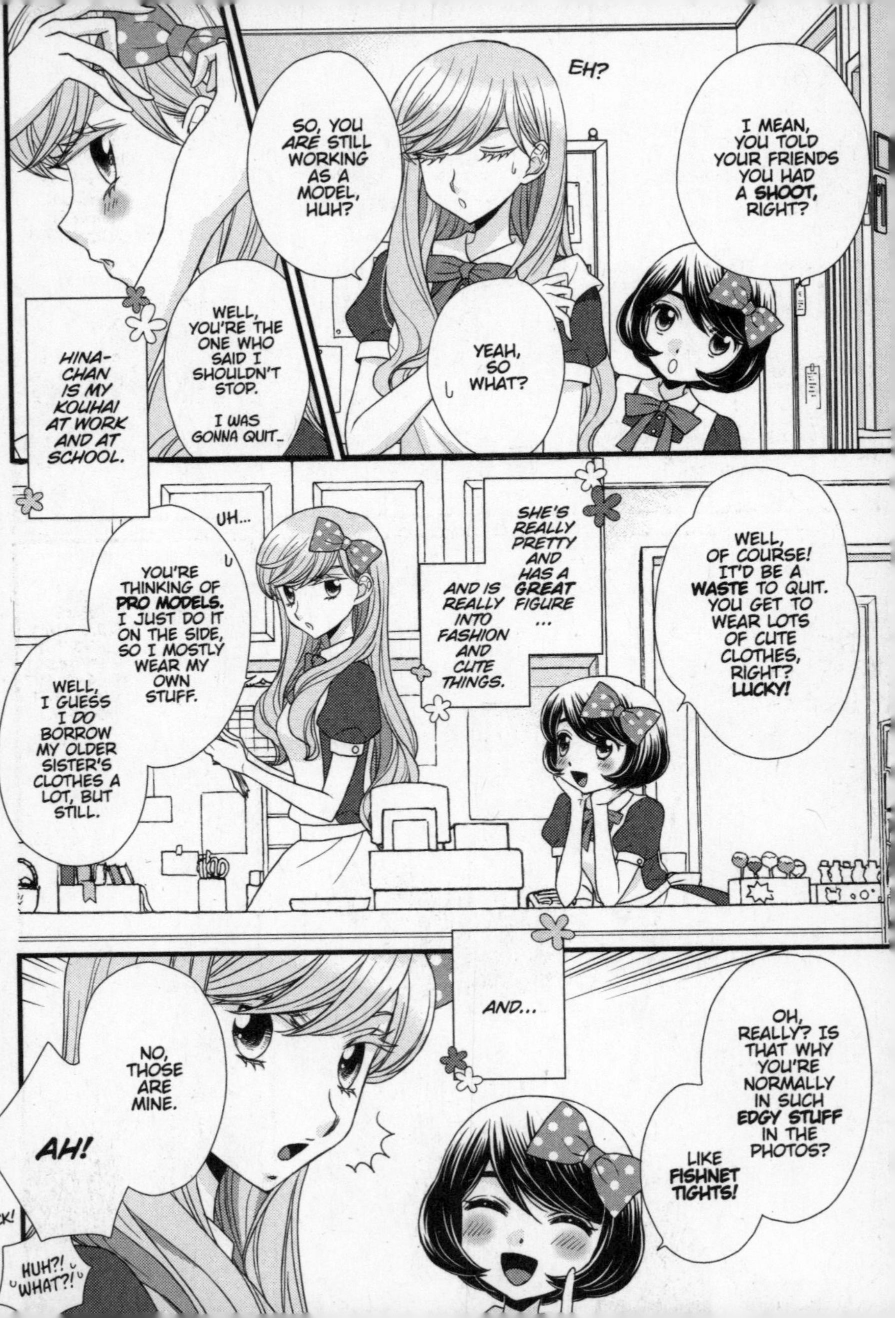
EH?
I MEAN, YOU TOLD YOUR FRIENDS YOU HAD A SHOOT, RIGHT?
SO, YOU ARE STILL WORKING AS A MODEL, HUH?
YEAH, SO WHAT?
WELL, YOU'RE THE ONE WHO SAID I SHOULDN'T STOP. I WAS GONNA QUIT...
HINA-CHAN IS MY KOUHAI AT WORK AND AT SCHOOL.
WELL, OF COURSE! IT'D BE A WASTE TO QUIT. YOU GET TO WEAR LOTS OF CUTE CLOTHES, RIGHT? LUCKY!
SHE'S REALLY PRETTY AND HAS A GREAT FIGURE ... AND IS REALLY INTO FASHION AND CUTE THINGS.
UH...
YOU'RE THINKING OF PRO MODELS. I JUST DO IT ON THE SIDE, SO I MOSTLY WEAR MY OWN STUFF.
WELL, I GUESS I DO BORROW MY OLDER SISTER'S CLOTHES A LOT, BUT STILL.
AND...
OH, REALLY? IS THAT WHY YOU'RE NORMALLY IN SUCH EDGY STUFF IN THE PHOTOS?
LIKE FISHNET TIGHTS!
NO, THOSE ARE MINE.
AH!
ACK!
HUH?! WHAT?!

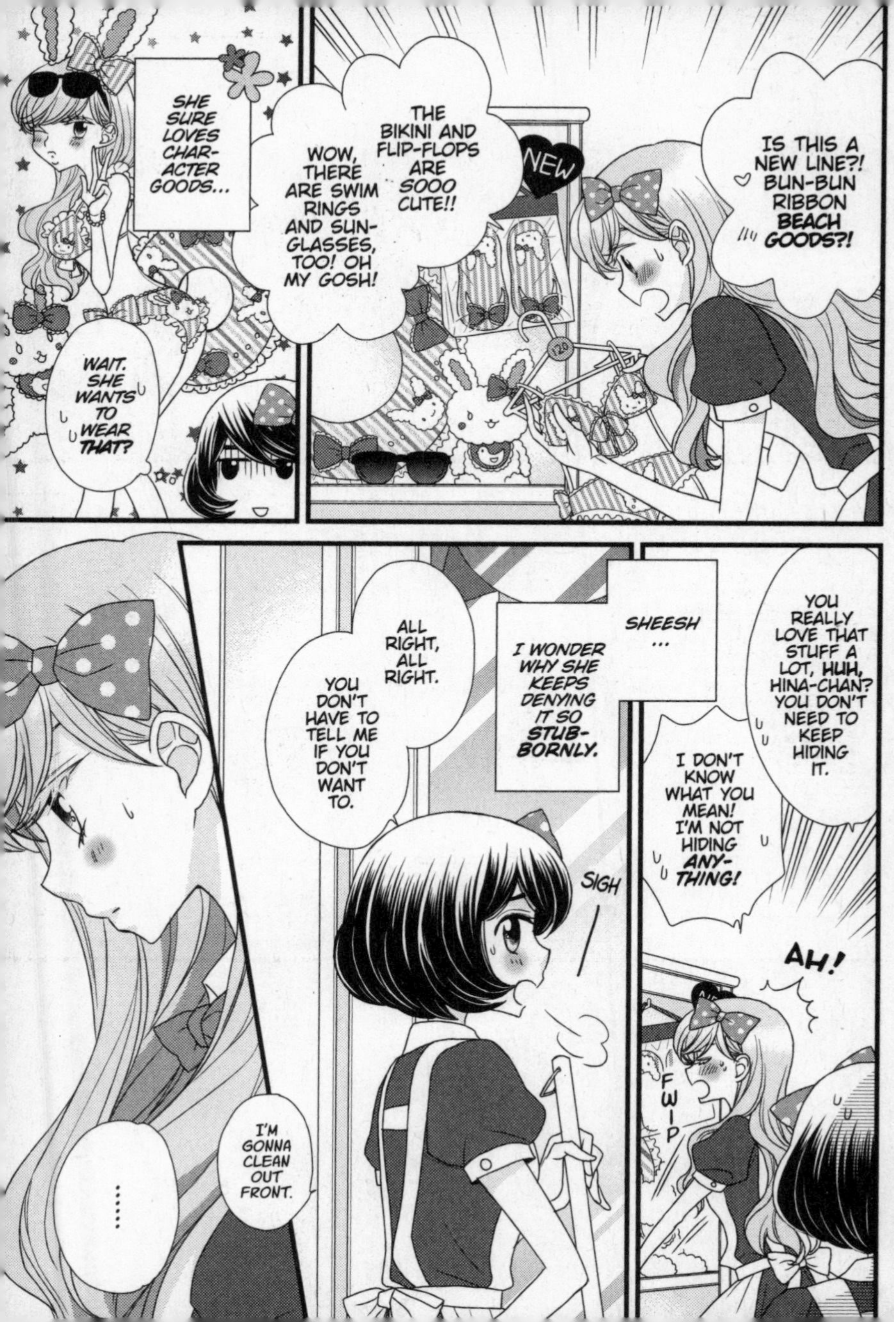
IS THIS A NEW LINE?! BUN-BUN RIBBON BEACH GOODS?!
NEW
THE BIKINI AND FLIP-FLOPS ARE SOOO CUTE!!
WOW, THERE ARE SWIM RINGS AND SUN-GLASSES, TOO! OH MY GOSH!
SHE SURE LOVES CHAR-ACTER GOODS...
WAIT. SHE WANTS TO WEAR THAT?
YOU REALLY LOVE THAT STUFF A LOT, HUH, HINA-CHAN? YOU DON'T NEED TO KEEP HIDING IT.
I DON'T KNOW WHAT YOU MEAN! I'M NOT HIDING ANY-THING!
AH!
FWIP
SHEESH ...
I WONDER WHY SHE KEEPS DENYING IT SO STUB-BORNLY.
SIGH
ALL RIGHT, ALL RIGHT.
YOU DON'T HAVE TO TELL ME IF YOU DON'T WANT TO.
I'M GONNA CLEAN OUT FRONT.
......

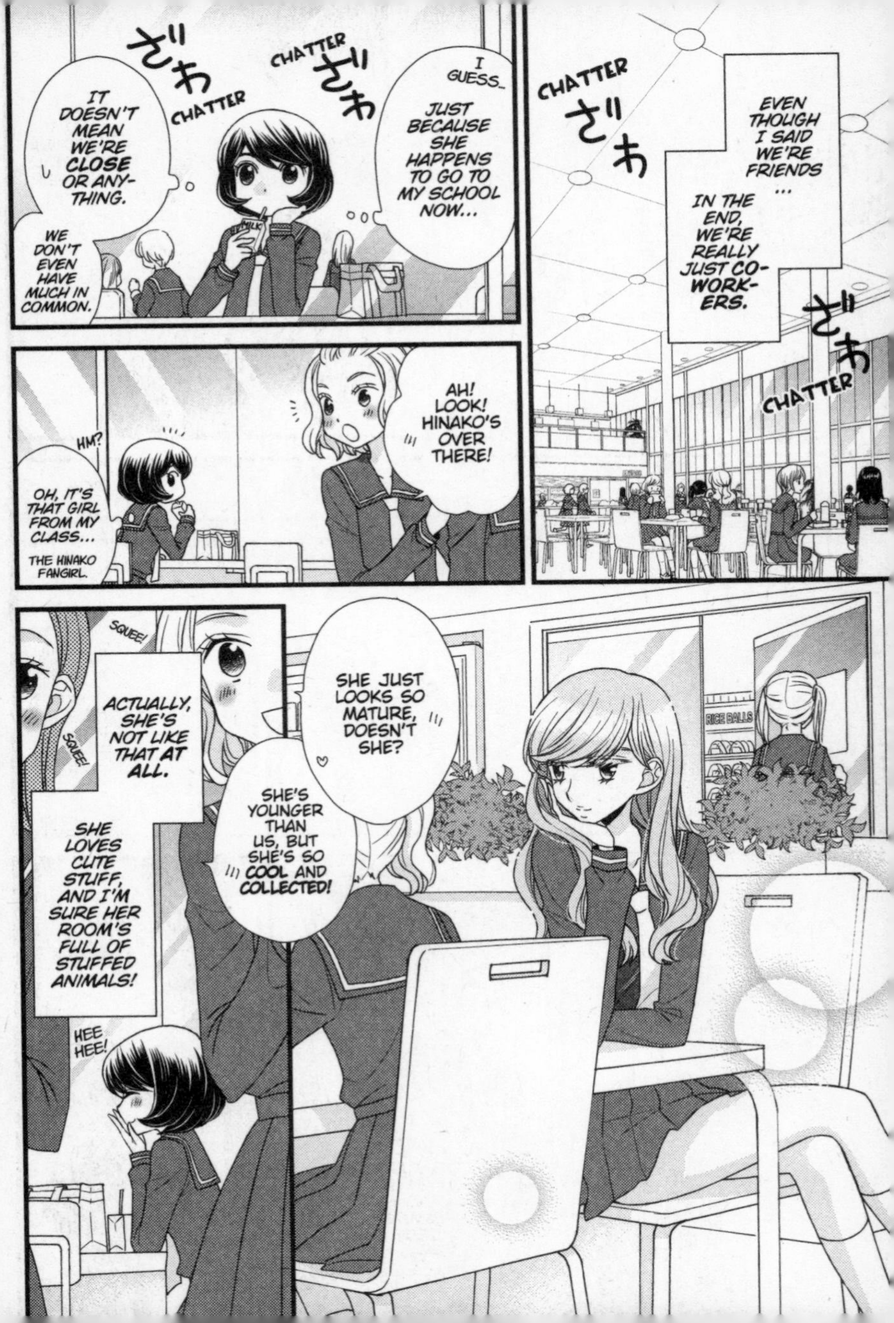
CHATTER
ざわ
EVEN THOUGH I SAID WE'RE FRIENDS...
IN THE END, WE'RE REALLY JUST CO-WORKERS.
ざわ
CHATTER
I GUESS...
JUST BECAUSE SHE HAPPENS TO GO TO MY SCHOOL NOW...
CHATTER
ざわ
MILK
ざわ
CHATTER
IT DOESN'T MEAN WE'RE CLOSE OR ANYTHING.
WE DON'T EVEN HAVE MUCH IN COMMON.
AH! LOOK! HINAKO'S OVER THERE!
HM?
OH, IT'S THAT GIRL FROM MY CLASS...
THE HINAKO FANGIRL.
RICE BALLS
SHE JUST LOOKS SO MATURE, DOESN'T SHE?
SHE'S YOUNGER THAN US, BUT SHE'S SO COOL AND COLLECTED!
SQUEE!
SQUEE!
ACTUALLY, SHE'S NOT LIKE THAT AT ALL.
SHE LOVES CUTE STUFF, AND I'M SURE HER ROOM'S FULL OF STUFFED ANIMALS!
HEE HEE!

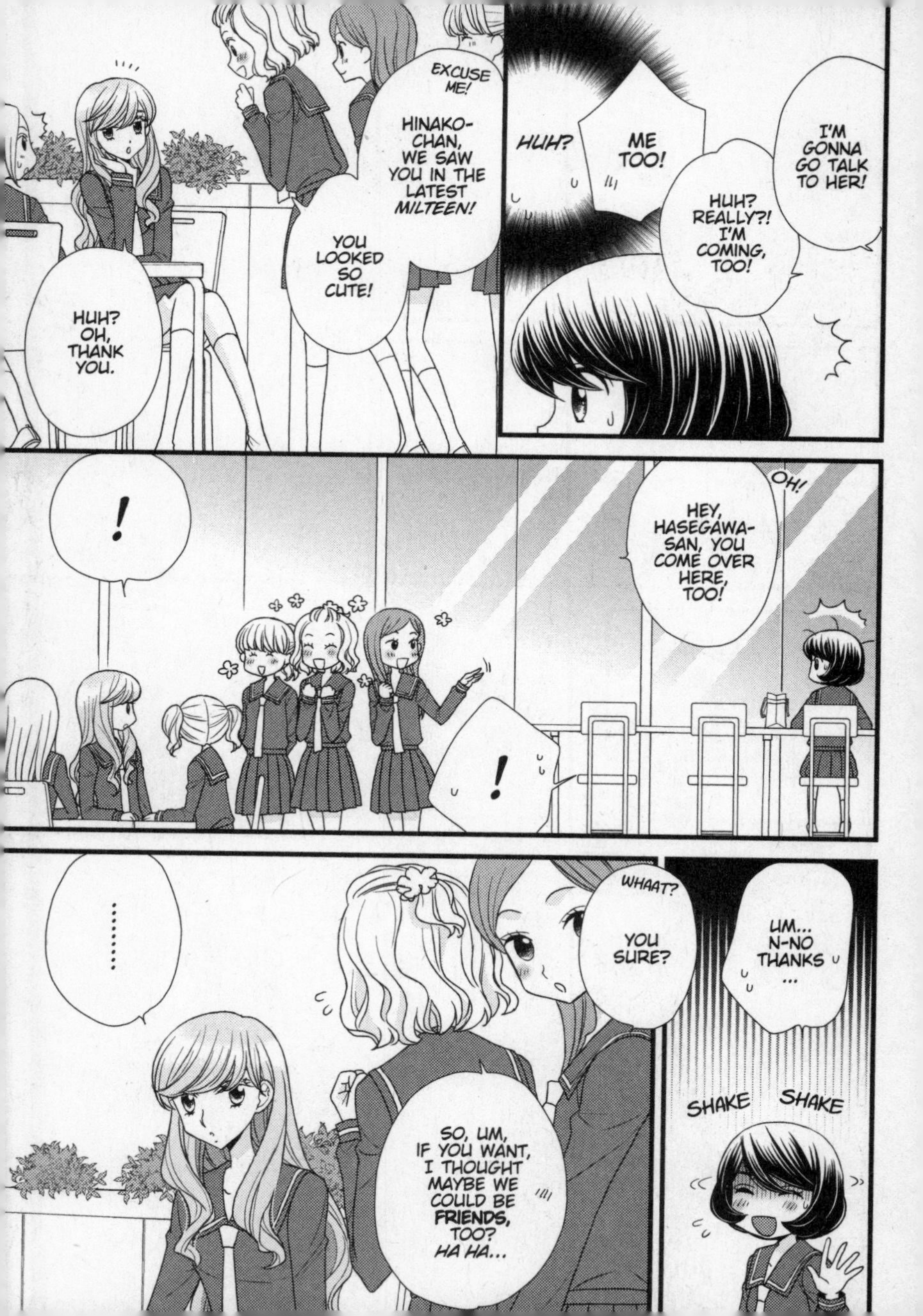
I'M GONNA GO TALK TO HER!
HUH? REALLY?! I'M COMING, TOO!
ME TOO!
HUH?
EXCUSE ME!
HINAKO-CHAN, WE SAW YOU IN THE LATEST *MILTEEN*!
YOU LOOKED SO CUTE!
HUH? OH, THANK YOU.
OH!
HEY, HASEGAWA-SAN, YOU COME OVER HERE, TOO!
!
!
UM... N-NO THANKS ...
SHAKE SHAKE
WHAAT?
YOU SURE?
SO, UM, IF YOU WANT, I THOUGHT MAYBE WE COULD BE **FRIENDS**, TOO? *HA HA...*
....

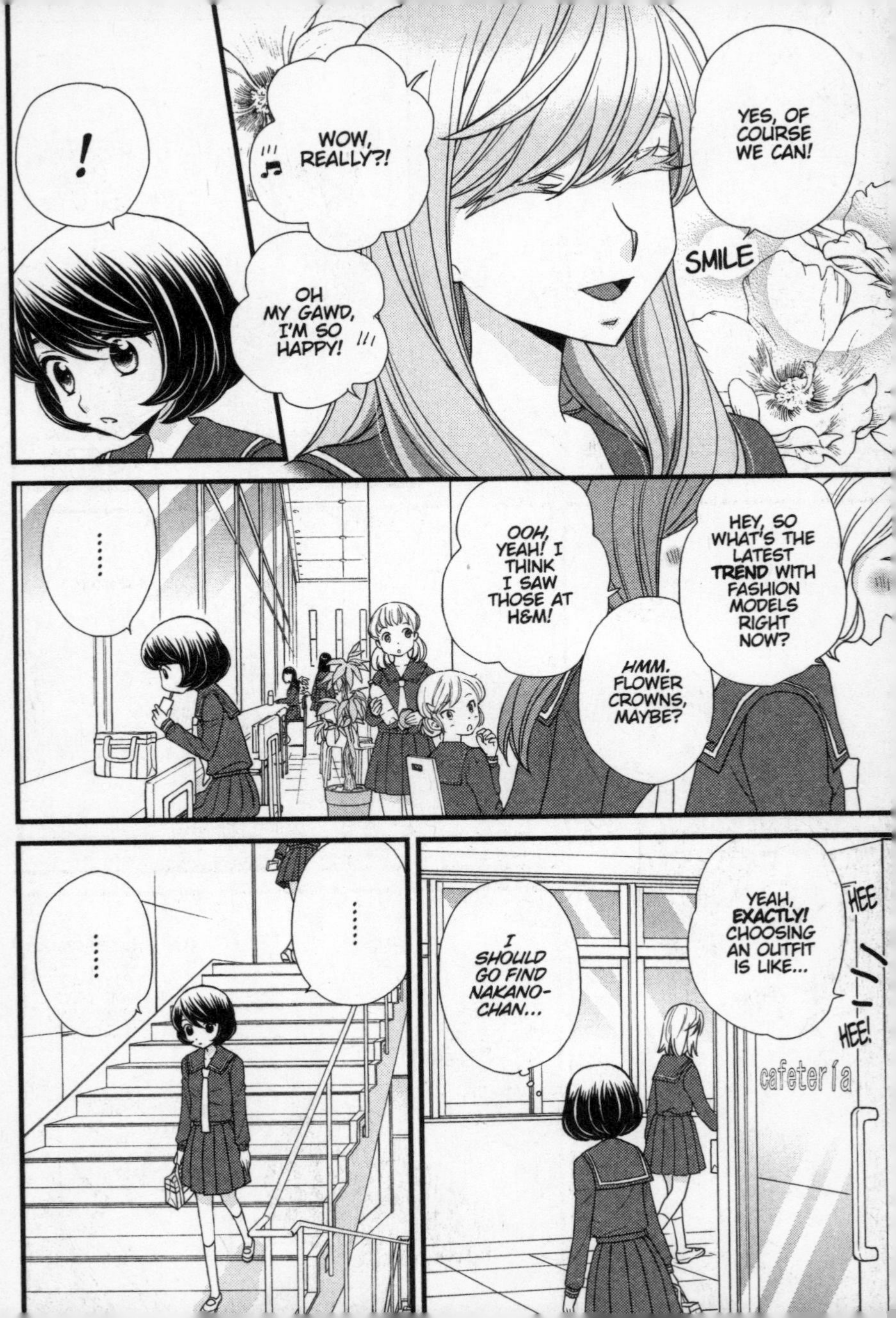
YES, OF COURSE WE CAN!
SMILE
WOW, REALLY?!
OH MY GAWD, I'M SO HAPPY!
!
HEY, SO WHAT'S THE LATEST TREND WITH FASHION MODELS RIGHT NOW?
HMM. FLOWER CROWNS, MAYBE?
OOH, YEAH! I THINK I SAW THOSE AT H&M!
......
YEAH, EXACTLY! CHOOSING AN OUTFIT IS LIKE...
HEE HEE!
cafeteria
I SHOULD GO FIND NAKANO-CHAN...
......
......

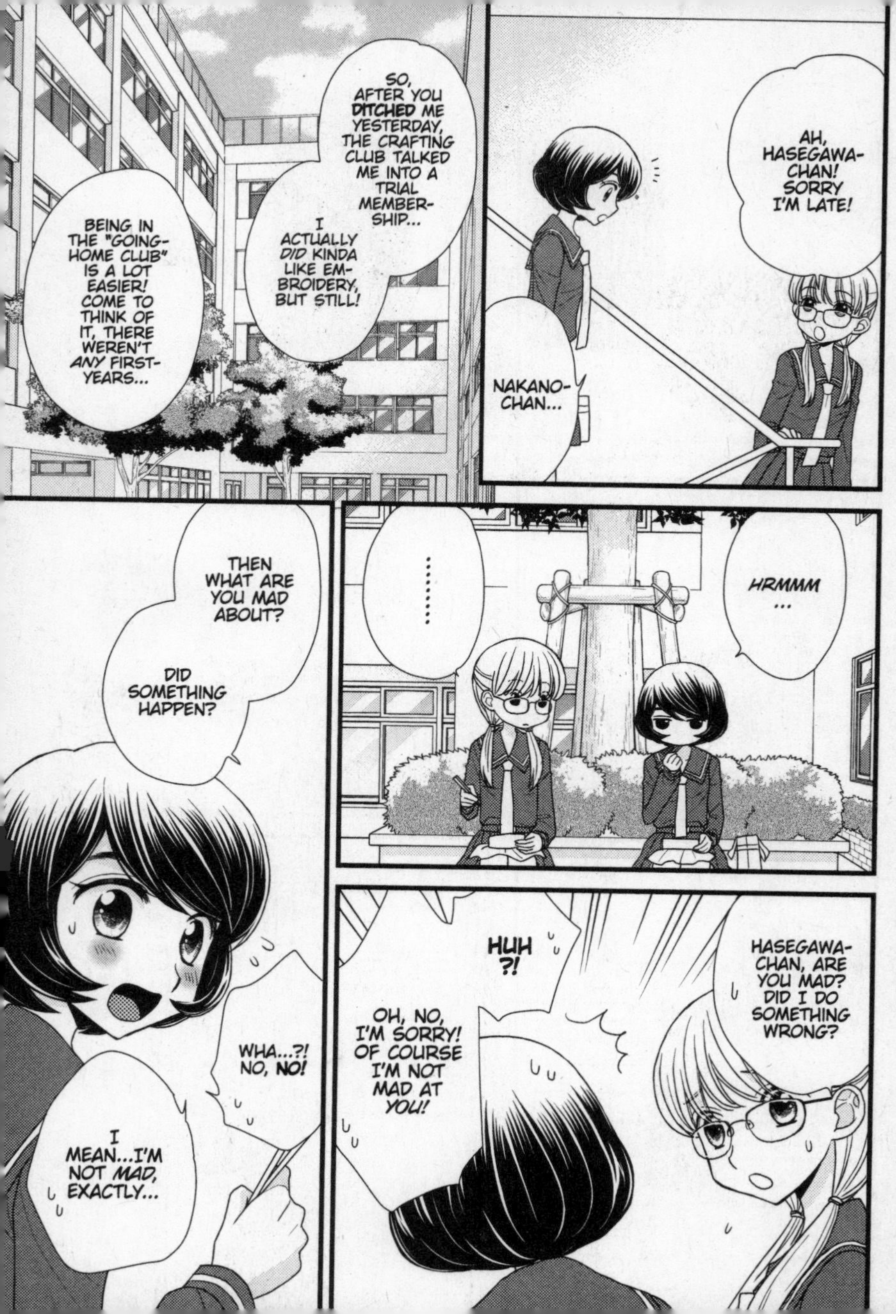

AH, HASEGAWA-CHAN! SORRY I'M LATE!
NAKANO-CHAN...
SO, AFTER YOU DITCHED ME YESTERDAY, THE CRAFTING CLUB TALKED ME INTO A TRIAL MEMBERSHIP...
I ACTUALLY DID KINDA LIKE EMBROIDERY, BUT STILL!
BEING IN THE "GOING-HOME CLUB" IS A LOT EASIER! COME TO THINK OF IT, THERE WEREN'T ANY FIRST-YEARS...
HRMMM ...
......
HASEGAWA-CHAN, ARE YOU MAD? DID I DO SOMETHING WRONG?
HUH ?!
OH, NO, I'M SORRY! OF COURSE I'M NOT MAD AT YOU!
THEN WHAT ARE YOU MAD ABOUT?
DID SOMETHING HAPPEN?
WHA...?! NO, NO!
I MEAN...I'M NOT MAD, EXACTLY...

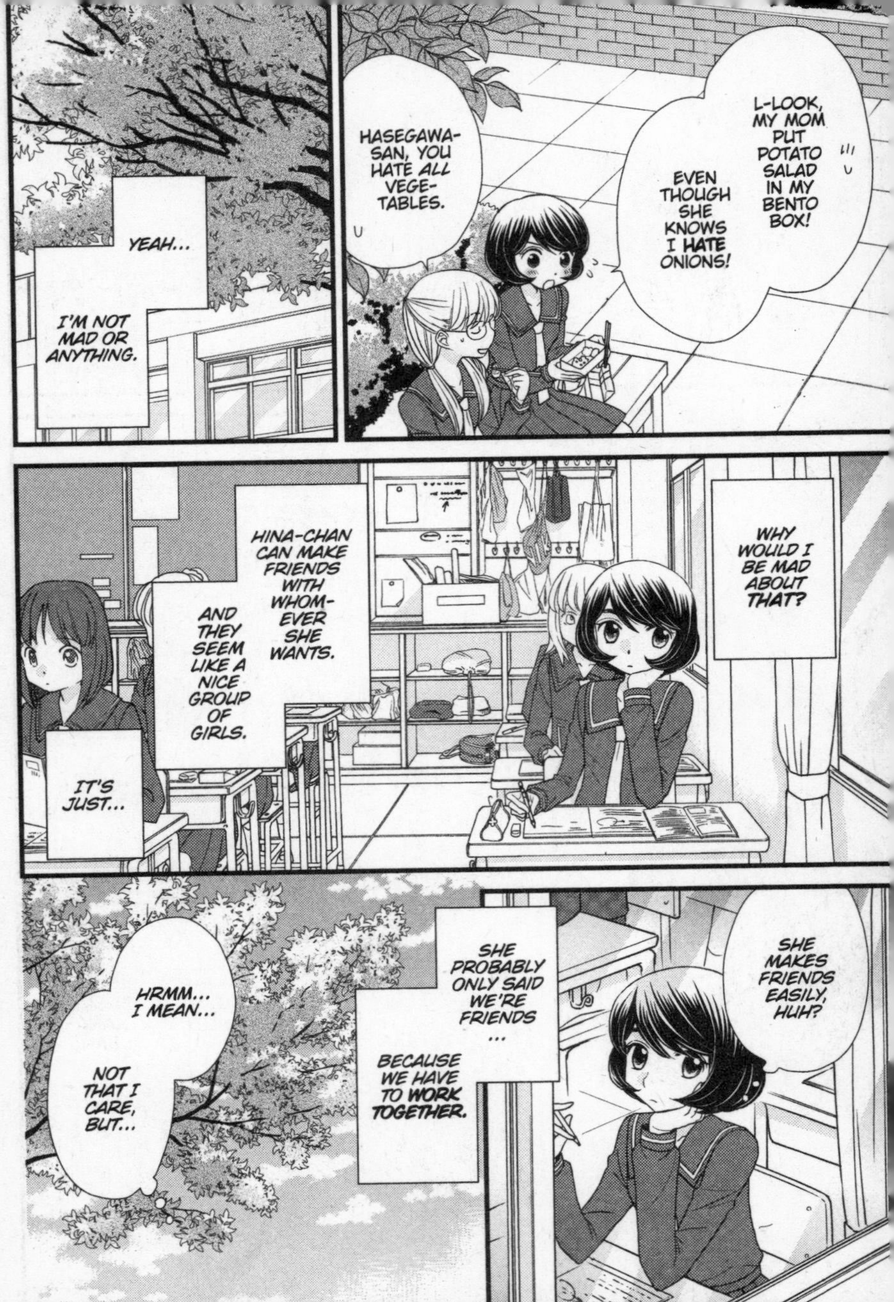
L-LOOK, MY MOM PUT POTATO SALAD IN MY BENTO BOX!
EVEN THOUGH SHE KNOWS I HATE ONIONS!
HASEGAWA-SAN, YOU HATE ALL VEGETABLES.
YEAH...
I'M NOT MAD OR ANYTHING.
WHY WOULD I BE MAD ABOUT THAT?
HINA-CHAN CAN MAKE FRIENDS WITH WHOMEVER SHE WANTS.
AND THEY SEEM LIKE A NICE GROUP OF GIRLS.
IT'S JUST...
SHE MAKES FRIENDS EASILY, HUH?
SHE PROBABLY ONLY SAID WE'RE FRIENDS ...
BECAUSE WE HAVE TO WORK TOGETHER.
HRMM... I MEAN...
NOT THAT I CARE, BUT...

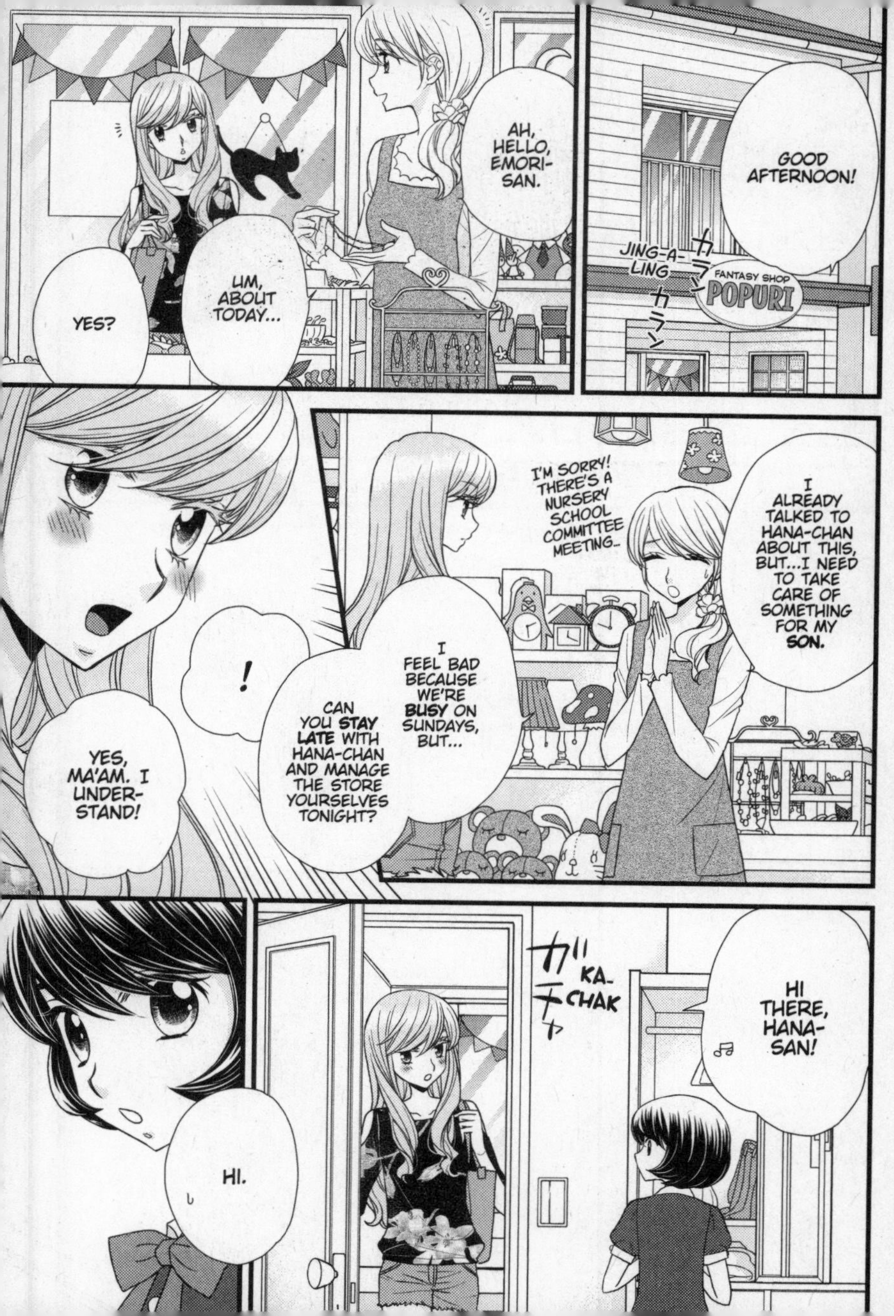
GOOD AFTERNOON!
JING-A-LING
カラン
カラン
FANTASY SHOP POPURI
AH, HELLO, EMORI-SAN.
UM, ABOUT TODAY...
YES?
I ALREADY TALKED TO HANA-CHAN ABOUT THIS, BUT...I NEED TO TAKE CARE OF SOMETHING FOR MY SON.
I'M SORRY! THERE'S A NURSERY SCHOOL COMMITTEE MEETING..
I FEEL BAD BECAUSE WE'RE BUSY ON SUNDAYS, BUT...
CAN YOU STAY LATE WITH HANA-CHAN AND MANAGE THE STORE YOURSELVES TONIGHT?
!
YES, MA'AM. I UNDERSTAND!
HI THERE, HANA-SAN!
ガチャ
KA-CHAK
HI.

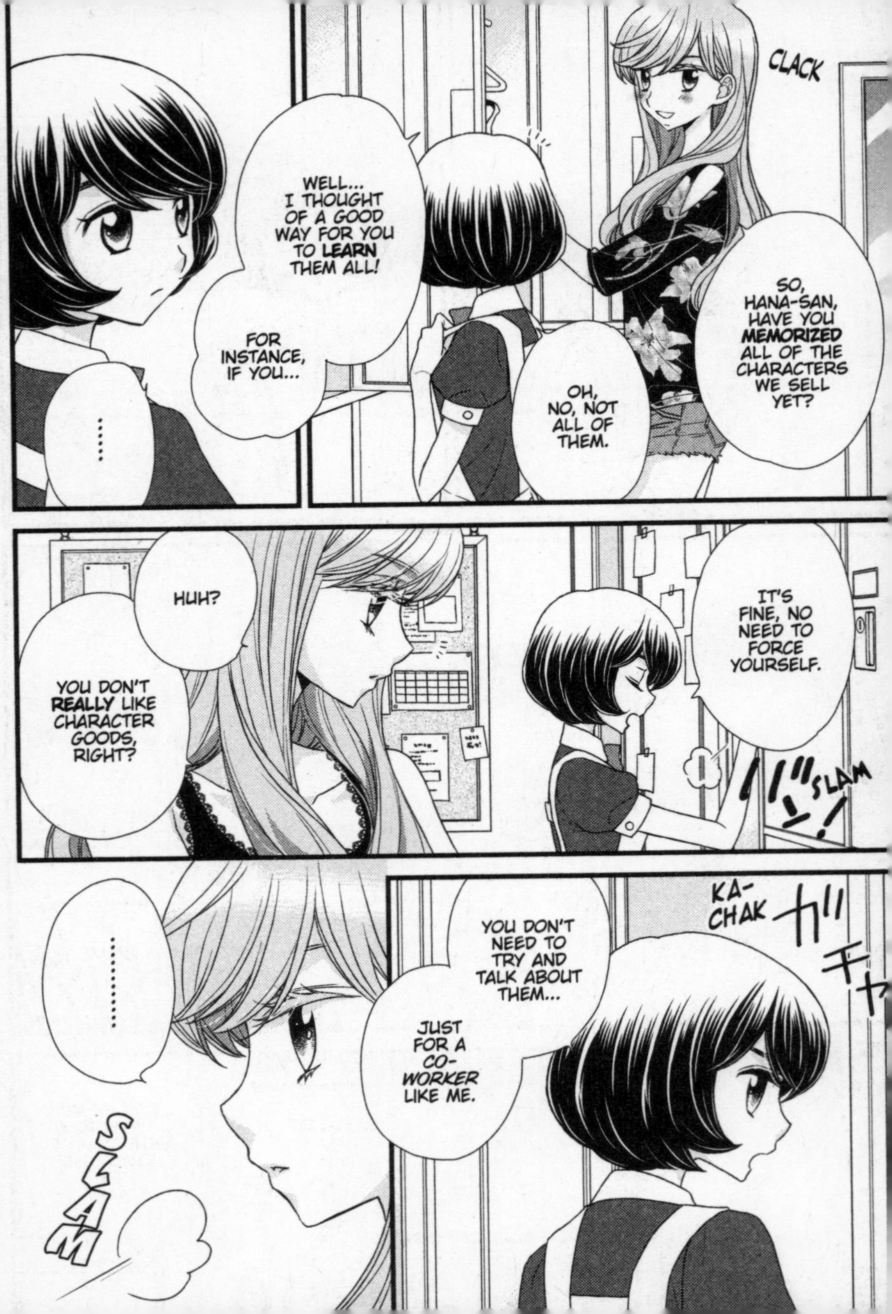
CLACK
SO, HANA-SAN, HAVE YOU MEMORIZED ALL OF THE CHARACTERS WE SELL YET?
OH, NO, NOT ALL OF THEM.
WELL... I THOUGHT OF A GOOD WAY FOR YOU TO LEARN THEM ALL!
FOR INSTANCE, IF YOU...
......
IT'S FINE, NO NEED TO FORCE YOURSELF.
SLAM
HUH?
YOU DON'T REALLY LIKE CHARACTER GOODS, RIGHT?
KA-CHAK
YOU DON'T NEED TO TRY AND TALK ABOUT THEM...
JUST FOR A CO-WORKER LIKE ME.
......
SLAM

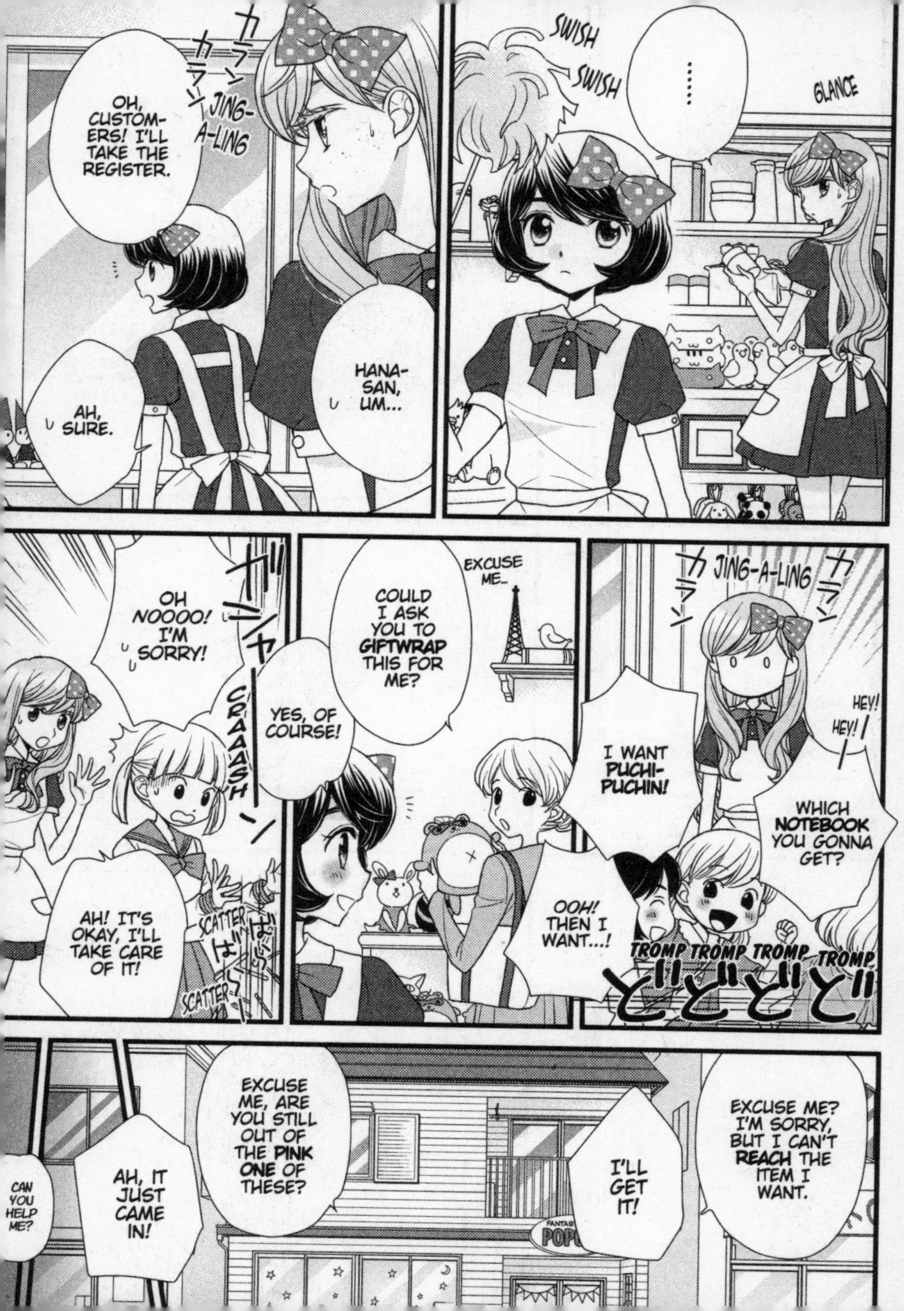
SWISH
SWISH
......
GLANCE
カラン
カラン
JING-A-LING
OH, CUSTOMERS! I'LL TAKE THE REGISTER.
HANA-SAN, UM...
AH, SURE.
カラン
JING-A-LING
カラン
HEY! HEY!
I WANT PUCHI-PUCHIN!
WHICH NOTEBOOK YOU GONNA GET?
OOH! THEN I WANT...!
TROMP TROMP TROMP TROMP
EXCUSE ME..
COULD I ASK YOU TO GIFTWRAP THIS FOR ME?
YES, OF COURSE!
CRAAASH
OH NOOOO! I'M SORRY!
AH! IT'S OKAY, I'LL TAKE CARE OF IT!
SCATTER
SCATTER
EXCUSE ME? I'M SORRY, BUT I CAN'T REACH THE ITEM I WANT.
I'LL GET IT!
EXCUSE ME, ARE YOU STILL OUT OF THE PINK ONE OF THESE?
AH, IT JUST CAME IN!
CAN YOU HELP ME?

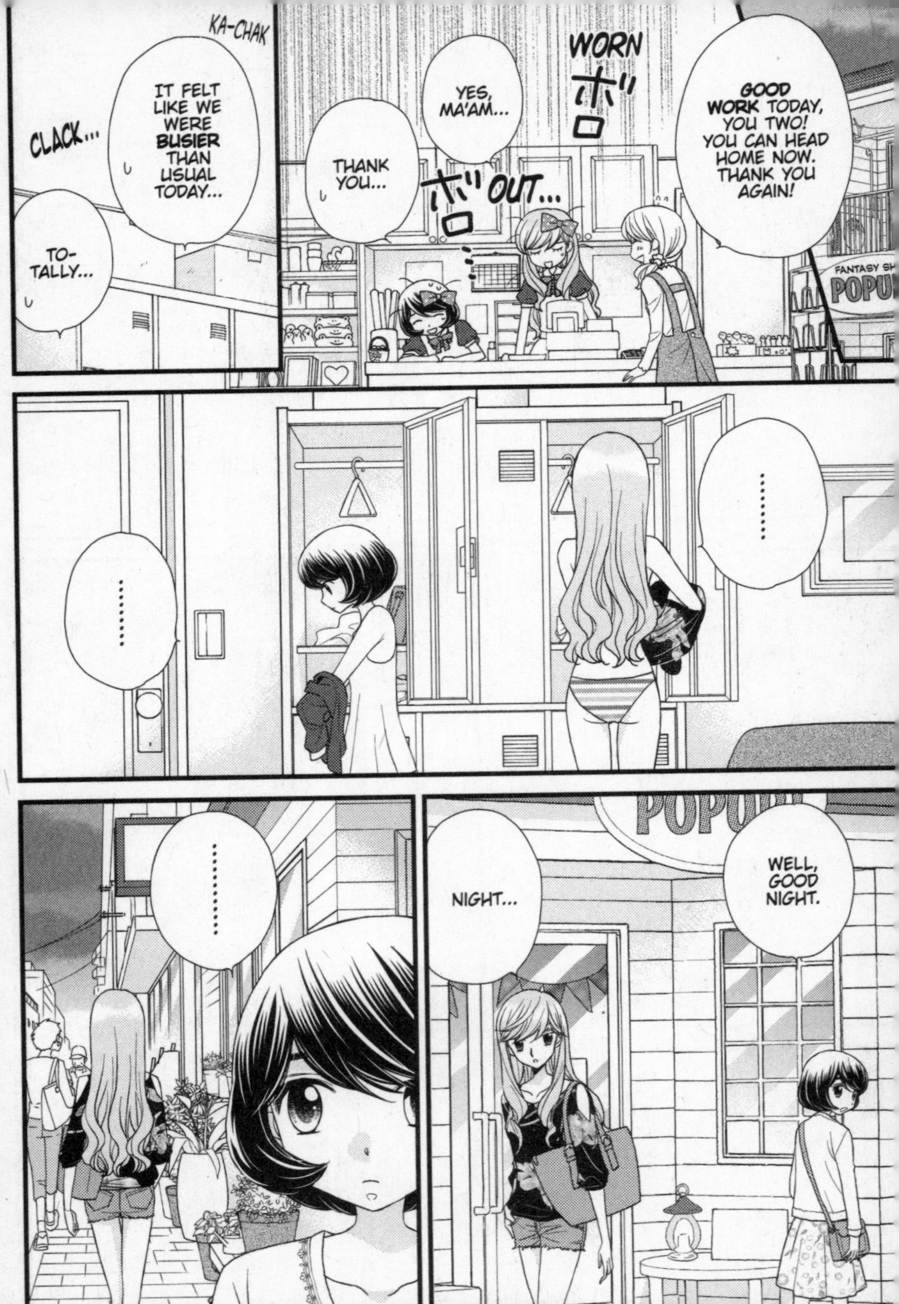
GOOD WORK TODAY, YOU TWO! YOU CAN HEAD HOME NOW. THANK YOU AGAIN!
WORN ボロ
YES, MA'AM...
ボロ OUT...
THANK YOU...
KA-CHAK
IT FELT LIKE WE WERE BUSIER THAN USUAL TODAY...
CLACK...
TO-TALLY...
......
......
WELL, GOOD NIGHT.
NIGHT...
....

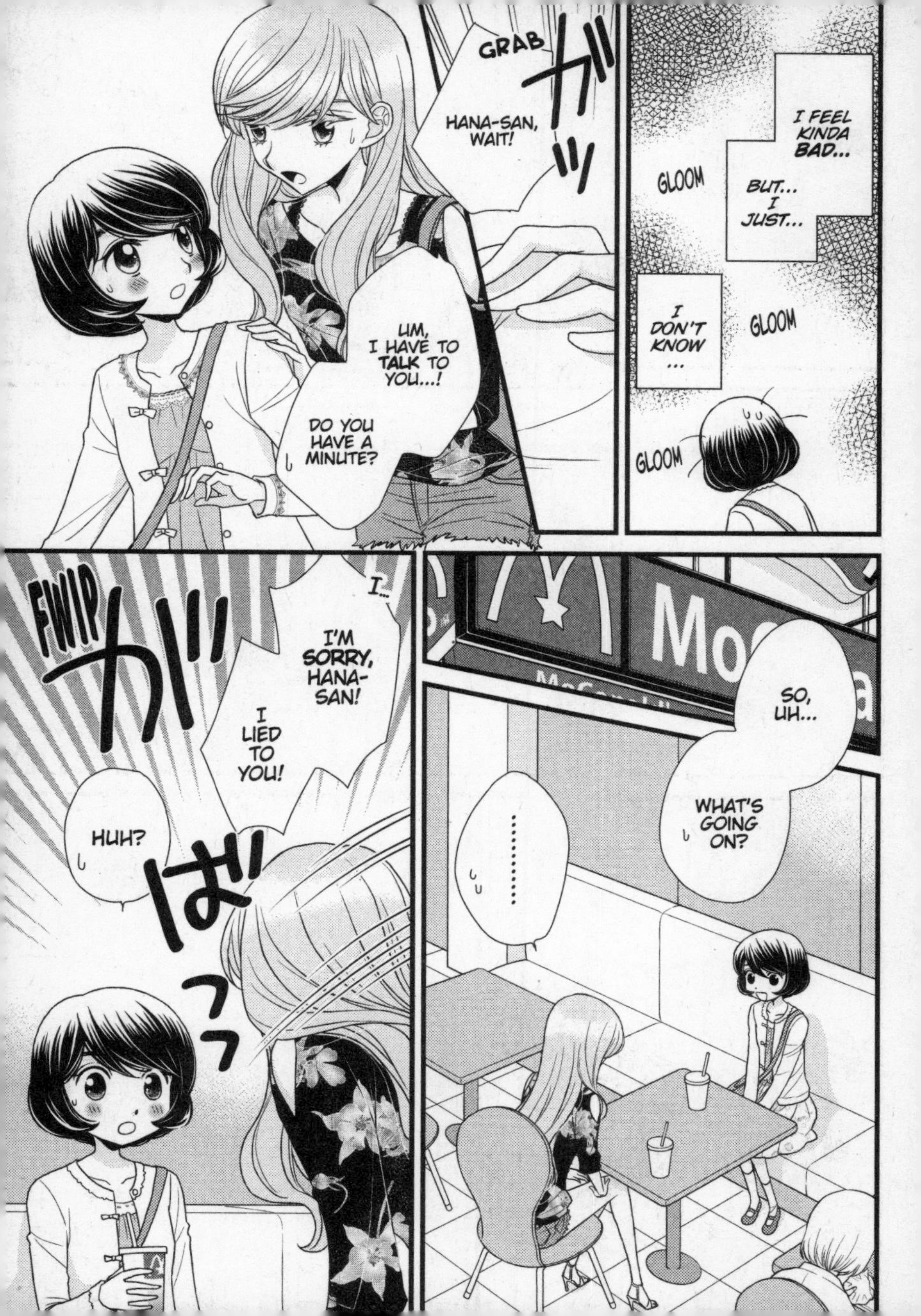
I FEEL KINDA BAD...
BUT... I JUST...
GLOOM
I DON'T KNOW ...
GLOOM
GLOOM
GRAB
HANA-SAN, WAIT!
UM, I HAVE TO TALK TO YOU...!
DO YOU HAVE A MINUTE?
SO, UH...
WHAT'S GOING ON?
......
I...
I'M SORRY, HANA-SAN!
I LIED TO YOU!
FWIP
HUH?

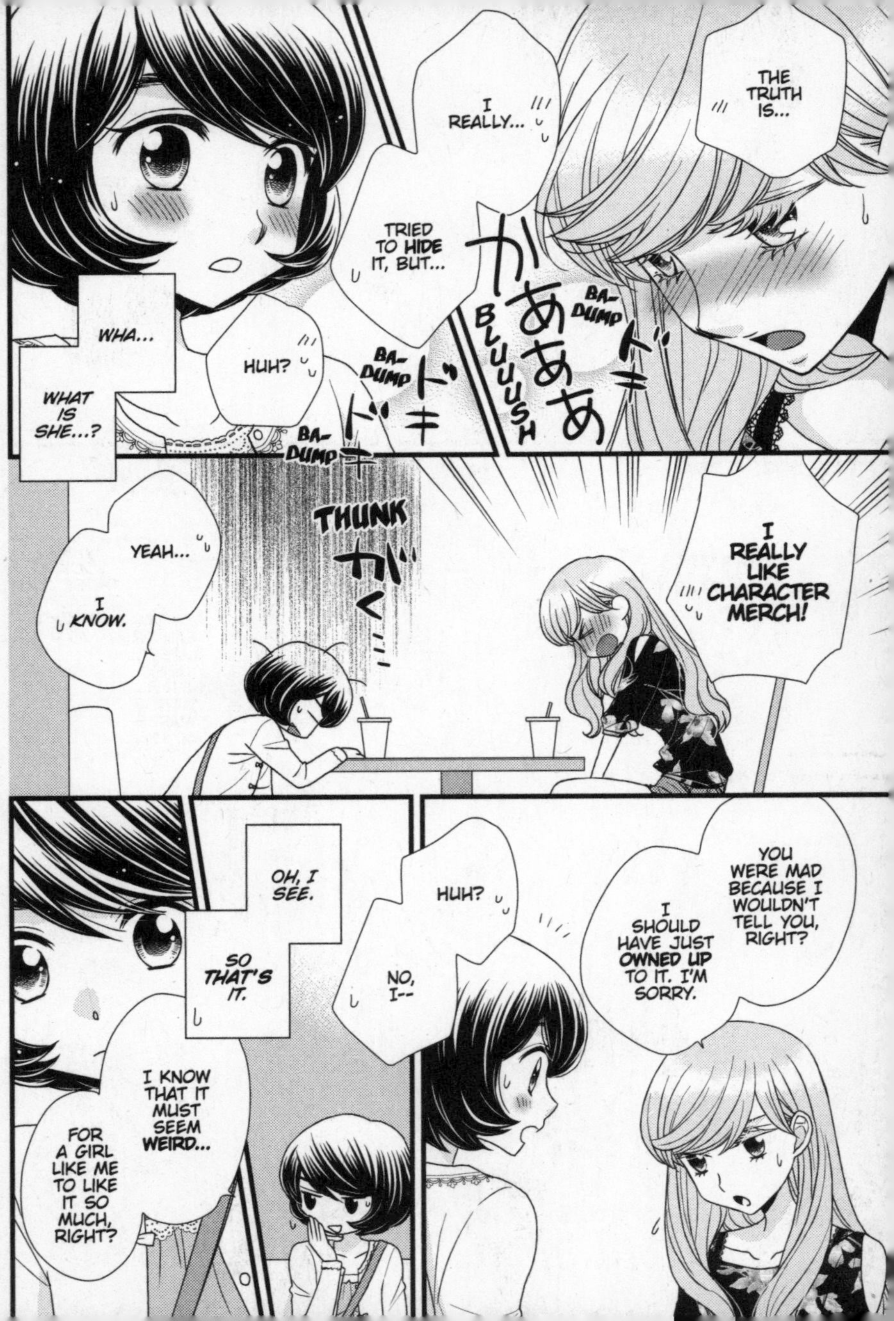
THE TRUTH IS...
I REALLY...
TRIED TO HIDE IT, BUT...
かあああ
BLUUUSH
ドキ
BA-DUMP
ドキ
BA-DUMP
ドキ
BA-DUMP
HUH?
WHA...
WHAT IS SHE...?
I REALLY LIKE CHARACTER MERCH!
がくっ
THUNK
YEAH...
I KNOW.
YOU WERE MAD BECAUSE I WOULDN'T TELL YOU, RIGHT?
I SHOULD HAVE JUST OWNED UP TO IT. I'M SORRY.
HUH?
NO, I--
OH, I SEE.
SO THAT'S IT.
I KNOW THAT IT MUST SEEM WEIRD...
FOR A GIRL LIKE ME TO LIKE IT SO MUCH, RIGHT?

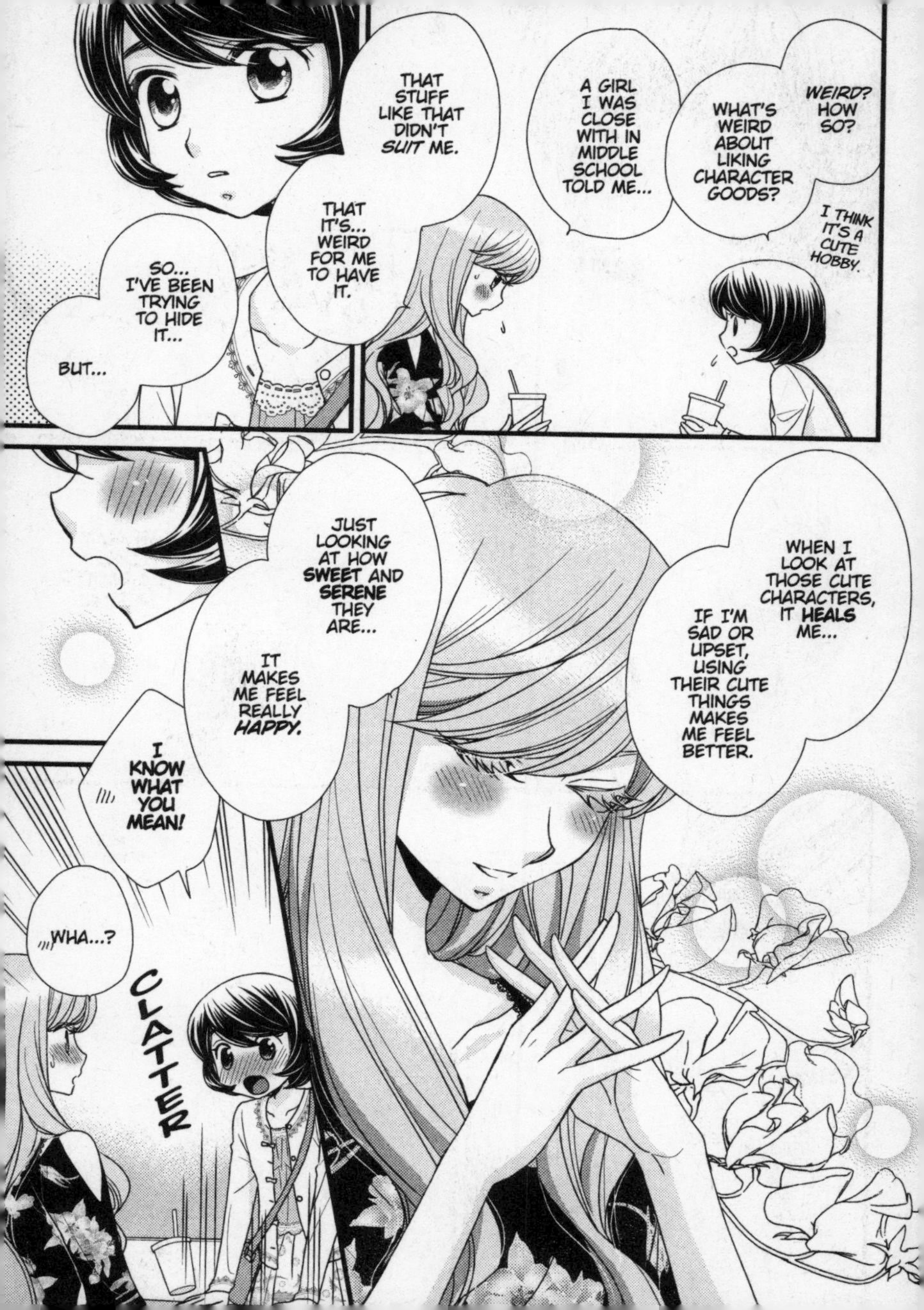
WEIRD? HOW SO?
WHAT'S WEIRD ABOUT LIKING CHARACTER GOODS?
I THINK IT'S A CUTE HOBBY.
A GIRL I WAS CLOSE WITH IN MIDDLE SCHOOL TOLD ME...
THAT IT'S... WEIRD FOR ME TO HAVE IT.
THAT STUFF LIKE THAT DIDN'T SUIT ME.
SO... I'VE BEEN TRYING TO HIDE IT...
BUT...
WHEN I LOOK AT THOSE CUTE CHARACTERS, IT HEALS ME...
IF I'M SAD OR UPSET, USING THEIR CUTE THINGS MAKES ME FEEL BETTER.
JUST LOOKING AT HOW SWEET AND SERENE THEY ARE...
IT MAKES ME FEEL REALLY HAPPY.
I KNOW WHAT YOU MEAN!
WHA...?
CLATTER

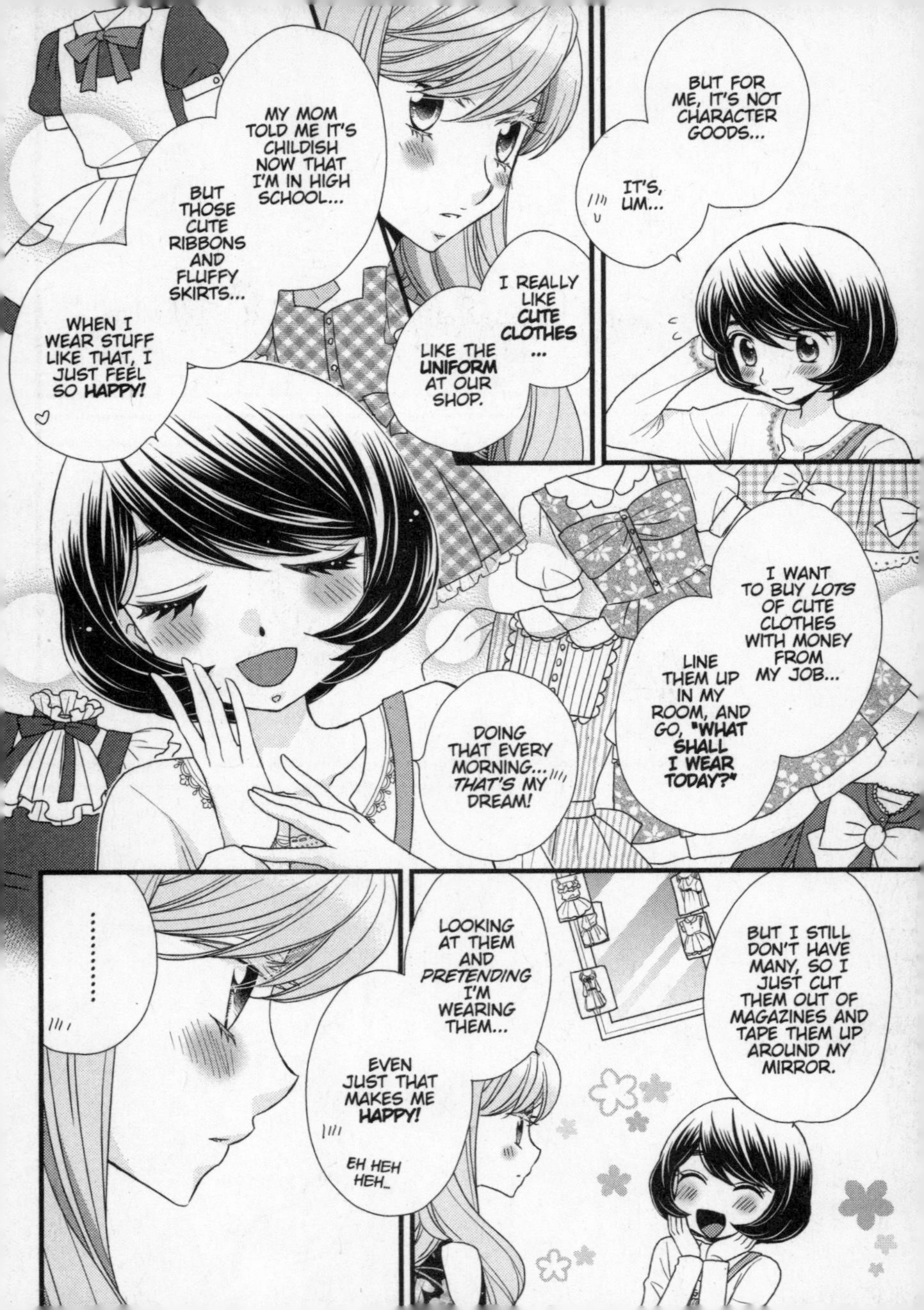
BUT FOR ME, IT'S NOT CHARACTER GOODS...
IT'S, UM...
I REALLY LIKE **CUTE CLOTHES**...
LIKE THE **UNIFORM** AT OUR SHOP.
MY MOM TOLD ME IT'S CHILDISH NOW THAT I'M IN HIGH SCHOOL...
BUT THOSE CUTE RIBBONS AND FLUFFY SKIRTS...
WHEN I WEAR STUFF LIKE THAT, I JUST FEEL SO **HAPPY!**
I WANT TO BUY *LOTS* OF CUTE CLOTHES WITH MONEY FROM MY JOB...
LINE THEM UP IN MY ROOM, AND GO, **"WHAT SHALL I WEAR TODAY?"**
DOING THAT EVERY MORNING... *THAT'S* MY DREAM!
BUT I STILL DON'T HAVE MANY, SO I JUST CUT THEM OUT OF MAGAZINES AND TAPE THEM UP AROUND MY MIRROR.
LOOKING AT THEM AND *PRETENDING* I'M WEARING THEM...
EVEN JUST THAT MAKES ME **HAPPY!**
EH HEH HEH..
....

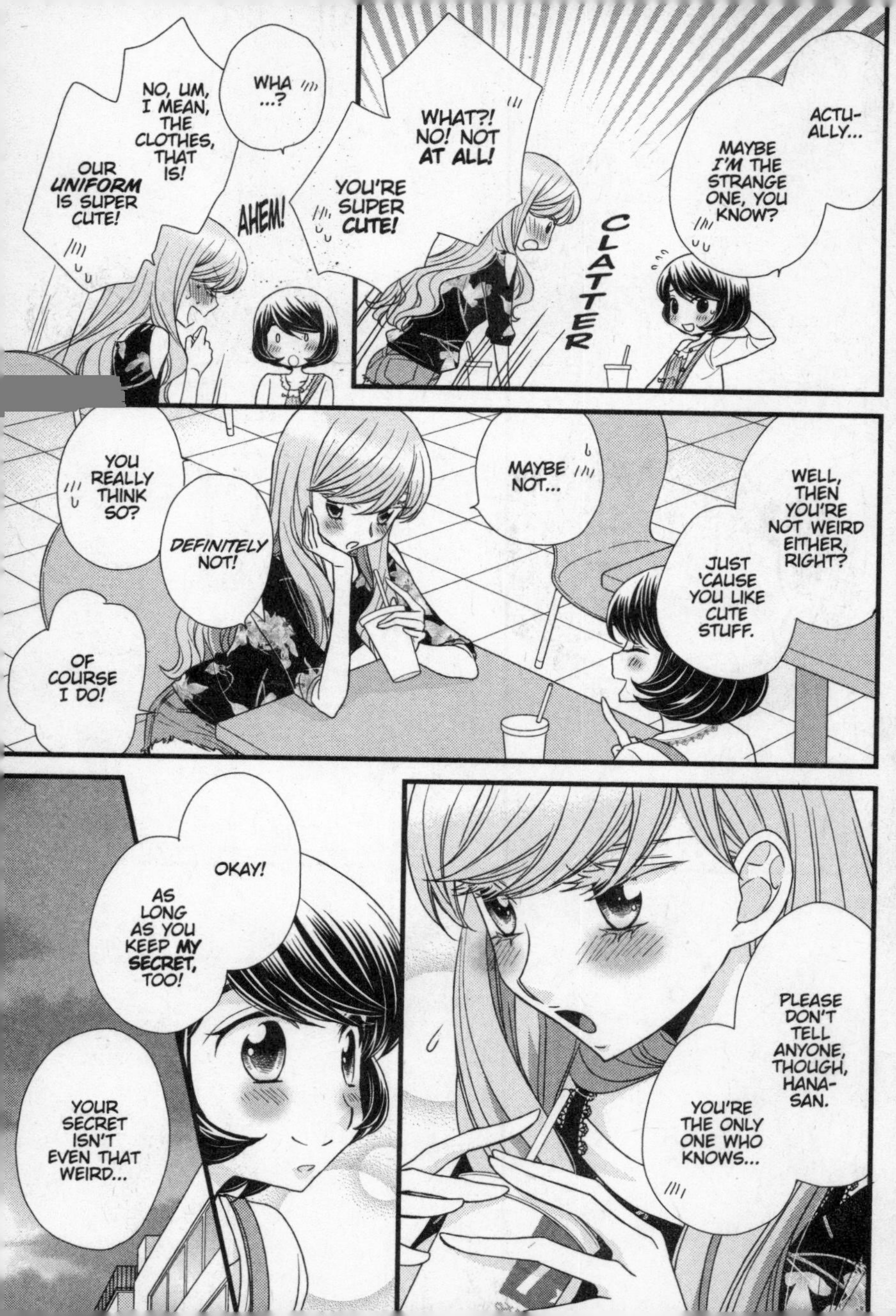
ACTU-ALLY...
MAYBE *I'M* THE STRANGE ONE, YOU KNOW?
CLATTER
WHAT?! NO! NOT AT ALL!
YOU'RE SUPER CUTE!
WHA...?
AHEM!
NO, UM, I MEAN, THE CLOTHES, THAT IS!
OUR *UNIFORM* IS SUPER CUTE!
WELL, THEN YOU'RE NOT WEIRD EITHER, RIGHT?
JUST 'CAUSE YOU LIKE CUTE STUFF.
MAYBE NOT...
YOU REALLY THINK SO?
DEFINITELY NOT!
OF COURSE I DO!
PLEASE DON'T TELL ANYONE, THOUGH, HANA-SAN.
YOU'RE THE ONLY ONE WHO KNOWS...
OKAY!
AS LONG AS YOU KEEP MY SECRET, TOO!
YOUR SECRET ISN'T EVEN THAT WEIRD...

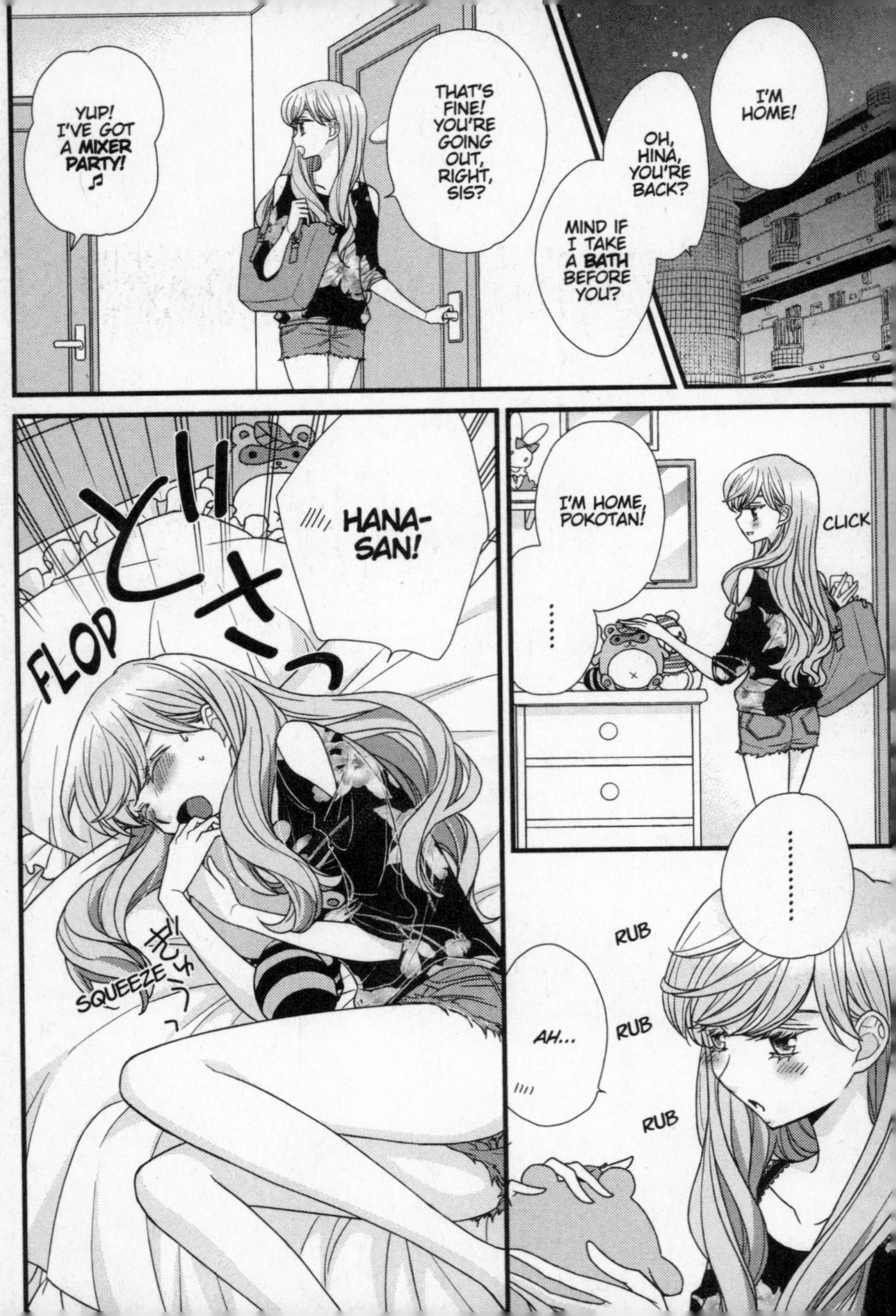

I'M HOME!
OH, HINA, YOU'RE BACK?
MIND IF I TAKE A BATH BEFORE YOU?
THAT'S FINE! YOU'RE GOING OUT, RIGHT, SIS?
YUP! I'VE GOT A MIXER PARTY! ♪
CLICK
I'M HOME, POKOTAN!
......
......
RUB
RUB
AH...
RUB
HANA-SAN!
どさっ
FLOP
ぎゅうっ
SQUEEZE

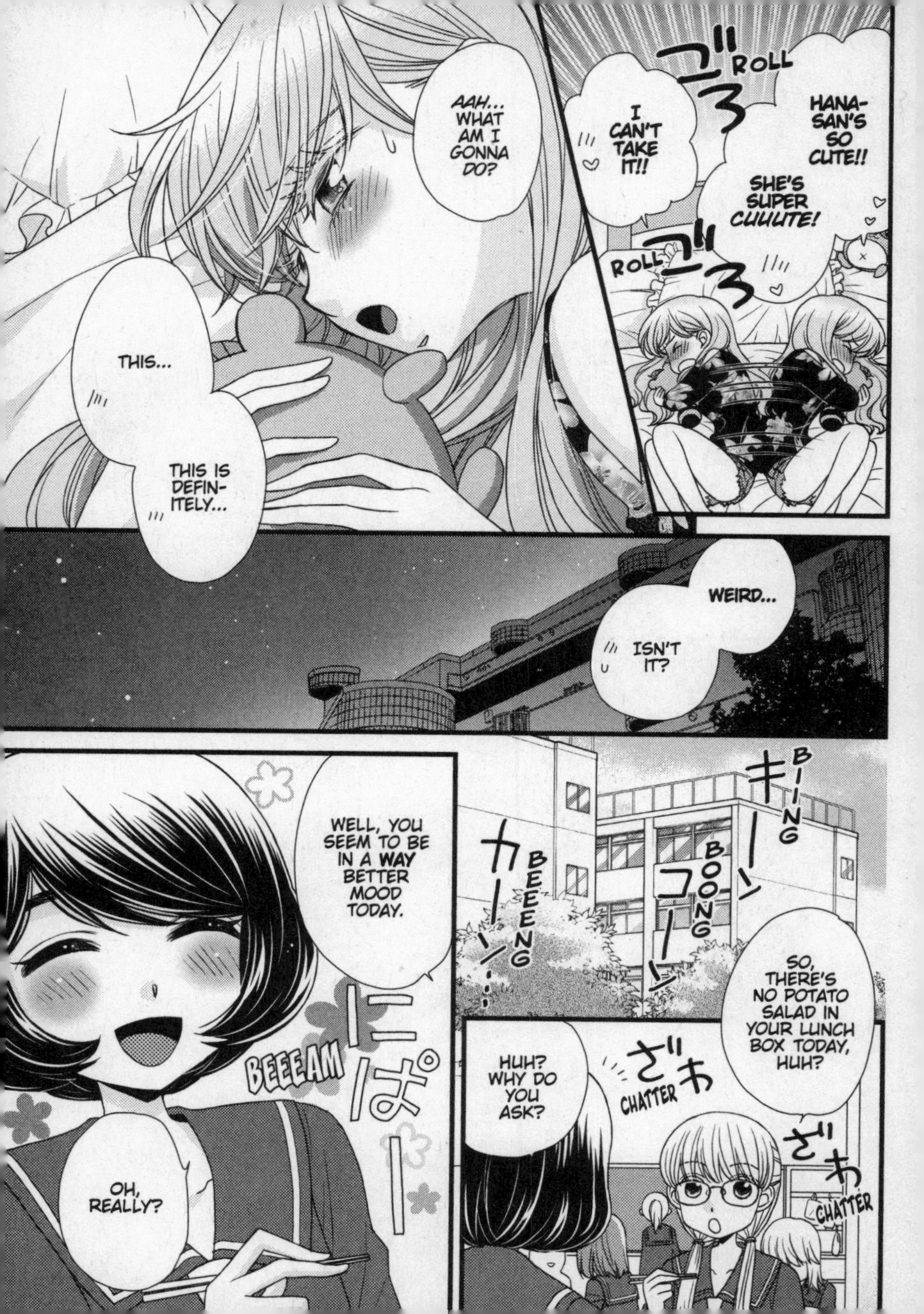

ROLL
HANA-SAN'S SO CUTE!!
I CAN'T TAKE IT!!
SHE'S SUPER CUUUTE!
ROLL
AAH... WHAT AM I GONNA DO?
THIS...
THIS IS DEFIN-ITELY...
WEIRD...
ISN'T IT?
BIING
BOONG
BEEEENG...
SO, THERE'S NO POTATO SALAD IN YOUR LUNCH BOX TODAY, HUH?
CHATTER
HUH? WHY DO YOU ASK?
CHATTER
WELL, YOU SEEM TO BE IN A WAY BETTER MOOD TODAY.
BEEEAM
OH, REALLY?

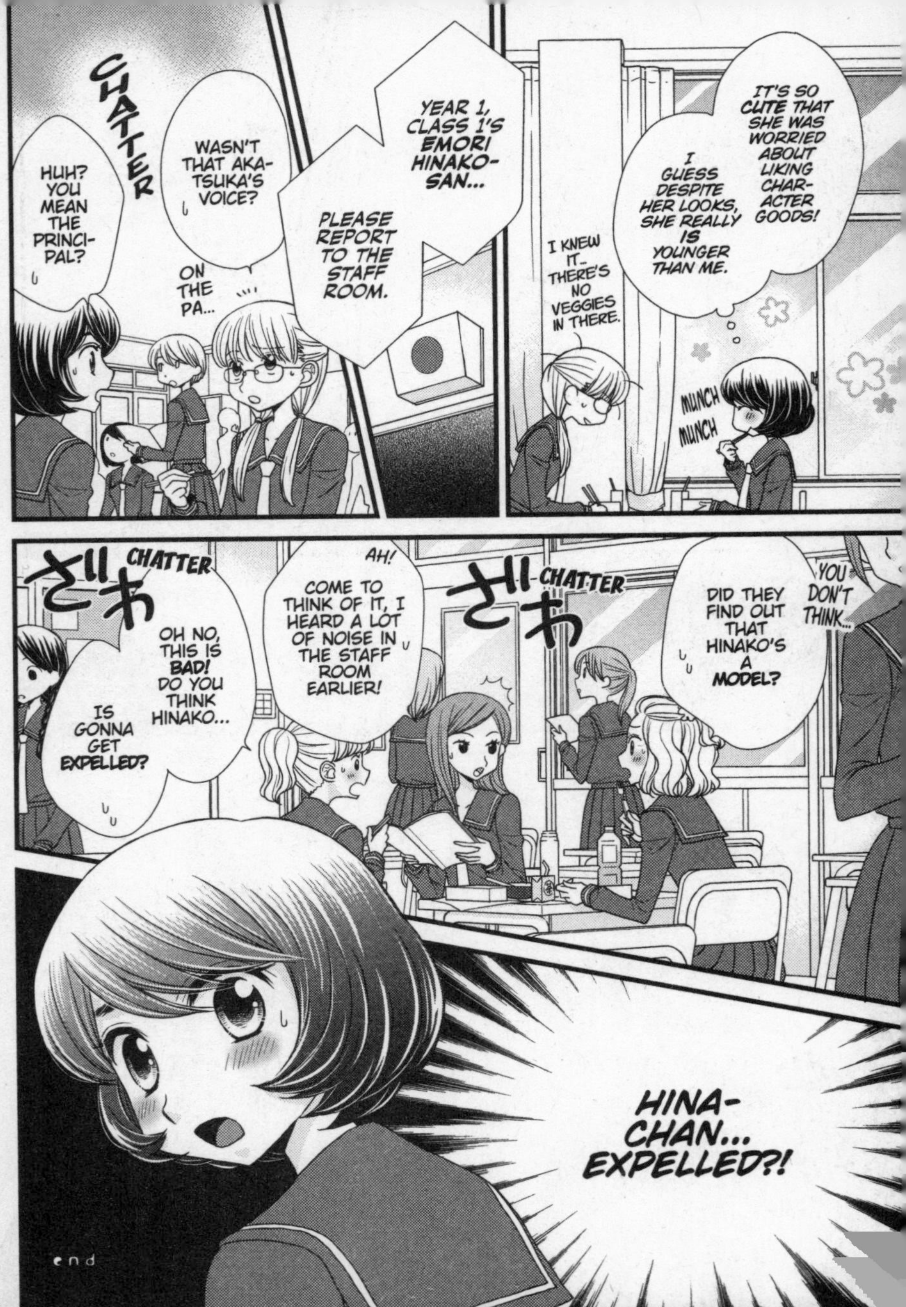

IT'S SO CUTE THAT SHE WAS WORRIED ABOUT LIKING CHARACTER GOODS!
I GUESS DESPITE HER LOOKS, SHE REALLY IS YOUNGER THAN ME.
I KNEW IT.. THERE'S NO VEGGIES IN THERE.
MUNCH MUNCH
YEAR 1, CLASS 1'S EMORI HINAKO-SAN...
PLEASE REPORT TO THE STAFF ROOM.
WASN'T THAT AKATSUKA'S VOICE?
ON THE PA...
CHATTER
HUH? YOU MEAN THE PRINCIPAL?
YOU DON'T THINK...
DID THEY FIND OUT THAT HINAKO'S A MODEL?
ざわ CHATTER
AH!
COME TO THINK OF IT, I HEARD A LOT OF NOISE IN THE STAFF ROOM EARLIER!
ざわ CHATTER
OH NO, THIS IS BAD! DO YOU THINK HINAKO...
IS GONNA GET EXPELLED?
HINA-CHAN... EXPELLED?!
end

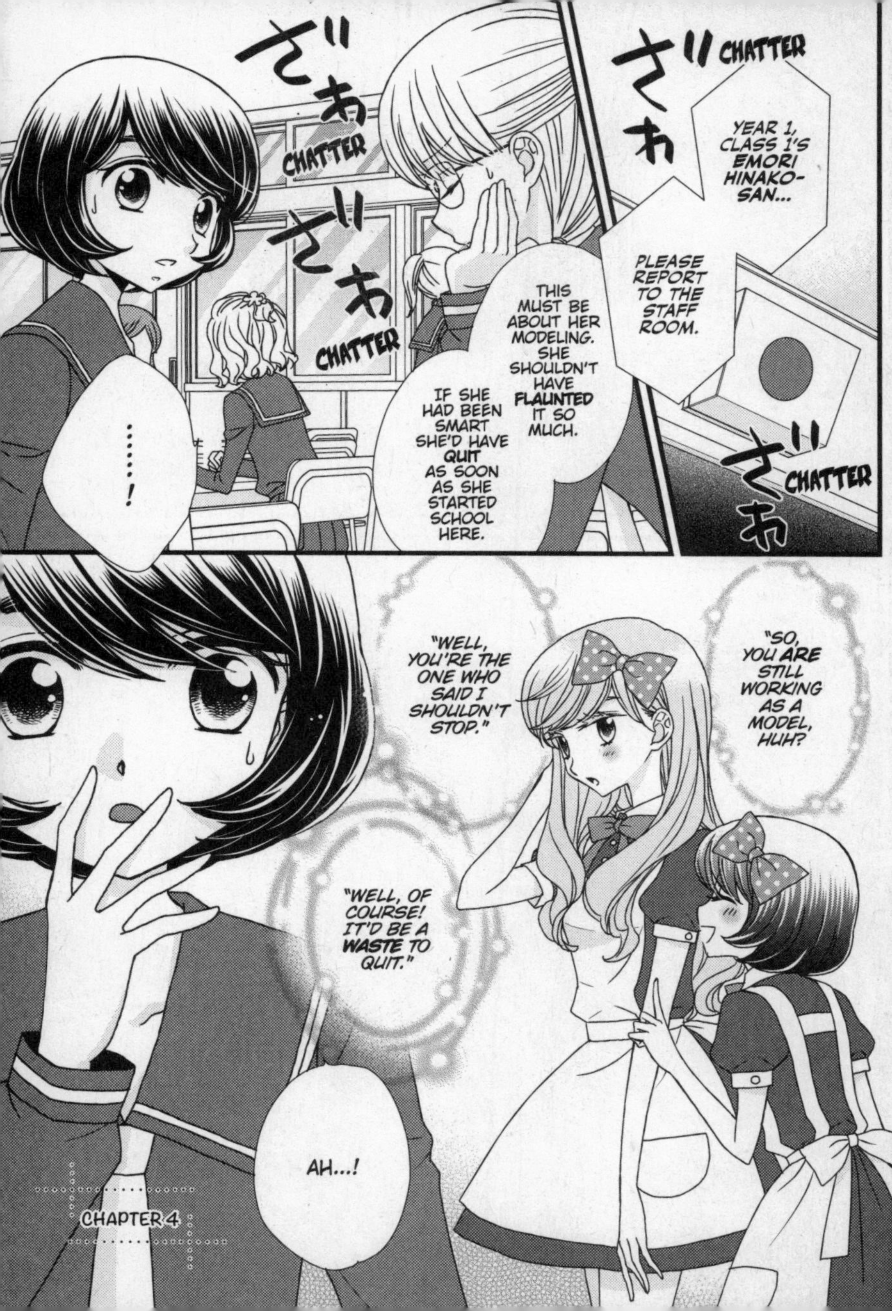
ざわ
CHATTER
YEAR 1, CLASS 1'S EMORI HINAKO-SAN...
PLEASE REPORT TO THE STAFF ROOM.
ざわ
CHATTER
THIS MUST BE ABOUT HER MODELING. SHE SHOULDN'T HAVE **FLAUNTED** IT SO MUCH.
IF SHE HAD BEEN SMART SHE'D HAVE **QUIT** AS SOON AS SHE STARTED SCHOOL HERE.
ざぁ
CHATTER
ざわ
CHATTER
......!
"SO, YOU **ARE** STILL WORKING AS A MODEL, HUH?
"WELL, YOU'RE THE ONE WHO SAID I SHOULDN'T STOP."
"WELL, OF COURSE! IT'D BE A **WASTE** TO QUIT."
AH...!
CHAPTER 4

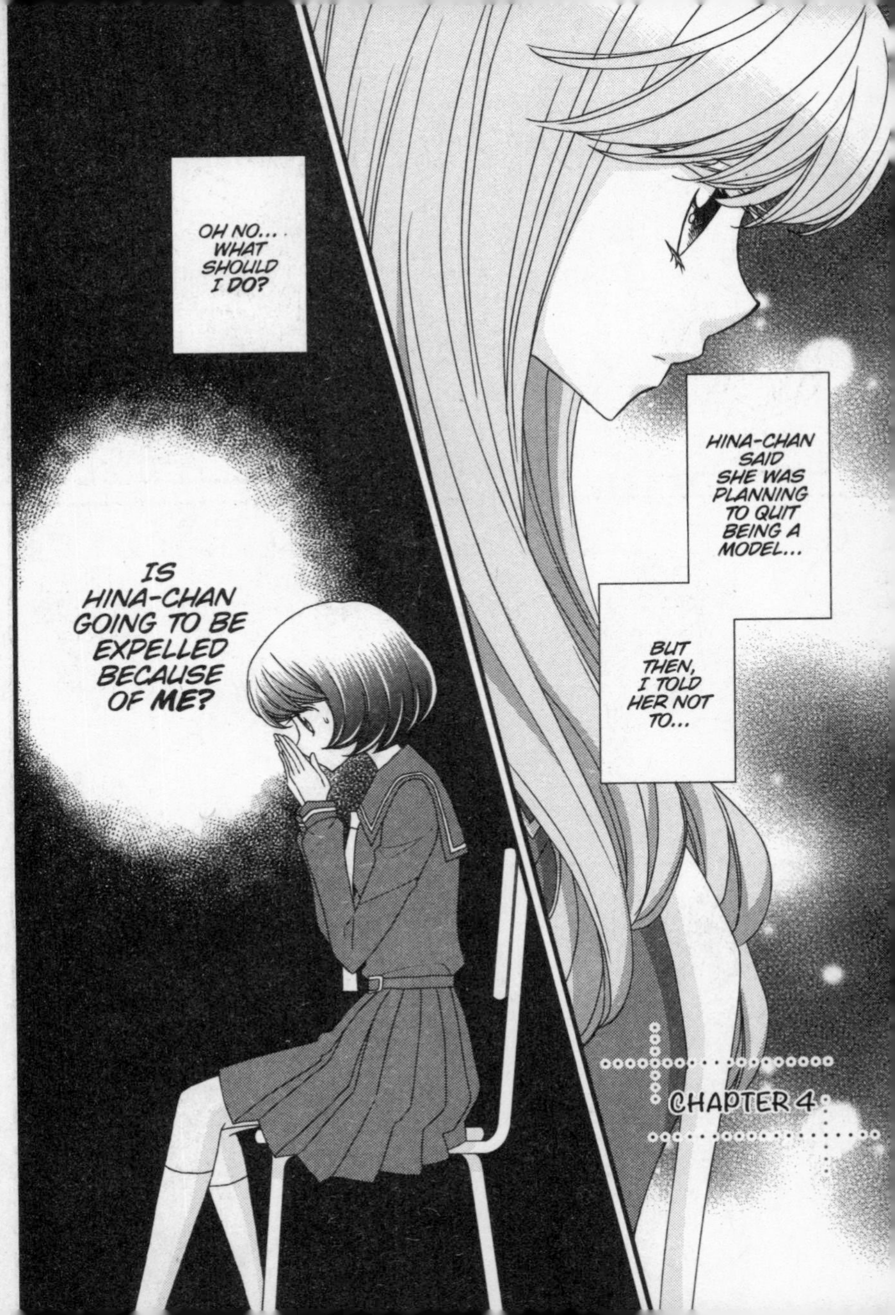
HINA-CHAN SAID SHE WAS PLANNING TO QUIT BEING A MODEL...
BUT THEN, I TOLD HER NOT TO...
OH NO... WHAT SHOULD I DO?
IS HINA-CHAN GOING TO BE EXPELLED BECAUSE OF ME?

CHAPTER 4

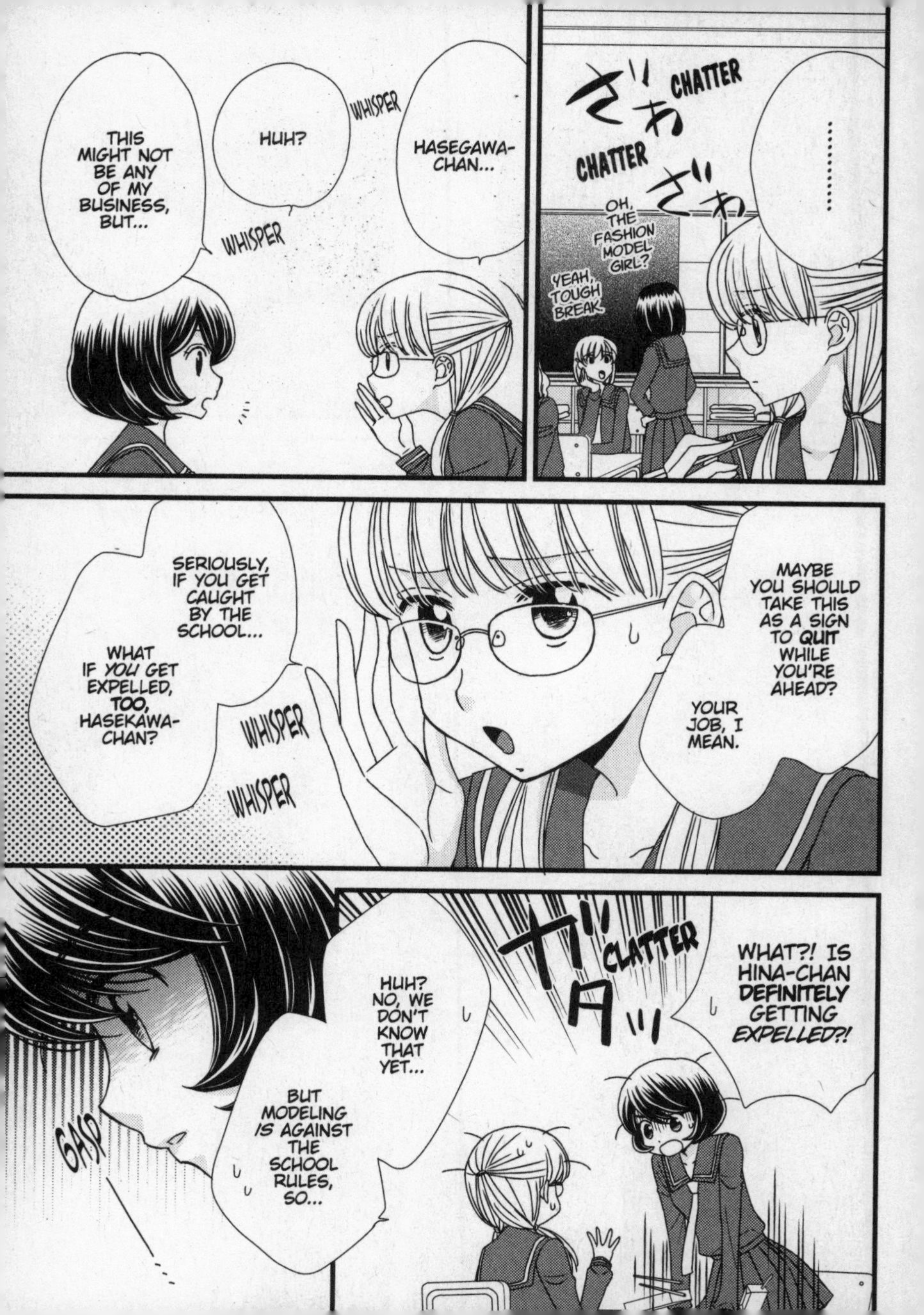
ざわ
CHATTER
ざわ
CHATTER
OH, THE FASHION MODEL GIRL?
YEAH, TOUGH BREAK.
......
HASEGAWA-CHAN...
WHISPER
HUH?
THIS MIGHT NOT BE ANY OF MY BUSINESS, BUT...
WHISPER
MAYBE YOU SHOULD TAKE THIS AS A SIGN TO QUIT WHILE YOU'RE AHEAD?
YOUR JOB, I MEAN.
SERIOUSLY, IF YOU GET CAUGHT BY THE SCHOOL...
WHAT IF YOU GET EXPELLED, TOO, HASEKAWA-CHAN?
WHISPER
WHISPER
WHAT?! IS HINA-CHAN DEFINITELY GETTING EXPELLED?!
ガタッ
CLATTER
HUH? NO, WE DON'T KNOW THAT YET...
BUT MODELING IS AGAINST THE SCHOOL RULES, SO...
GASP

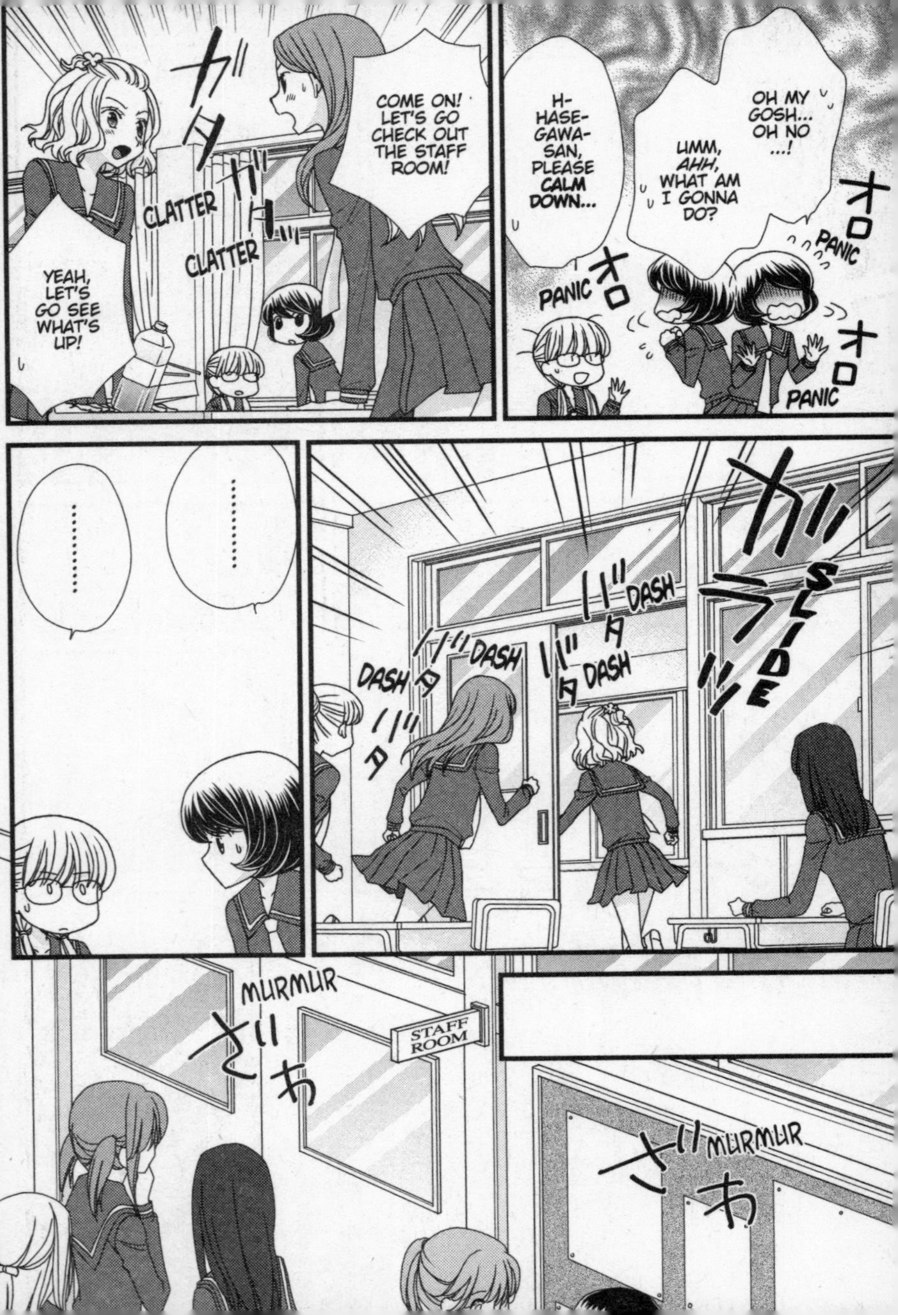
OH MY GOSH... OH NO ...!
UMM, AHH, WHAT AM I GONNA DO?
PANIC
H-HASE-GAWA-SAN, PLEASE CALM DOWN...
PANIC
PANIC
COME ON! LET'S GO CHECK OUT THE STAFF ROOM!
CLATTER
CLATTER
YEAH, LET'S GO SEE WHAT'S UP!
SLIDE
DASH
DASH
DASH
DASH
......
......
MURMUR
STAFF ROOM
MURMUR

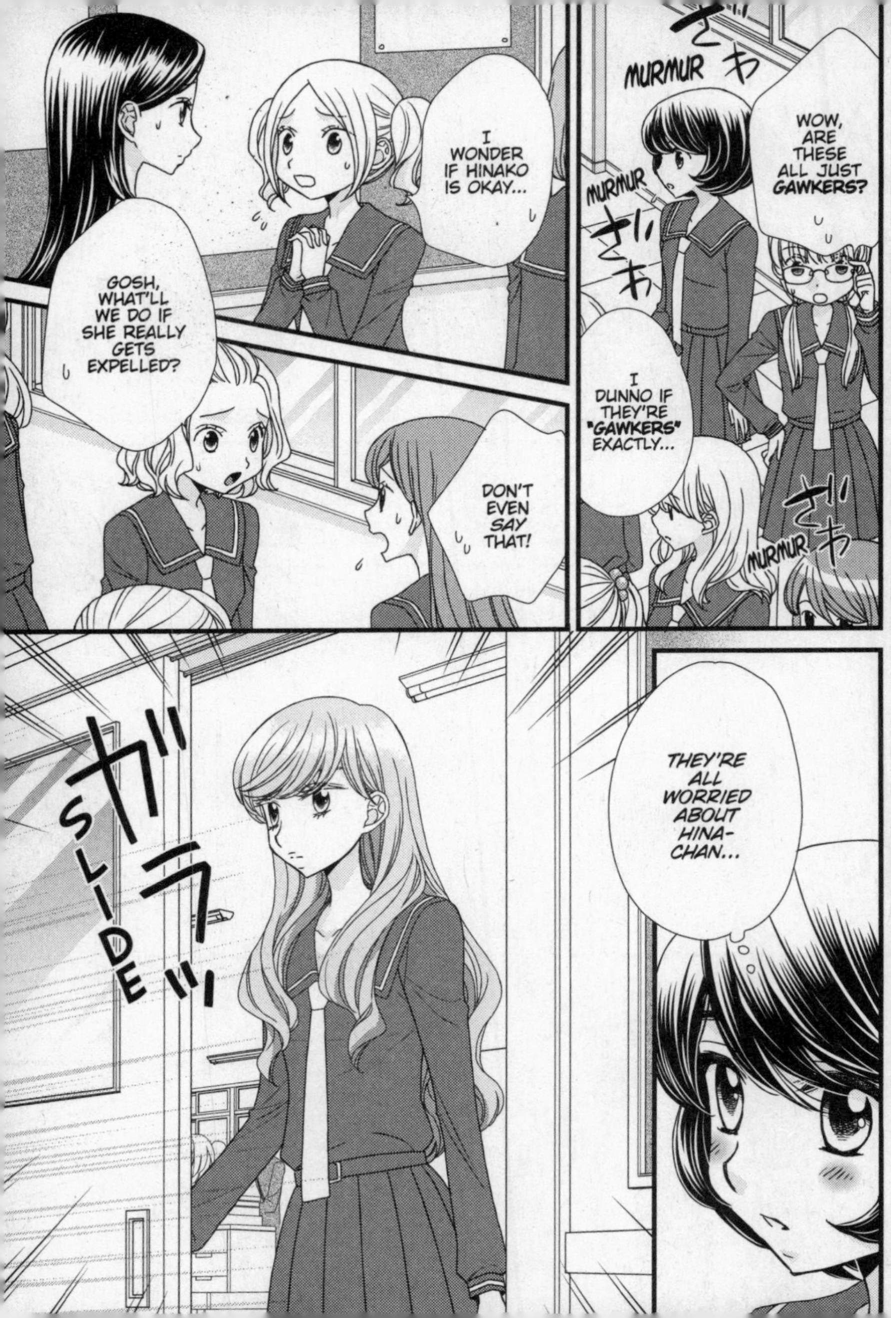

ざわ
MURMUR
WOW, ARE THESE ALL JUST GAWKERS?
MURMUR
ざわ
I DUNNO IF THEY'RE "GAWKERS" EXACTLY...
ざわ
MURMUR
I WONDER IF HINAKO IS OKAY...
GOSH, WHAT'LL WE DO IF SHE REALLY GETS EXPELLED?
DON'T EVEN SAY THAT!
THEY'RE ALL WORRIED ABOUT HINA-CHAN...
SLIDE

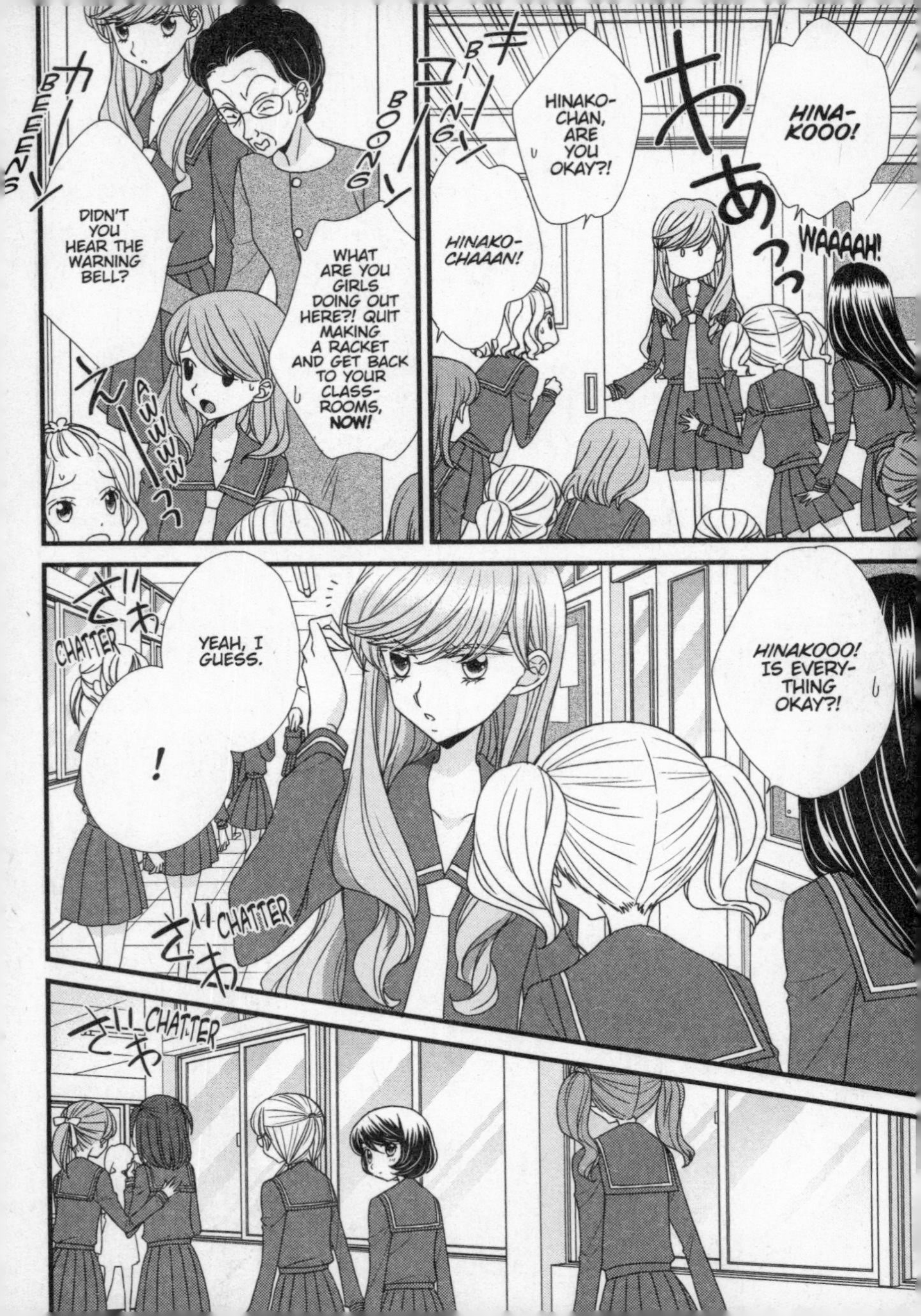
HINA-KOOO!
WAAAAH!
HINAKO-CHAN, ARE YOU OKAY?!
HINAKO-CHAAAN!
BIIING
BOOONG
WHAT ARE YOU GIRLS DOING OUT HERE?! QUIT MAKING A RACKET AND GET BACK TO YOUR CLASSROOMS, NOW!
DIDN'T YOU HEAR THE WARNING BELL?
AWWWW
HINAKOOO! IS EVERY-THING OKAY?!
YEAH, I GUESS.
!
CHATTER
CHATTER
CHATTER

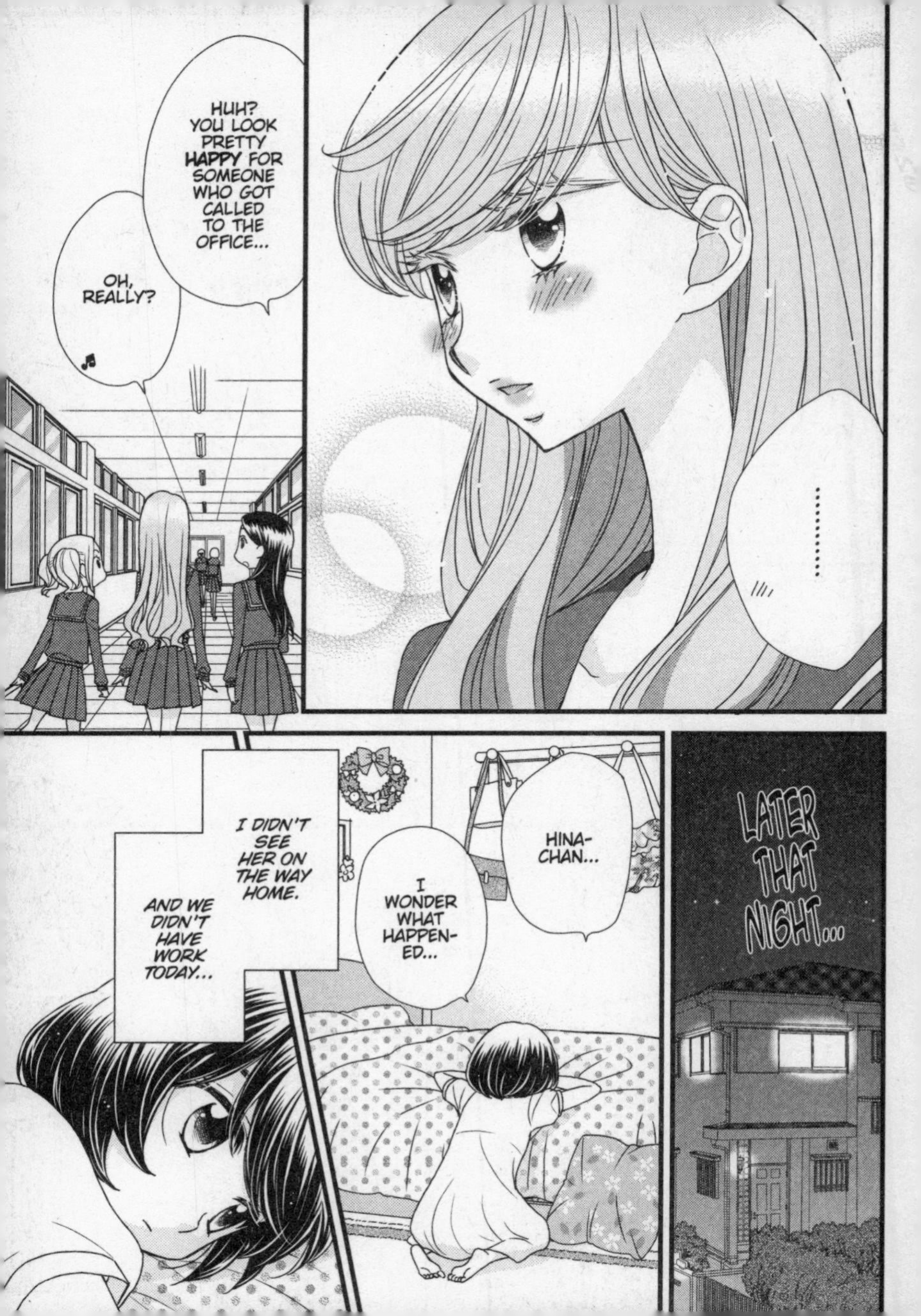
......
HUH? YOU LOOK PRETTY **HAPPY** FOR SOMEONE WHO GOT CALLED TO THE OFFICE...
OH, REALLY? ♪
LATER THAT NIGHT...
HINA-CHAN...
I WONDER WHAT HAPPEN-ED...
I DIDN'T SEE HER ON THE WAY HOME.
AND WE DIDN'T HAVE WORK TODAY...

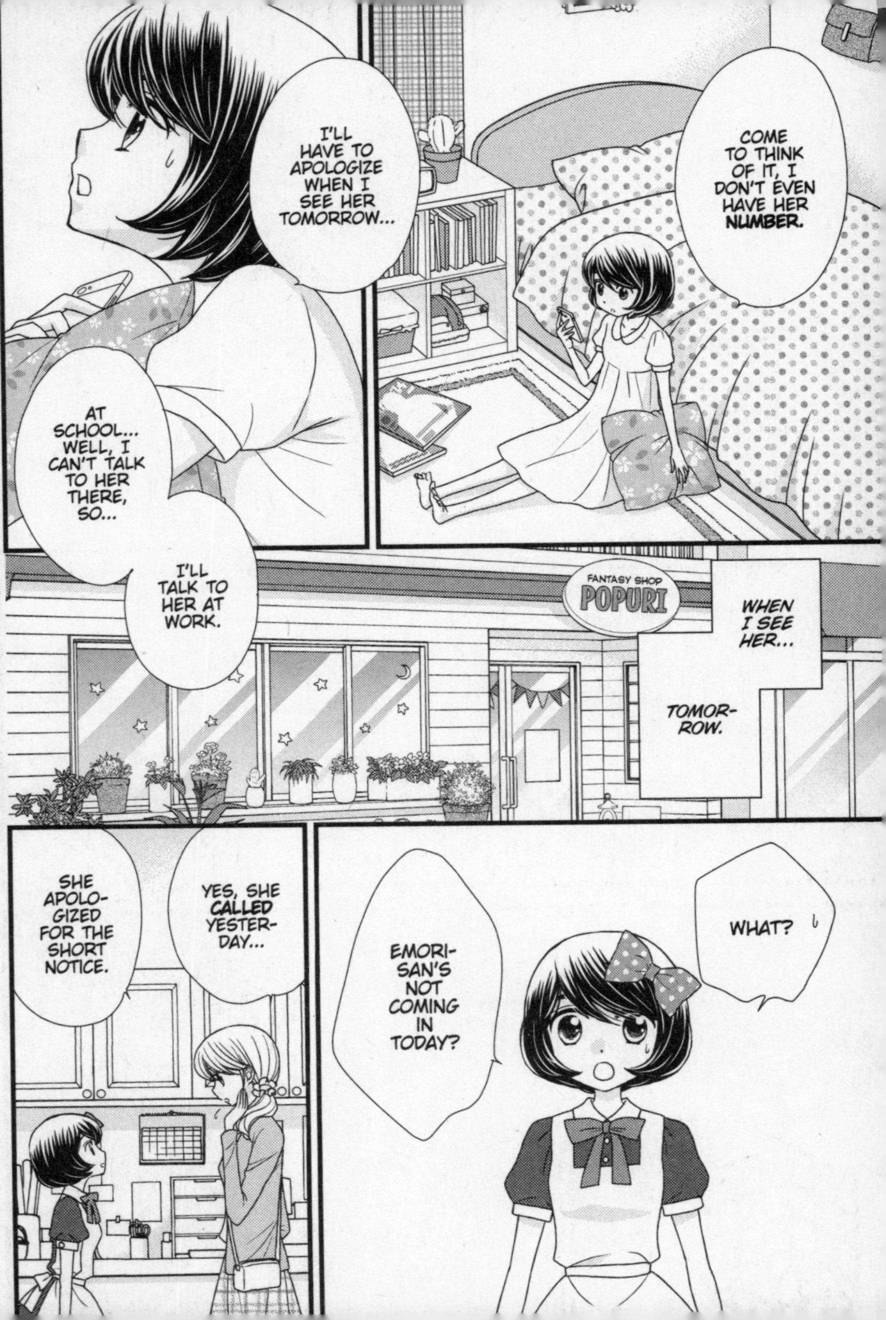
COME TO THINK OF IT, I DON'T EVEN HAVE HER NUMBER.
I'LL HAVE TO APOLOGIZE WHEN I SEE HER TOMORROW...
AT SCHOOL... WELL, I CAN'T TALK TO HER THERE, SO...
I'LL TALK TO HER AT WORK.
FANTASY SHOP POPURI
WHEN I SEE HER...
TOMOR-ROW.
WHAT?
EMORI-SAN'S NOT COMING IN TODAY?
YES, SHE CALLED YESTER-DAY...
SHE APOLO-GIZED FOR THE SHORT NOTICE.

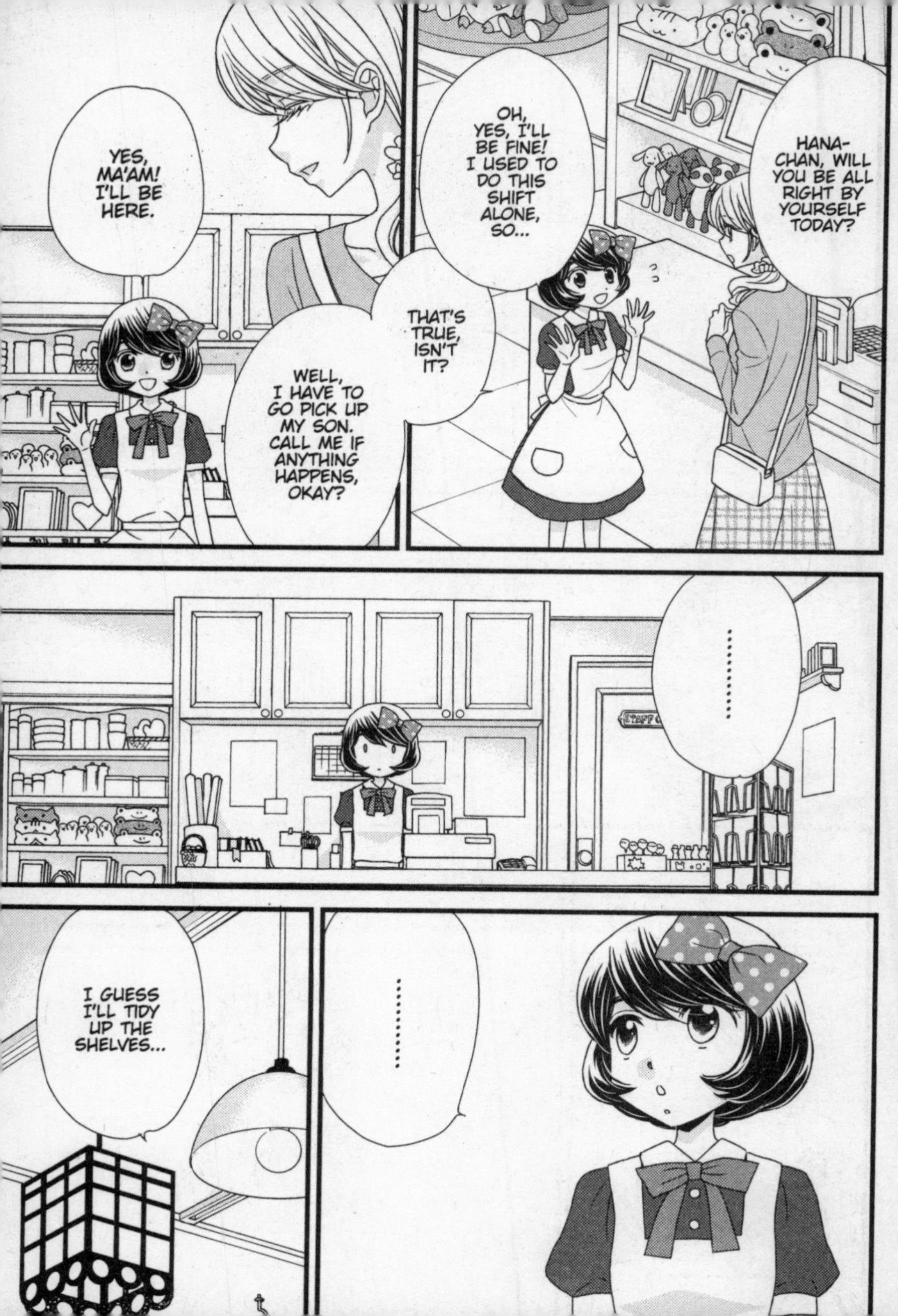
HANA-CHAN, WILL YOU BE ALL RIGHT BY YOURSELF TODAY?
OH, YES, I'LL BE FINE! I USED TO DO THIS SHIFT ALONE, SO...
THAT'S TRUE, ISN'T IT?
WELL, I HAVE TO GO PICK UP MY SON. CALL ME IF ANYTHING HAPPENS, OKAY?
YES, MA'AM! I'LL BE HERE.
......
STAFF
......
I GUESS I'LL TIDY UP THE SHELVES...

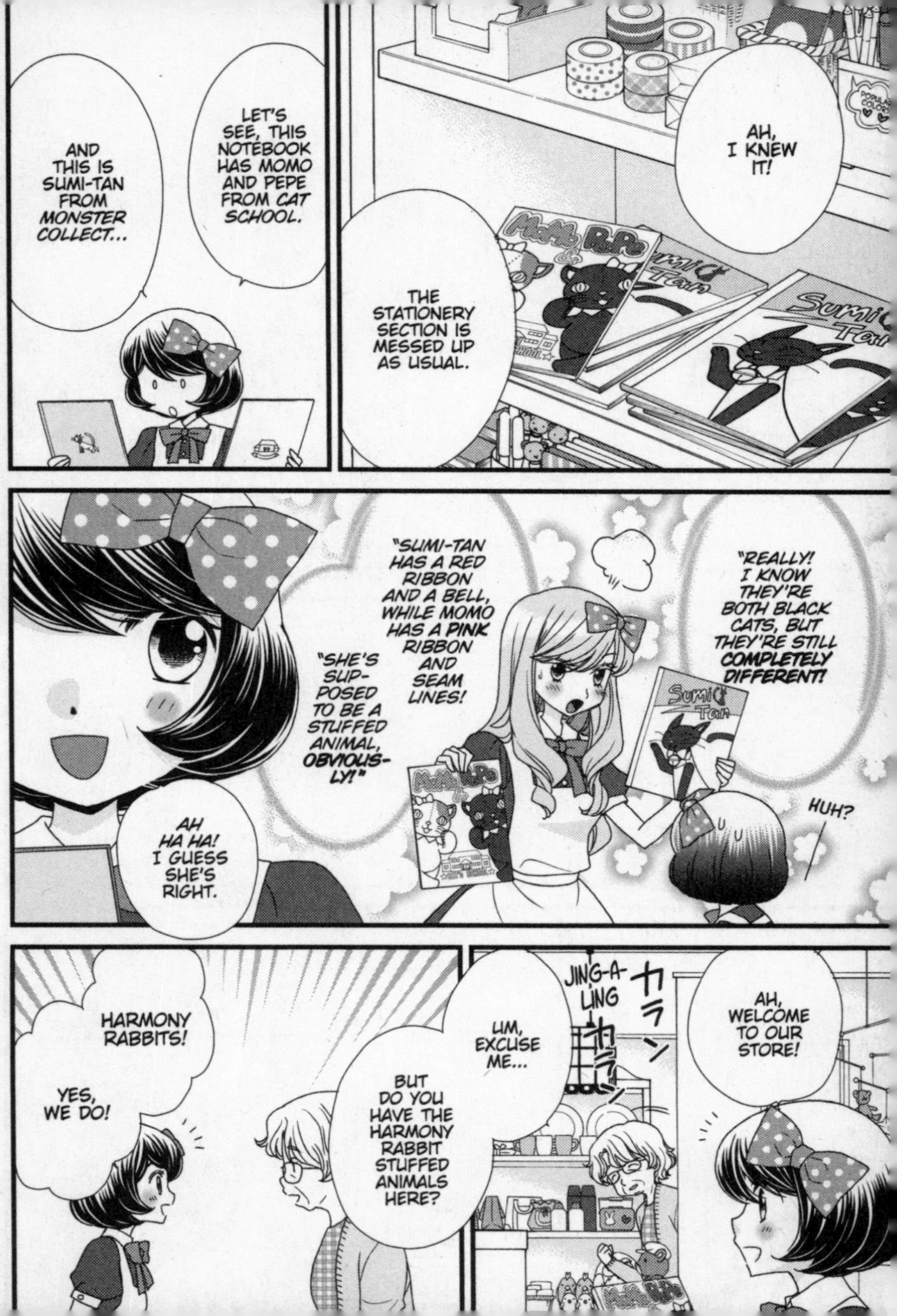
AH, I KNEW IT!
THE STATIONERY SECTION IS MESSED UP AS USUAL.
LET'S SEE, THIS NOTEBOOK HAS MOMO AND PEPE FROM CAT SCHOOL.
AND THIS IS SUMI-TAN FROM MONSTER COLLECT...
"REALLY! I KNOW THEY'RE BOTH BLACK CATS, BUT THEY'RE STILL COMPLETELY DIFFERENT!
HUH?
"SUMI-TAN HAS A RED RIBBON AND A BELL, WHILE MOMO HAS A PINK RIBBON AND SEAM LINES!
"SHE'S SUP-POSED TO BE A STUFFED ANIMAL, OBVIOUS-LY!"
AH HA HA! I GUESS SHE'S RIGHT.
AH, WELCOME TO OUR STORE!
JING-A-LING
カラン カラン
UM, EXCUSE ME...
BUT DO YOU HAVE THE HARMONY RABBIT STUFFED ANIMALS HERE?
HARMONY RABBITS!
YES, WE DO!

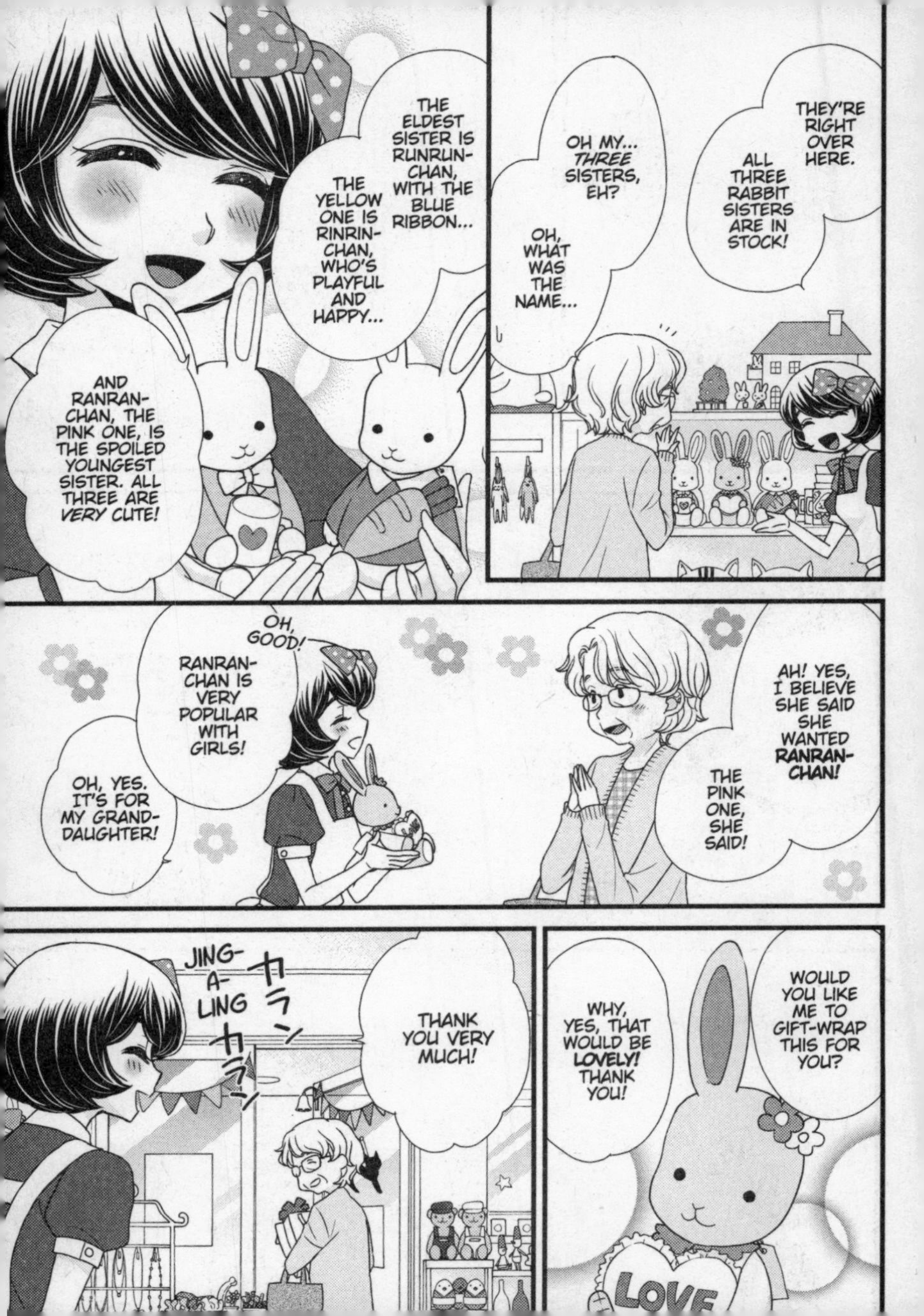
THEY'RE RIGHT OVER HERE.
ALL THREE RABBIT SISTERS ARE IN STOCK!
OH MY... *THREE* SISTERS, EH?
OH, WHAT WAS THE NAME...
THE ELDEST SISTER IS RUNRUN-CHAN, WITH THE BLUE RIBBON...
THE YELLOW ONE IS RINRIN-CHAN, WHO'S PLAYFUL AND HAPPY...
AND RANRAN-CHAN, THE PINK ONE, IS THE SPOILED YOUNGEST SISTER. ALL THREE ARE *VERY CUTE!*
AH! YES, I BELIEVE SHE SAID SHE WANTED **RANRAN-CHAN!**
THE PINK ONE, SHE SAID!
OH, GOOD!
RANRAN-CHAN IS VERY POPULAR WITH GIRLS!
OH, YES. IT'S FOR MY GRAND-DAUGHTER!
WOULD YOU LIKE ME TO GIFT-WRAP THIS FOR YOU?
WHY, YES, THAT WOULD BE **LOVELY!** THANK YOU!
LOVE
THANK YOU VERY MUCH!
JING-A-LING
カラン
カラン

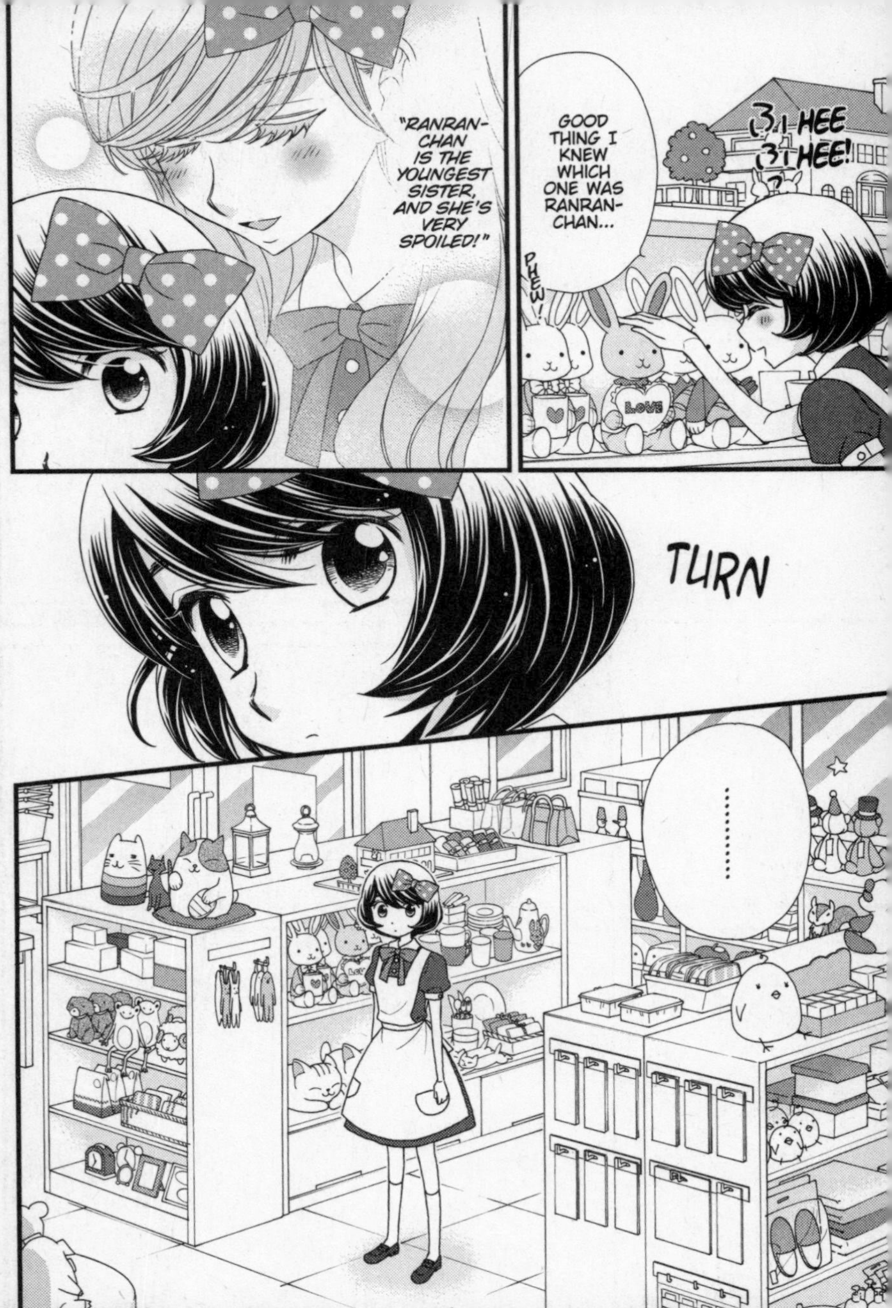
HEE HEE!
HEE HEE!
GOOD THING I KNEW WHICH ONE WAS RANRAN-CHAN...
PHEW!
"RANRAN-CHAN IS THE YOUNGEST SISTER, AND SHE'S VERY SPOILED!"
TURN
......

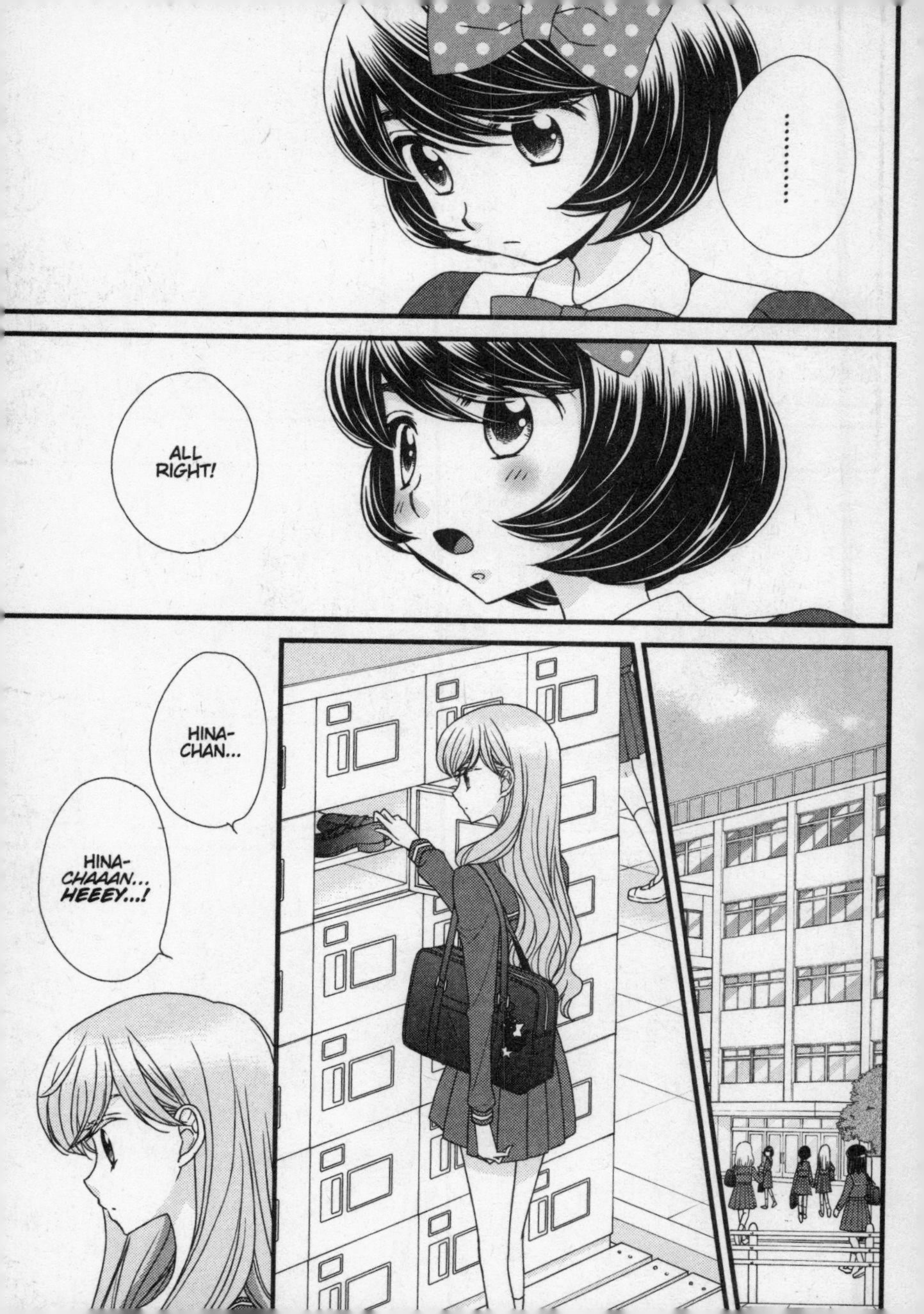

....
ALL RIGHT!
HINA-CHAN...
HINA-CHAAAN... HEEEY...!

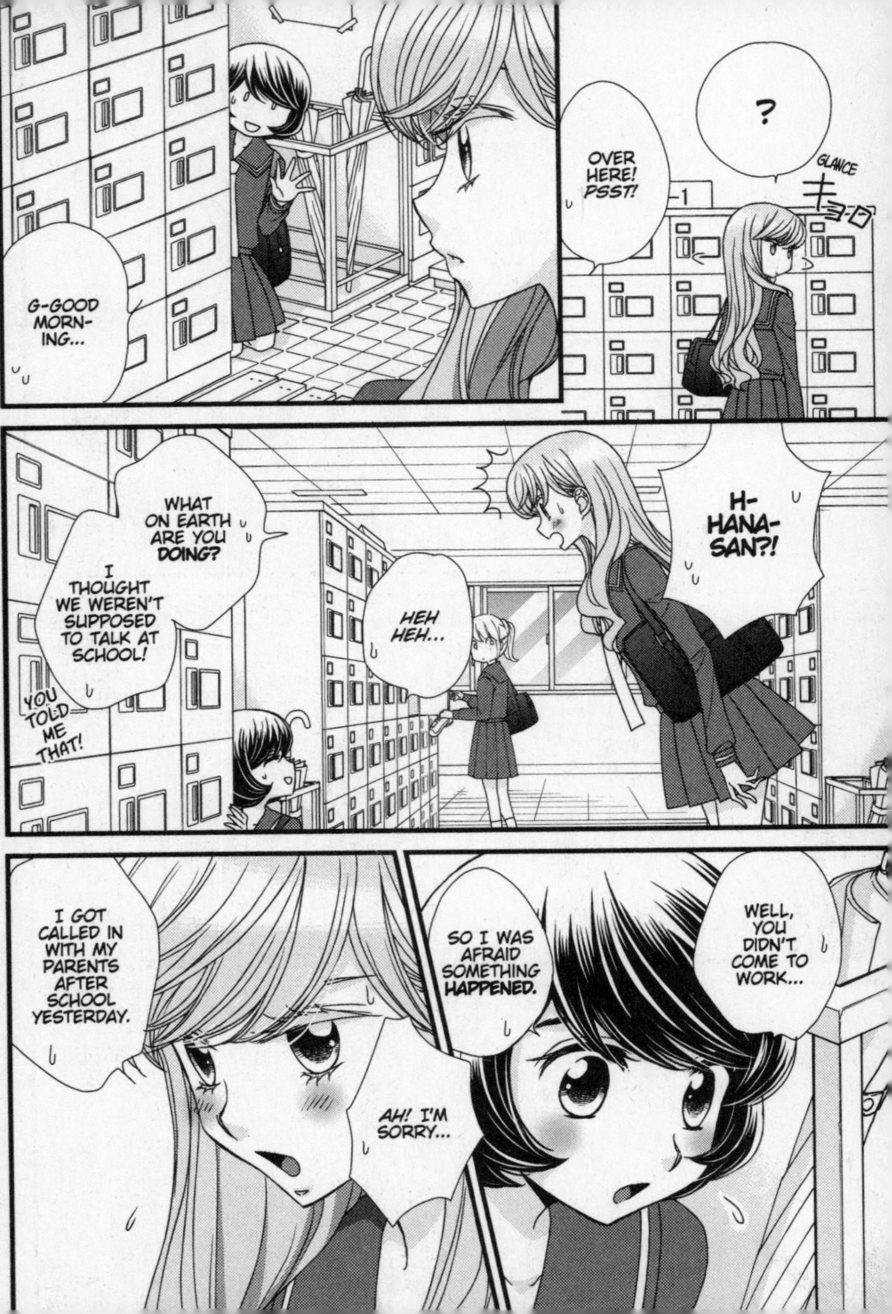
?
GLANCE
OVER HERE! PSST!
G-GOOD MORNING...
H-HANA-SAN?!
HEH HEH...
WHAT ON EARTH ARE YOU DOING?
I THOUGHT WE WEREN'T SUPPOSED TO TALK AT SCHOOL!
YOU TOLD ME THAT!
WELL, YOU DIDN'T COME TO WORK...
SO I WAS AFRAID SOMETHING HAPPENED.
AH! I'M SORRY...
I GOT CALLED IN WITH MY PARENTS AFTER SCHOOL YESTERDAY.

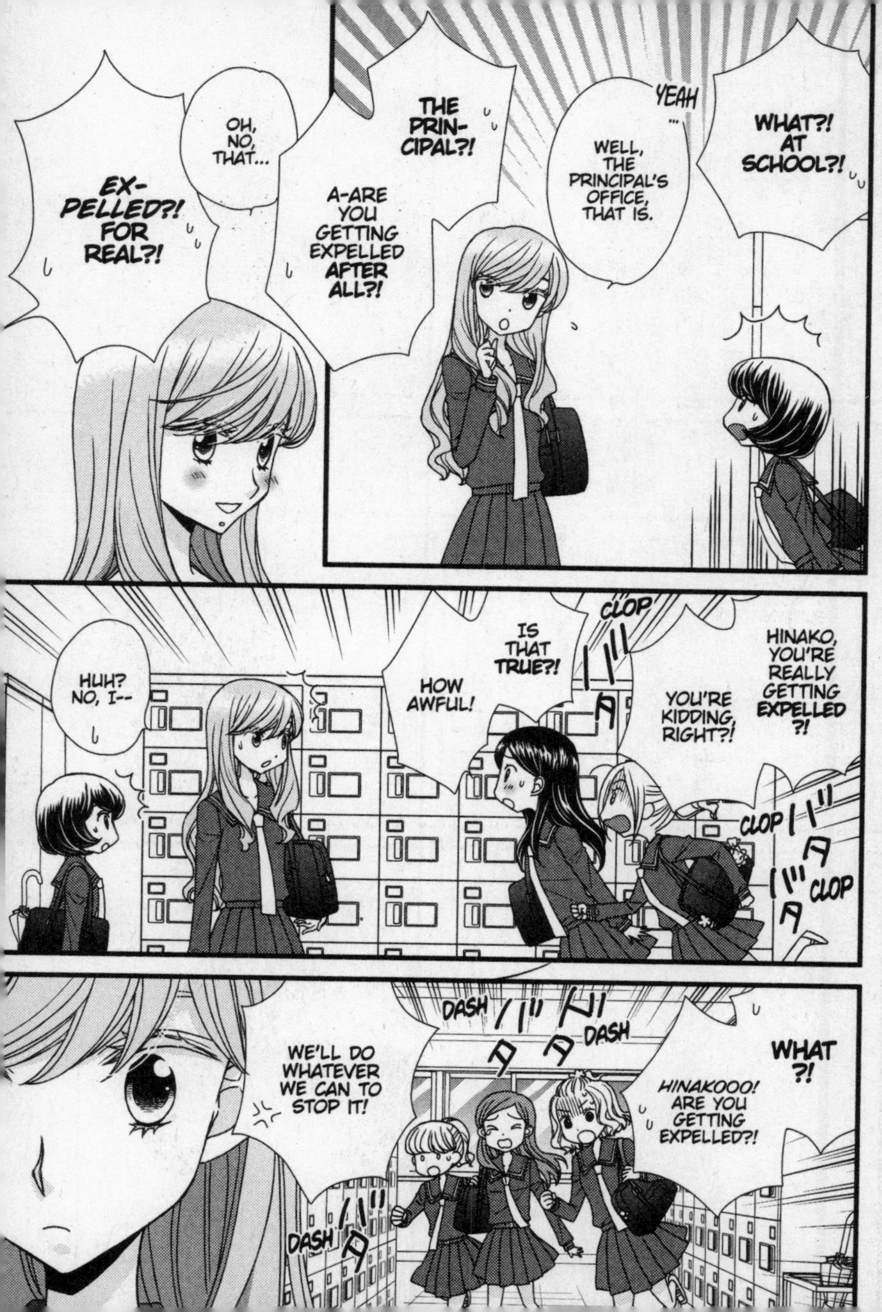
WHAT?! AT SCHOOL?!
YEAH...
WELL, THE PRINCIPAL'S OFFICE, THAT IS.
THE PRIN-CIPAL?!
A-ARE YOU GETTING EXPELLED AFTER ALL?!
OH, NO, THAT...
EX-PELLED?! FOR REAL?!
HINAKO, YOU'RE REALLY GETTING EXPELLED?!
CLOP
YOU'RE KIDDING, RIGHT?!
IS THAT TRUE?!
HOW AWFUL!
CLOP
CLOP
HUH? NO, I--
WHAT?!
HINAKOOO! ARE YOU GETTING EXPELLED?!
DASH
DASH
WE'LL DO WHATEVER WE CAN TO STOP IT!
DASH

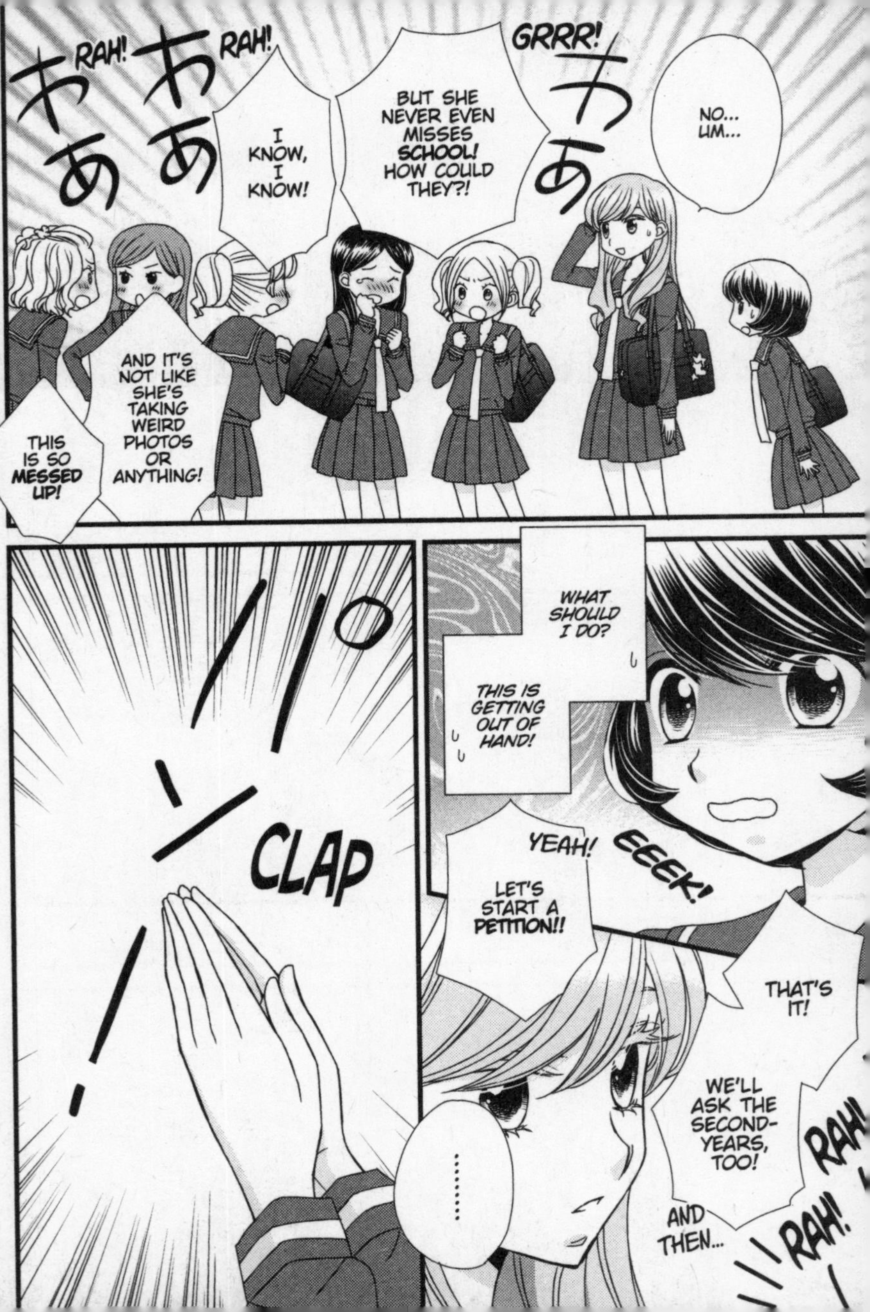
GRRR!
わあ
NO... UM...
BUT SHE NEVER EVEN MISSES SCHOOL! HOW COULD THEY?!
I KNOW, I KNOW!
RAH!
わあ
RAH!
わあ
AND IT'S NOT LIKE SHE'S TAKING WEIRD PHOTOS OR ANYTHING!
THIS IS SO MESSED UP!
WHAT SHOULD I DO?
THIS IS GETTING OUT OF HAND!
EEEK!
YEAH!
LET'S START A PETITION!!
THAT'S IT!
WE'LL ASK THE SECOND-YEARS, TOO!
AND THEN...
RAH!
RAH!
......
CLAP

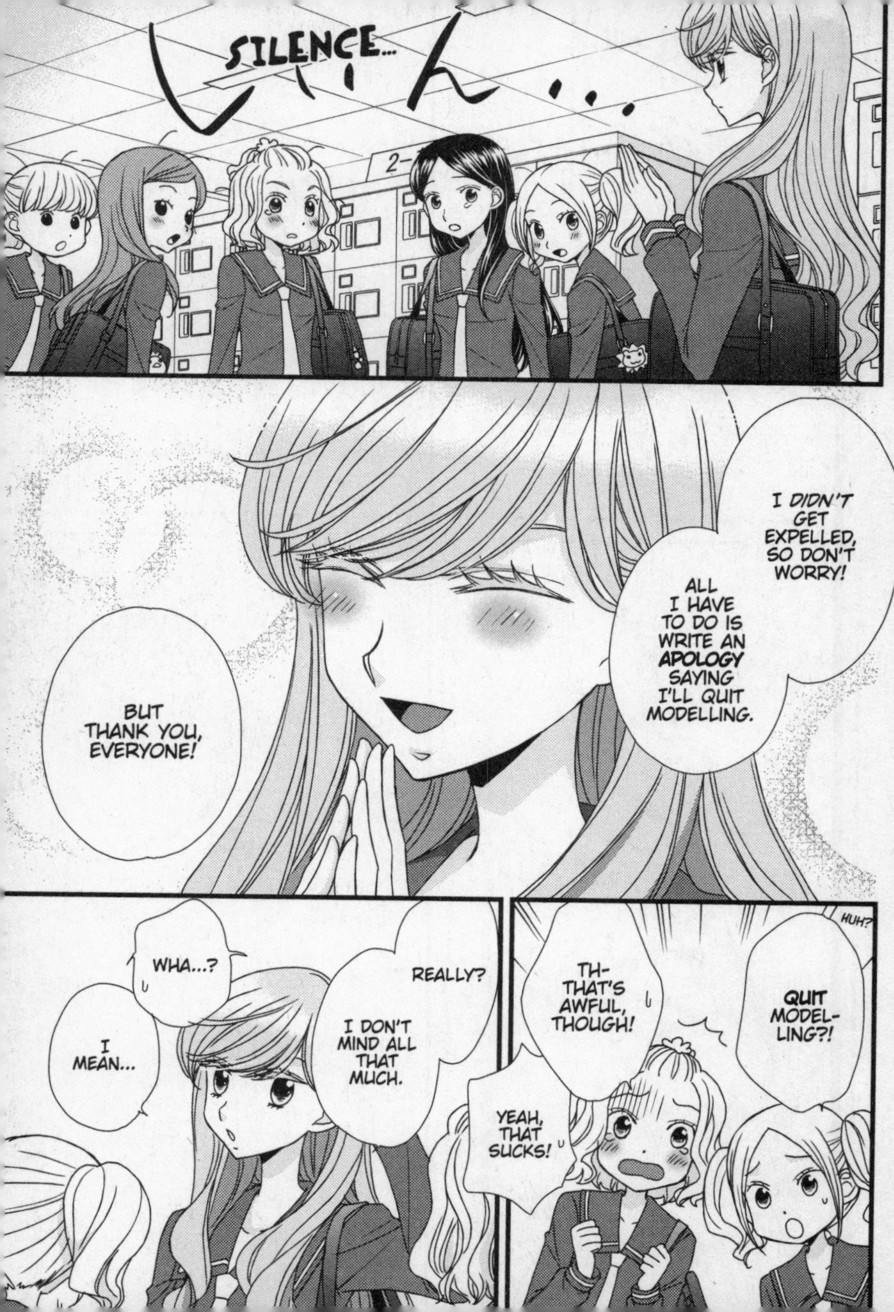
SILENCE...
I DIDN'T GET EXPELLED, SO DON'T WORRY!
ALL I HAVE TO DO IS WRITE AN APOLOGY SAYING I'LL QUIT MODELLING.
BUT THANK YOU, EVERYONE!
HUH?
QUIT MODEL-LING?!
TH-THAT'S AWFUL, THOUGH!
YEAH, THAT SUCKS!
REALLY?
I DON'T MIND ALL THAT MUCH.
WHA...?
I MEAN...

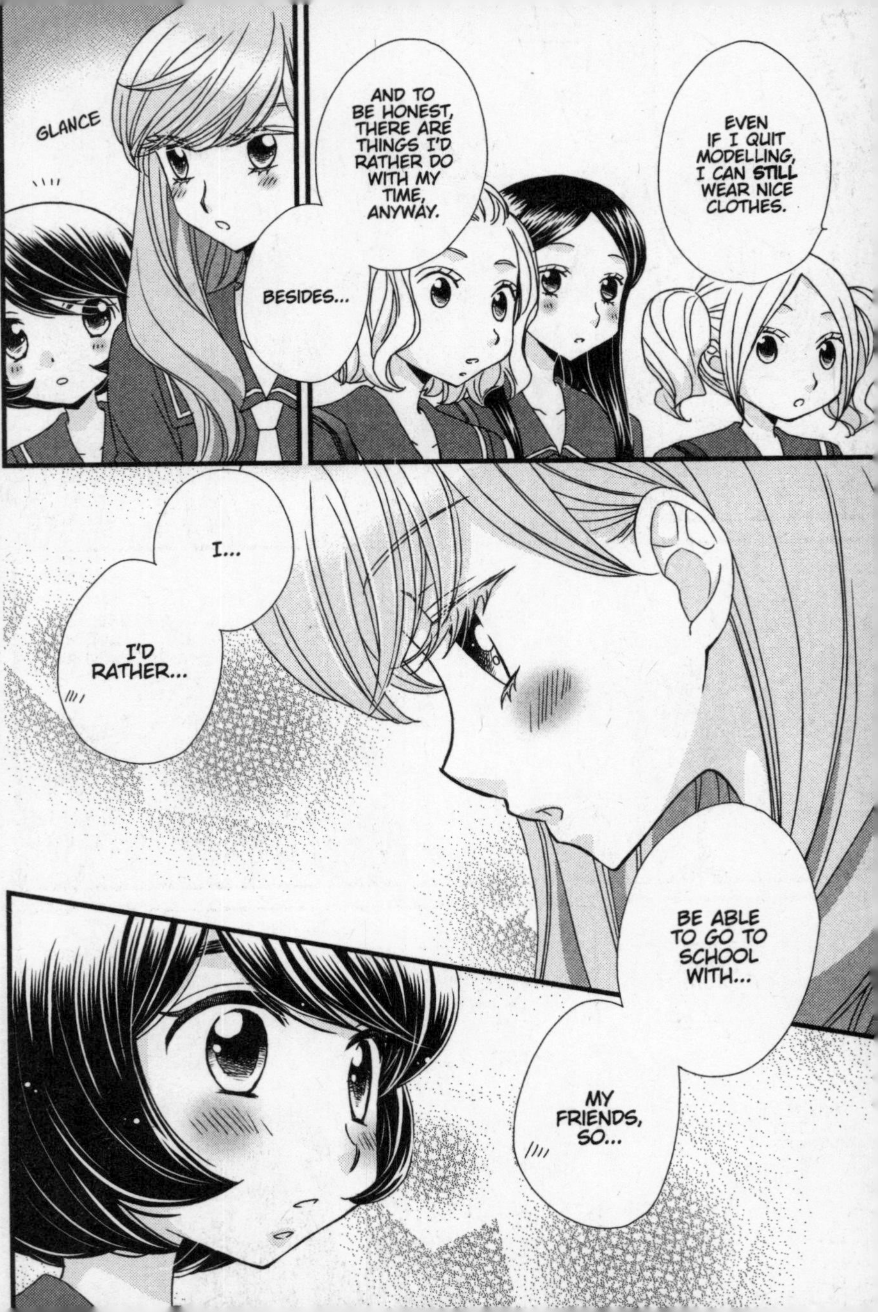
EVEN IF I QUIT MODELLING, I CAN STILL WEAR NICE CLOTHES.
AND TO BE HONEST, THERE ARE THINGS I'D RATHER DO WITH MY TIME, ANYWAY.
BESIDES...
GLANCE
I...
I'D RATHER...
BE ABLE TO GO TO SCHOOL WITH...
MY FRIENDS, SO...

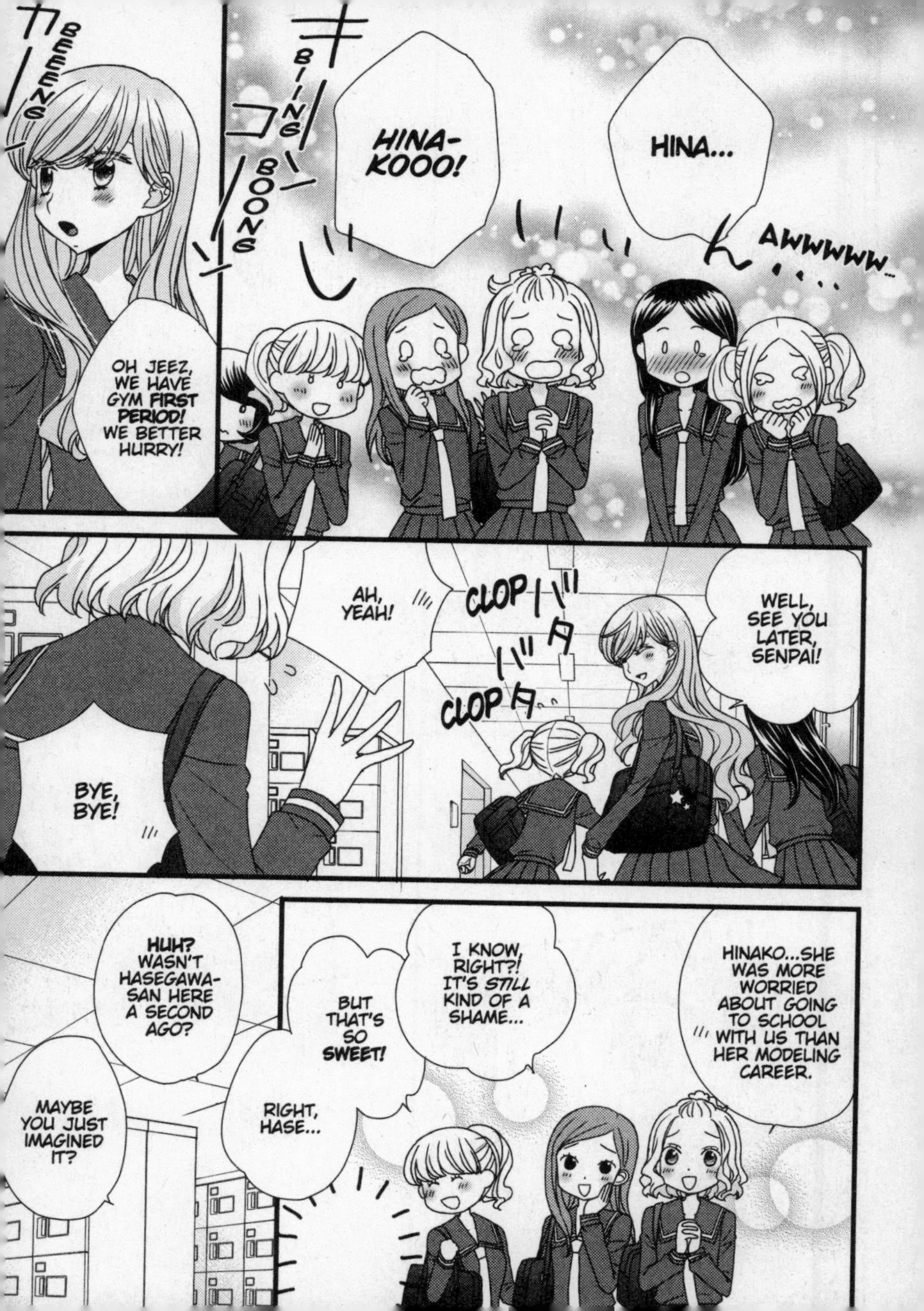
AWWWWW...
HINA...
HINA-KOOO!
BIING
BOOONG
BEEEENG
OH JEEZ, WE HAVE GYM FIRST PERIOD! WE BETTER HURRY!
WELL, SEE YOU LATER, SENPAI!
CLOP
CLOP
AH, YEAH!
BYE, BYE!
HINAKO...SHE WAS MORE WORRIED ABOUT GOING TO SCHOOL WITH US THAN HER MODELING CAREER.
I KNOW, RIGHT?! IT'S STILL KIND OF A SHAME...
BUT THAT'S SO SWEET!
RIGHT, HASE...
HUH? WASN'T HASEGAWA-SAN HERE A SECOND AGO?
MAYBE YOU JUST IMAGINED IT?

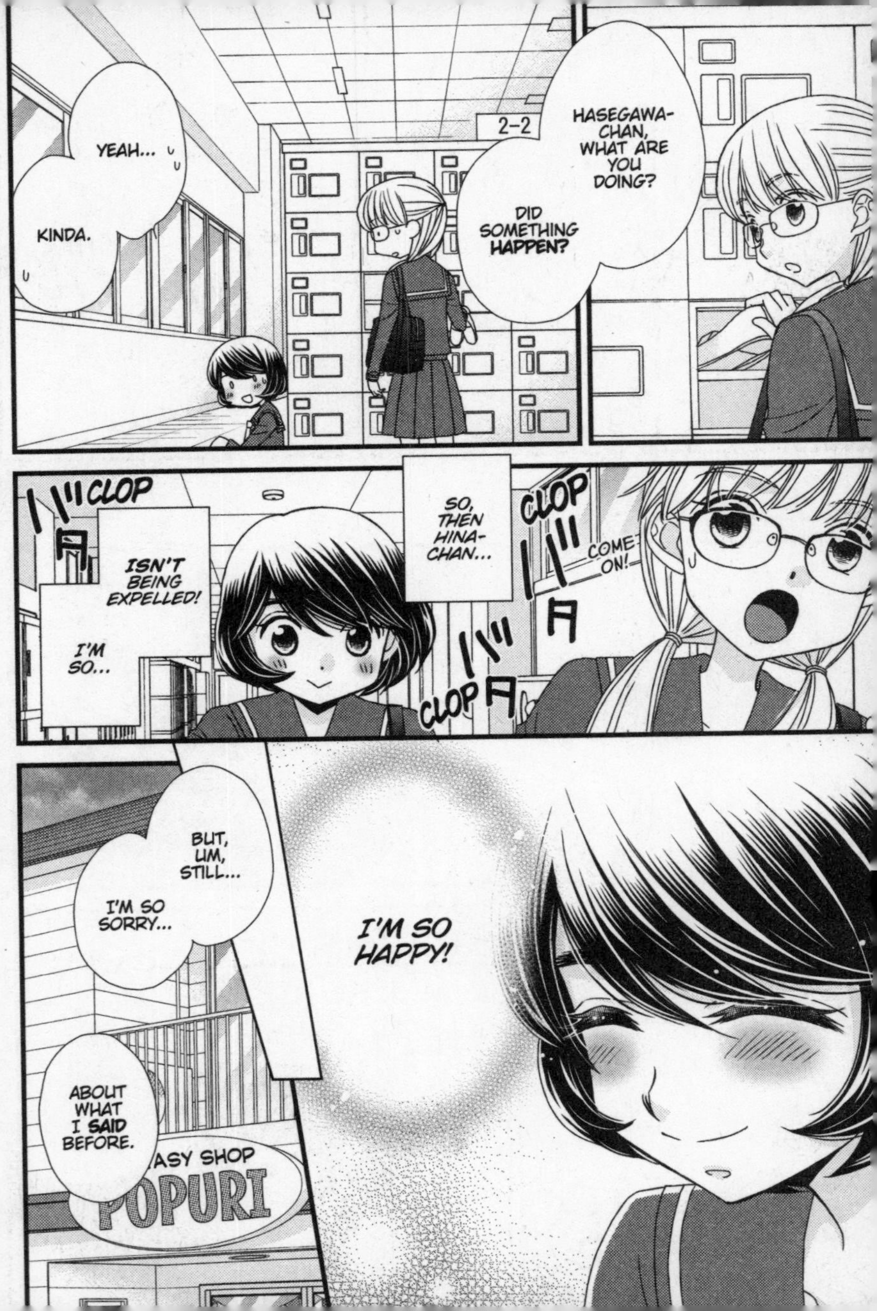
HASEGAWA-CHAN, WHAT ARE YOU DOING?
DID SOMETHING HAPPEN?
YEAH...
KINDA.
CLOP
COME ON!
CLOP
SO, THEN HINA-CHAN...
CLOP
ISN'T BEING EXPELLED!
I'M SO...
I'M SO HAPPY!
BUT, UM, STILL...
I'M SO SORRY...
ABOUT WHAT I SAID BEFORE.
ASY SHOP
POPURI

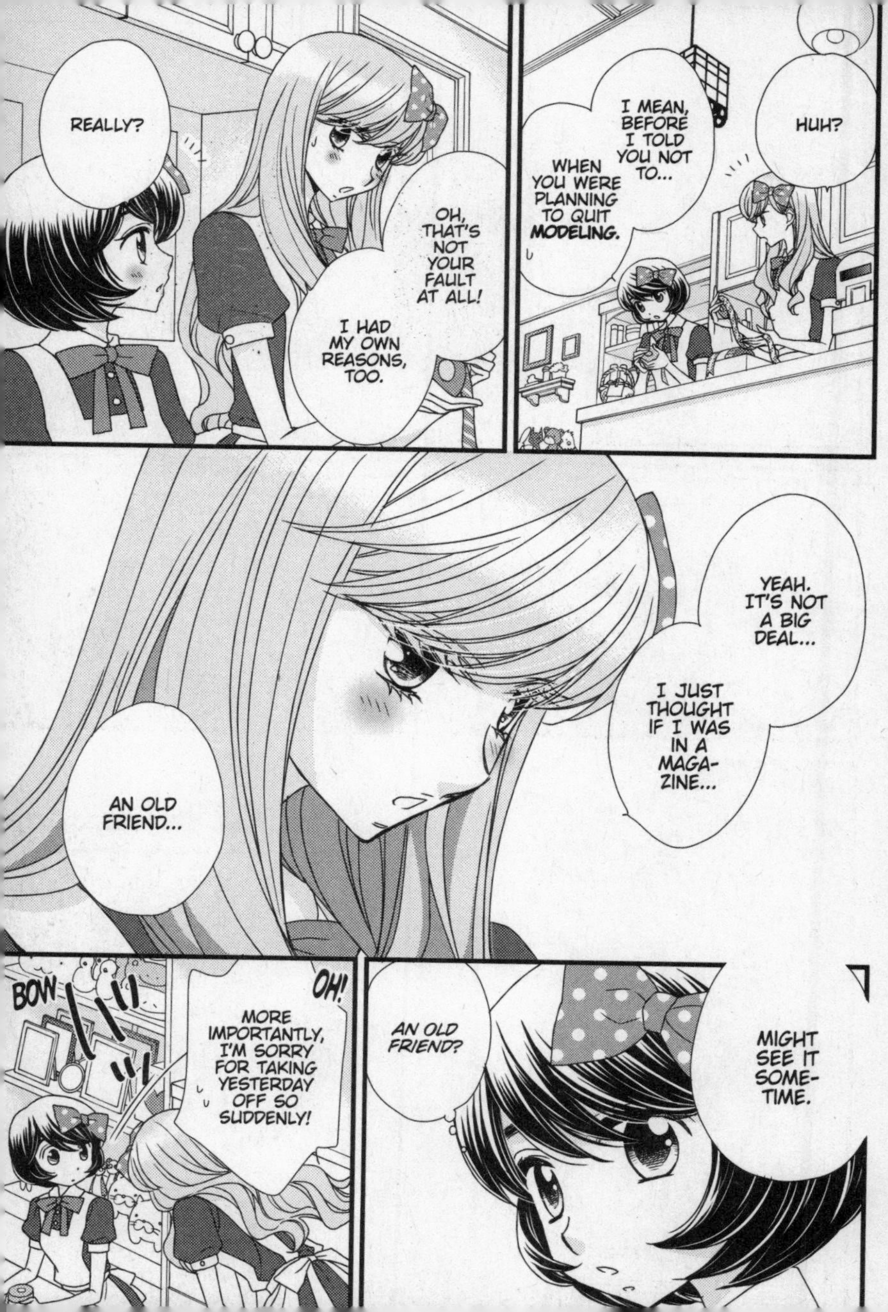
HUH?
I MEAN, BEFORE I TOLD YOU NOT TO...
WHEN YOU WERE PLANNING TO QUIT **MODELING**.
OH, THAT'S NOT YOUR FAULT AT ALL!
I HAD MY OWN REASONS, TOO.
REALLY?
YEAH. IT'S NOT A BIG DEAL...
I JUST THOUGHT IF I WAS IN A MAGAZINE...
AN OLD FRIEND...
MIGHT SEE IT SOMETIME.
AN OLD FRIEND?
OH!
MORE IMPORTANTLY, I'M SORRY FOR TAKING YESTERDAY OFF SO SUDDENLY!
BOW

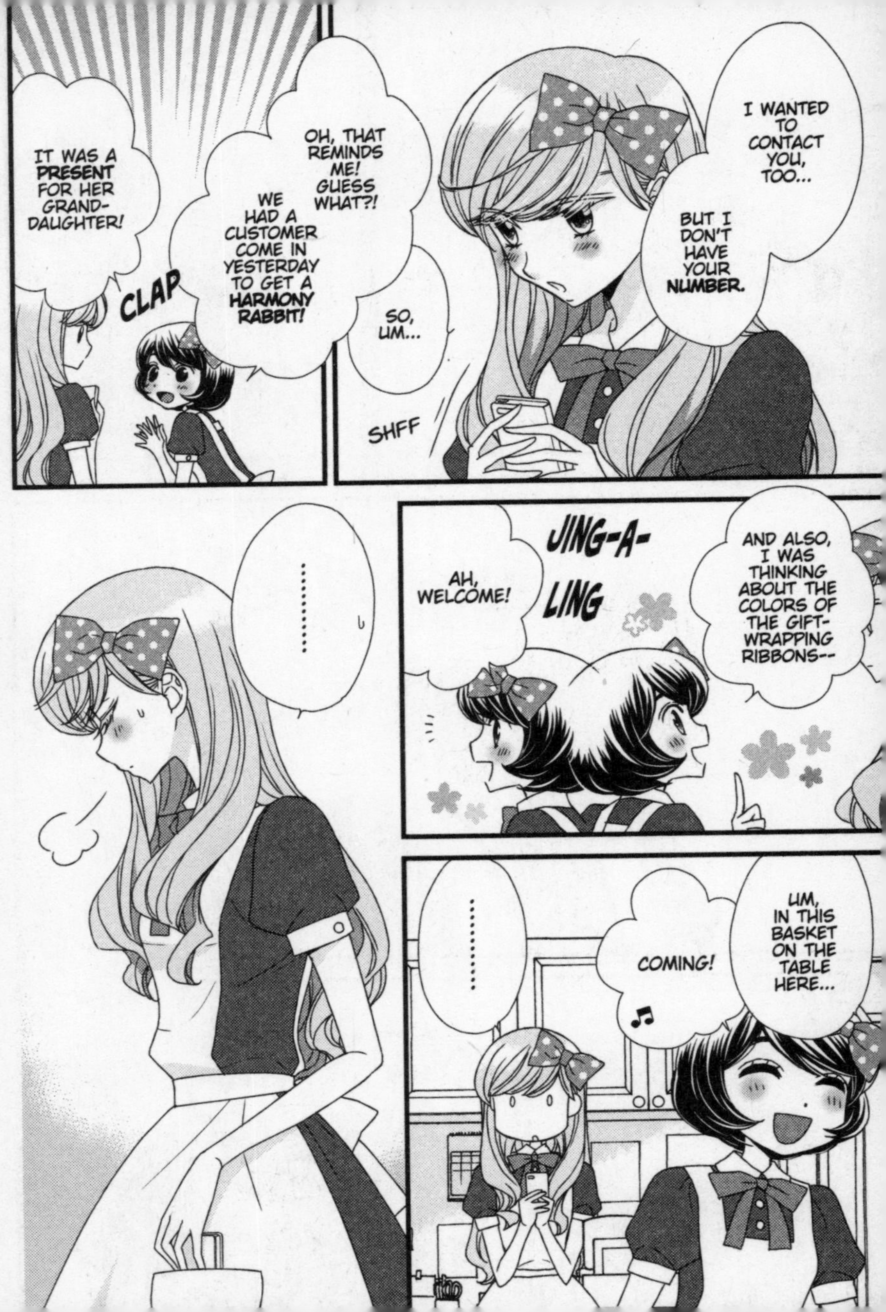
I WANTED TO CONTACT YOU, TOO...
BUT I DON'T HAVE YOUR NUMBER.
SO, UM...
SHFF
OH, THAT REMINDS ME! GUESS WHAT?!
WE HAD A CUSTOMER COME IN YESTERDAY TO GET A HARMONY RABBIT!
CLAP
IT WAS A PRESENT FOR HER GRAND-DAUGHTER!
AND ALSO, I WAS THINKING ABOUT THE COLORS OF THE GIFT-WRAPPING RIBBONS--
JING-A-LING
AH, WELCOME!
UM, IN THIS BASKET ON THE TABLE HERE...
COMING!
......
......

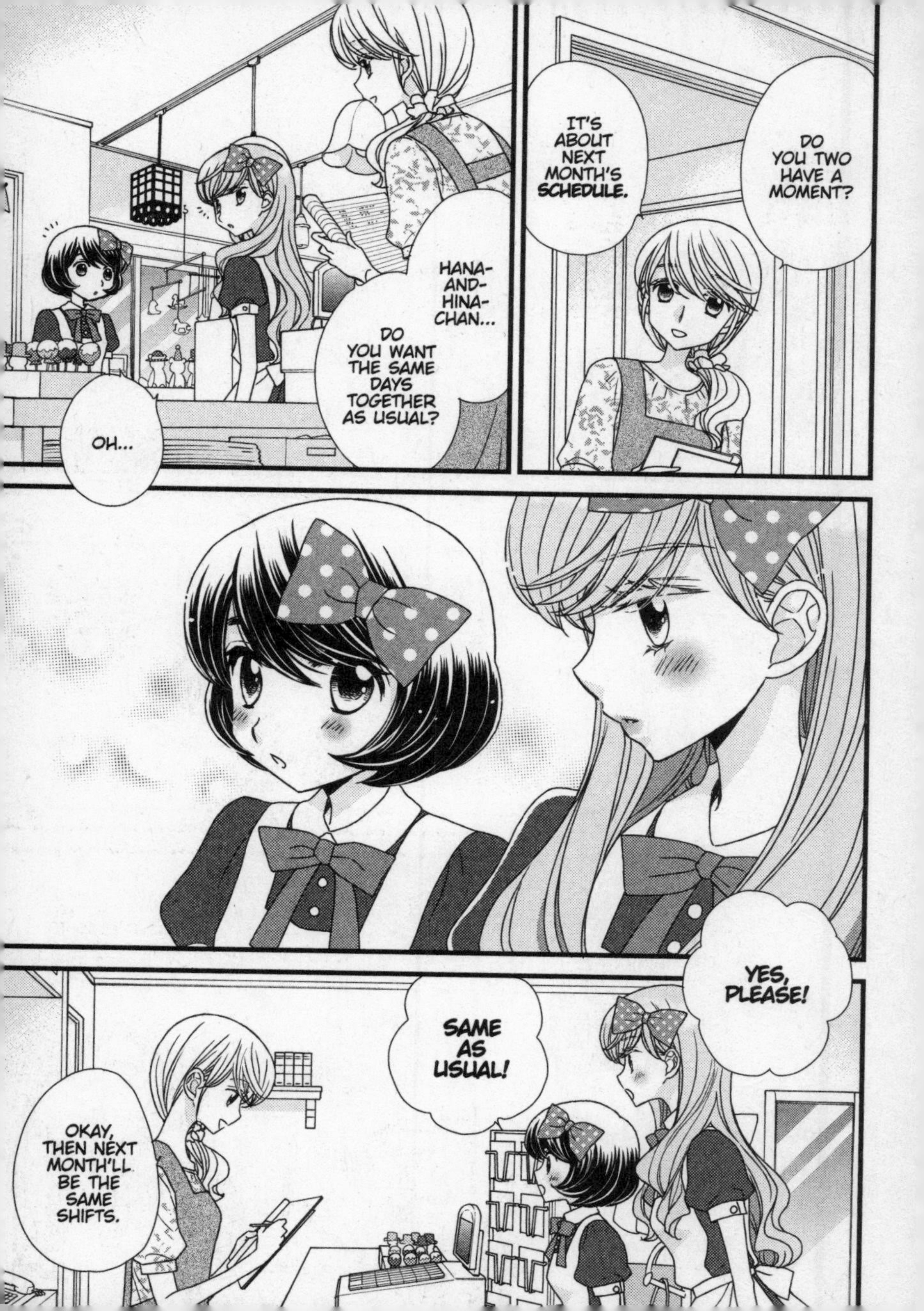
DO YOU TWO HAVE A MOMENT?
IT'S ABOUT NEXT MONTH'S SCHEDULE.
HANA-AND-HINA-CHAN...
DO YOU WANT THE SAME DAYS TOGETHER AS USUAL?
OH...
YES, PLEASE!
SAME AS USUAL!
OKAY, THEN NEXT MONTH'LL BE THE SAME SHIFTS.

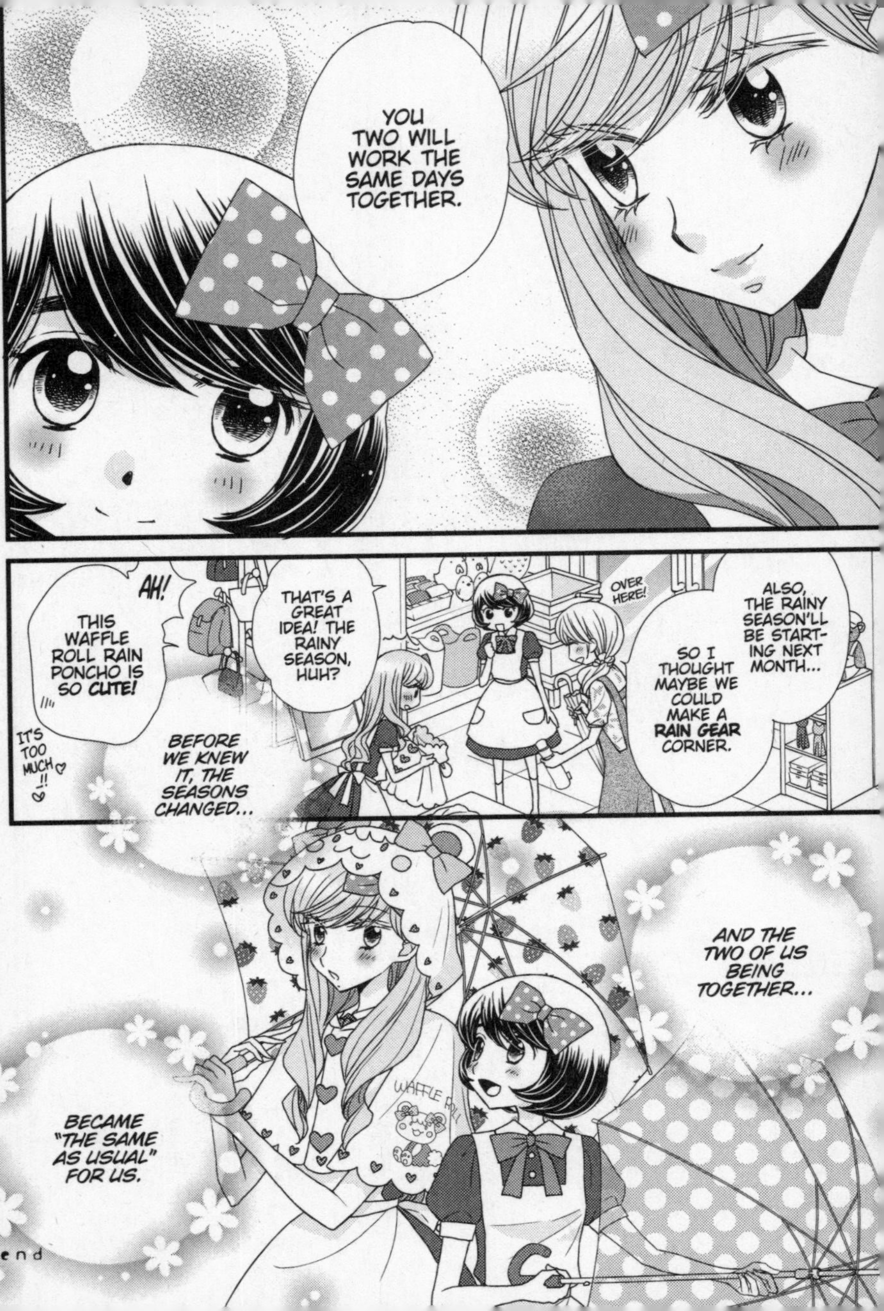
YOU TWO WILL WORK THE SAME DAYS TOGETHER.
ALSO, THE RAINY SEASON'LL BE STARTING NEXT MONTH...
SO I THOUGHT MAYBE WE COULD MAKE A **RAIN GEAR** CORNER.
OVER HERE!
THAT'S A GREAT IDEA! THE RAINY SEASON, HUH?
AH!
THIS WAFFLE ROLL RAIN PONCHO IS SO **CUTE!**
IT'S TOO MUCH!!
BEFORE WE KNEW IT, THE SEASONS CHANGED...
AND THE TWO OF US BEING TOGETHER...
BECAME "THE SAME AS USUAL" FOR US.
WAFFLE ROLL
end

Hana & Hina AFTER ♥ SCHOOL

Hana & Hina AFTER♥SCHOOL

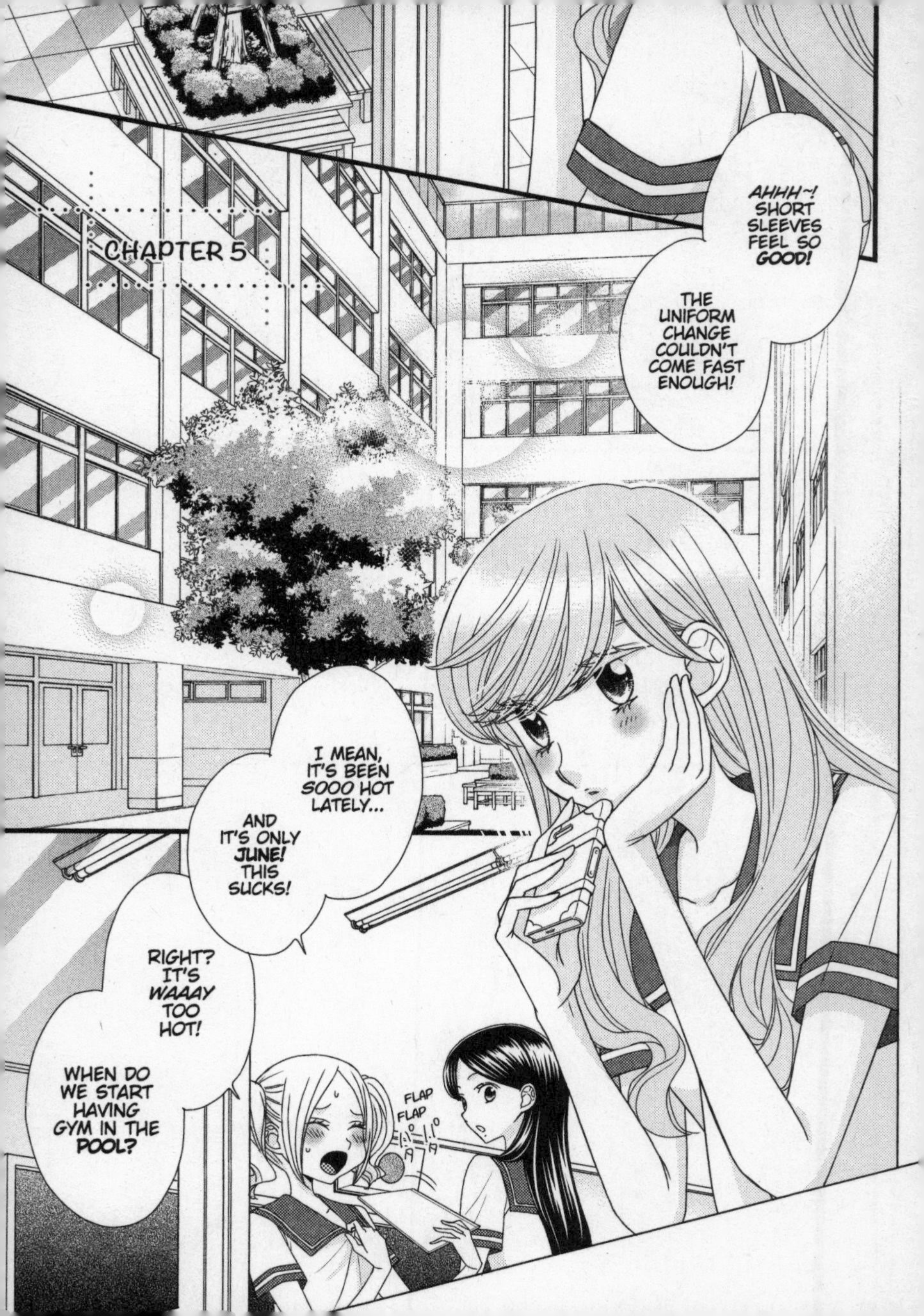
CHAPTER 5
AHHH~! SHORT SLEEVES FEEL SO GOOD!
THE UNIFORM CHANGE COULDN'T COME FAST ENOUGH!
I MEAN, IT'S BEEN SOOO HOT LATELY...
AND IT'S ONLY JUNE! THIS SUCKS!
RIGHT? IT'S WAAAY TOO HOT!
WHEN DO WE START HAVING GYM IN THE POOL?
FLAP FLAP

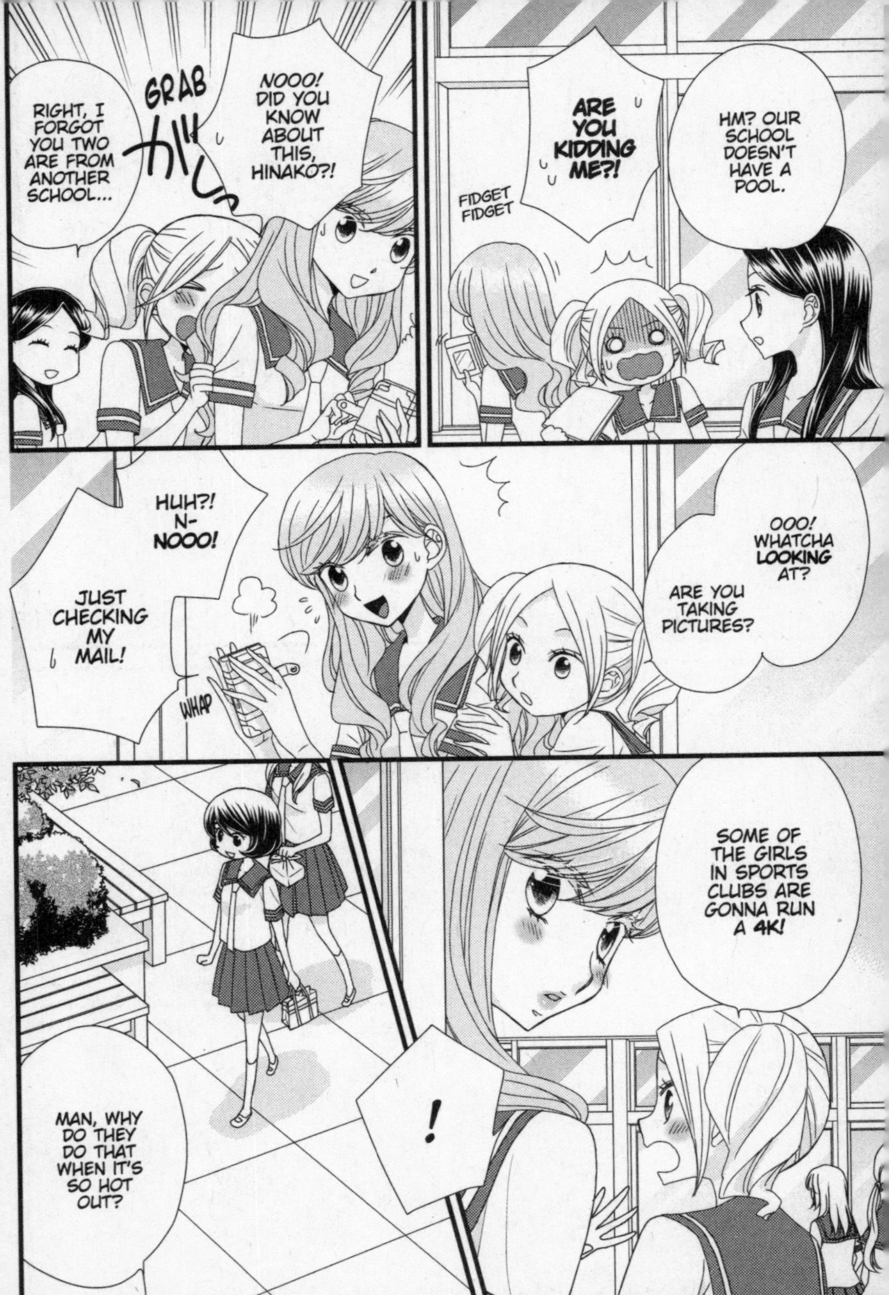
HM? OUR SCHOOL DOESN'T HAVE A POOL.
ARE YOU KIDDING ME?!
FIDGET FIDGET
NOOO! DID YOU KNOW ABOUT THIS, HINAKO?!
GRAB
RIGHT, I FORGOT YOU TWO ARE FROM ANOTHER SCHOOL...
OOO! WHATCHA LOOKING AT?
ARE YOU TAKING PICTURES?
HUH?! N-NOOO!
JUST CHECKING MY MAIL!
WHAP
SOME OF THE GIRLS IN SPORTS CLUBS ARE GONNA RUN A 4K!
!
MAN, WHY DO THEY DO THAT WHEN IT'S SO HOT OUT?

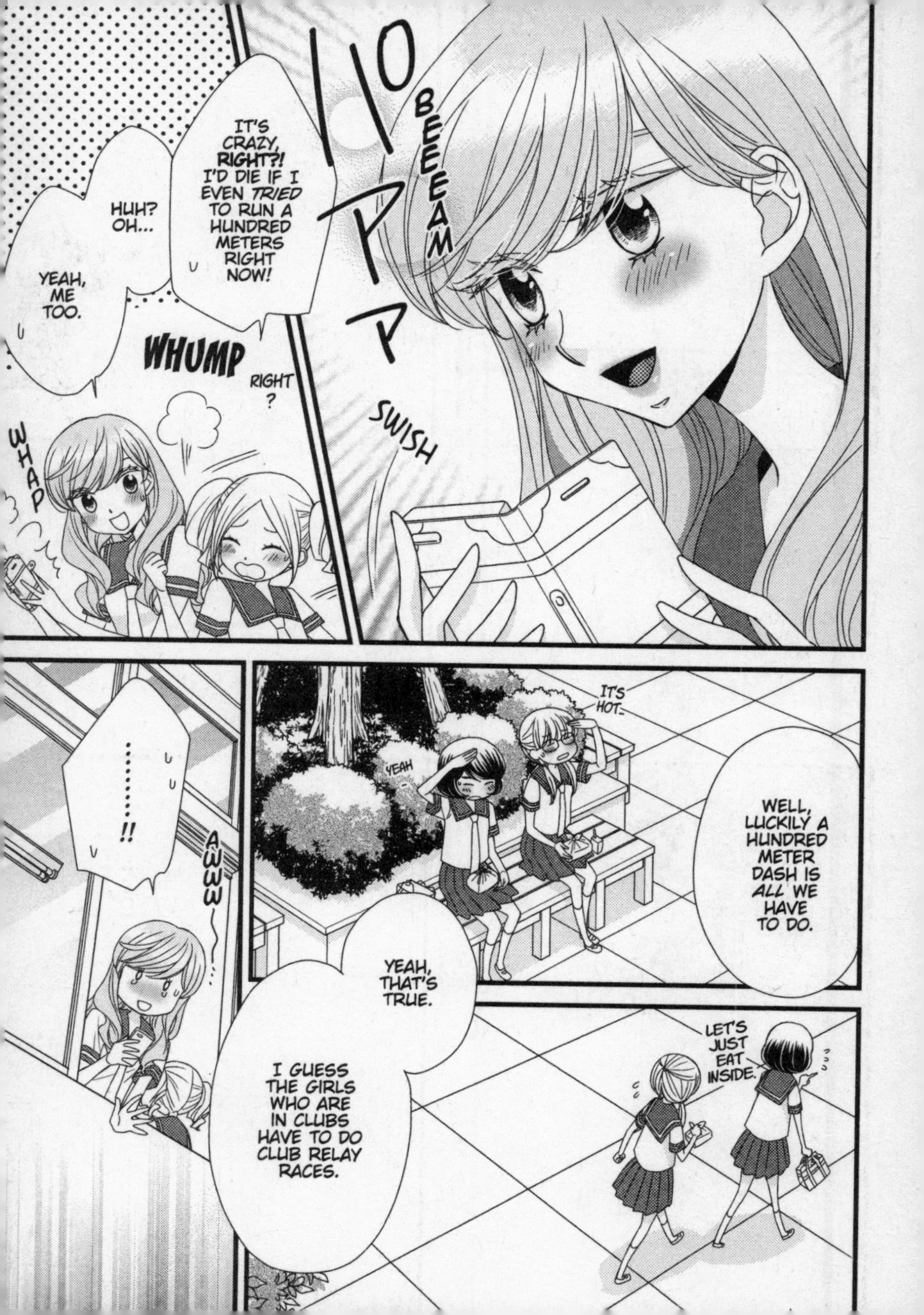
110
BEEEAM
PAP
SWISH
IT'S CRAZY, **RIGHT?!** I'D DIE IF I EVEN *TRIED* TO RUN A HUNDRED METERS RIGHT NOW!
HUH? OH...
YEAH, ME TOO.
WHUMP
RIGHT?
WHAP
IT'S HOT...
YEAH
WELL, LUCKILY A HUNDRED METER DASH IS *ALL* WE HAVE TO DO.
YEAH, THAT'S TRUE.
I GUESS THE GIRLS WHO ARE IN CLUBS HAVE TO DO CLUB RELAY RACES.
LET'S JUST EAT INSIDE.
.......!!
AWWW~...

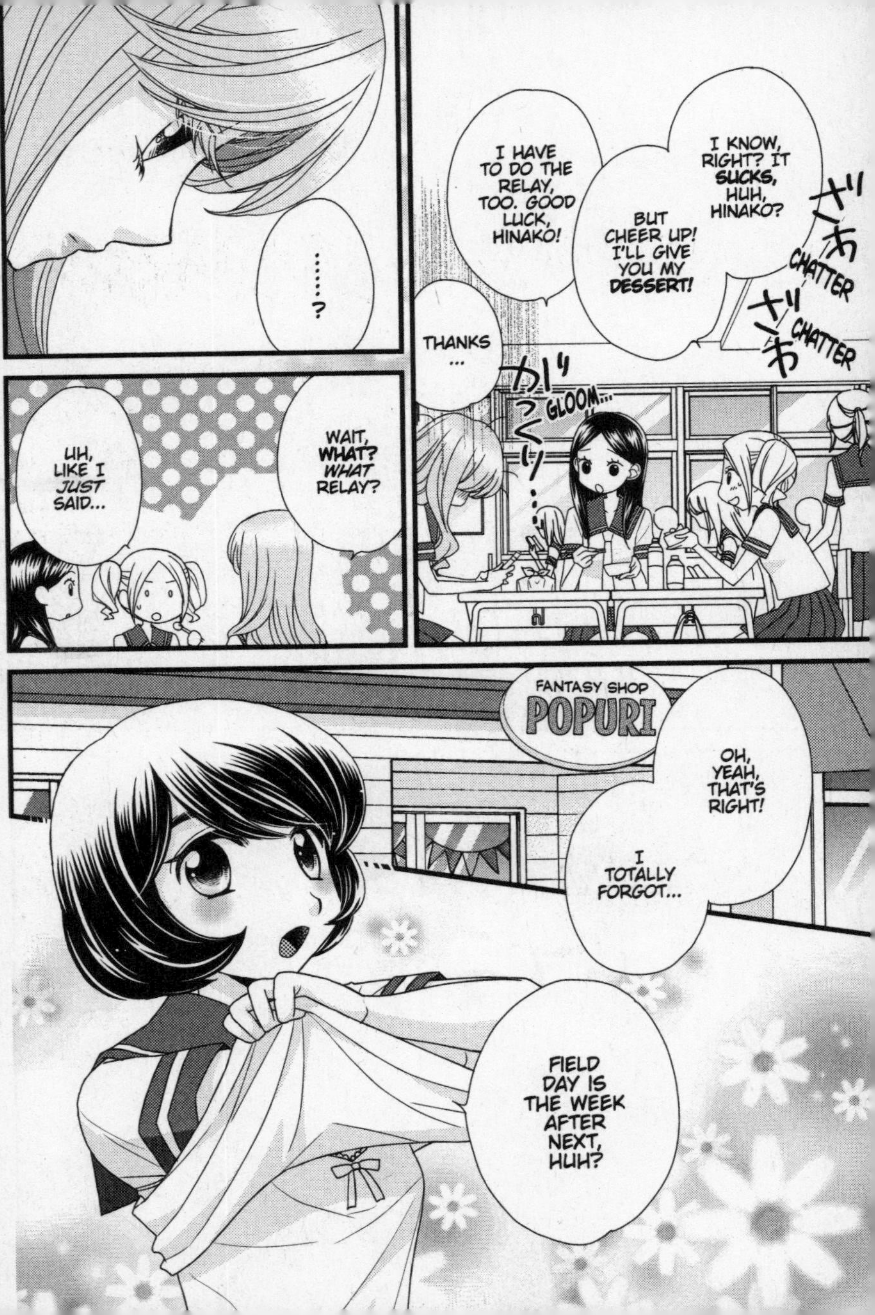
I KNOW, RIGHT? IT SUCKS, HUH, HINAKO?
BUT CHEER UP! I'LL GIVE YOU MY DESSERT!
CHATTER
CHATTER
I HAVE TO DO THE RELAY, TOO. GOOD LUCK, HINAKO!
THANKS ...
GLOOM...
......?
WAIT, WHAT? WHAT RELAY?
UH, LIKE I JUST SAID...
FANTASY SHOP POPURI
OH, YEAH, THAT'S RIGHT!
I TOTALLY FORGOT...
FIELD DAY IS THE WEEK AFTER NEXT, HUH?

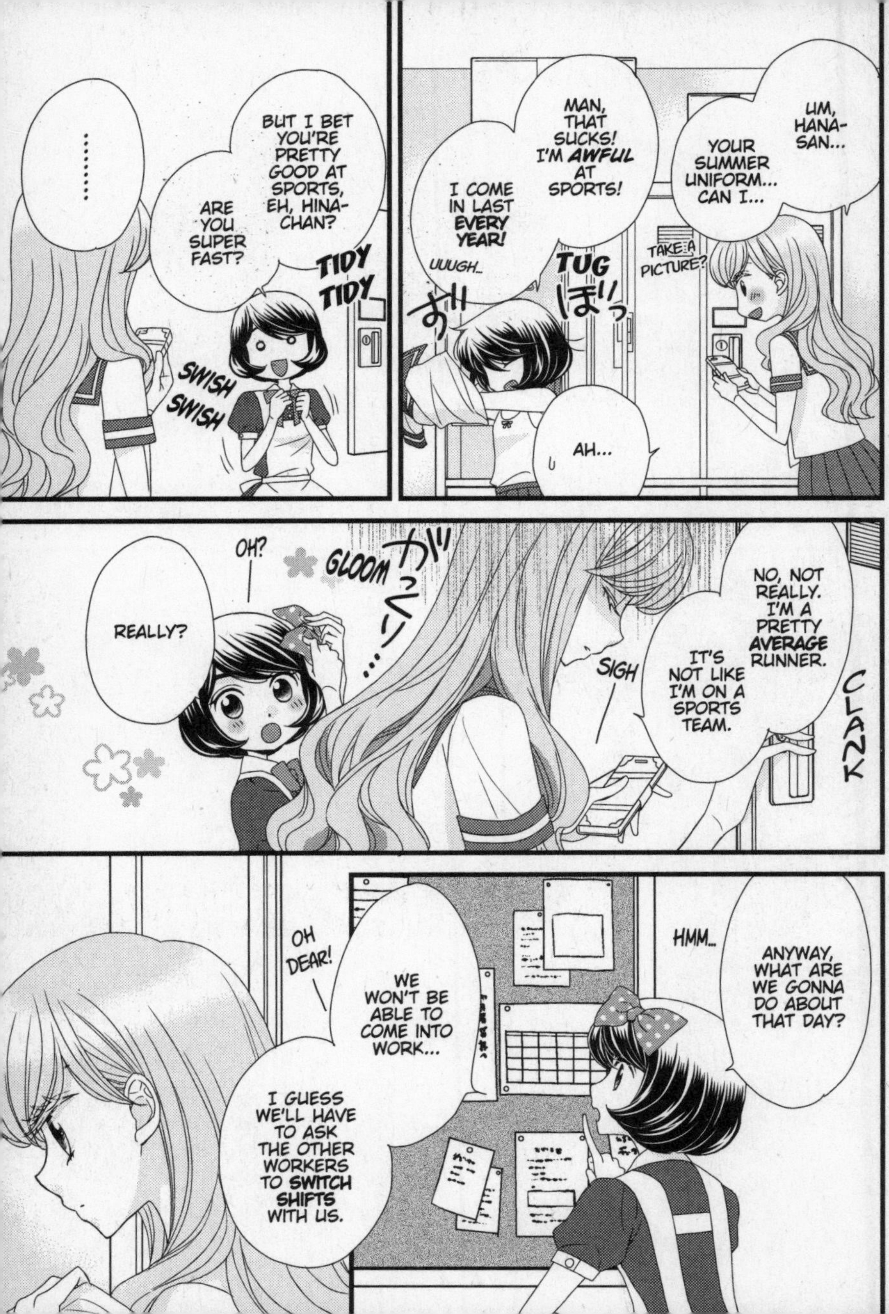
UM, HANA-SAN...
YOUR SUMMER UNIFORM... CAN I...
TAKE A PICTURE?
MAN, THAT SUCKS! I'M AWFUL AT SPORTS!
I COME IN LAST EVERY YEAR!
TUG
UUUGH...
AH...
BUT I BET YOU'RE PRETTY GOOD AT SPORTS, EH, HINA-CHAN?
ARE YOU SUPER FAST?
......
TIDY TIDY
SWISH SWISH
CLANK
NO, NOT REALLY. I'M A PRETTY AVERAGE RUNNER.
IT'S NOT LIKE I'M ON A SPORTS TEAM.
SIGH
GLOOM
がっくり…
OH?
REALLY?
ANYWAY, WHAT ARE WE GONNA DO ABOUT THAT DAY?
HMM...
OH DEAR!
WE WON'T BE ABLE TO COME INTO WORK...
I GUESS WE'LL HAVE TO ASK THE OTHER WORKERS TO SWITCH SHIFTS WITH US.

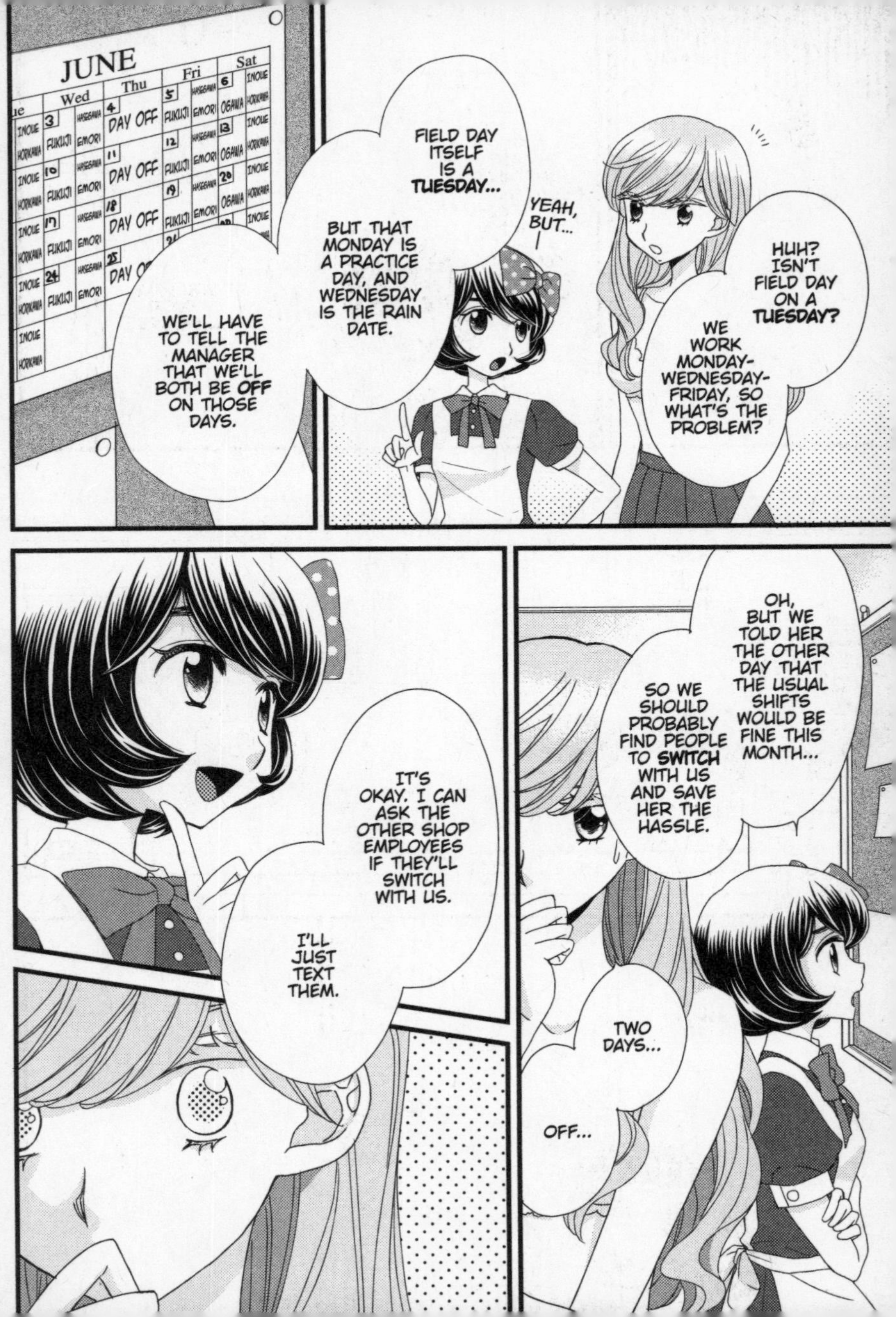

HUH? ISN'T FIELD DAY ON A TUESDAY?
WE WORK MONDAY-WEDNESDAY-FRIDAY, SO WHAT'S THE PROBLEM?
YEAH, BUT...
FIELD DAY ITSELF IS A TUESDAY...
BUT THAT MONDAY IS A PRACTICE DAY, AND WEDNESDAY IS THE RAIN DATE.
JUNE
Wed Thu Fri Sat
DAY OFF
WE'LL HAVE TO TELL THE MANAGER THAT WE'LL BOTH BE OFF ON THOSE DAYS.
OH, BUT WE TOLD HER THE OTHER DAY THAT THE USUAL SHIFTS WOULD BE FINE THIS MONTH...
SO WE SHOULD PROBABLY FIND PEOPLE TO SWITCH WITH US AND SAVE HER THE HASSLE.
TWO DAYS...
OFF...
IT'S OKAY. I CAN ASK THE OTHER SHOP EMPLOYEES IF THEY'LL SWITCH WITH US.
I'LL JUST TEXT THEM.

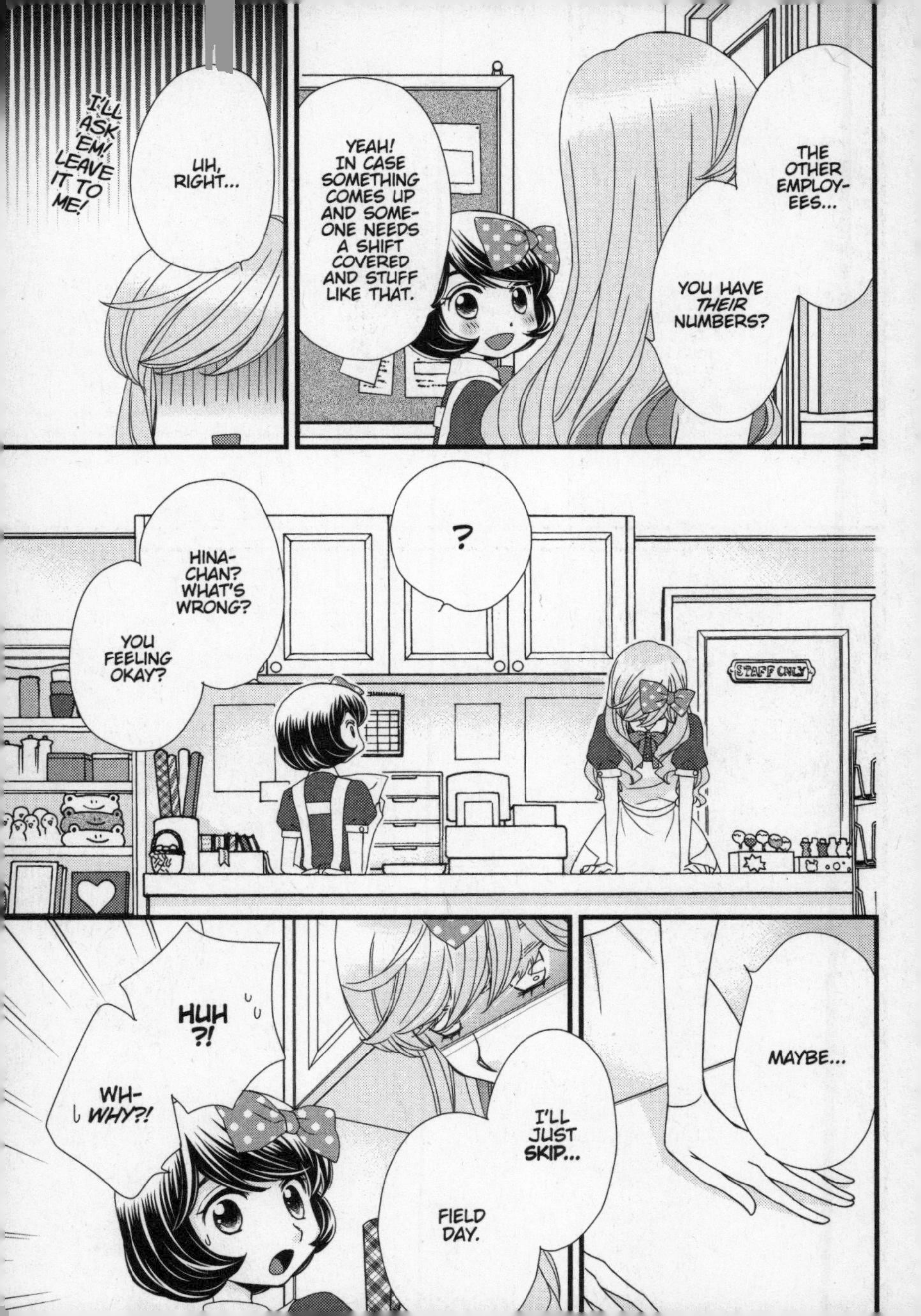
THE OTHER EMPLOYEES...
YOU HAVE *THEIR* NUMBERS?
YEAH! IN CASE SOMETHING COMES UP AND SOMEONE NEEDS A SHIFT COVERED AND STUFF LIKE THAT.
UH, RIGHT...
I'LL ASK 'EM! LEAVE IT TO ME!
?
HINA-CHAN? WHAT'S WRONG?
YOU FEELING OKAY?
STAFF ONLY
MAYBE...
I'LL JUST SKIP...
FIELD DAY.
HUH?!
WH- *WHY?!*

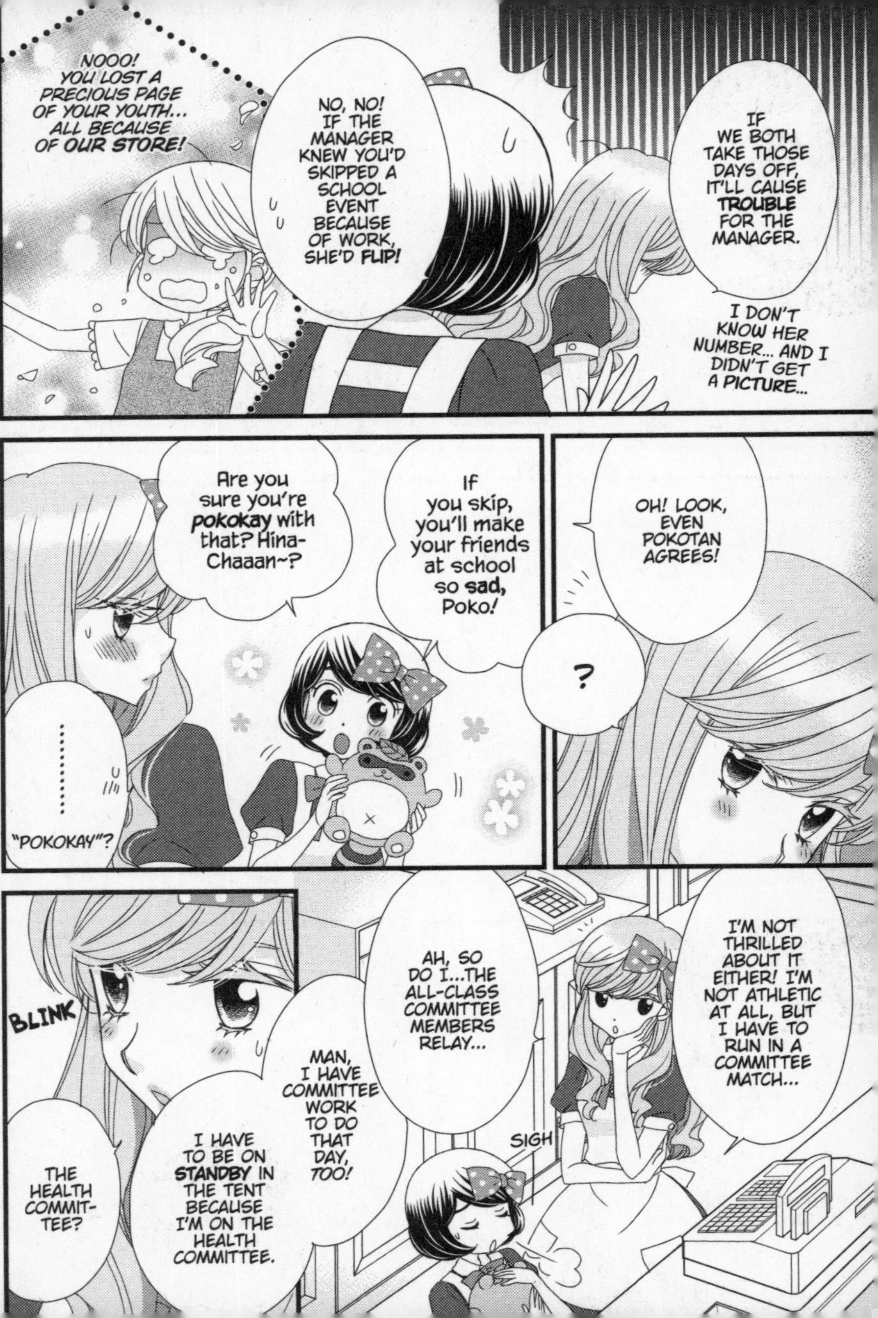
IF WE BOTH TAKE THOSE DAYS OFF, IT'LL CAUSE TROUBLE FOR THE MANAGER.
I DON'T KNOW HER NUMBER... AND I DIDN'T GET A PICTURE...
NO, NO! IF THE MANAGER KNEW YOU'D SKIPPED A SCHOOL EVENT BECAUSE OF WORK, SHE'D FLIP!
NOOO! YOU LOST A PRECIOUS PAGE OF YOUR YOUTH... ALL BECAUSE OF OUR STORE!
OH! LOOK, EVEN POKOTAN AGREES!
?
If you skip, you'll make your friends at school so sad, Poko!
Are you sure you're pokokay with that? Hina-Chaaan~?
......
"POKOKAY"?
I'M NOT THRILLED ABOUT IT EITHER! I'M NOT ATHLETIC AT ALL, BUT I HAVE TO RUN IN A COMMITTEE MATCH...
AH, SO DO I...THE ALL-CLASS COMMITTEE MEMBERS RELAY...
SIGH
MAN, I HAVE COMMITTEE WORK TO DO THAT DAY, TOO!
I HAVE TO BE ON STANDBY IN THE TENT BECAUSE I'M ON THE HEALTH COMMITTEE.
BLINK
THE HEALTH COMMIT-TEE?

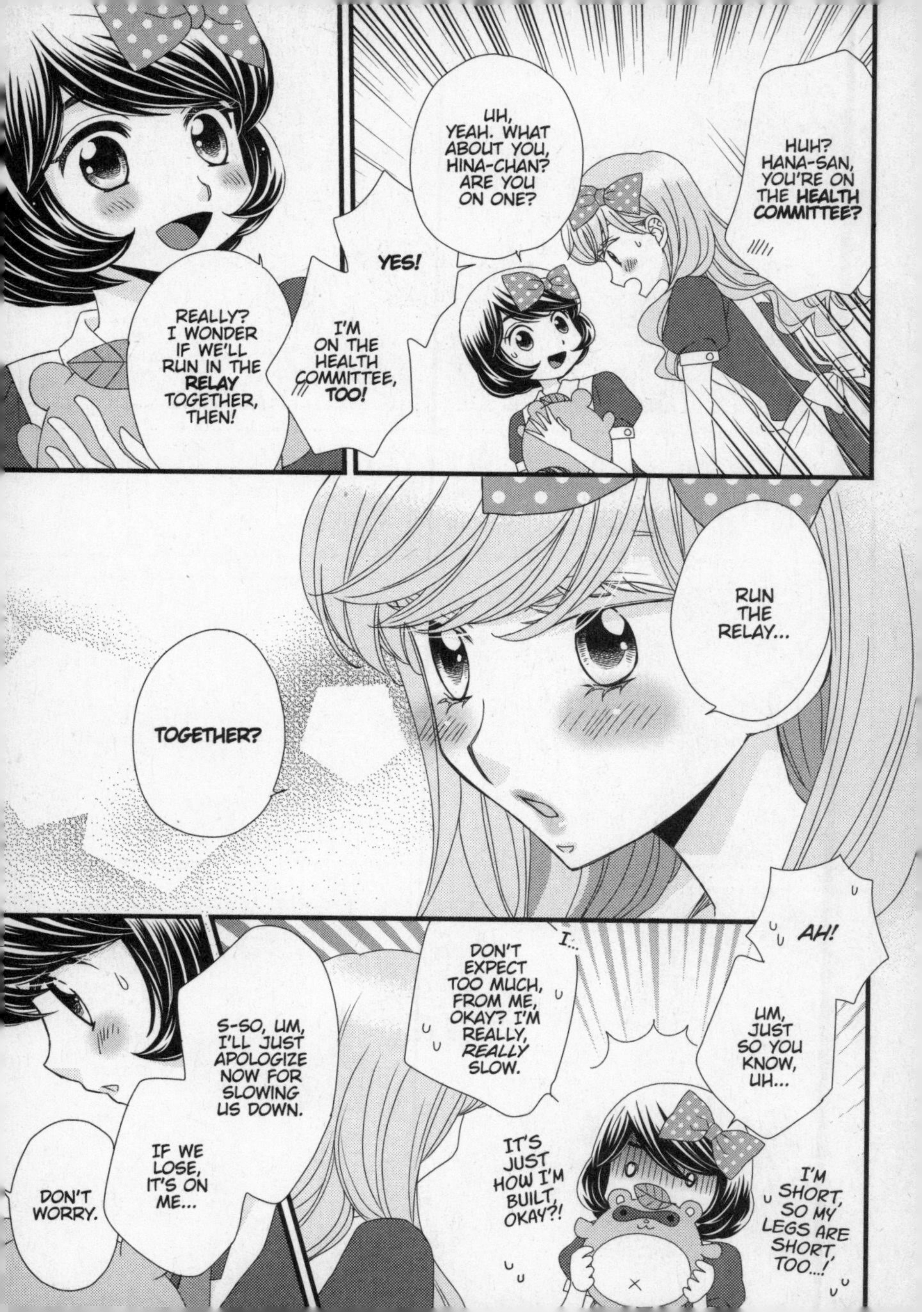
HUH? HANA-SAN, YOU'RE ON THE **HEALTH COMMITTEE?**
UH, YEAH. WHAT ABOUT YOU, HINA-CHAN? ARE YOU ON ONE?
YES!
I'M ON THE HEALTH COMMITTEE, **TOO!**
REALLY? I WONDER IF WE'LL RUN IN THE **RELAY** TOGETHER, THEN!
RUN THE RELAY...
TOGETHER?
AH!
UM, JUST SO YOU KNOW, UH...
I'M SHORT, SO MY LEGS ARE SHORT, TOO...!
IT'S JUST HOW I'M BUILT, OKAY?!
I...
DON'T EXPECT TOO MUCH, FROM ME, OKAY? I'M REALLY, *REALLY* SLOW.
S-SO, UM, I'LL JUST APOLOGIZE NOW FOR SLOWING US DOWN.
IF WE LOSE, IT'S ON ME...
DON'T WORRY.

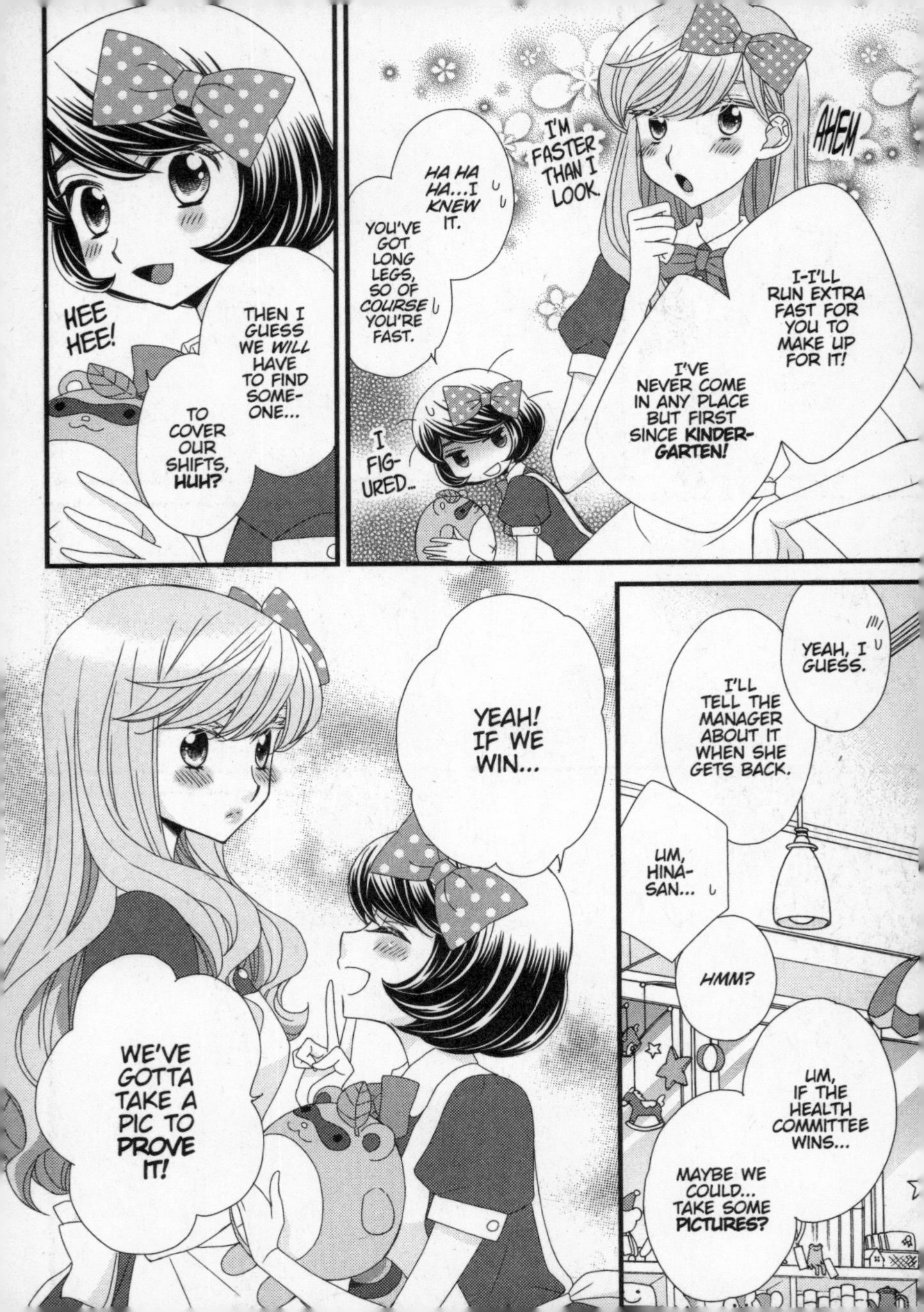
AHEM
I'M FASTER THAN I LOOK.
HA HA HA...I KNEW IT.
YOU'VE GOT LONG LEGS, SO OF COURSE YOU'RE FAST.
I-I'LL RUN EXTRA FAST FOR YOU TO MAKE UP FOR IT!
I'VE NEVER COME IN ANY PLACE BUT FIRST SINCE KINDERGARTEN!
I FIGURED...
THEN I GUESS WE WILL HAVE TO FIND SOMEONE...
TO COVER OUR SHIFTS, HUH?
HEE HEE!
YEAH, I GUESS.
I'LL TELL THE MANAGER ABOUT IT WHEN SHE GETS BACK.
UM, HINA-SAN...
HMM?
UM, IF THE HEALTH COMMITTEE WINS...
MAYBE WE COULD... TAKE SOME PICTURES?
YEAH! IF WE WIN...
WE'VE GOTTA TAKE A PIC TO PROVE IT!

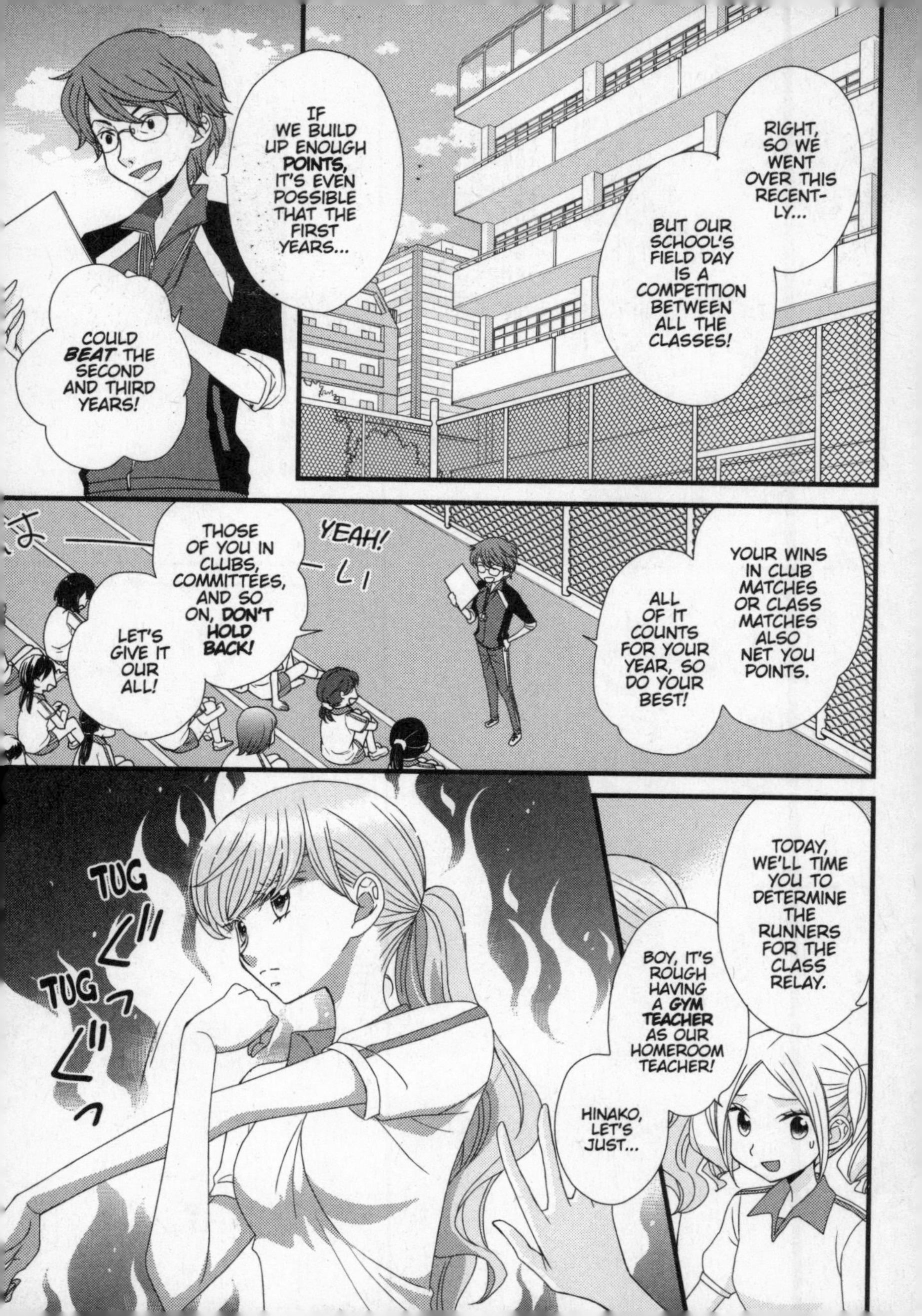
RIGHT, SO WE WENT OVER THIS RECENTLY...
BUT OUR SCHOOL'S FIELD DAY IS A COMPETITION BETWEEN ALL THE CLASSES!
IF WE BUILD UP ENOUGH **POINTS,** IT'S EVEN POSSIBLE THAT THE FIRST YEARS...
COULD ***BEAT*** THE SECOND AND THIRD YEARS!
YOUR WINS IN CLUB MATCHES OR CLASS MATCHES ALSO NET YOU POINTS.
ALL OF IT COUNTS FOR YOUR YEAR, SO DO YOUR BEST!
THOSE OF YOU IN CLUBS, COMMITTEES, AND SO ON, **DON'T HOLD BACK!**
LET'S GIVE IT OUR ALL!
YEAH!
TODAY, WE'LL TIME YOU TO DETERMINE THE RUNNERS FOR THE CLASS RELAY.
BOY, IT'S ROUGH HAVING A **GYM TEACHER** AS OUR HOMEROOM TEACHER!
HINAKO, LET'S JUST...
TUG
TUG

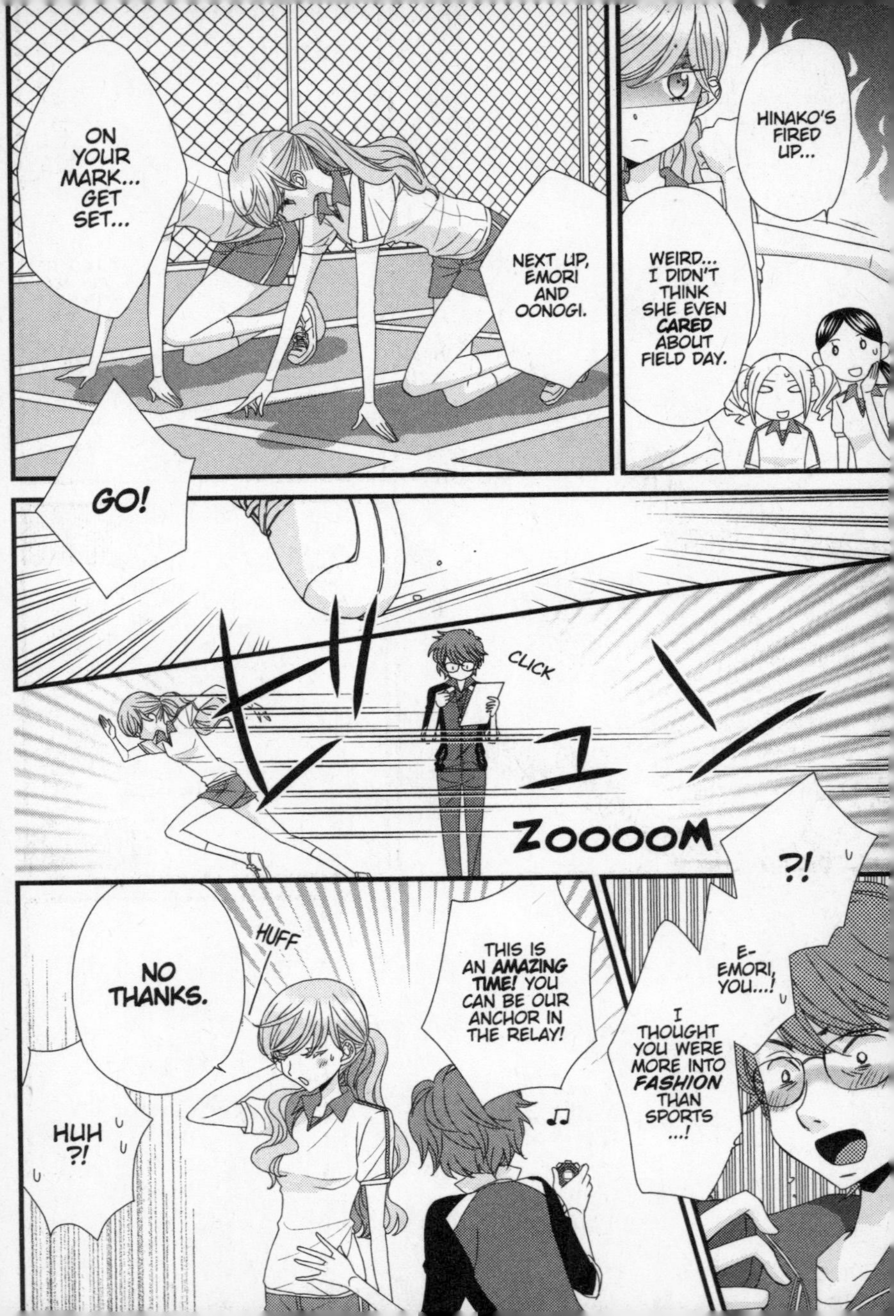
HINAKO'S FIRED UP...
WEIRD... I DIDN'T THINK SHE EVEN CARED ABOUT FIELD DAY.
NEXT UP, EMORI AND OONOGI.
ON YOUR MARK... GET SET...
GO!
CLICK
ZOOOOM
?!
E-EMORI, YOU...!
I THOUGHT YOU WERE MORE INTO FASHION THAN SPORTS ...!
THIS IS AN AMAZING TIME! YOU CAN BE OUR ANCHOR IN THE RELAY!
HUFF
NO THANKS.
HUH ?!

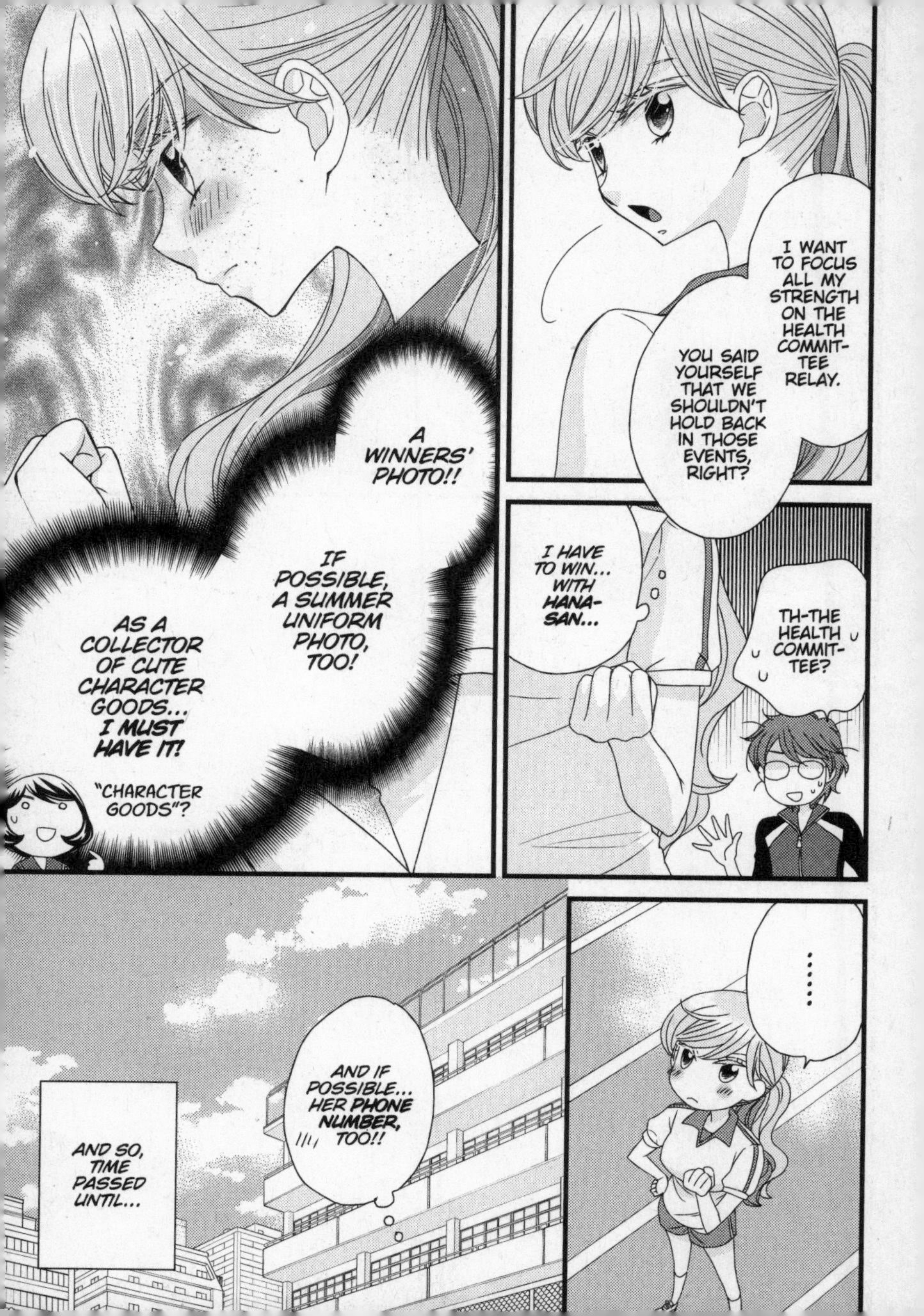
I WANT TO FOCUS ALL MY STRENGTH ON THE HEALTH COMMIT-TEE RELAY.
YOU SAID YOURSELF THAT WE SHOULDN'T HOLD BACK IN THOSE EVENTS, RIGHT?
TH-THE HEALTH COMMIT-TEE?
I HAVE TO WIN... WITH HANA-SAN...
A WINNERS' PHOTO!!
IF POSSIBLE, A SUMMER UNIFORM PHOTO, TOO!
AS A COLLECTOR OF CUTE CHARACTER GOODS... I MUST HAVE IT!
"CHARACTER GOODS"?
......
AND IF POSSIBLE... HER PHONE NUMBER, TOO!!
AND SO, TIME PASSED UNTIL...

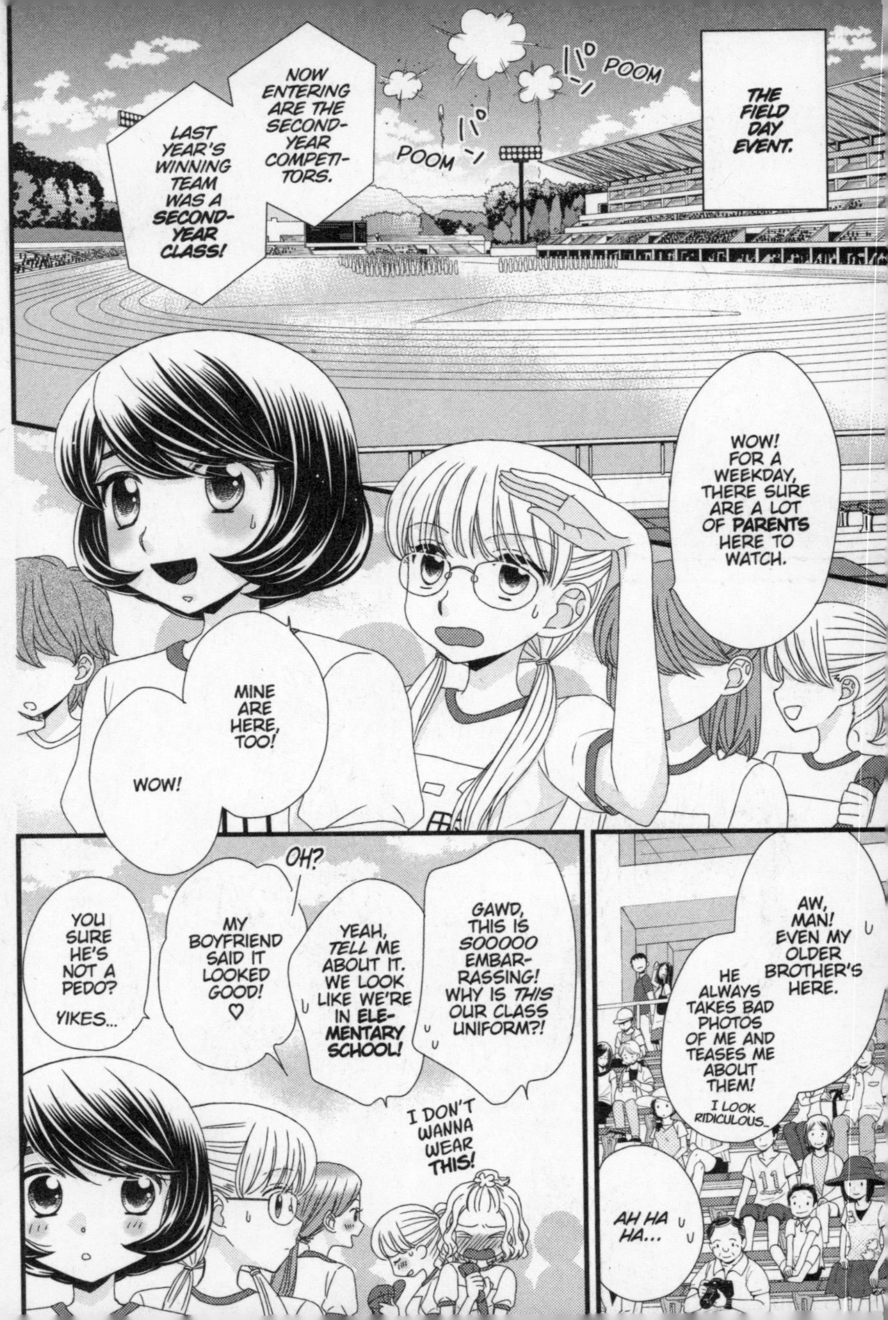
THE FIELD DAY EVENT.
パ POOM
パ POOM
NOW ENTERING ARE THE SECOND-YEAR COMPETITORS.
LAST YEAR'S WINNING TEAM WAS A SECOND-YEAR CLASS!
WOW! FOR A WEEKDAY, THERE SURE ARE A LOT OF PARENTS HERE TO WATCH.
MINE ARE HERE, TOO!
WOW!
AW, MAN! EVEN MY OLDER BROTHER'S HERE.
HE ALWAYS TAKES BAD PHOTOS OF ME AND TEASES ME ABOUT THEM!
I LOOK RIDICULOUS...
AH HA HA...
GAWD, THIS IS SOOOOO EMBARRASSING! WHY IS THIS OUR CLASS UNIFORM?!
YEAH, TELL ME ABOUT IT. WE LOOK LIKE WE'RE IN ELEMENTARY SCHOOL!
OH?
MY BOYFRIEND SAID IT LOOKED GOOD! ♡
YOU SURE HE'S NOT A PEDO?
YIKES...
I DON'T WANNA WEAR THIS!

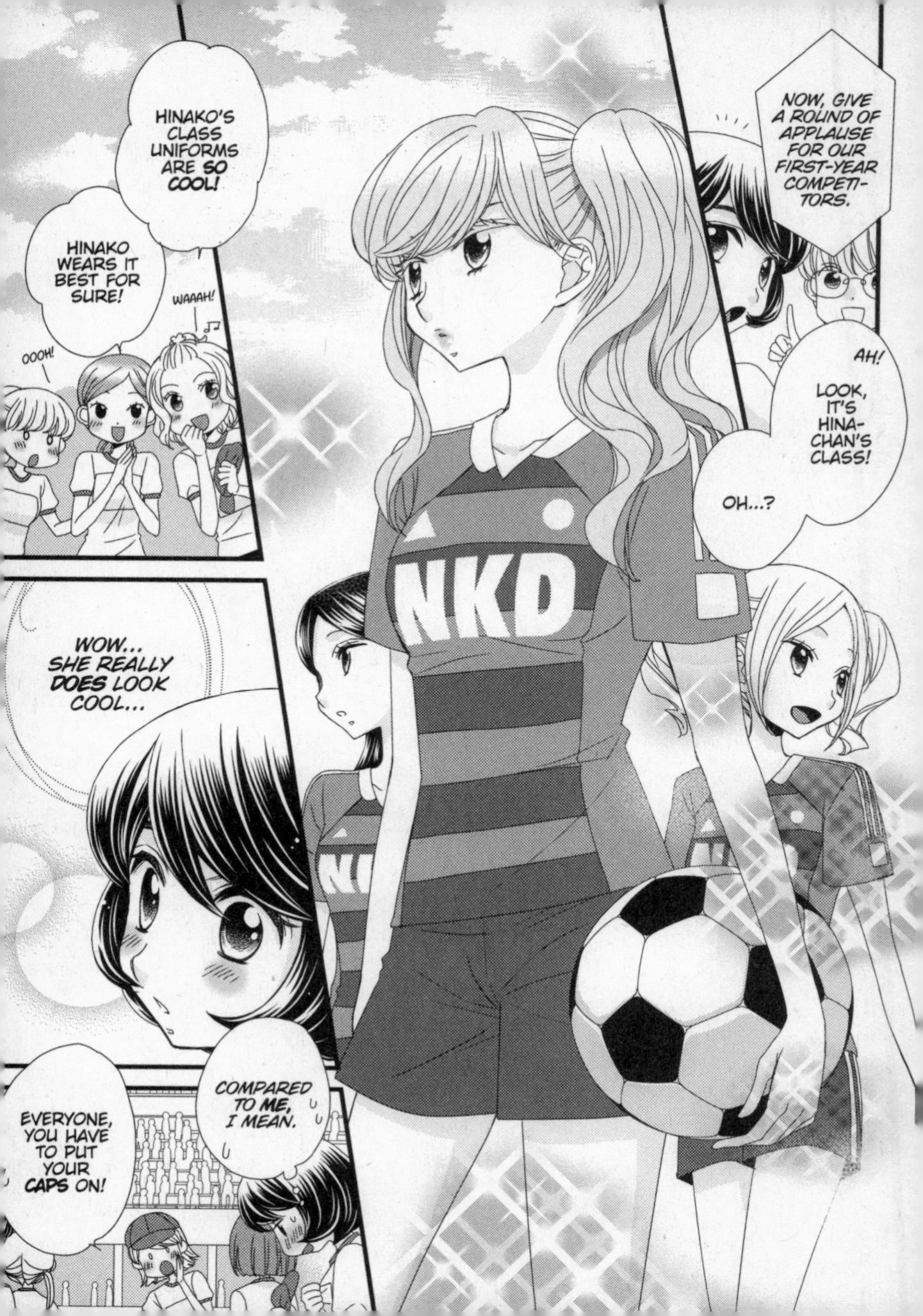
NOW, GIVE A ROUND OF APPLAUSE FOR OUR FIRST-YEAR COMPETI-TORS.
AH!
LOOK, IT'S HINA-CHAN'S CLASS!
OH...?
HINAKO'S CLASS UNIFORMS ARE SO COOL!
HINAKO WEARS IT BEST FOR SURE!
WAAAH!
OOOH!
NKD
WOW... SHE REALLY DOES LOOK COOL...
COMPARED TO ME, I MEAN.
EVERYONE, YOU HAVE TO PUT YOUR CAPS ON!

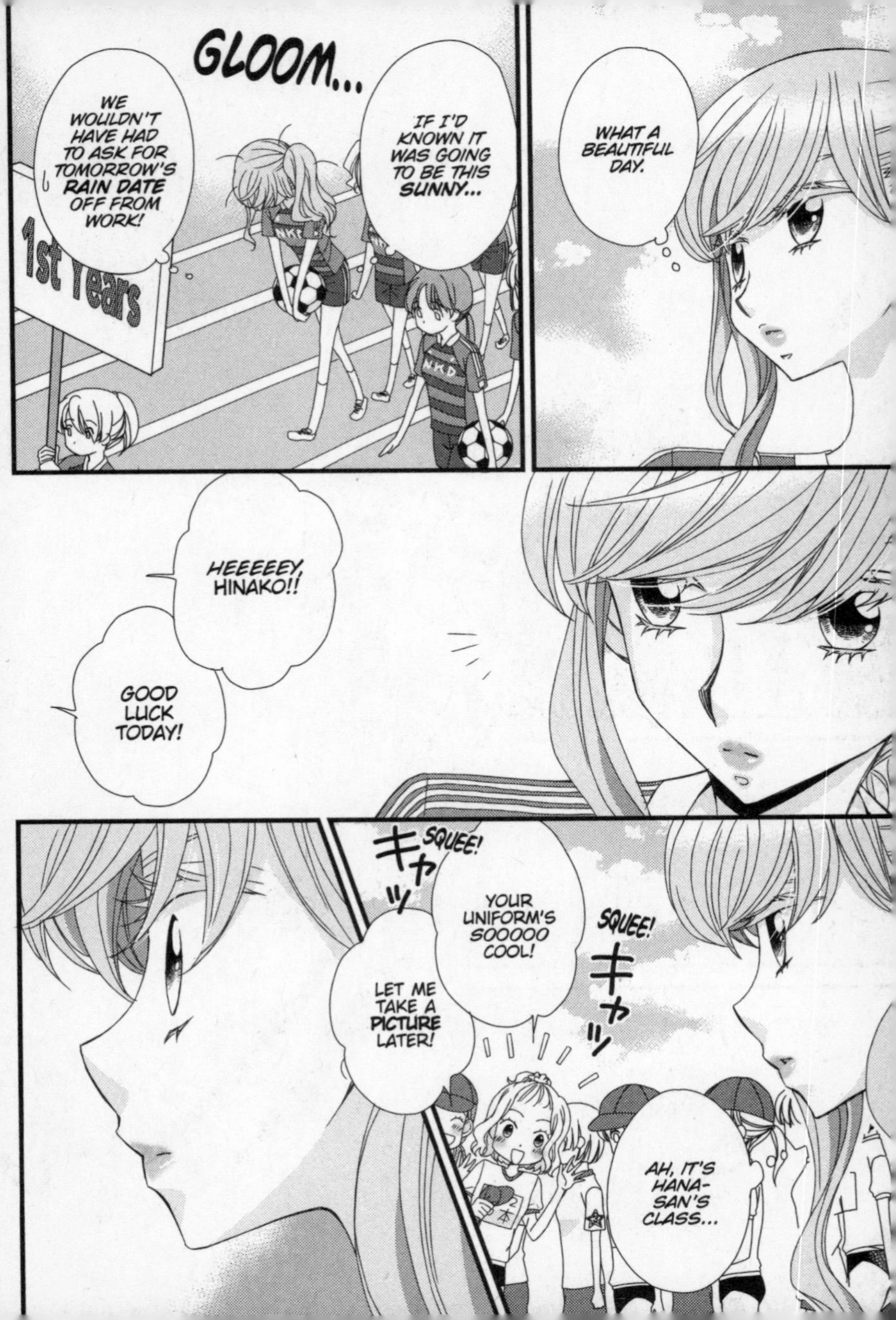
WHAT A BEAUTIFUL DAY.
GLOOM...
IF I'D KNOWN IT WAS GOING TO BE THIS SUNNY...
WE WOULDN'T HAVE HAD TO ASK FOR TOMORROW'S RAIN DATE OFF FROM WORK!
1st Years
HEEEEEY, HINAKO!!
GOOD LUCK TODAY!
SQUEE!
キャッ
YOUR UNIFORM'S SOOOOO COOL!
SQUEE!
キャッ
LET ME TAKE A PICTURE LATER!
AH, IT'S HANA-SAN'S CLASS...

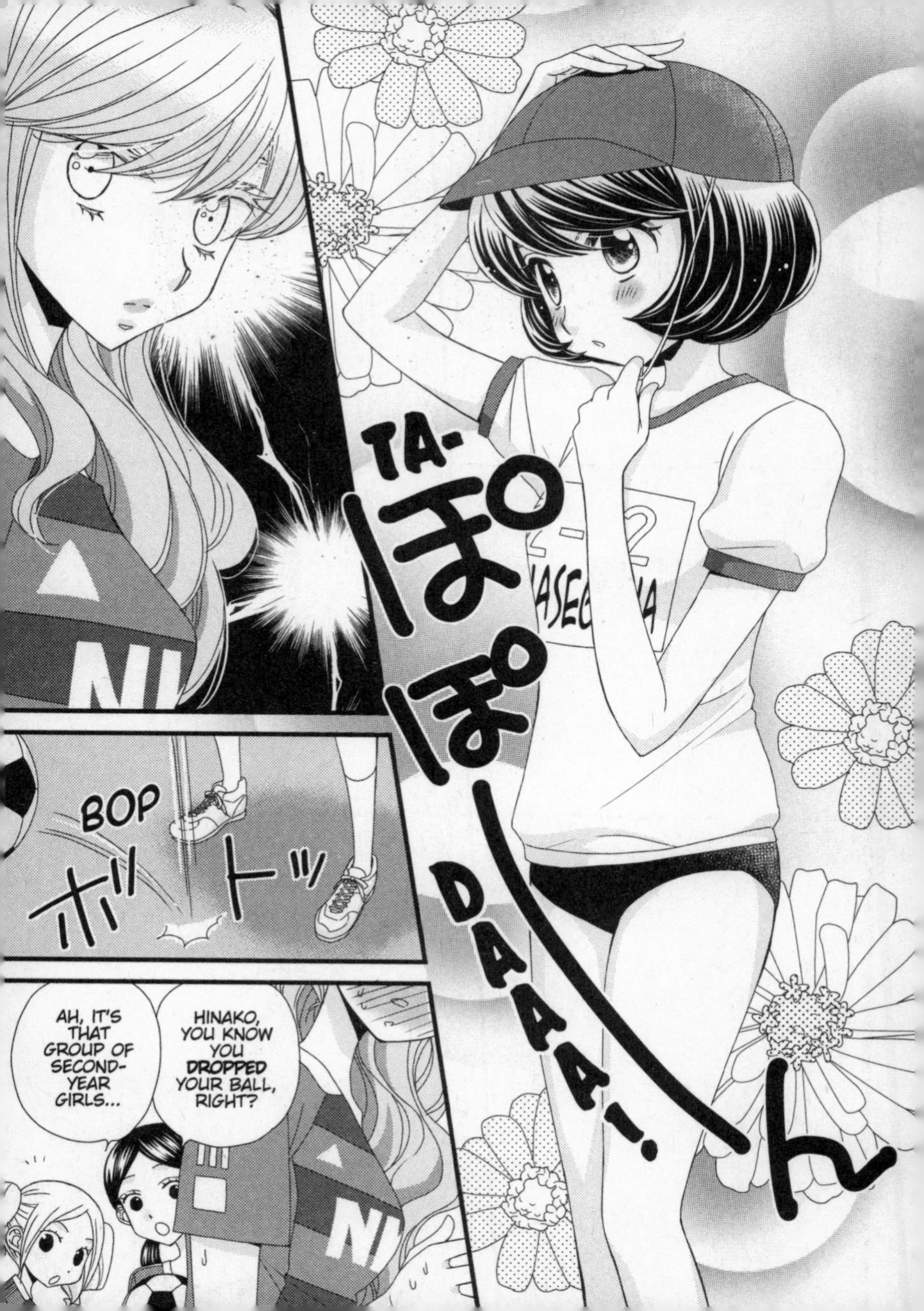

TA-
ぽーぽーーん
DAAA!!
BOP
ボトッ
HINAKO, YOU KNOW YOU **DROPPED** YOUR BALL, RIGHT?
AH, IT'S THAT GROUP OF SECOND-YEAR GIRLS...

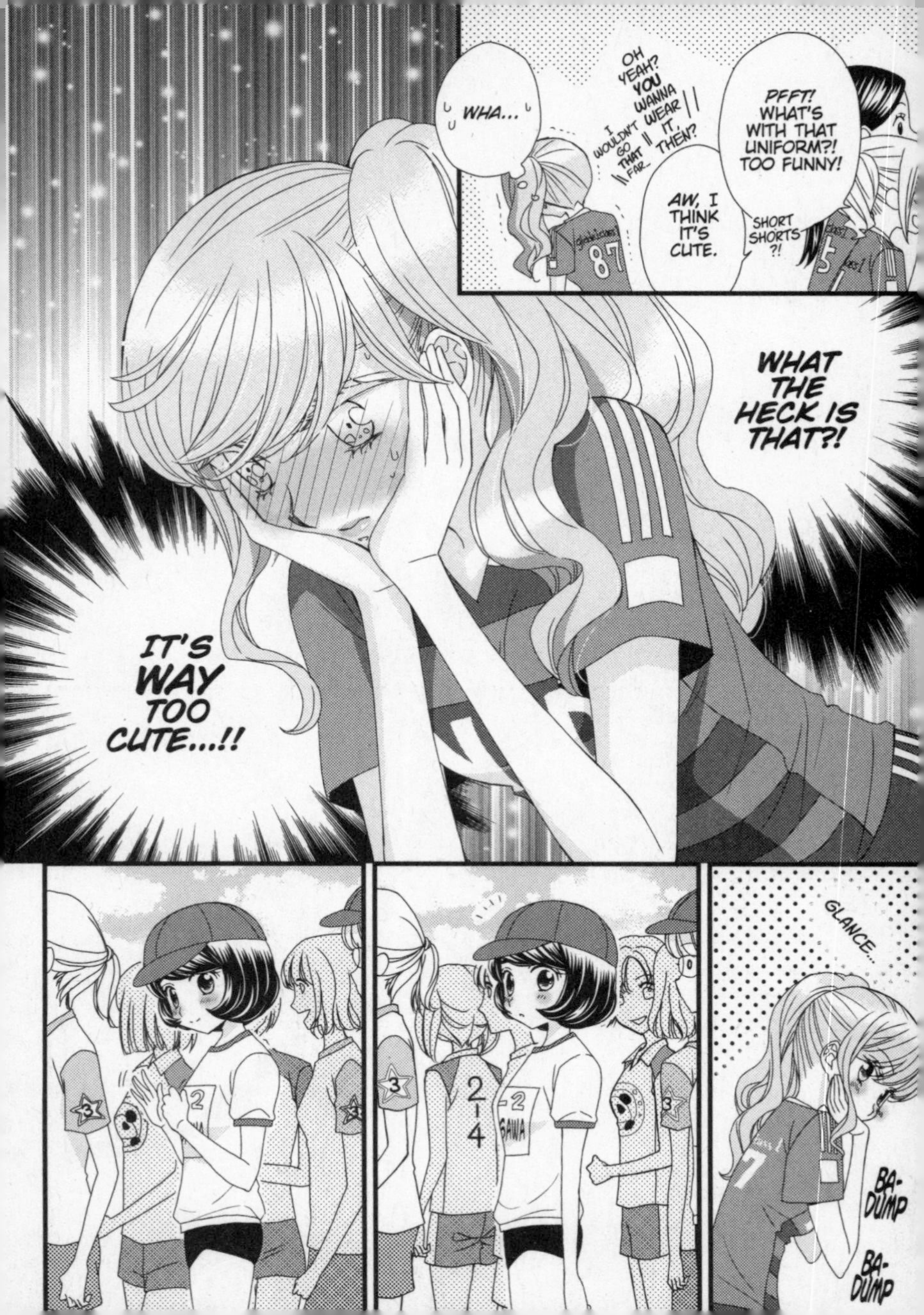
PFFT! WHAT'S WITH THAT UNIFORM?! TOO FUNNY!
SHORT SHORTS?!
AW, I THINK IT'S CUTE.
OH YEAH? YOU WANNA WEAR IT, THEN?
I WOULDN'T GO THAT FAR_
WHA...
WHAT THE HECK IS THAT?!
IT'S WAY TOO CUTE...!!
GLANCE...
BA-DUMP
BA-DUMP

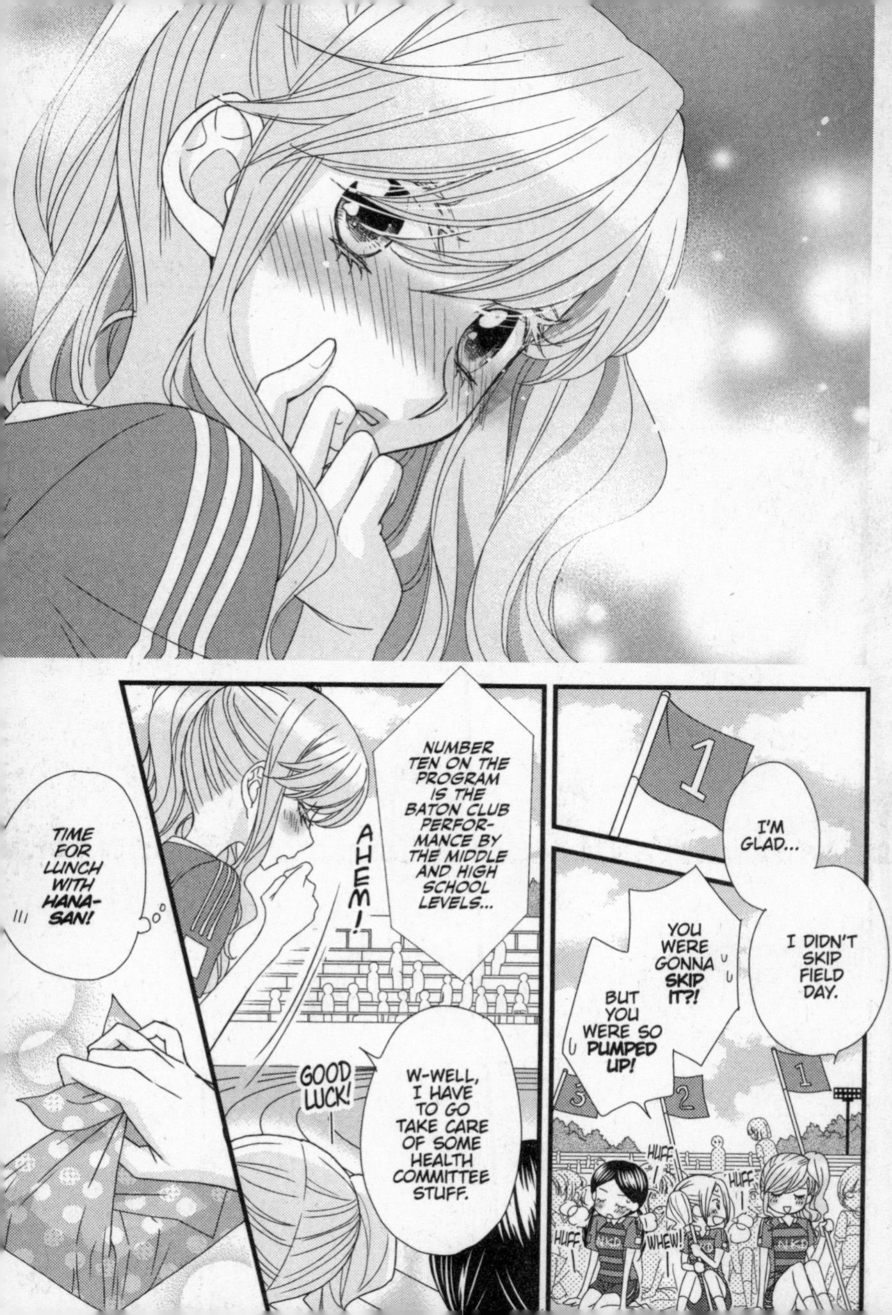
I'M GLAD...
I DIDN'T SKIP FIELD DAY.
YOU WERE GONNA SKIP IT?!
BUT YOU WERE SO PUMPED UP!
HUFF
HUFF
HUFF
WHEW!
NUMBER TEN ON THE PROGRAM IS THE BATON CLUB PERFORMANCE BY THE MIDDLE AND HIGH SCHOOL LEVELS...
AHEM!
W-WELL, I HAVE TO GO TAKE CARE OF SOME HEALTH COMMITTEE STUFF.
GOOD LUCK!
TIME FOR LUNCH WITH HANA-SAN!

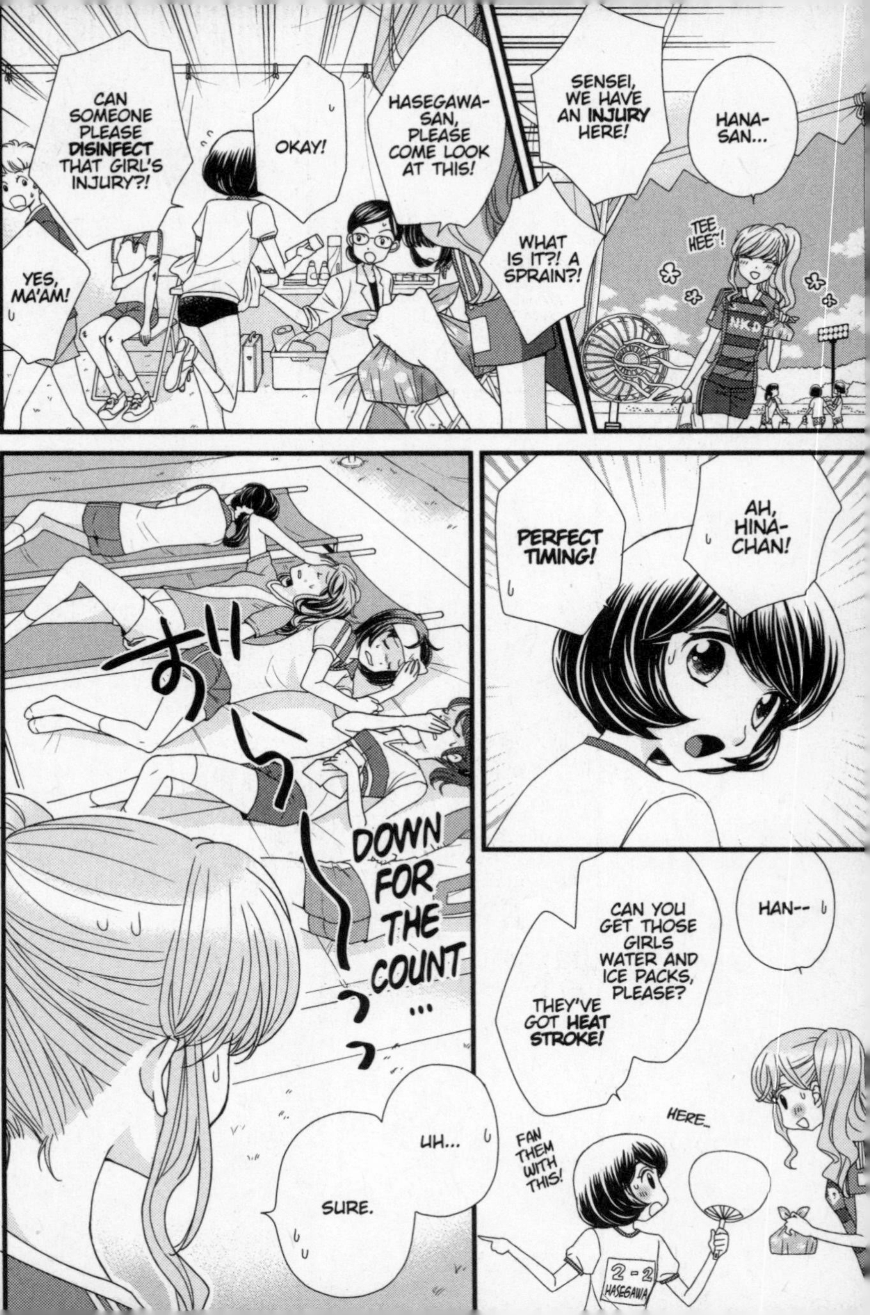
HANA-SAN...
TEE HEE~!
SENSEI, WE HAVE AN INJURY HERE!
WHAT IS IT?! A SPRAIN?!
HASEGAWA-SAN, PLEASE COME LOOK AT THIS!
OKAY!
CAN SOMEONE PLEASE DISINFECT THAT GIRL'S INJURY?!
YES, MA'AM!
AH, HINA-CHAN!
PERFECT TIMING!
ずーん
DOWN FOR THE COUNT...
HAN--
CAN YOU GET THOSE GIRLS WATER AND ICE PACKS, PLEASE?
THEY'VE GOT HEAT STROKE!
HERE..
FAN THEM WITH THIS!
2-2
HASEGAWA
UH...
SURE.

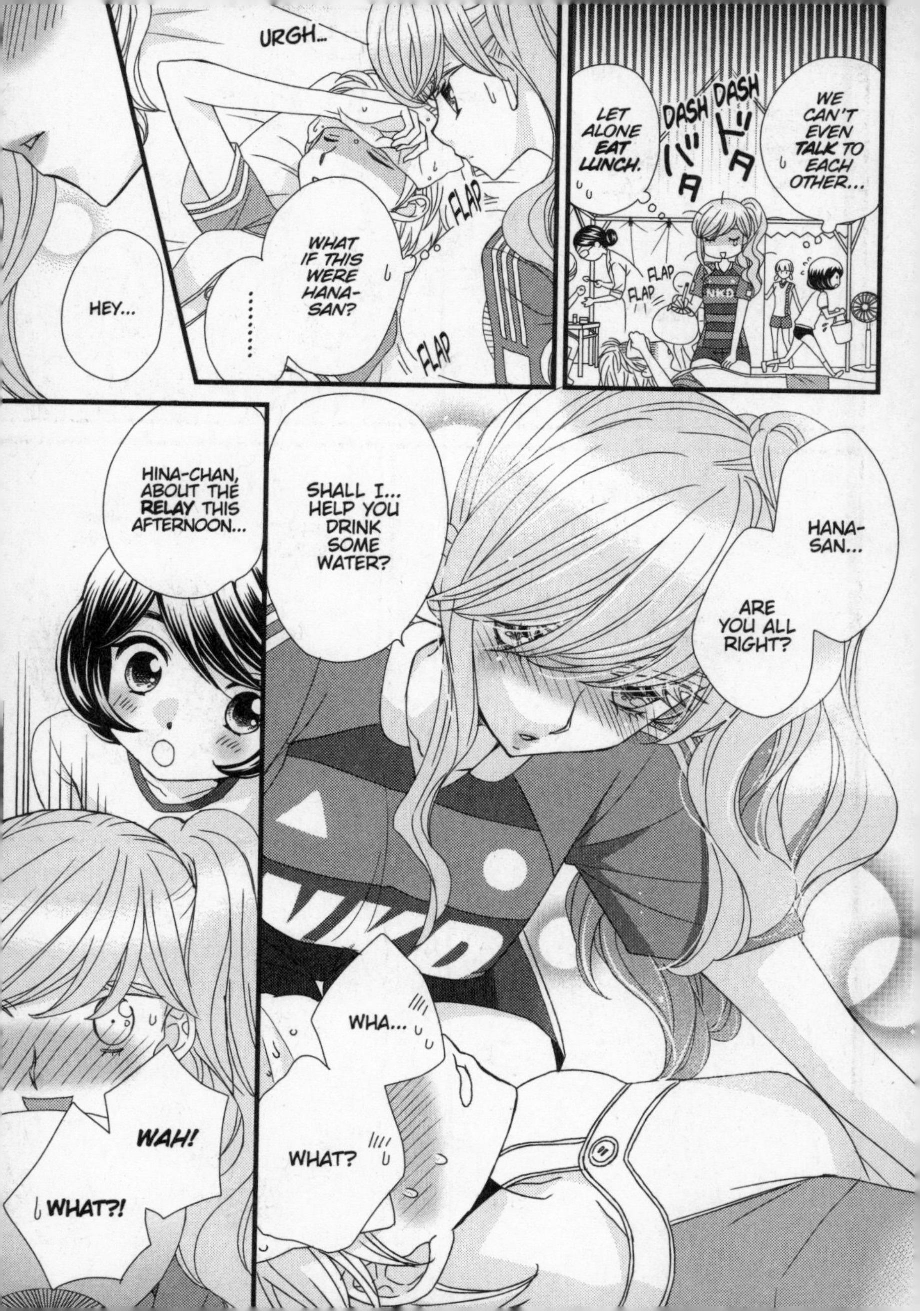
WE CAN'T EVEN TALK TO EACH OTHER...
DASH DASH
LET ALONE EAT LUNCH.
FLAP
FLAP
URGH...
FLAP
WHAT IF THIS WERE HANA-SAN?
......
FLAP
HEY...
HANA-SAN...
ARE YOU ALL RIGHT?
SHALL I... HELP YOU DRINK SOME WATER?
WHA...
WHAT?
HINA-CHAN, ABOUT THE RELAY THIS AFTERNOON...
WAH!
WHAT?!

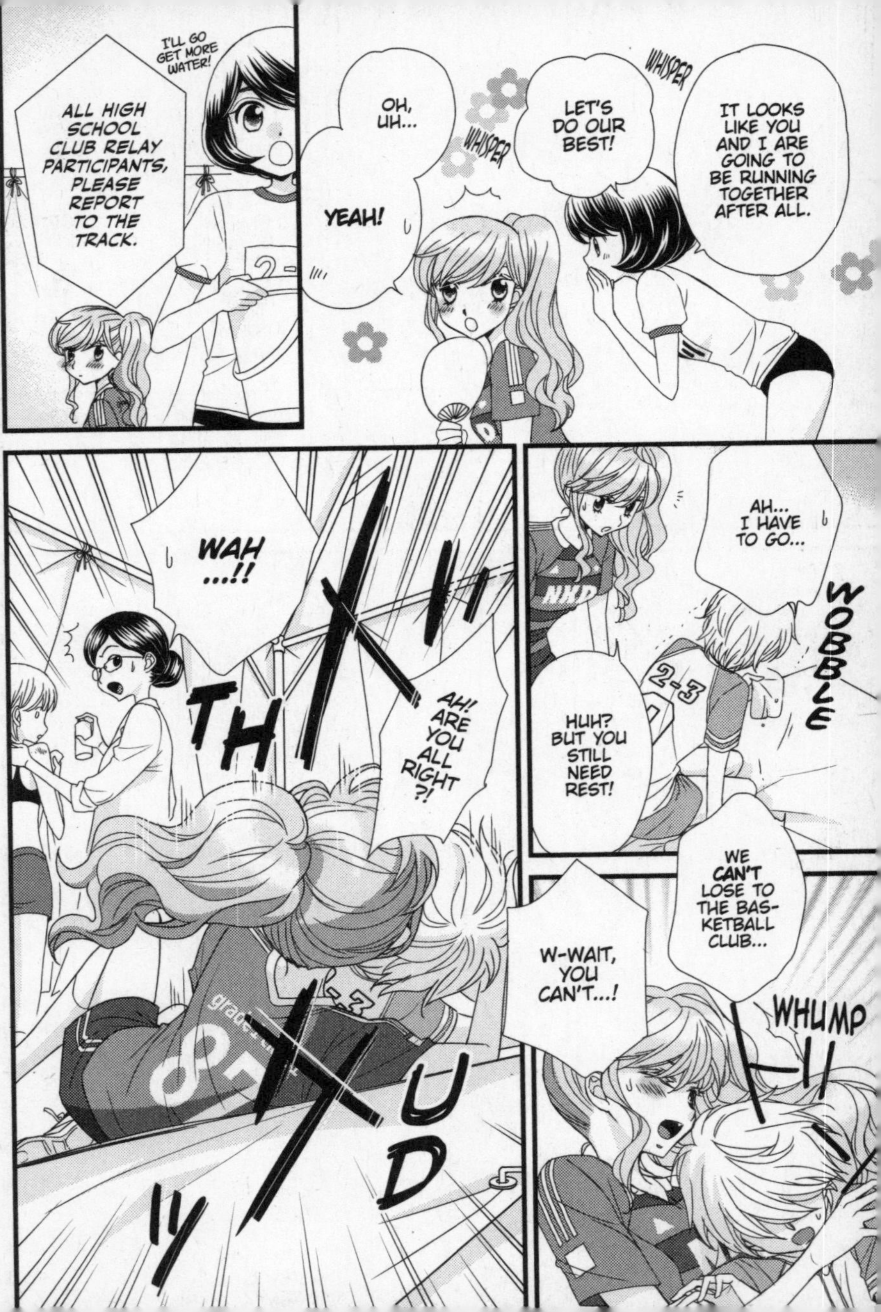
IT LOOKS LIKE YOU AND I ARE GOING TO BE RUNNING TOGETHER AFTER ALL.
WHISPER
LET'S DO OUR BEST!
WHISPER
OH, UH...
YEAH!
I'LL GO GET MORE WATER!
ALL HIGH SCHOOL CLUB RELAY PARTICIPANTS, PLEASE REPORT TO THE TRACK.
AH... I HAVE TO GO...
WOBBLE
HUH? BUT YOU STILL NEED REST!
WE CAN'T LOSE TO THE BAS-KETBALL CLUB...
WHUMP
W-WAIT, YOU CAN'T...!
AH! ARE YOU ALL RIGHT?!
WAH ...!!
THUD

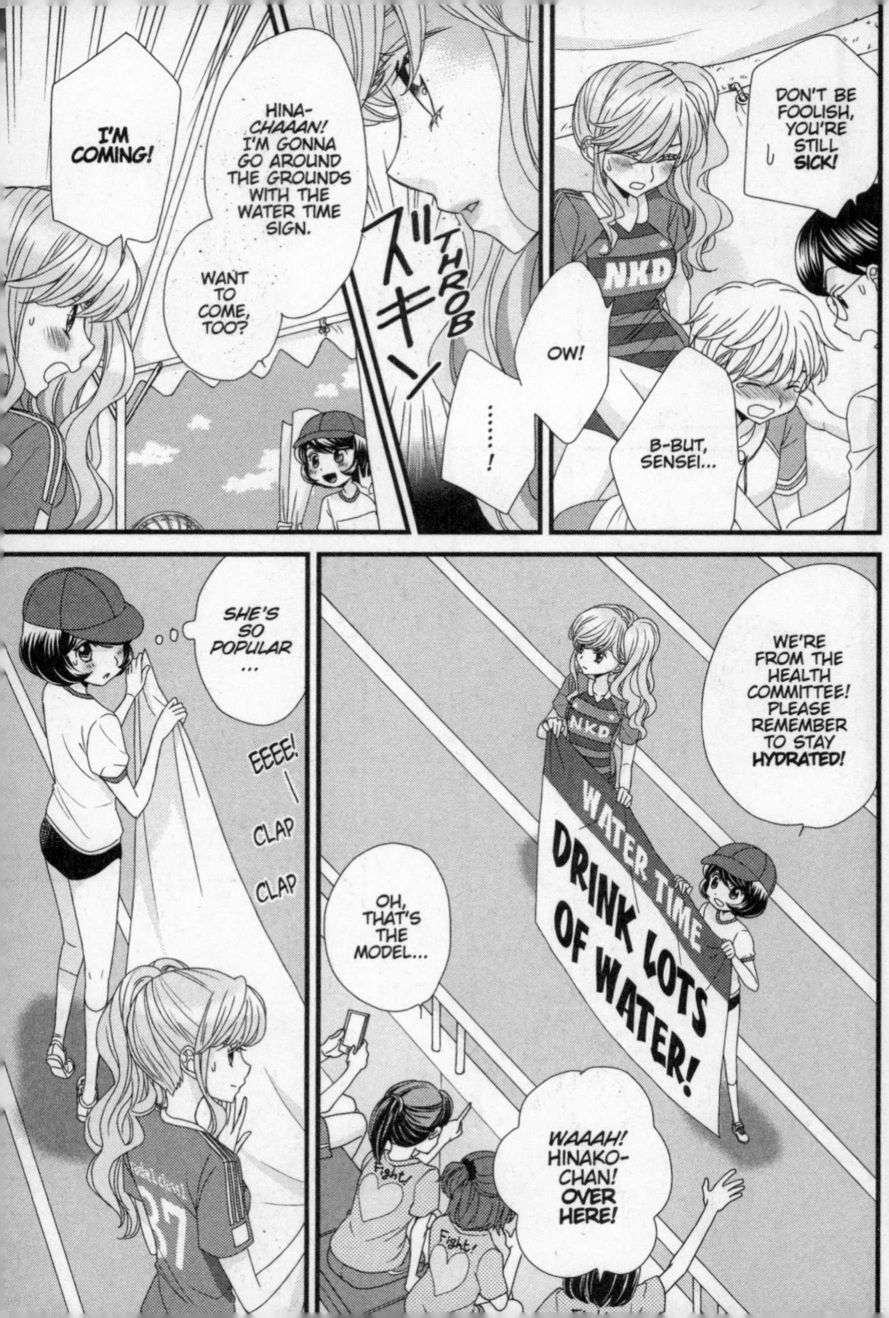
DON'T BE FOOLISH, YOU'RE STILL SICK!
OW!
B-BUT, SENSEI...
THROB
......!
HINA-CHAAAN! I'M GONNA GO AROUND THE GROUNDS WITH THE WATER TIME SIGN.
WANT TO COME, TOO?
I'M COMING!
WE'RE FROM THE HEALTH COMMITTEE! PLEASE REMEMBER TO STAY HYDRATED!
NKD
WATER TIME
DRINK LOTS OF WATER!
OH, THAT'S THE MODEL...
WAAAH! HINAKO-CHAN! OVER HERE!
Fight!
Fight!
SHE'S SO POPULAR...
EEEE!
CLAP
CLAP

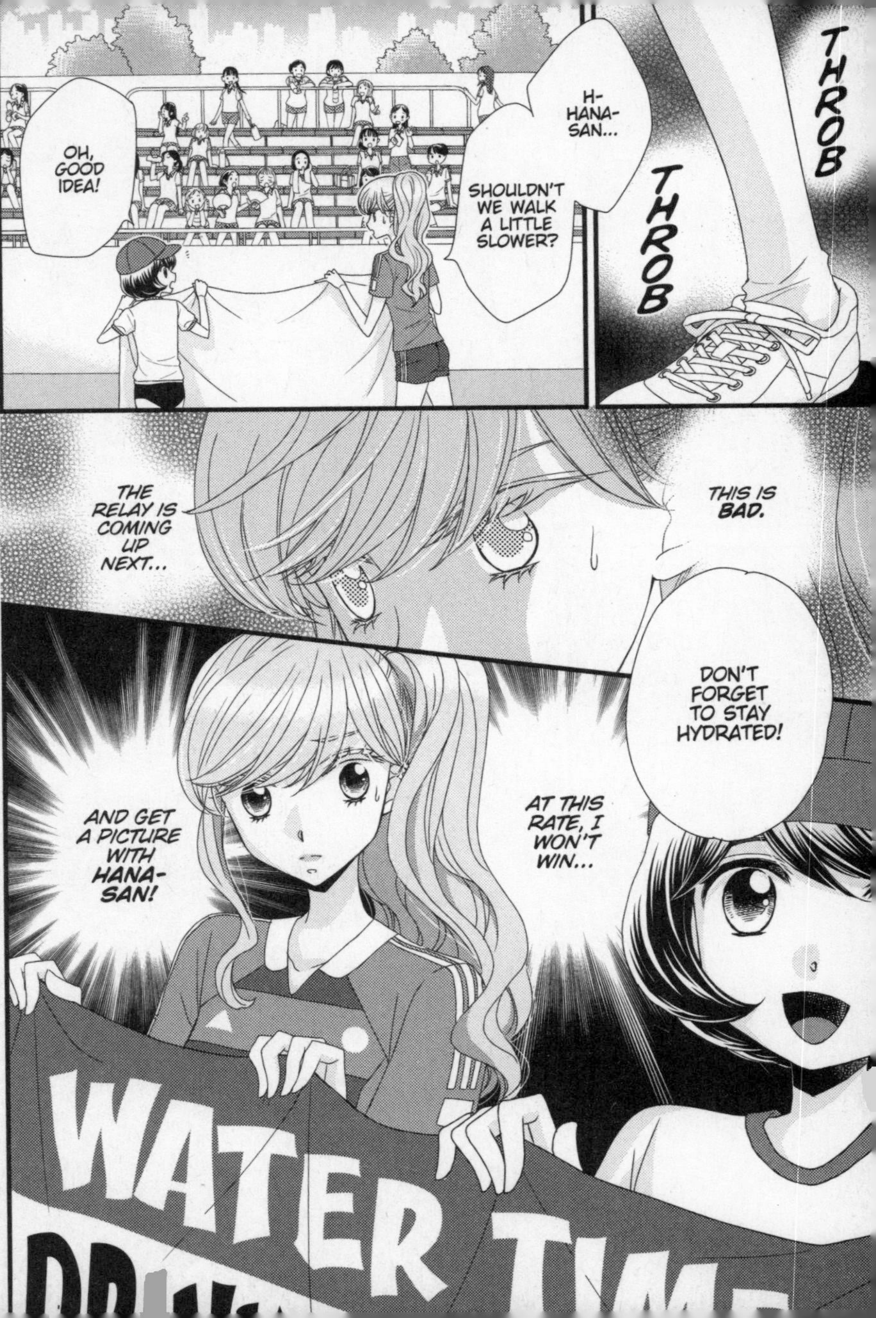
THROB
THROB
H-HANA-SAN...
SHOULDN'T WE WALK A LITTLE SLOWER?
OH, GOOD IDEA!
THIS IS BAD.
THE RELAY IS COMING UP NEXT...
DON'T FORGET TO STAY HYDRATED!
AT THIS RATE, I WON'T WIN...
AND GET A PICTURE WITH HANA-SAN!
WATER TIME

end

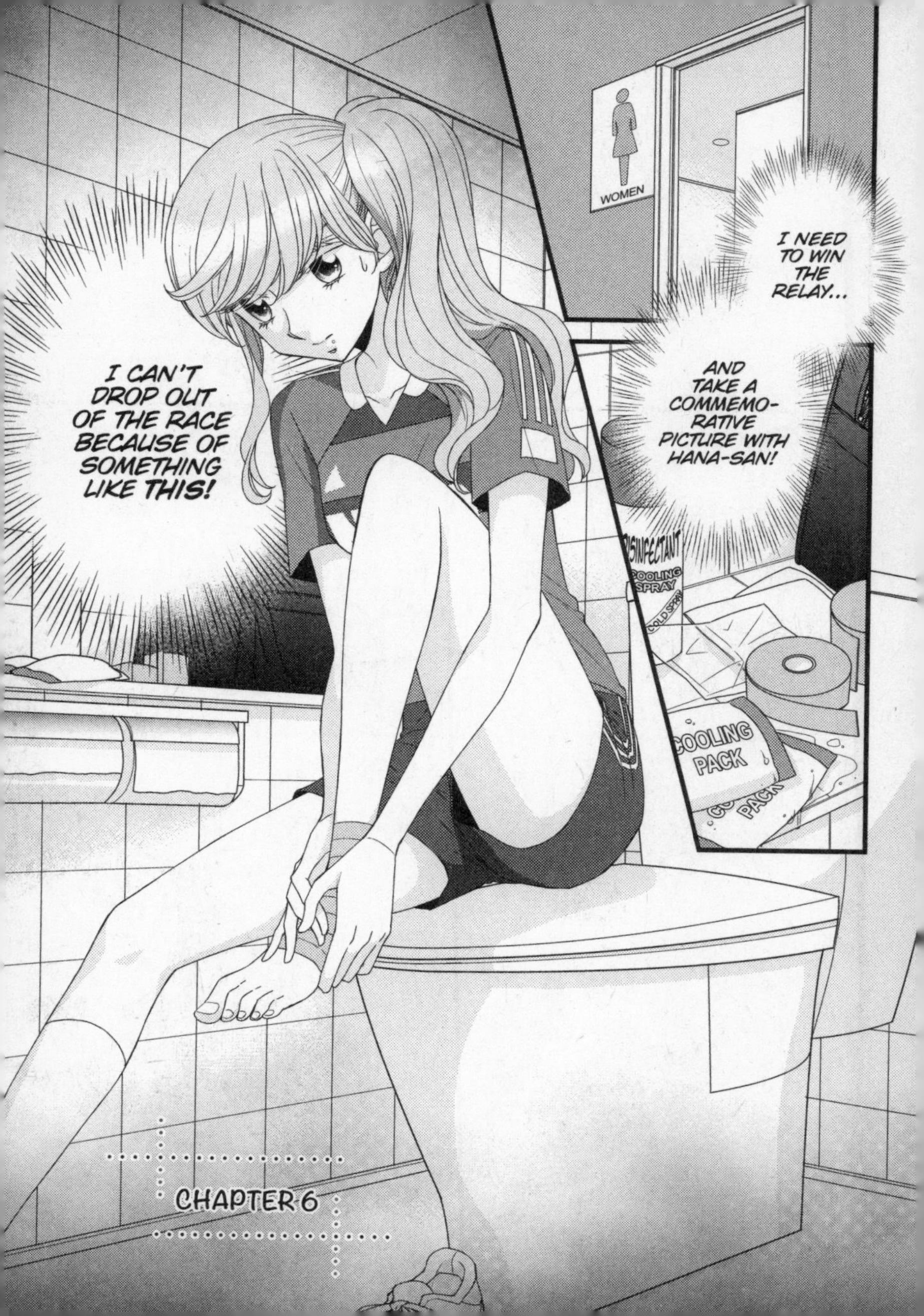
WOMEN
I NEED TO WIN THE RELAY...
AND TAKE A COMMEMO-RATIVE PICTURE WITH HANA-SAN!
I CAN'T DROP OUT OF THE RACE BECAUSE OF SOMETHING LIKE THIS!
DISINFECTANT
COOLING SPRAY
COLD SPRAY
COOLING PACK
PACK
CHAPTER 6

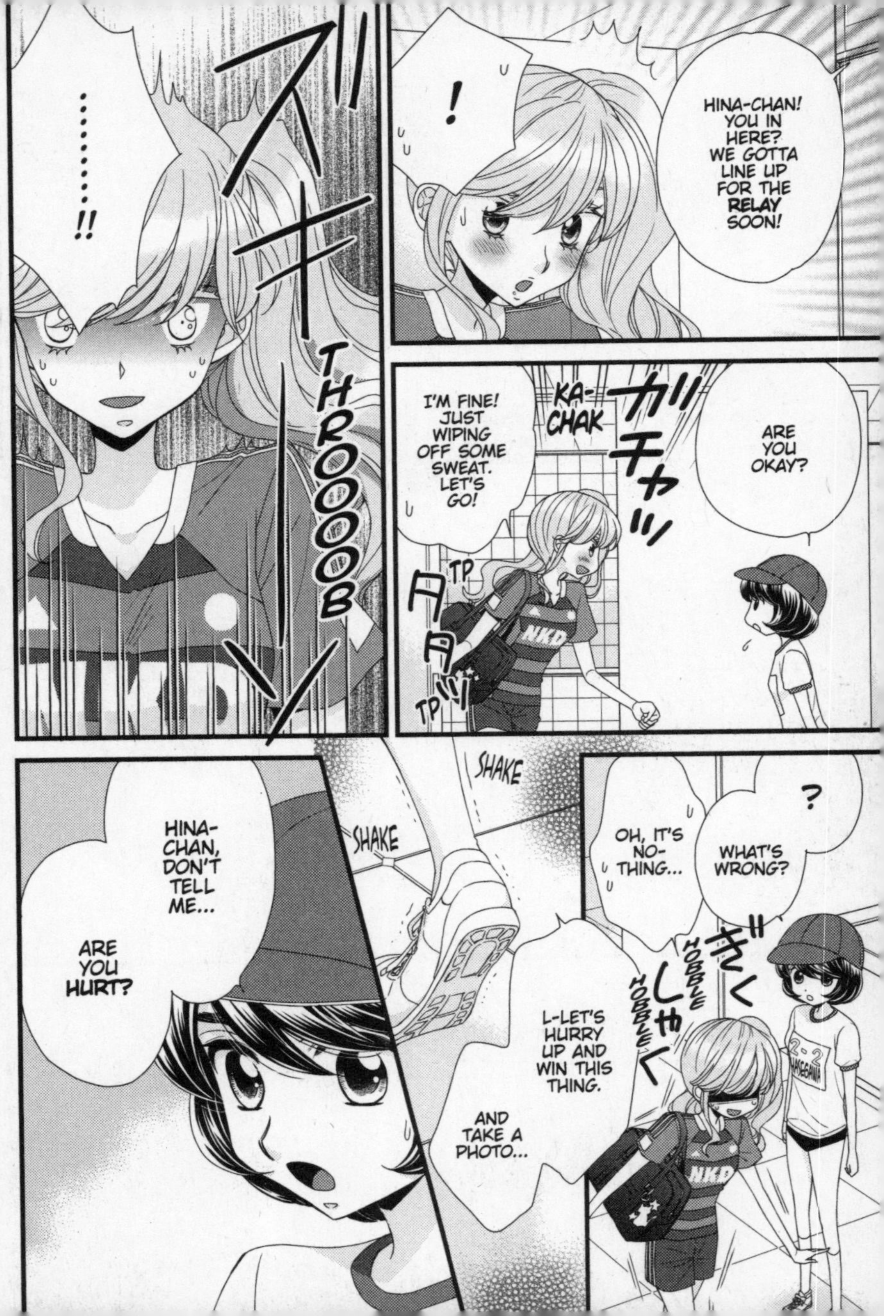
HINA-CHAN! YOU IN HERE? WE GOTTA LINE UP FOR THE RELAY SOON!
!
ARE YOU OKAY?
KA-CHAK
I'M FINE! JUST WIPING OFF SOME SWEAT. LET'S GO!
TP TP
......!!
THROOOOOB
?
WHAT'S WRONG?
OH, IT'S NO-THING...
HOBBLE HOBBLE
L-LET'S HURRY UP AND WIN THIS THING.
AND TAKE A PHOTO...
SHAKE
SHAKE
HINA-CHAN, DON'T TELL ME...
ARE YOU HURT?

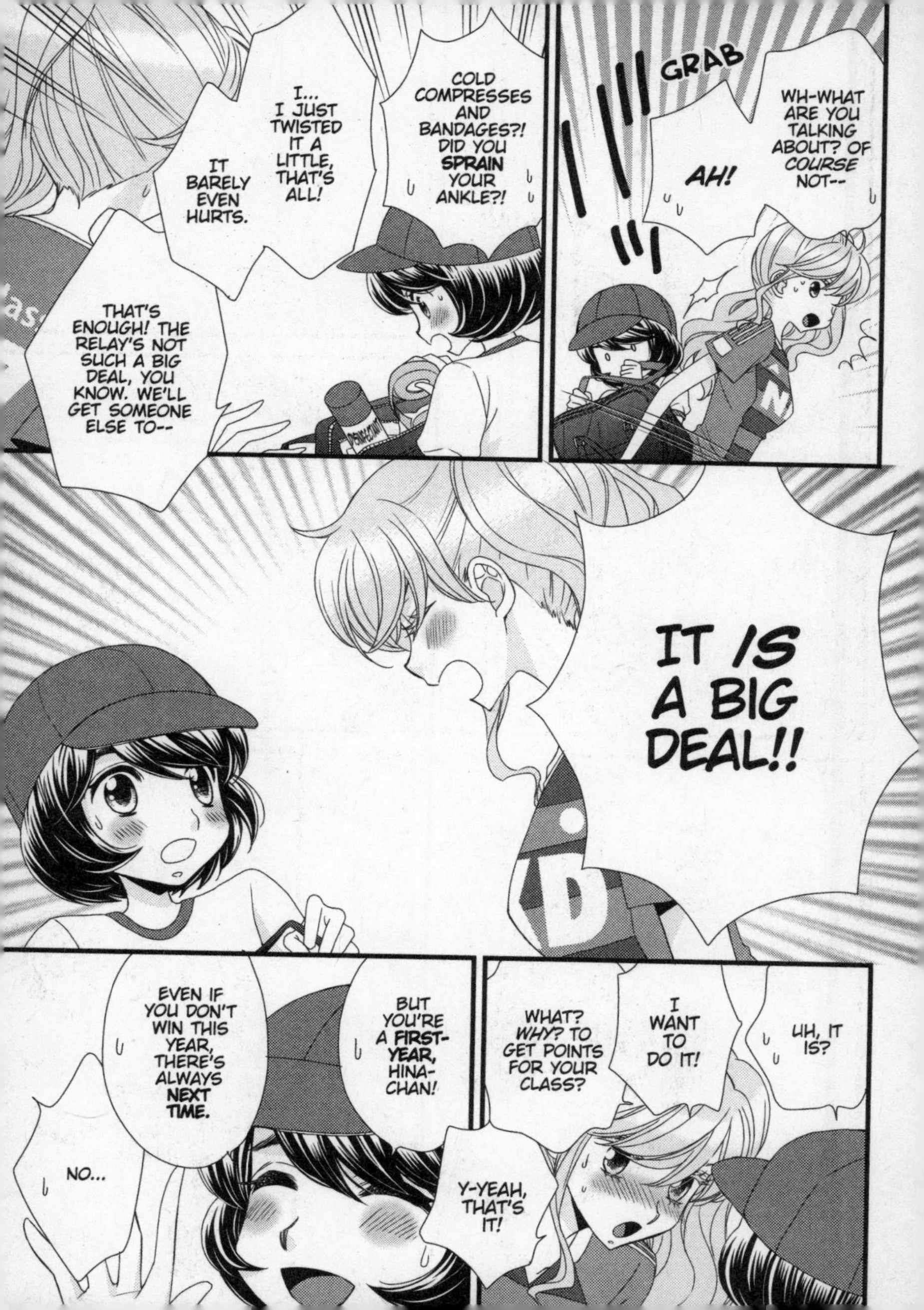

WH-WHAT ARE YOU TALKING ABOUT? OF COURSE NOT--
GRAB
AH!
COLD COMPRESSES AND BANDAGES?! DID YOU SPRAIN YOUR ANKLE?!
I... I JUST TWISTED IT A LITTLE, THAT'S ALL!
IT BARELY EVEN HURTS.
THAT'S ENOUGH! THE RELAY'S NOT SUCH A BIG DEAL, YOU KNOW. WE'LL GET SOMEONE ELSE TO--
IT IS A BIG DEAL!!
UH, IT IS?
I WANT TO DO IT!
WHAT? WHY? TO GET POINTS FOR YOUR CLASS?
Y-YEAH, THAT'S IT!
BUT YOU'RE A FIRST-YEAR, HINA-CHAN!
EVEN IF YOU DON'T WIN THIS YEAR, THERE'S ALWAYS NEXT TIME.
NO...

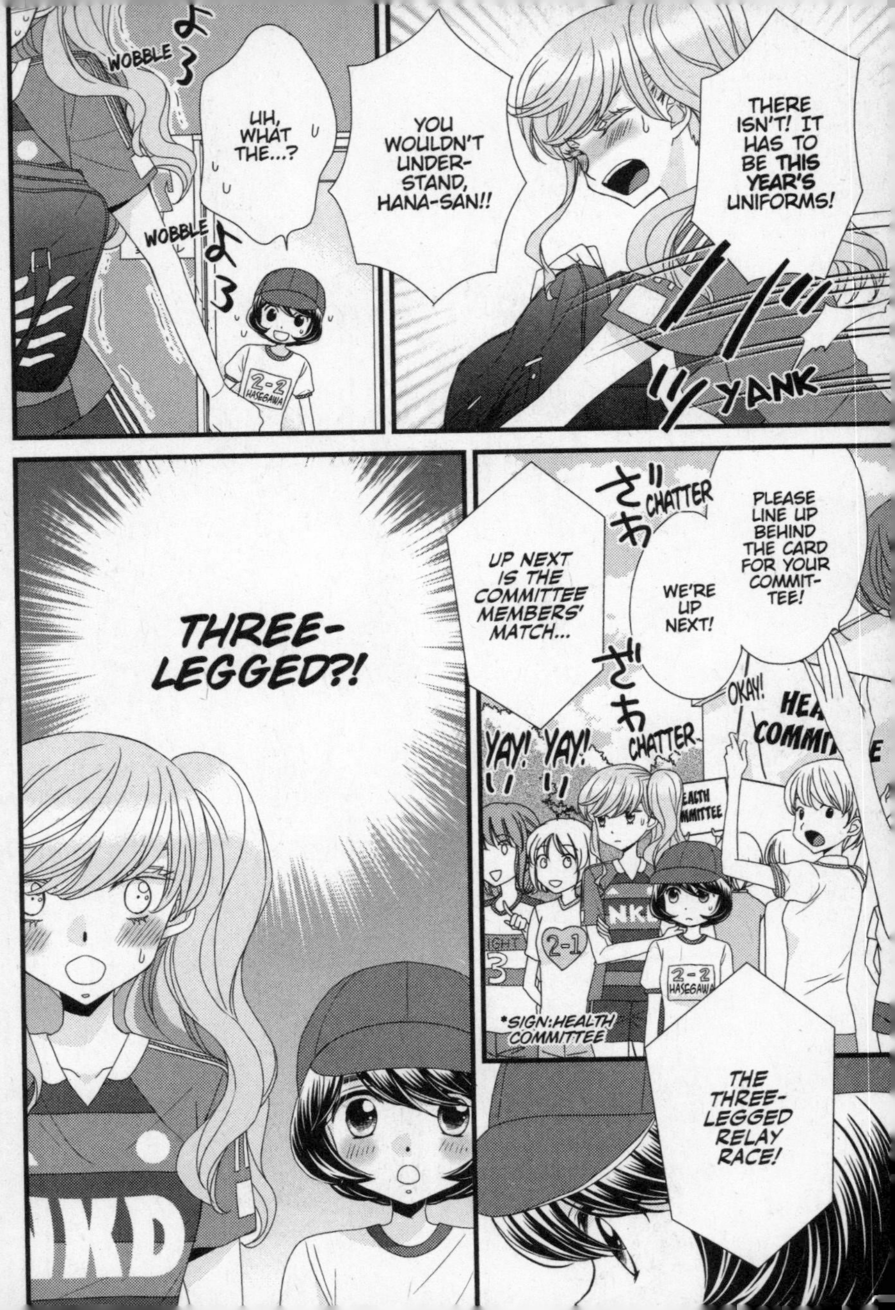
THERE ISN'T! IT HAS TO BE THIS YEAR'S UNIFORMS!
YANK
YOU WOULDN'T UNDERSTAND, HANA-SAN!!
UH, WHAT THE...?
WOBBLE
WOBBLE
PLEASE LINE UP BEHIND THE CARD FOR YOUR COMMITTEE!
WE'RE UP NEXT!
CHATTER
UP NEXT IS THE COMMITTEE MEMBERS' MATCH...
CHATTER
OKAY!
YAY! YAY!
HEALTH COMMITTEE
*SIGN:HEALTH COMMITTEE
THE THREE-LEGGED RELAY RACE!
THREE-LEGGED?!

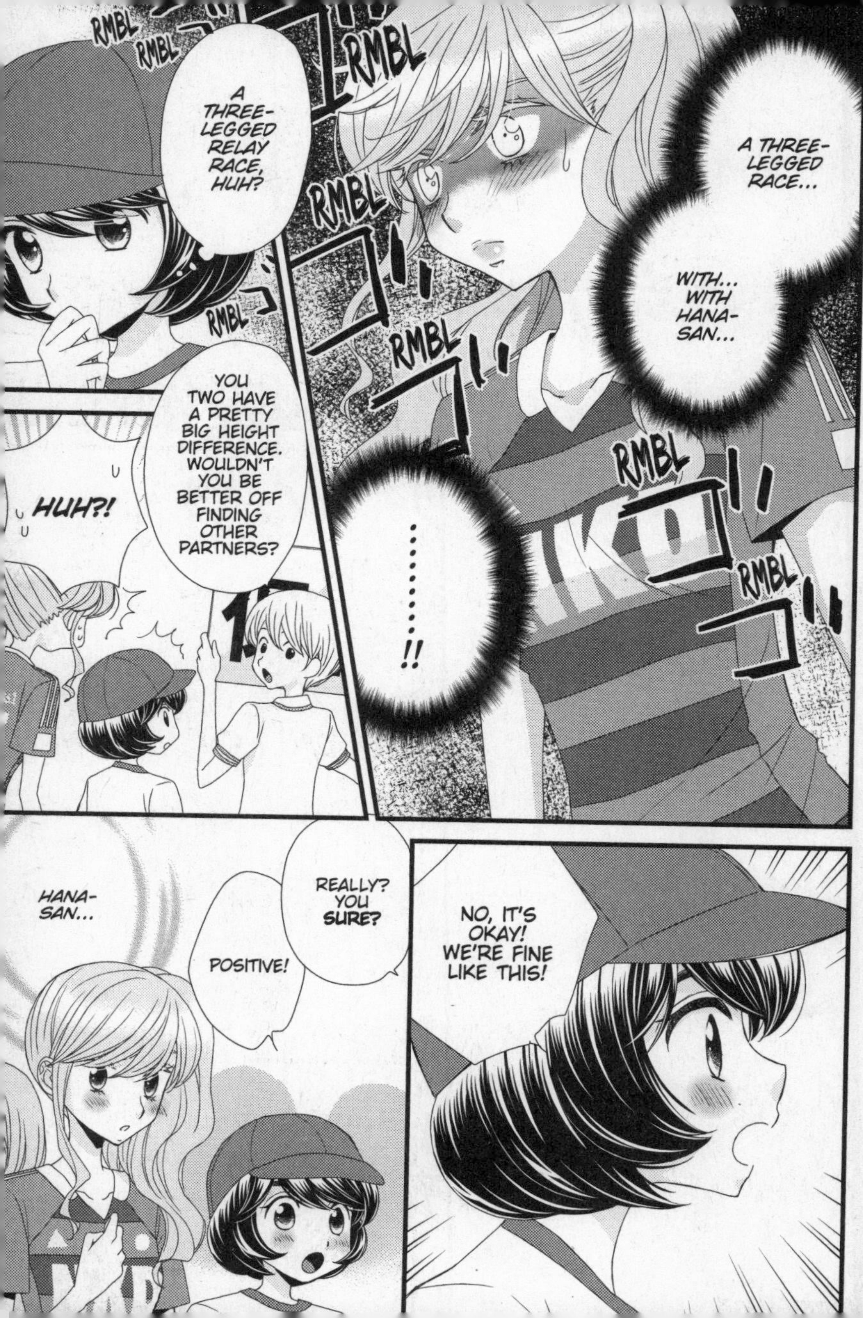
RMBL
A THREE-LEGGED RACE...
WITH... WITH HANA-SAN...
RMBL
RMBL
RMBL
RMBL
......!!
RMBL
RMBL
A THREE-LEGGED RELAY RACE, HUH?
RMBL
YOU TWO HAVE A PRETTY BIG HEIGHT DIFFERENCE. WOULDN'T YOU BE BETTER OFF FINDING OTHER PARTNERS?
HUH?!
NO, IT'S OKAY! WE'RE FINE LIKE THIS!
REALLY? YOU SURE?
POSITIVE!
HANA-SAN...

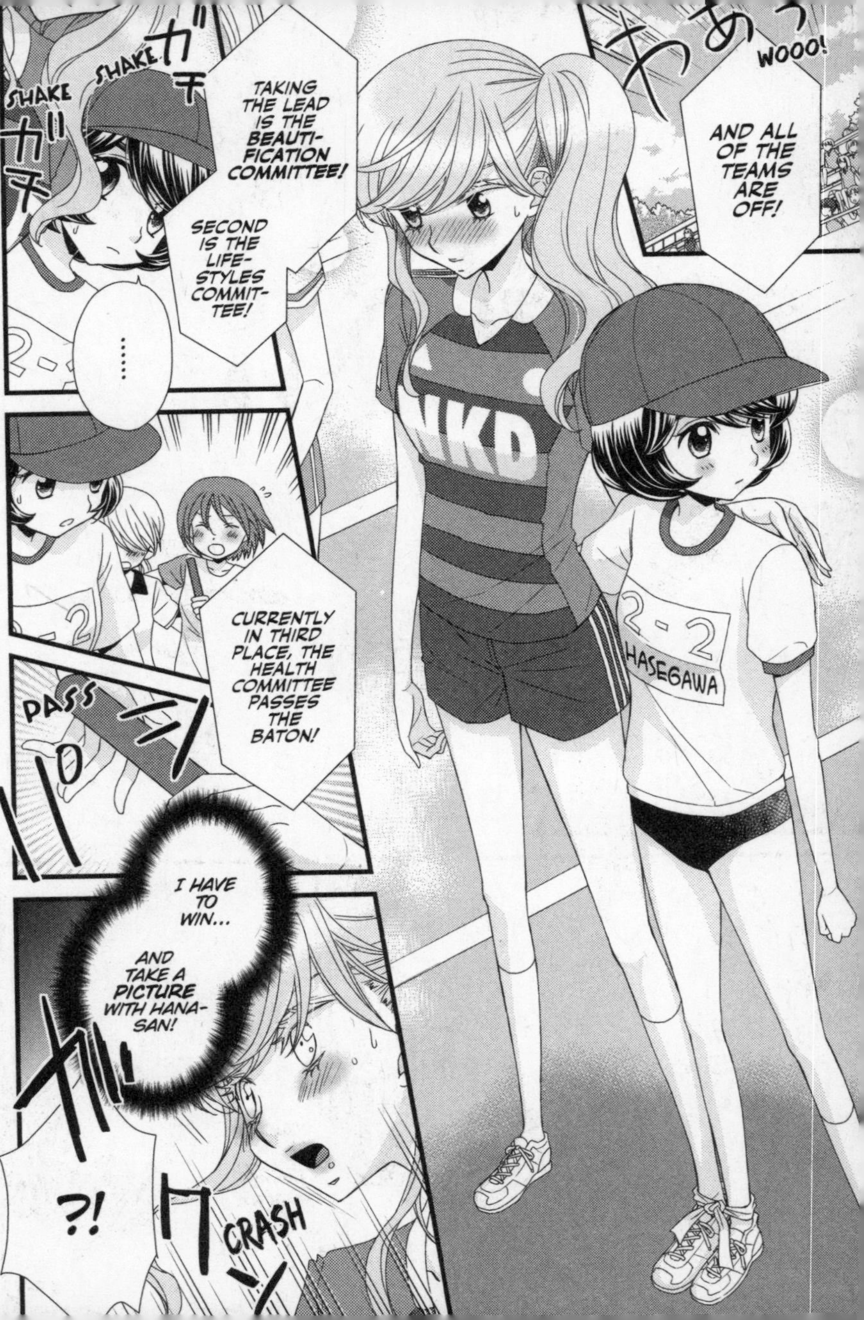
WOOO!
AND ALL OF THE TEAMS ARE OFF!
TAKING THE LEAD IS THE BEAUTIFICATION COMMITTEE!
SECOND IS THE LIFESTYLES COMMITTEE!
SHAKE
SHAKE
......
CURRENTLY IN THIRD PLACE, THE HEALTH COMMITTEE PASSES THE BATON!
PASS
I HAVE TO WIN...
AND TAKE A PICTURE WITH HANA-SAN!
?!
CRASH

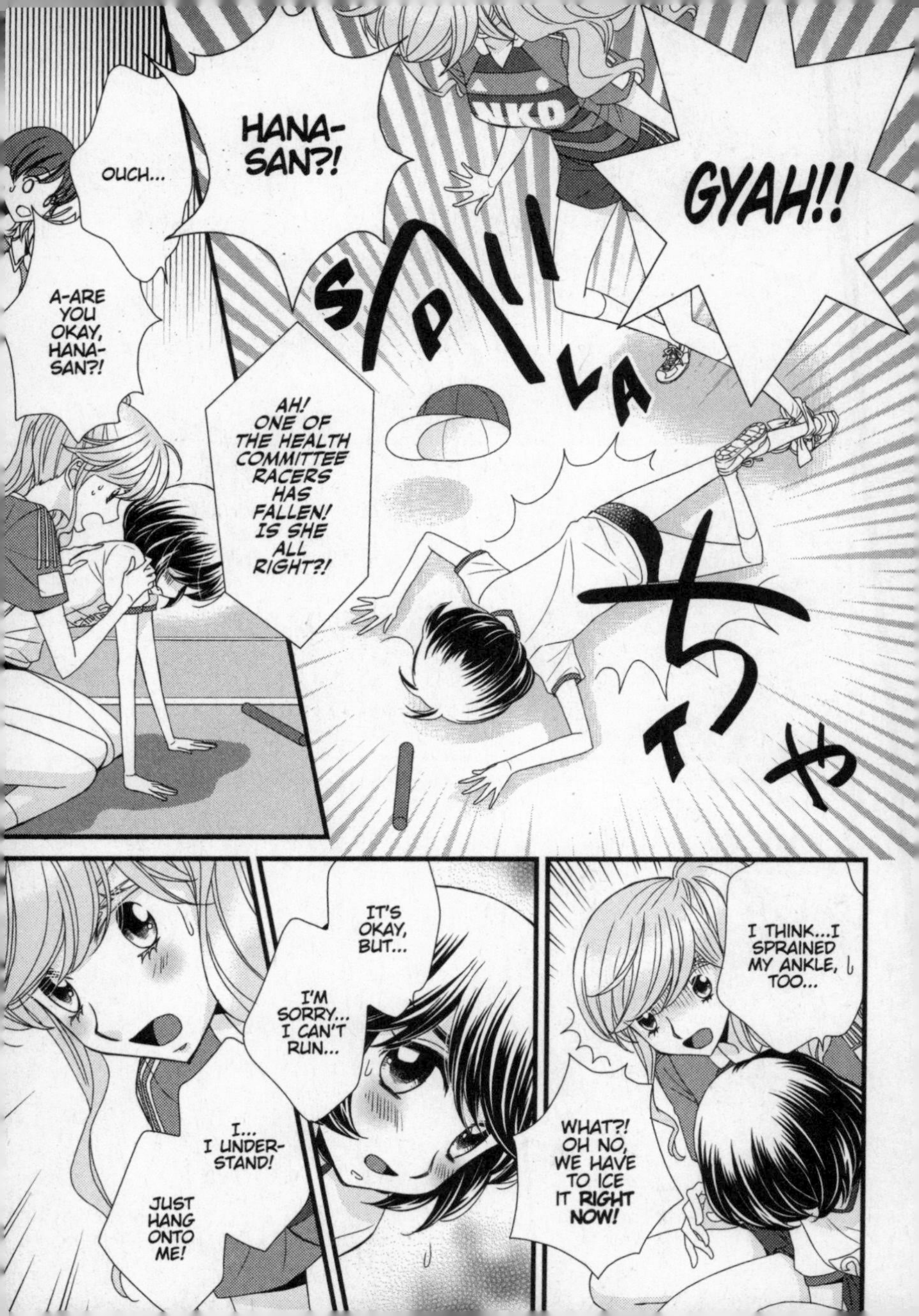
GYAH!!
SPLAT
ちや
HANA-SAN?!
AH! ONE OF THE HEALTH COMMITTEE RACERS HAS FALLEN! IS SHE ALL RIGHT?!
OUCH...
A-ARE YOU OKAY, HANA-SAN?!
I THINK...I SPRAINED MY ANKLE, TOO...
WHAT?! OH NO, WE HAVE TO ICE IT RIGHT NOW!
IT'S OKAY, BUT...
I'M SORRY... I CAN'T RUN...
I... I UNDERSTAND!
JUST HANG ONTO ME!

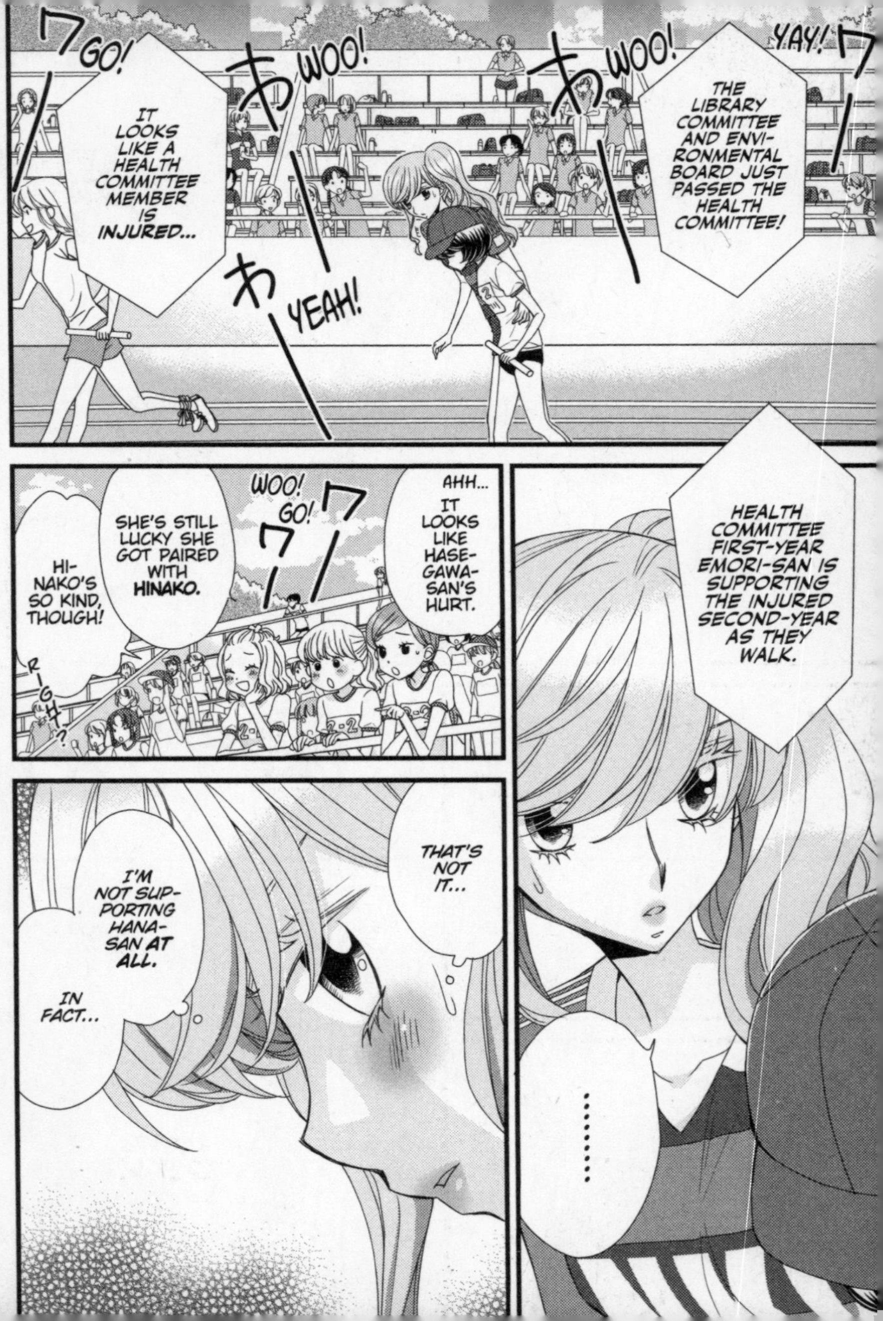

ワ
YAY!
THE LIBRARY COMMITTEE AND ENVIRONMENTAL BOARD JUST PASSED THE HEALTH COMMITTEE!
わ
WOO!
わ
YEAH!
わ
WOO!
IT LOOKS LIKE A HEALTH COMMITTEE MEMBER IS INJURED...
ワ
GO!
HEALTH COMMITTEE FIRST-YEAR EMORI-SAN IS SUPPORTING THE INJURED SECOND-YEAR AS THEY WALK.
....
AHH... IT LOOKS LIKE HASEGAWA-SAN'S HURT.
ワー
ワー
WOO! GO!
SHE'S STILL LUCKY SHE GOT PAIRED WITH HINAKO.
HINAKO'S SO KIND, THOUGH!
RIGHT?
THAT'S NOT IT...
I'M NOT SUPPORTING HANA-SAN AT ALL.
IN FACT...

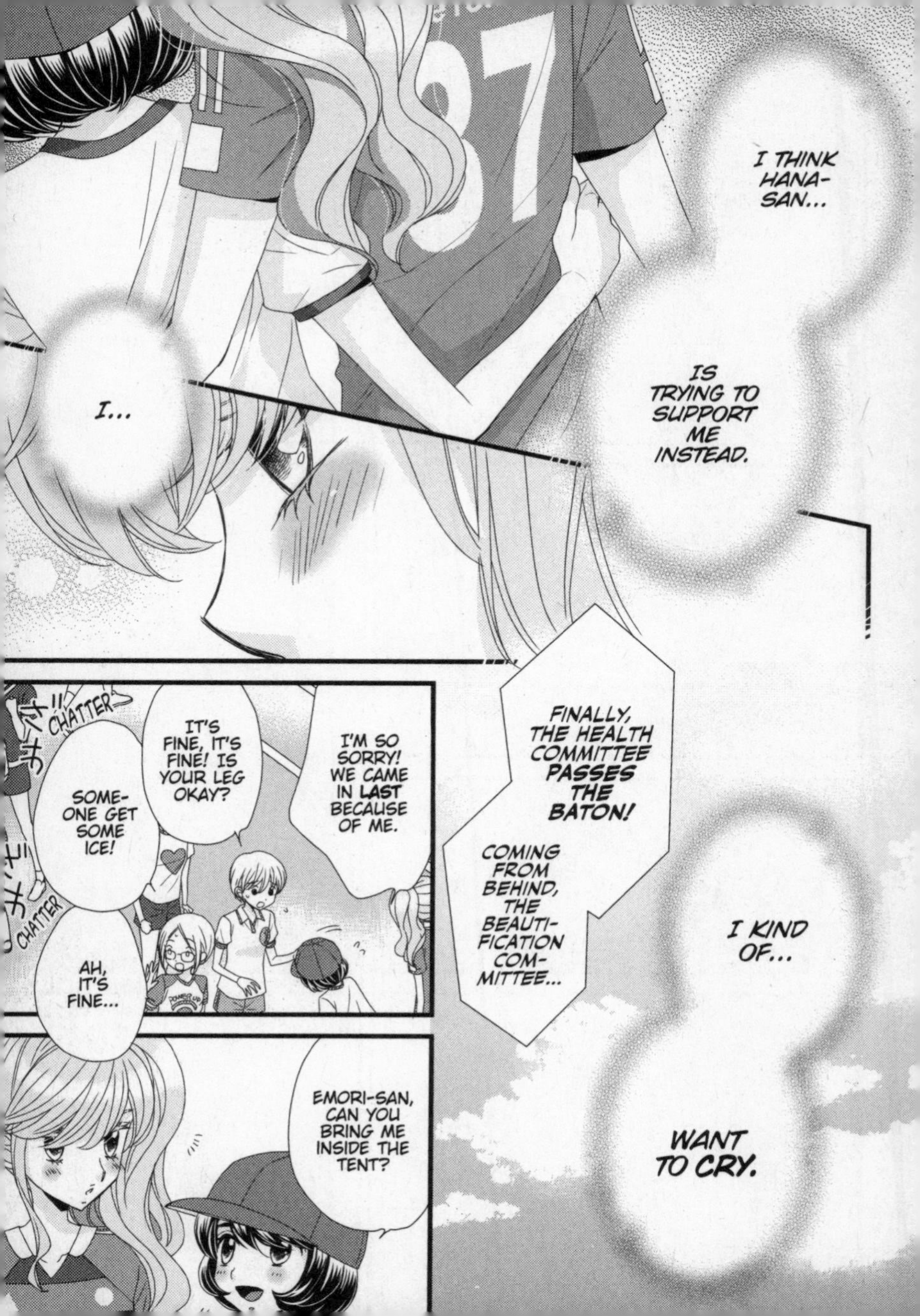
I THINK HANA-SAN...
IS TRYING TO SUPPORT ME INSTEAD.
I...
FINALLY, THE HEALTH COMMITTEE PASSES THE BATON!
COMING FROM BEHIND, THE BEAUTIFICATION COMMITTEE...
I KIND OF...
WANT TO CRY.
I'M SO SORRY! WE CAME IN LAST BECAUSE OF ME.
IT'S FINE, IT'S FINE! IS YOUR LEG OKAY?
SOME-ONE GET SOME ICE!
CHATTER
CHATTER
AH, IT'S FINE...
EMORI-SAN, CAN YOU BRING ME INSIDE THE TENT?

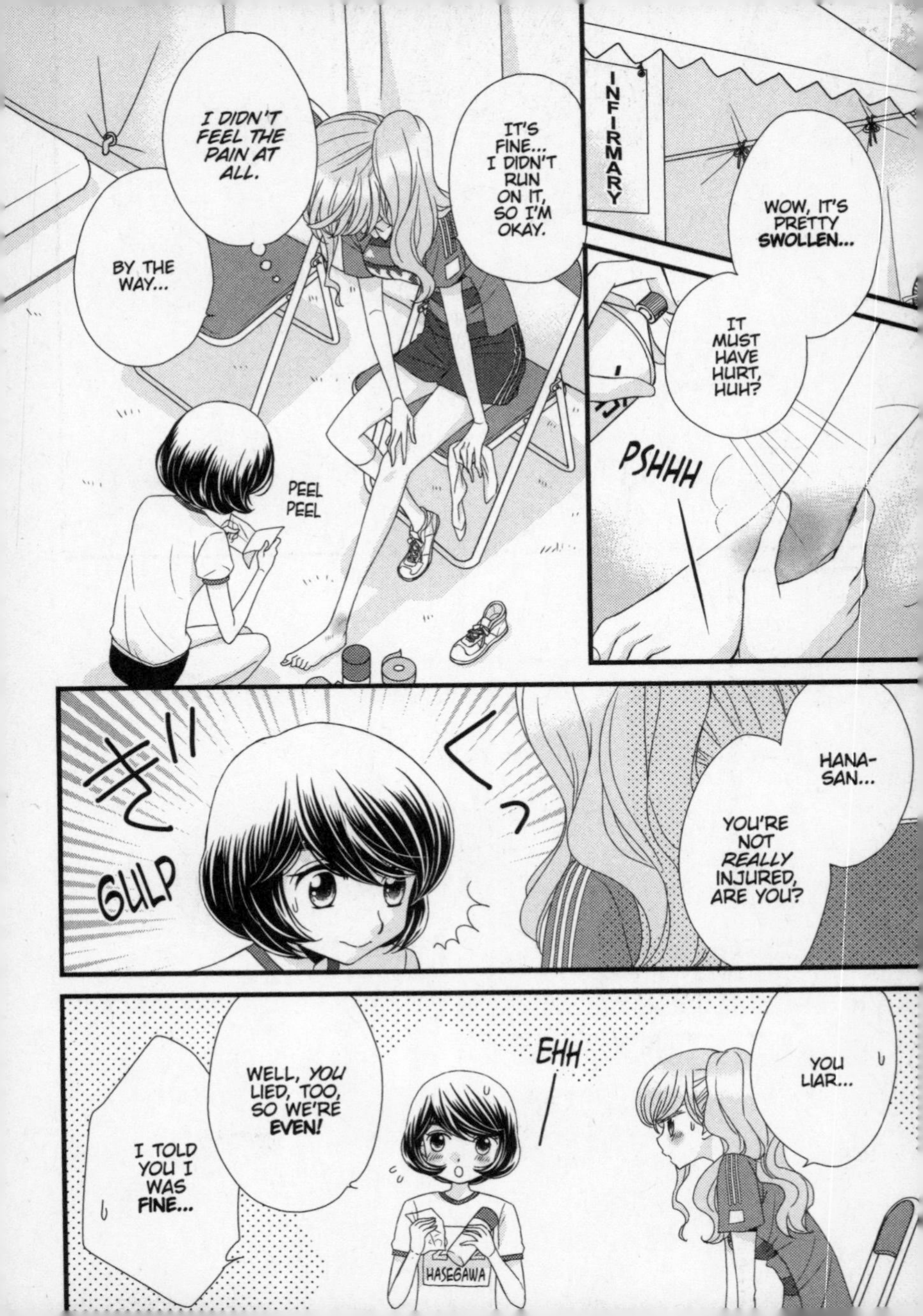
INFIRMARY
WOW, IT'S PRETTY SWOLLEN...
IT MUST HAVE HURT, HUH?
PSHHH
IT'S FINE... I DIDN'T RUN ON IT, SO I'M OKAY.
I DIDN'T FEEL THE PAIN AT ALL.
BY THE WAY...
PEEL PEEL
HANA-SAN...
YOU'RE NOT REALLY INJURED, ARE YOU?
GULP
YOU LIAR...
EHH
WELL, YOU LIED, TOO, SO WE'RE EVEN!
HASEGAWA
I TOLD YOU I WAS FINE...

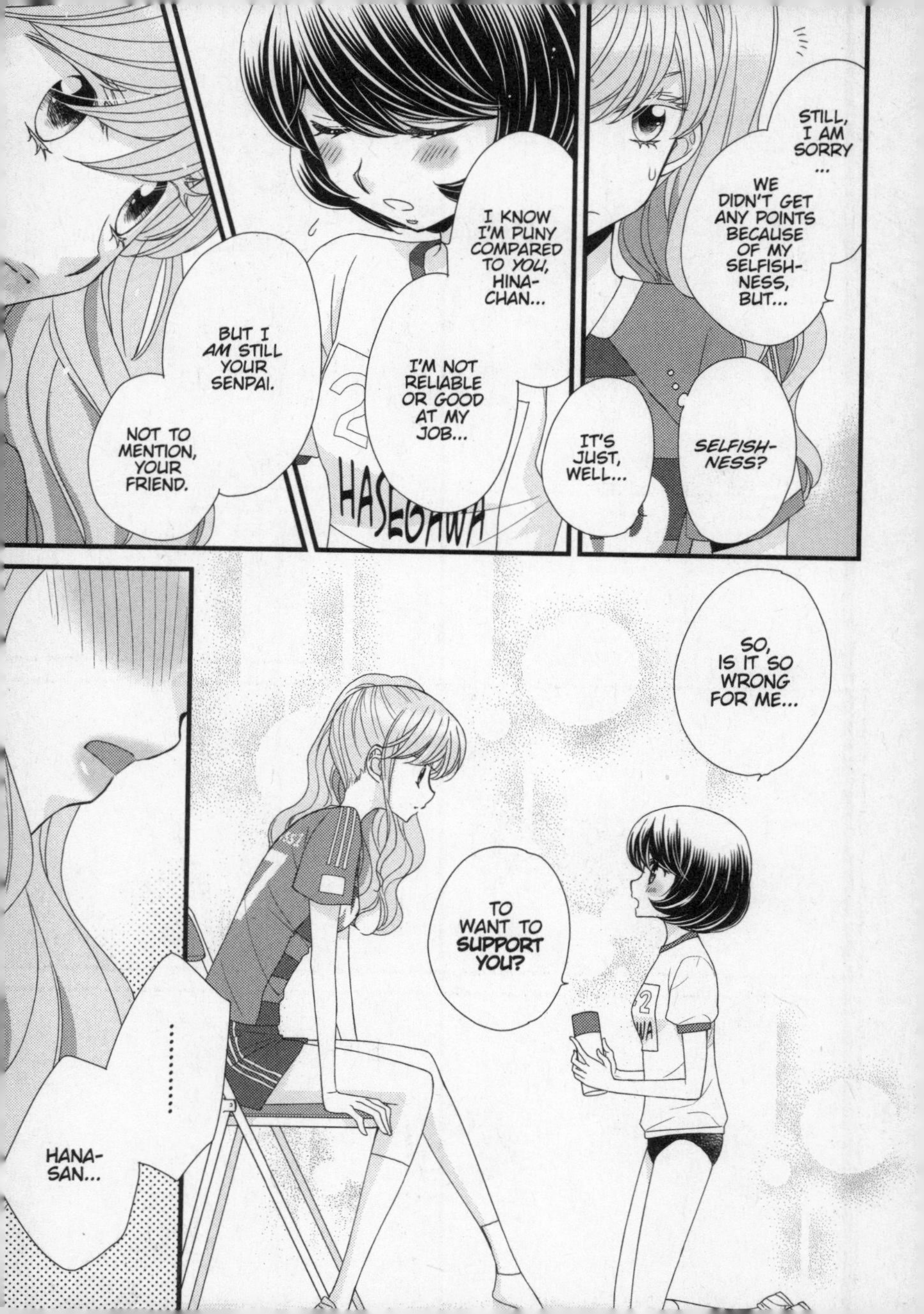
STILL, I AM SORRY ...
WE DIDN'T GET ANY POINTS BECAUSE OF MY SELFISHNESS, BUT...
SELFISHNESS?
IT'S JUST, WELL...
I KNOW I'M PUNY COMPARED TO *YOU*, HINA-CHAN...
I'M NOT RELIABLE OR GOOD AT MY JOB...
HASEGAWA
BUT I *AM* STILL YOUR SENPAI.
NOT TO MENTION, YOUR FRIEND.
SO, IS IT SO WRONG FOR ME...
TO WANT TO **SUPPORT YOU?**
......
HANA-SAN...

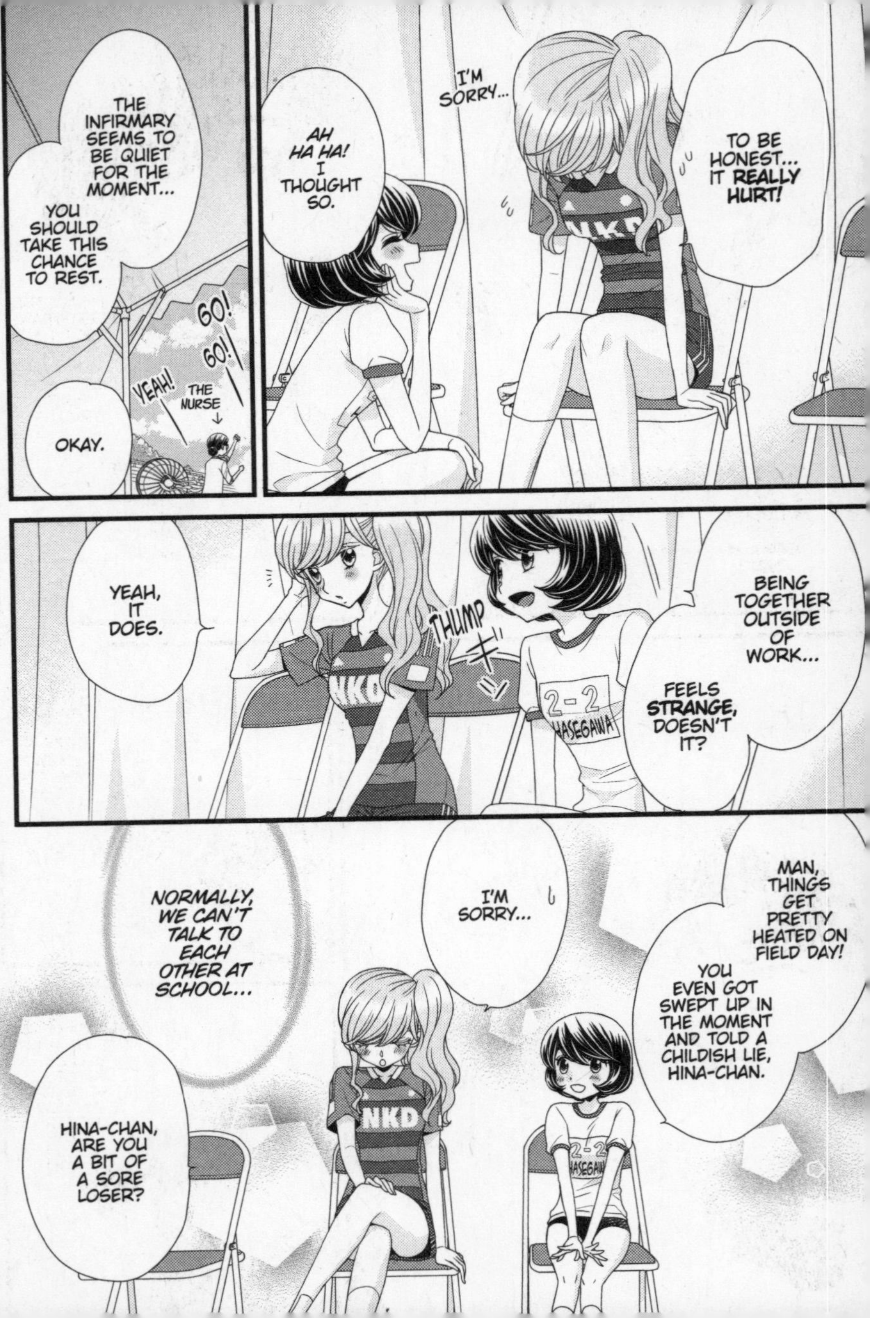

TO BE HONEST... IT REALLY HURT!
I'M SORRY...
AH HA HA! I THOUGHT SO.
THE INFIRMARY SEEMS TO BE QUIET FOR THE MOMENT...
YOU SHOULD TAKE THIS CHANCE TO REST.
GO! GO!
YEAH!
THE NURSE
OKAY.
BEING TOGETHER OUTSIDE OF WORK...
FEELS STRANGE, DOESN'T IT?
THUMP
YEAH, IT DOES.
MAN, THINGS GET PRETTY HEATED ON FIELD DAY!
YOU EVEN GOT SWEPT UP IN THE MOMENT AND TOLD A CHILDISH LIE, HINA-CHAN.
I'M SORRY...
NORMALLY, WE CAN'T TALK TO EACH OTHER AT SCHOOL...
HINA-CHAN, ARE YOU A BIT OF A SORE LOSER?

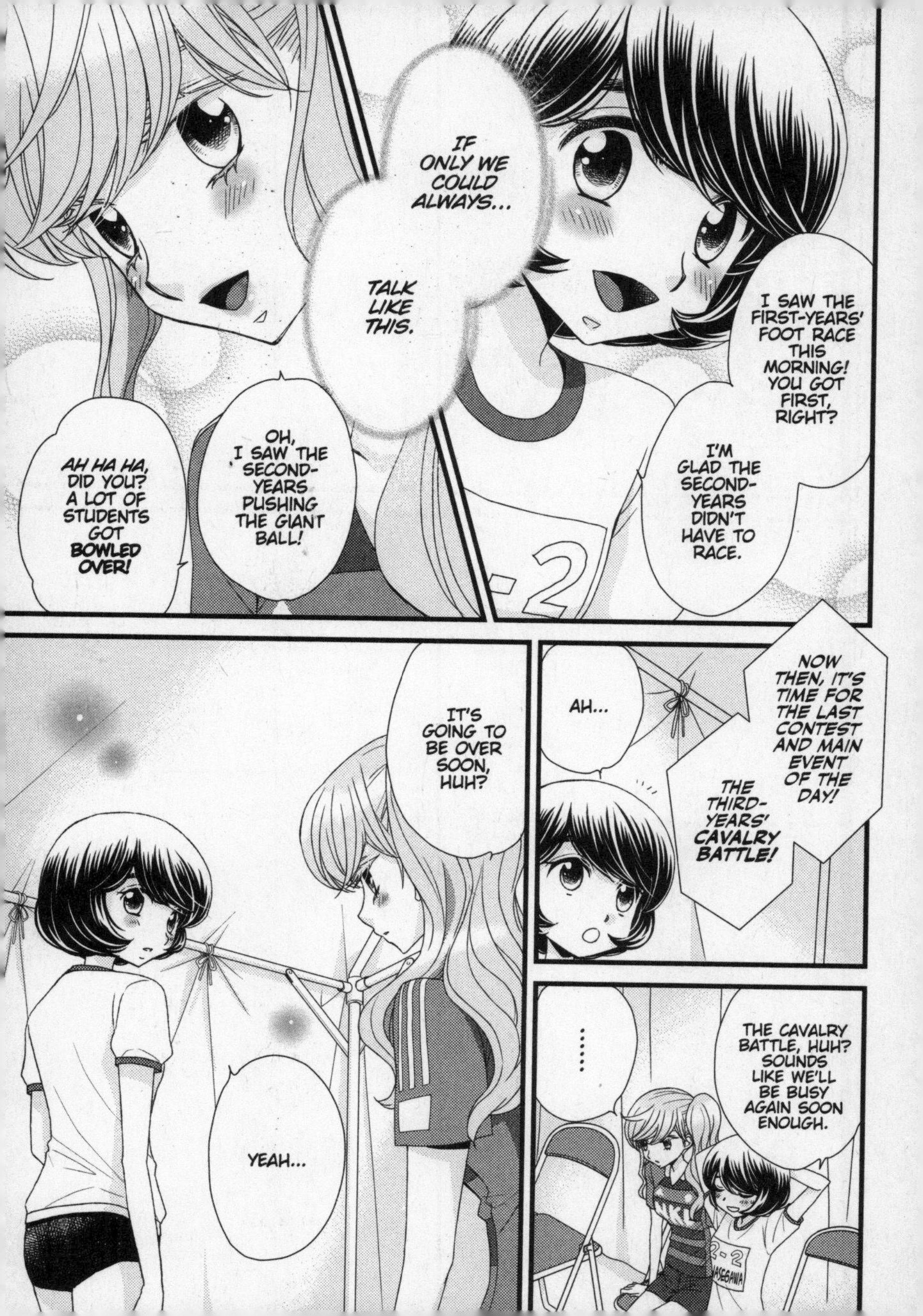

I SAW THE FIRST-YEARS' FOOT RACE THIS MORNING! YOU GOT FIRST, RIGHT?
I'M GLAD THE SECOND-YEARS DIDN'T HAVE TO RACE.
OH, I SAW THE SECOND-YEARS PUSHING THE GIANT BALL!
AH HA HA, DID YOU? A LOT OF STUDENTS GOT **BOWLED OVER!**
IF ONLY WE COULD ALWAYS...
TALK LIKE THIS.
NOW THEN, IT'S TIME FOR THE LAST CONTEST AND MAIN EVENT OF THE DAY!
THE THIRD-YEARS' **CAVALRY BATTLE!**
AH...
THE CAVALRY BATTLE, HUH? SOUNDS LIKE WE'LL BE BUSY AGAIN SOON ENOUGH.
......
IT'S GOING TO BE OVER SOON, HUH?
YEAH...

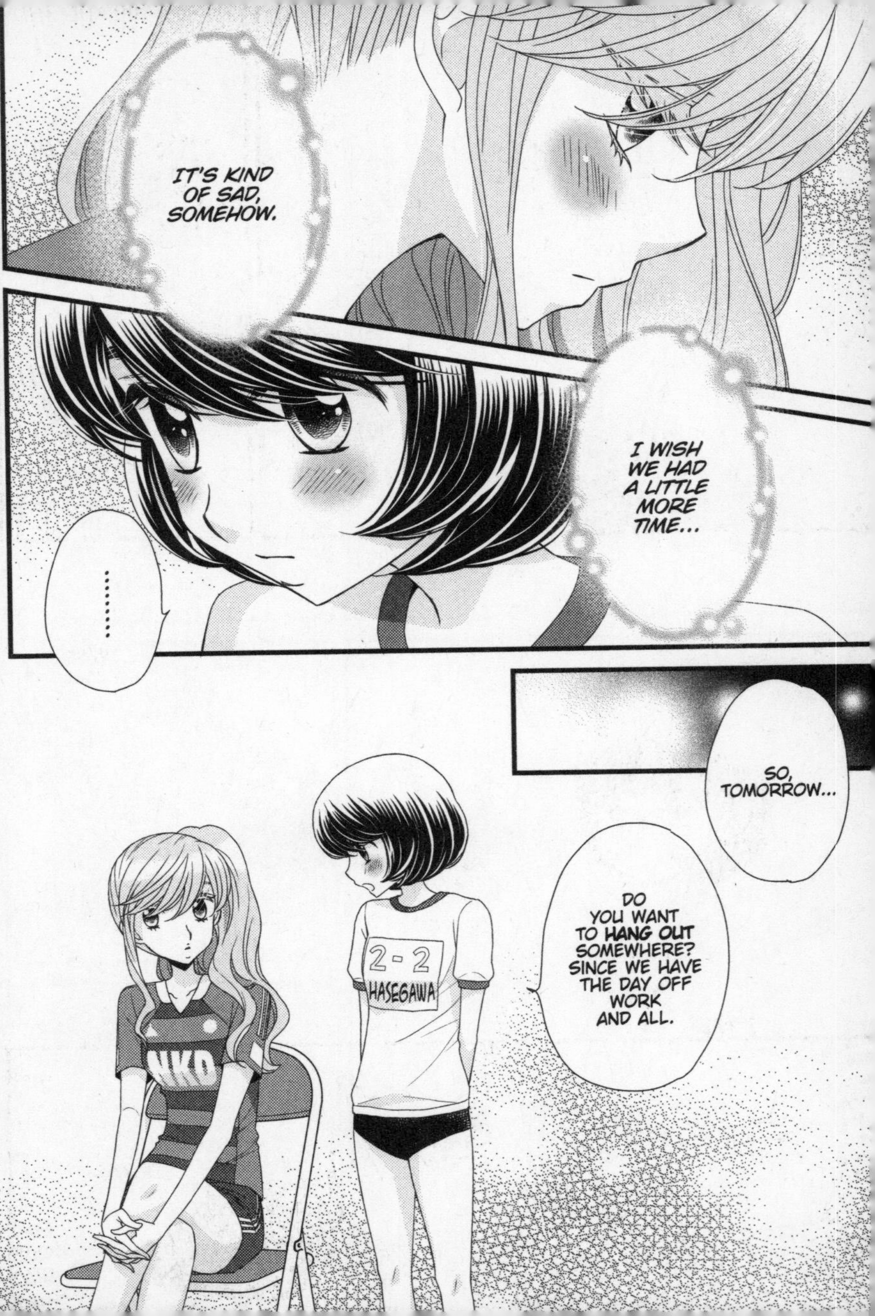
IT'S KIND OF SAD, SOMEHOW.
I WISH WE HAD A LITTLE MORE TIME...
......
SO, TOMORROW...
DO YOU WANT TO HANG OUT SOMEWHERE? SINCE WE HAVE THE DAY OFF WORK AND ALL.
2-2
HASEGAWA

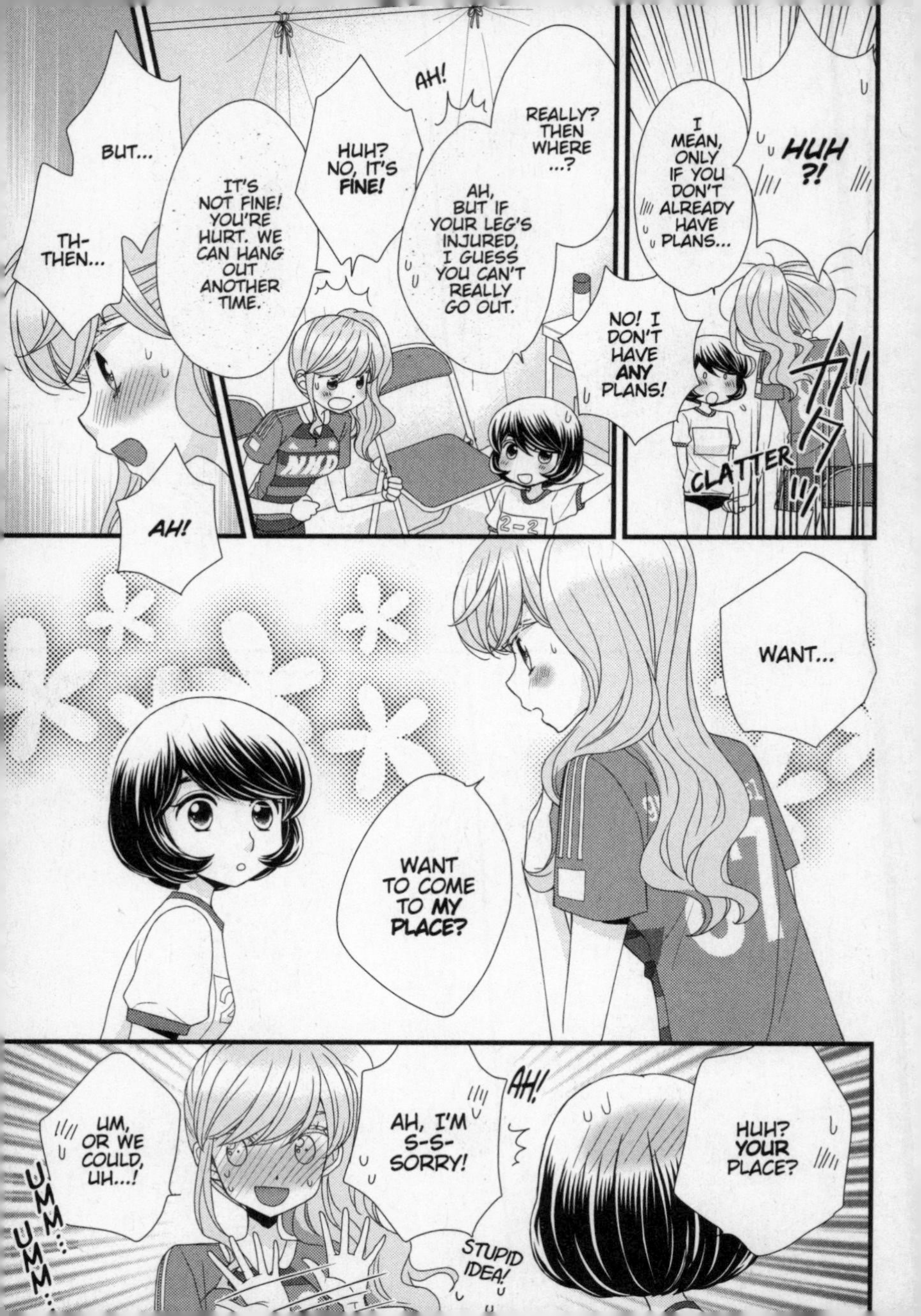
HUH ?!
I MEAN, ONLY IF YOU DON'T ALREADY HAVE PLANS...
NO! I DON'T HAVE ANY PLANS!
CLATTER
REALLY? THEN WHERE ...?
AH, BUT IF YOUR LEG'S INJURED, I GUESS YOU CAN'T REALLY GO OUT.
AH!
HUH? NO, IT'S FINE!
IT'S NOT FINE! YOU'RE HURT. WE CAN HANG OUT ANOTHER TIME.
BUT...
TH- THEN...
AH!
WANT...
WANT TO COME TO MY PLACE?
HUH? YOUR PLACE?
AH!
AH, I'M S-S-SORRY!
STUPID IDEA!
UM, OR WE COULD, UH...!
UMM... UMM...

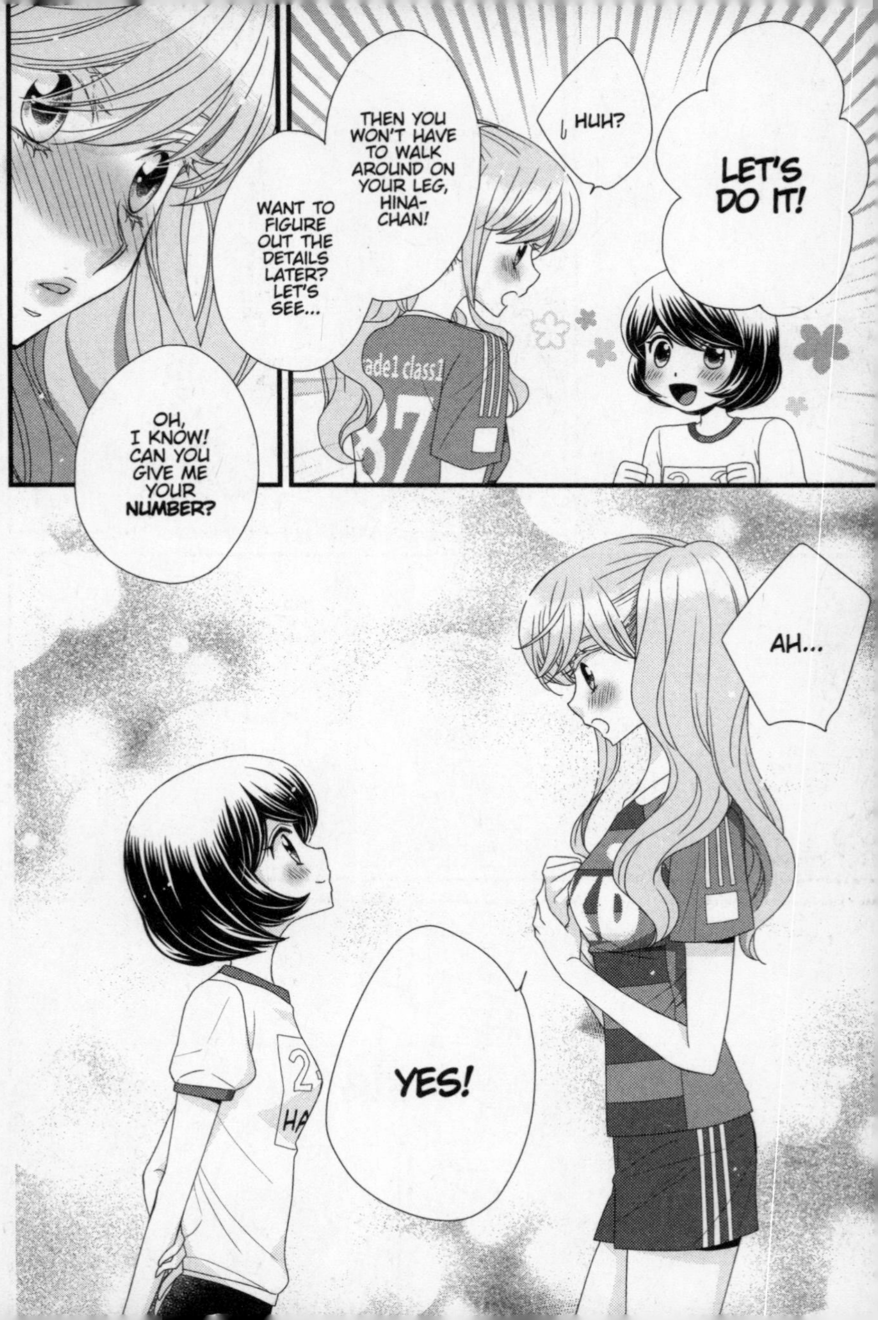
LET'S DO IT!
HUH?
THEN YOU WON'T HAVE TO WALK AROUND ON YOUR LEG, HINA-CHAN!
WANT TO FIGURE OUT THE DETAILS LATER? LET'S SEE...
OH, I KNOW! CAN YOU GIVE ME YOUR NUMBER?
AH...
YES!

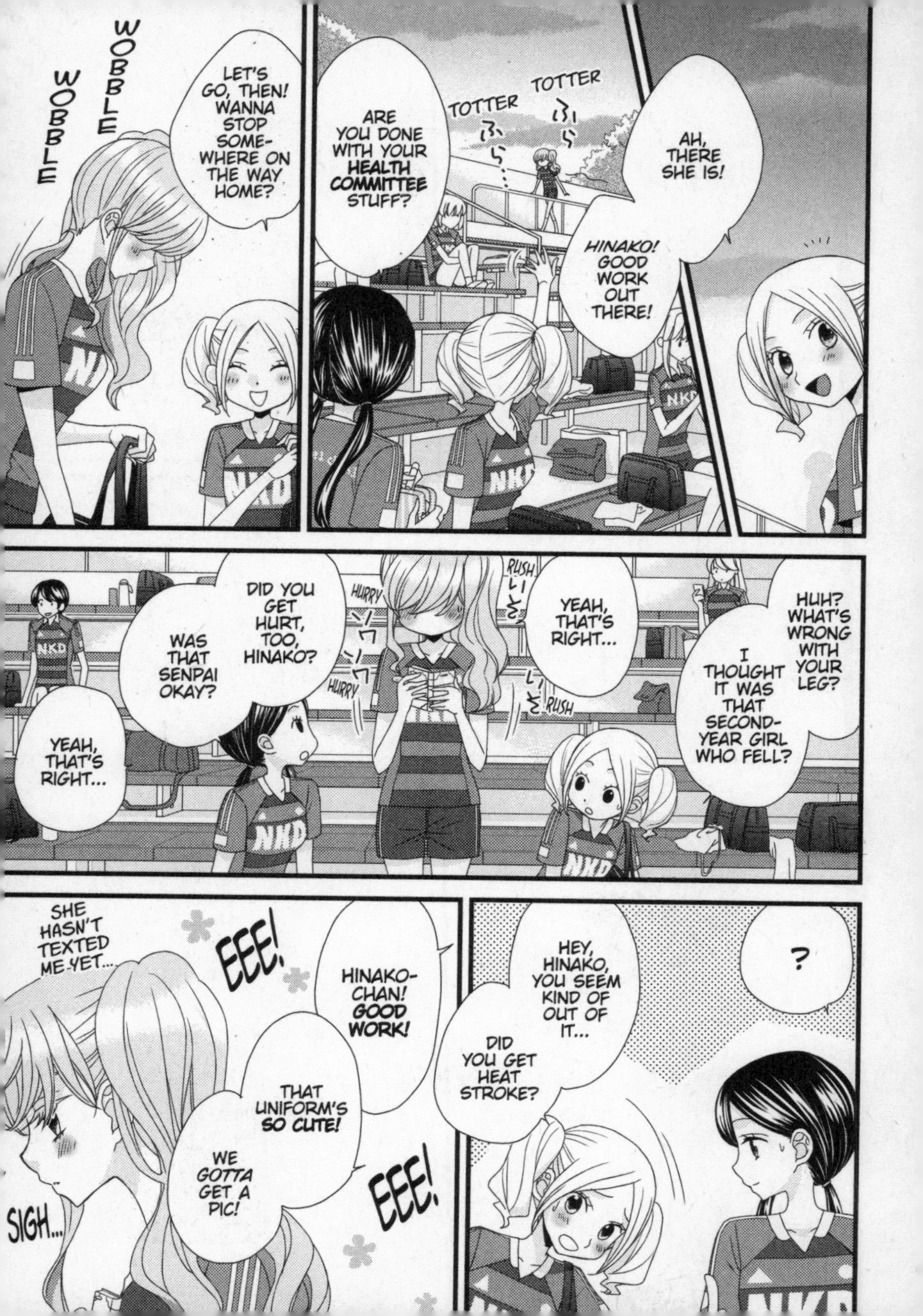
AH, THERE SHE IS!
HINAKO! GOOD WORK OUT THERE!
TOTTER TOTTER
TOTTER
ARE YOU DONE WITH YOUR **HEALTH COMMITTEE** STUFF?
LET'S GO, THEN! WANNA STOP SOME-WHERE ON THE WAY HOME?
WOBBLE WOBBLE
HUH? WHAT'S WRONG WITH YOUR LEG?
I THOUGHT IT WAS THAT SECOND-YEAR GIRL WHO FELL?
YEAH, THAT'S RIGHT...
RUSH
RUSH
HURRY
HURRY
DID YOU GET HURT, TOO, HINAKO?
WAS THAT SENPAI OKAY?
YEAH, THAT'S RIGHT...
?
HEY, HINAKO, YOU SEEM KIND OF OUT OF IT...
DID YOU GET HEAT STROKE?
HINAKO-CHAN! **GOOD WORK!**
EEE!
THAT UNIFORM'S **SO CUTE!**
WE GOTTA GET A PIC!
EEE!
SHE HASN'T TEXTED ME YET...
SIGH...

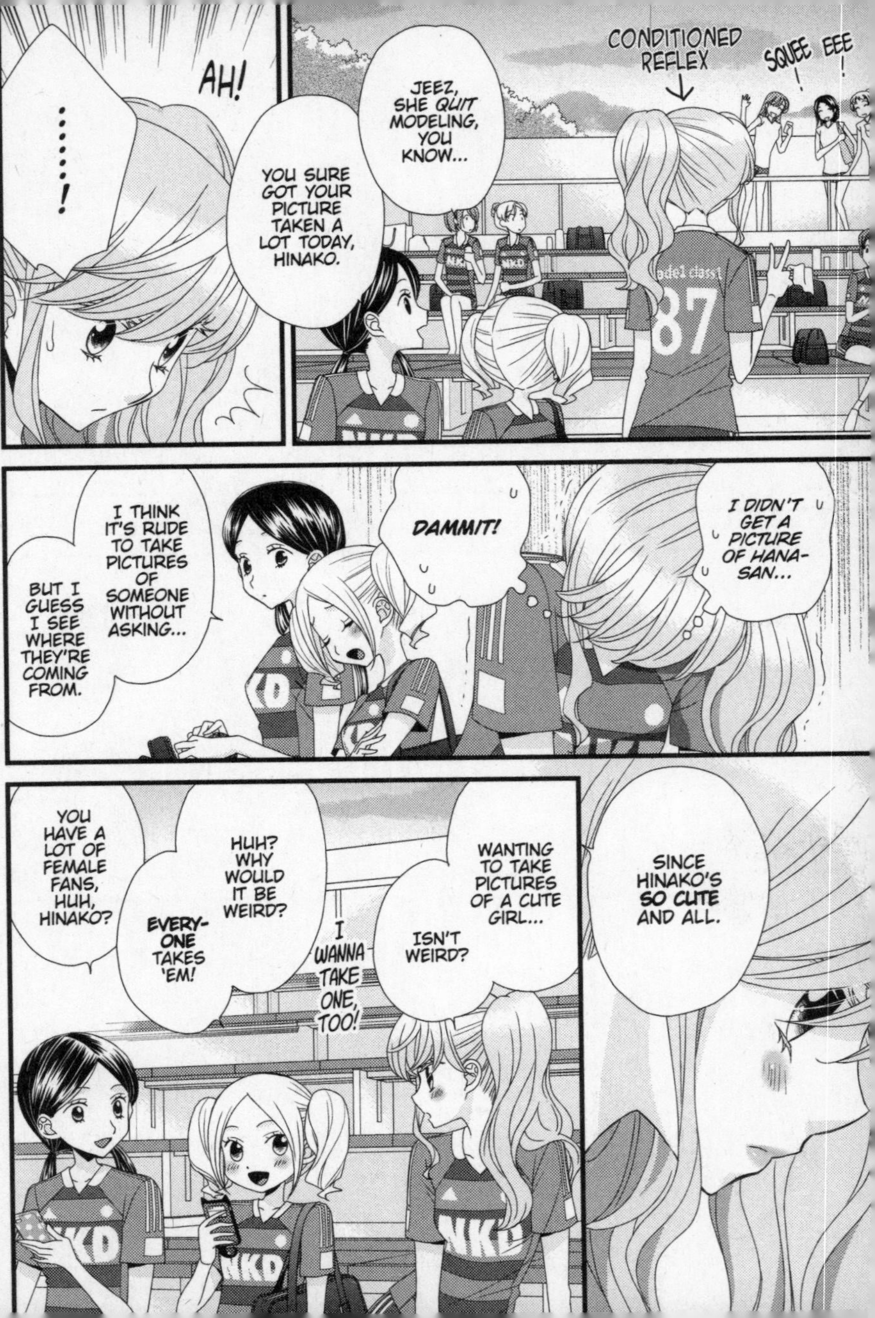
SQUEE EEE!
CONDITIONED REFLEX
JEEZ, SHE QUIT MODELING, YOU KNOW...
YOU SURE GOT YOUR PICTURE TAKEN A LOT TODAY, HINAKO.
AH!
......!
I DIDN'T GET A PICTURE OF HANA-SAN...
DAMMIT!
I THINK IT'S RUDE TO TAKE PICTURES OF SOMEONE WITHOUT ASKING...
BUT I GUESS I SEE WHERE THEY'RE COMING FROM.
SINCE HINAKO'S SO CUTE AND ALL.
WANTING TO TAKE PICTURES OF A CUTE GIRL...
ISN'T WEIRD?
I WANNA TAKE ONE, TOO!
HUH? WHY WOULD IT BE WEIRD?
EVERYONE TAKES 'EM!
YOU HAVE A LOT OF FEMALE FANS, HUH, HINAKO?

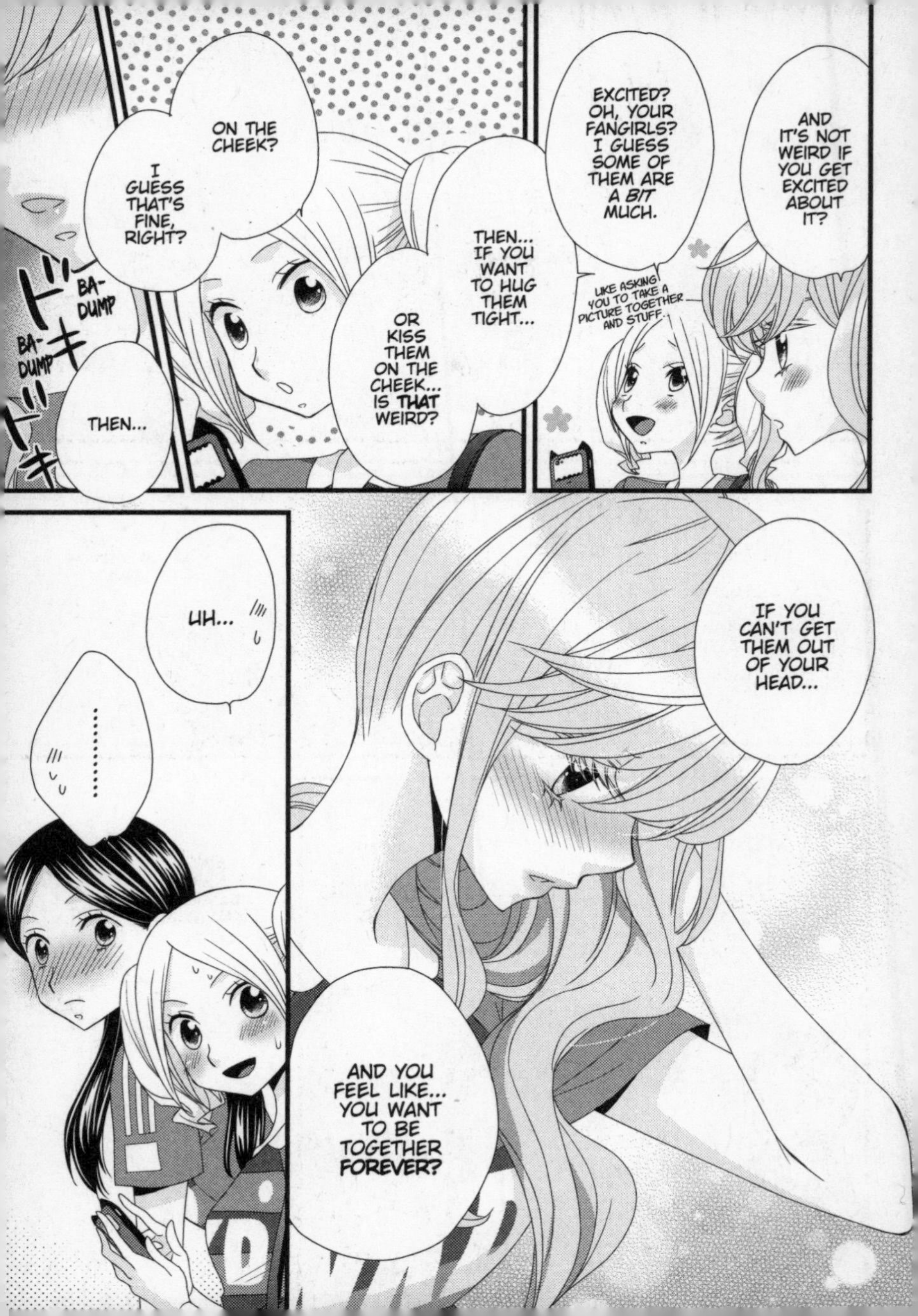
AND IT'S NOT WEIRD IF YOU GET EXCITED ABOUT IT?
EXCITED? OH, YOUR FANGIRLS? I GUESS SOME OF THEM ARE A *BIT* MUCH.
LIKE ASKING YOU TO TAKE A PICTURE TOGETHER AND STUFF...
THEN... IF YOU WANT TO HUG THEM TIGHT...
OR KISS THEM ON THE CHEEK... IS **THAT** WEIRD?
ON THE CHEEK?
I GUESS THAT'S FINE, RIGHT?
BA-DUMP
BA-DUMP
THEN...
IF YOU CAN'T GET THEM OUT OF YOUR HEAD...
AND YOU FEEL LIKE... YOU WANT TO BE TOGETHER **FOREVER?**
UH...
......

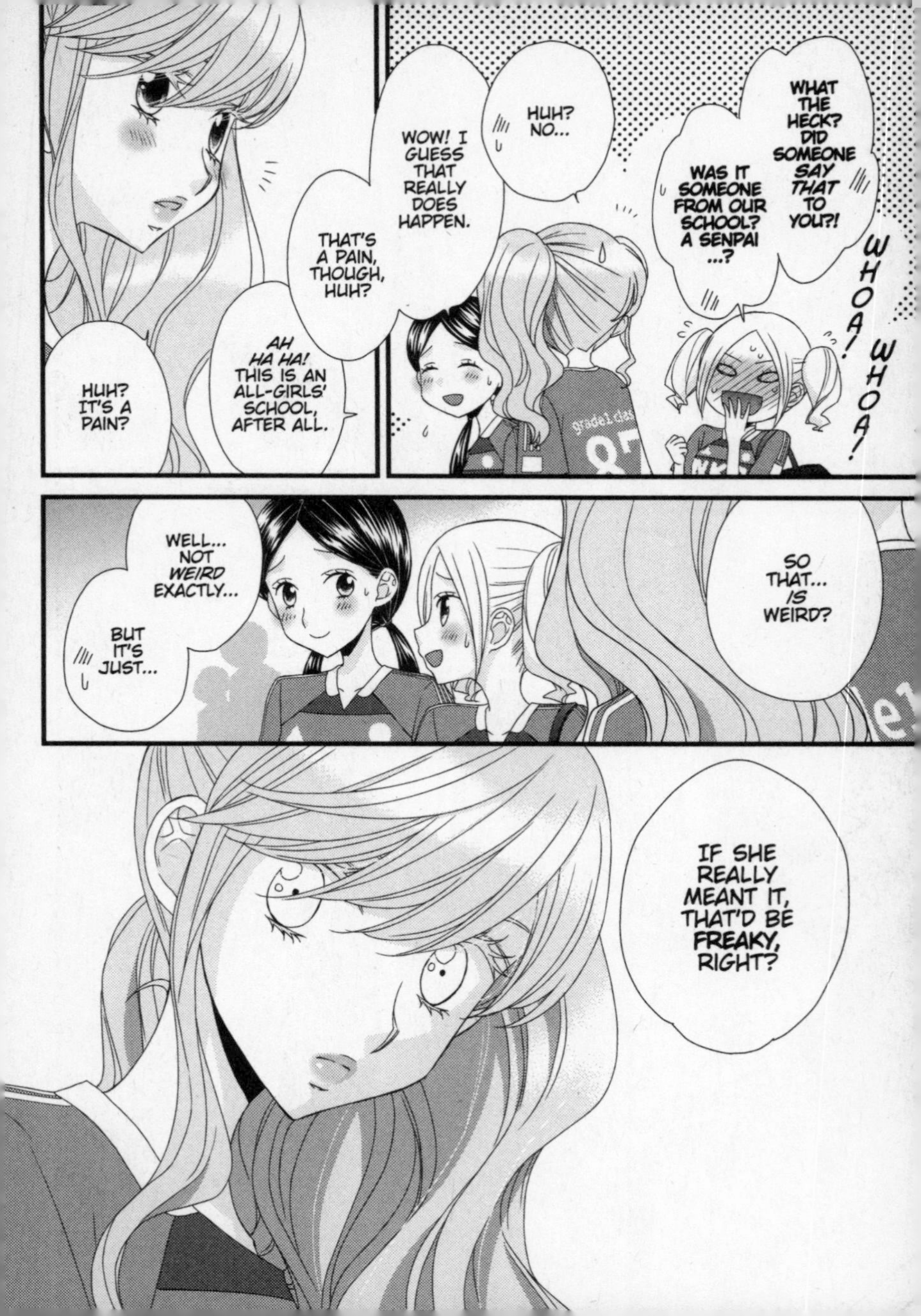
WHAT THE HECK? DID SOMEONE *SAY THAT* TO YOU?!
WHOA! WHOA!
WAS IT SOMEONE FROM OUR SCHOOL? A SENPAI ...?
HUH? NO...
WOW! I GUESS THAT REALLY DOES HAPPEN.
THAT'S A PAIN, THOUGH, HUH?
AH HA HA! THIS IS AN ALL-GIRLS' SCHOOL, AFTER ALL.
HUH? IT'S A PAIN?
SO THAT... *IS* WEIRD?
WELL... NOT *WEIRD* EXACTLY...
BUT IT'S JUST...
IF SHE REALLY MEANT IT, THAT'D BE **FREAKY**, RIGHT?

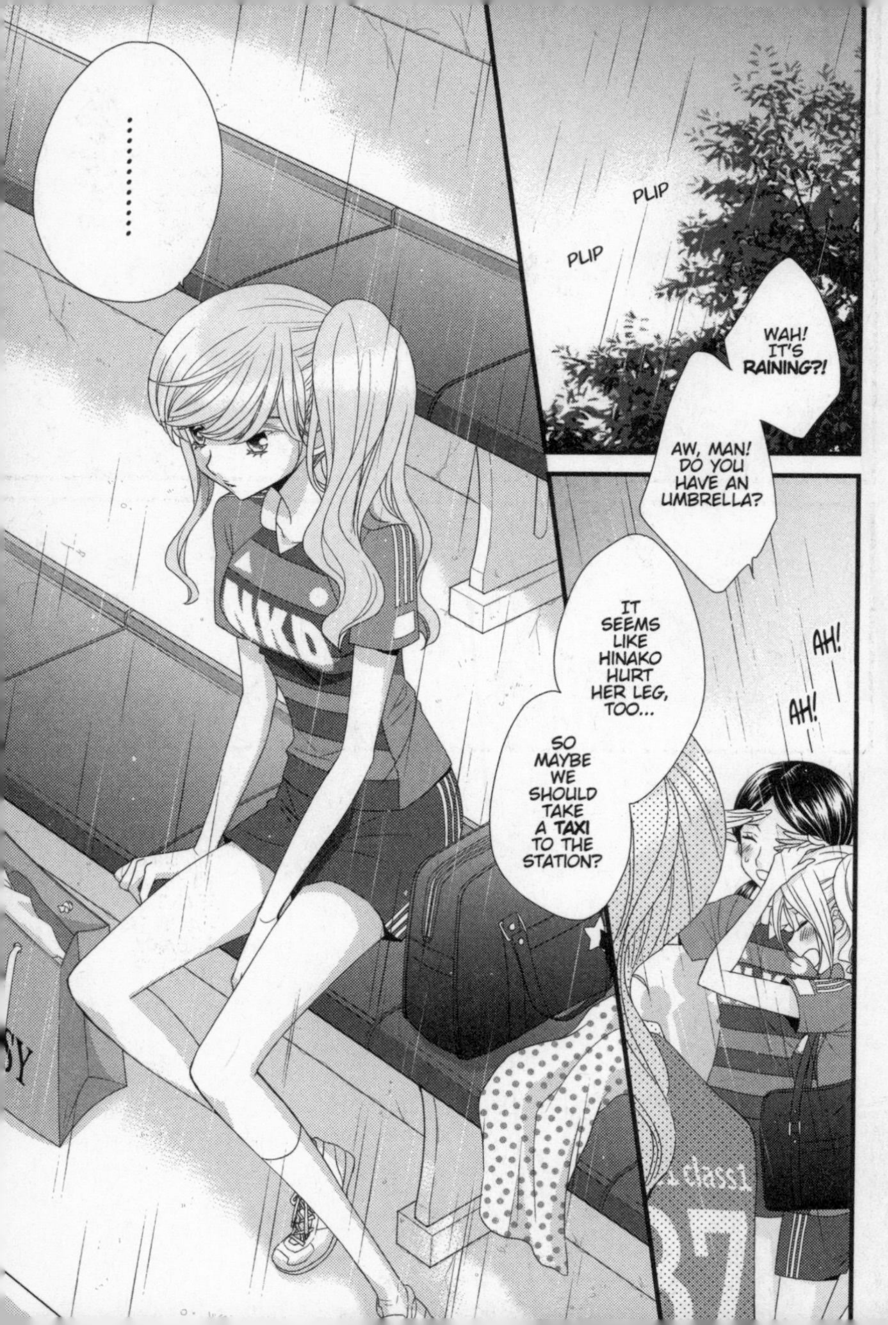
PLIP
PLIP
WAH! IT'S RAINING?!
AW, MAN! DO YOU HAVE AN UMBRELLA?
AH!
AH!
IT SEEMS LIKE HINAKO HURT HER LEG, TOO...
SO MAYBE WE SHOULD TAKE A TAXI TO THE STATION?
....

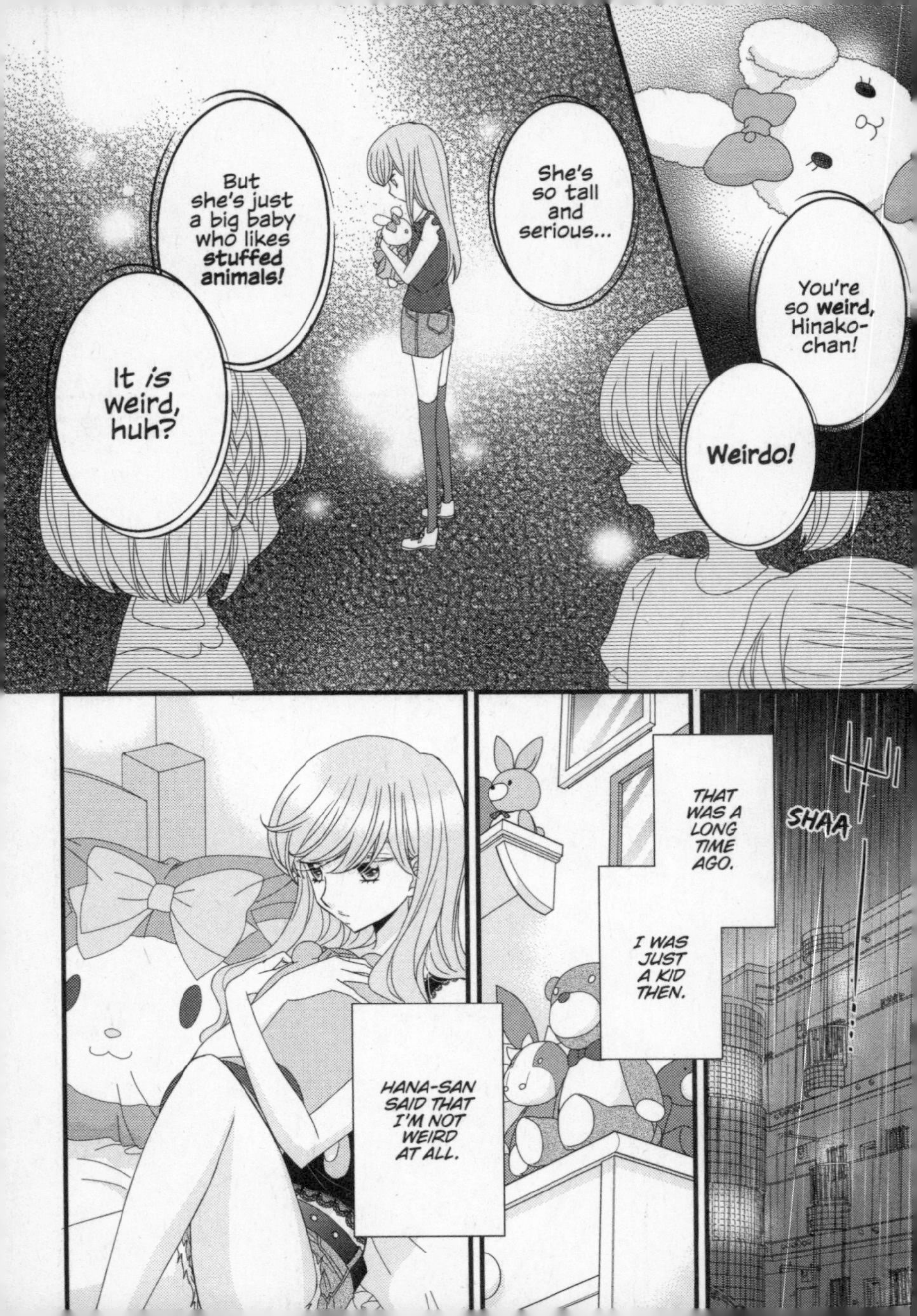
She's so tall and serious...
But she's just a big baby who likes stuffed animals!
It *is* weird, huh?
You're so weird, Hinako-chan!
Weirdo!
SHAA
THAT WAS A LONG TIME AGO.
I WAS JUST A KID THEN.
HANA-SAN SAID THAT I'M NOT WEIRD AT ALL.

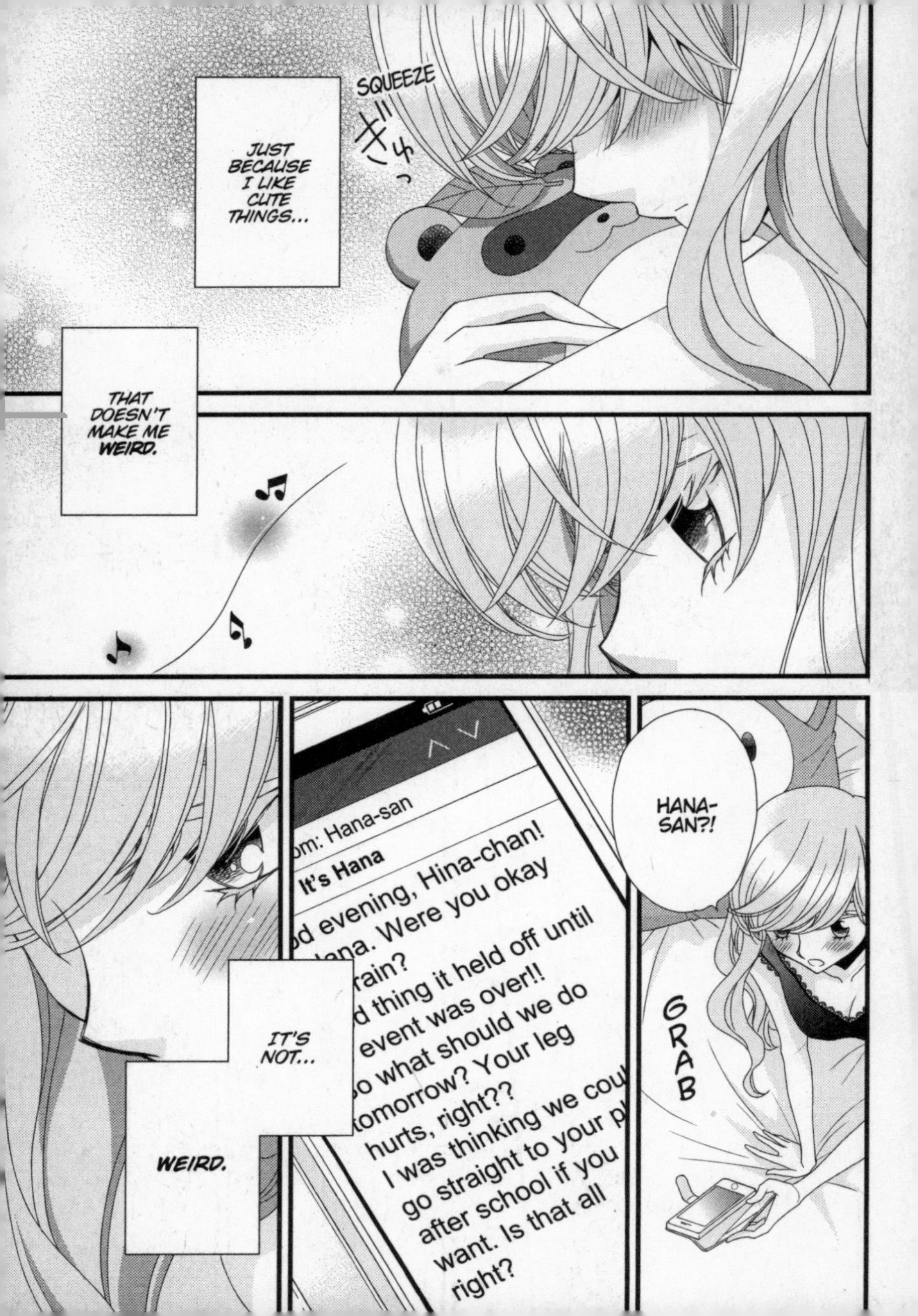
SQUEEZE
JUST BECAUSE I LIKE CUTE THINGS...
THAT DOESN'T MAKE ME WEIRD.
HANA-SAN?!
GRAB
om: Hana-san
It's Hana
od evening, Hina-chan!
ana. Were you okay
rain?
d thing it held off until
event was over!!
o what should we do
tomorrow? Your leg
hurts, right??
I was thinking we cou
go straight to your p
after school if you
want. Is that all
right?
IT'S NOT...
WEIRD.

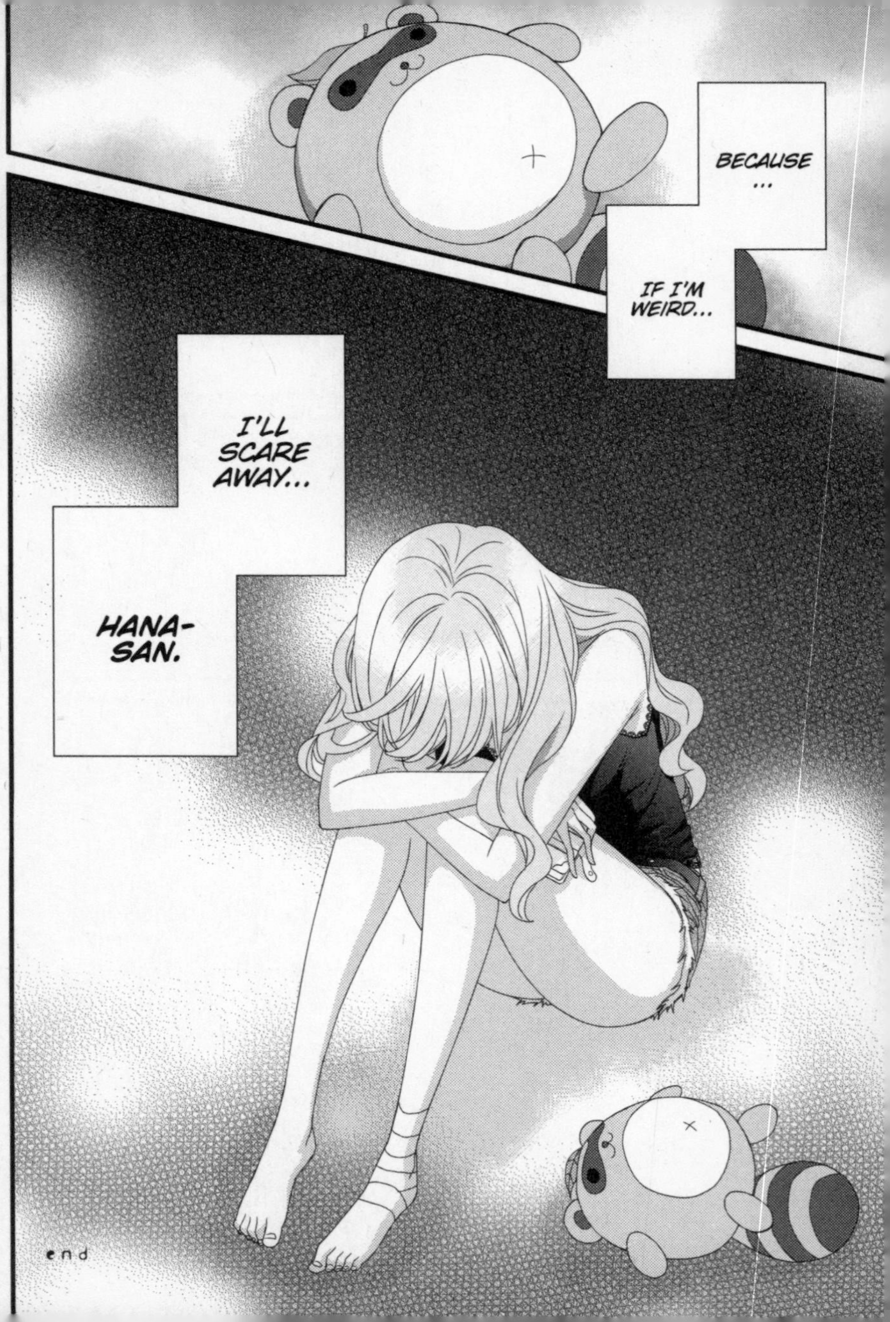
BECAUSE ...
IF I'M WEIRD...
I'LL SCARE AWAY...
HANA-SAN.
end

Hana & Hina AFTER ♡ SCHOOL

TO BE CONTINUED...

AFTERWORD

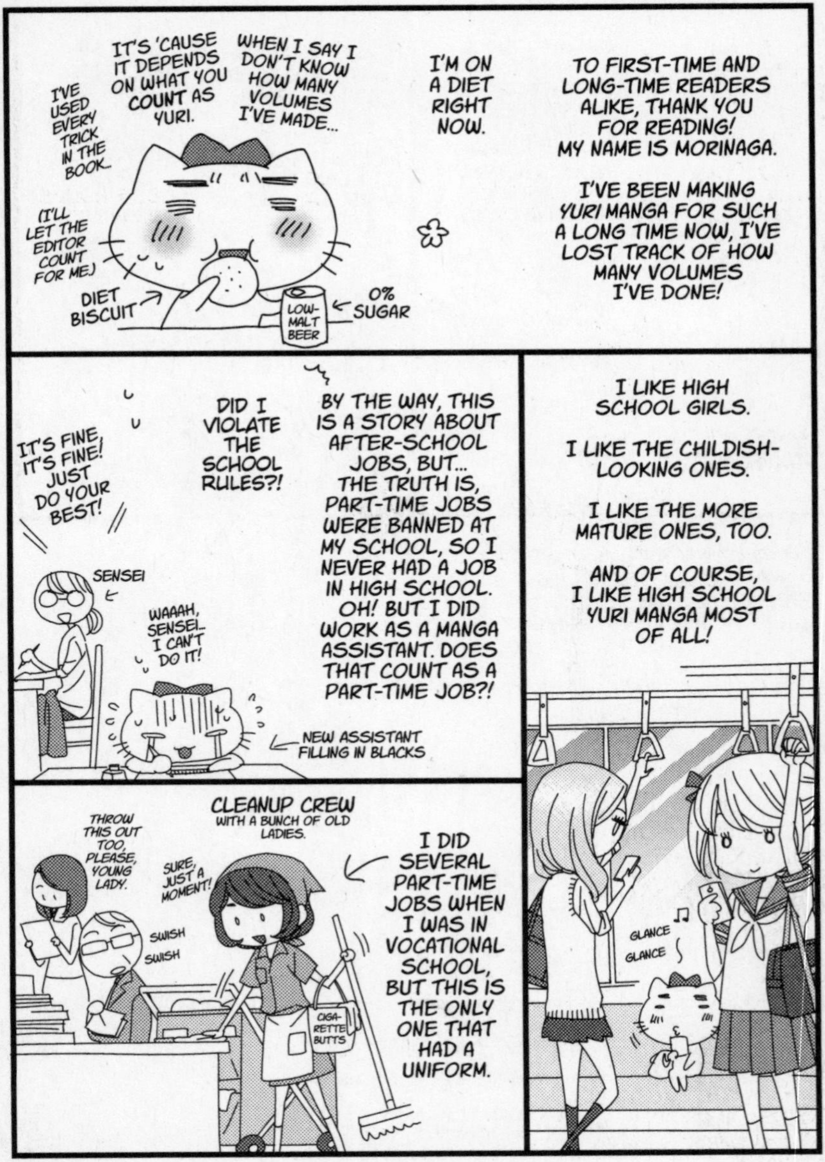
TO FIRST-TIME AND LONG-TIME READERS ALIKE, THANK YOU FOR READING! MY NAME IS MORINAGA.
I'VE BEEN MAKING YURI MANGA FOR SUCH A LONG TIME NOW, I'VE LOST TRACK OF HOW MANY VOLUMES I'VE DONE!
I'M ON A DIET RIGHT NOW.
WHEN I SAY I DON'T KNOW HOW MANY VOLUMES I'VE MADE...
IT'S 'CAUSE IT DEPENDS ON WHAT YOU COUNT AS YURI.
I'VE USED EVERY TRICK IN THE BOOK..
(I'LL LET THE EDITOR COUNT FOR ME)
0% SUGAR
LOW-MALT BEER
DIET BISCUIT
I LIKE HIGH SCHOOL GIRLS.
I LIKE THE CHILDISH-LOOKING ONES.
I LIKE THE MORE MATURE ONES, TOO.
AND OF COURSE, I LIKE HIGH SCHOOL YURI MANGA MOST OF ALL!
GLANCE
GLANCE
BY THE WAY, THIS IS A STORY ABOUT AFTER-SCHOOL JOBS, BUT... THE TRUTH IS, PART-TIME JOBS WERE BANNED AT MY SCHOOL, SO I NEVER HAD A JOB IN HIGH SCHOOL. OH! BUT I DID WORK AS A MANGA ASSISTANT. DOES THAT COUNT AS A PART-TIME JOB?!
DID I VIOLATE THE SCHOOL RULES?!
IT'S FINE, IT'S FINE! JUST DO YOUR BEST!
SENSEI
WAAAH, SENSEI.. I CAN'T DO IT!
NEW ASSISTANT FILLING IN BLACKS
I DID SEVERAL PART-TIME JOBS WHEN I WAS IN VOCATIONAL SCHOOL, BUT THIS IS THE ONLY ONE THAT HAD A UNIFORM.
CLEANUP CREW
WITH A BUNCH OF OLD LADIES.
SURE, JUST A MOMENT!
THROW THIS OUT TOO, PLEASE, YOUNG LADY.
SWISH
SWISH
CIGARETTE BUTTS